# DISCRIMINATION AND DISADVANTAGE IN EMPLOYMENT:
# THE EXPERIENCE OF BLACK WORKERS

**WEST LONDON INSTITUTE
OF HIGHER EDUCATION**

SERVITE IN LÆTITIA

**EX LIBRIS**

# DISCRIMINATION AND DISADVANTAGE IN EMPLOYMENT: THE EXPERIENCE OF BLACK WORKERS

A Reader edited by
Peter Braham, Ed Rhodes and
Michael Pearn

**Harper & Row, Publishers**
*in association with*
The Open University Press

Selection and editorial material
copyright © The Open University 1981

Harper & Row Ltd
28 Tavistock Street
London WC2E 7PN

British Library Cataloguing in Publication Data

Discrimination and disadvantage.
　1. Minorities – Employment – Addresses, essays, lectures
　I. Braham, Peter　　II. Rhodes, Ed
　III. Pearn, Michael
　331.6　　HD6305.M5

　ISBN 0-06-318193-2
　ISBN 0-06-318194-0 PbK

Phototypesetting by Parkway Group, London and Abingdon
Printed and bound by The Pitman Press, Bath

# CONTENTS

# PREFACE

Three companion volumes of readings have been prepared for the Open University course *Ethnic Minorities and Community Relations* (E354). The other two are *The School in the Multi-cultural Society* and *Social and Community work in a Multi-Racial Society*.

The readers form one component of the course which also includes correspondence texts, radio and television programmes and personal tuition.

The editors wish to acknowledge the help of the course team and its consultants in the compilation of these readers. Opinions expressed in the readers are, of course, not necessarily those of the course team or of the University.

# GENERAL INTRODUCTION

This reader is one of three produced in conjunction with the Open University course, 'Ethnic Minorities and Community Relations'. The choice of employment as the subject of this book and as one of the central themes of the course lies partly in the significance for the individual of experience in the workplace itself and in the relationship between paid employment – or its absence – and life outside the workplace. The kinds of jobs done by workers in terms of pay levels, skills, status, levels of autonomy and involvement, physical conditions, fringe benefits – the whole pattern of extrinsic and intrinsic rewards from work – are a fundamental part of, and fundamental to, their whole experience of life as well as that of the lives of their dependants. Access to the educational system and to leisure facilities, patterns of housing and health, and many other areas of social concern are all likely to be related to employment location in one way or another.

But this is the case for the population as a whole: to what extent is it either valid or useful to distinguish groups of workers in terms of their ethnicity and to examine their case as in some way a discrete issue? The answer lies partly within the historical experience of migrant workers throughout the world, whether they have moved within national and tribal frontiers or across them. In general, migrants moving voluntarily or otherwise tend to be disproportionately disadvantaged within the receiving societies and also tend to become a stigmatized group that is prone to acts of discrimination. In many cases both disadvantage and discrimination have persisted well beyond the immediate period of immigration. Beside this general experience there is the specific case of the United Kingdom where historical experience has been reinforced in the migration, largely of black workers from New Commonwealth countries, which took place mainly between the 1950s and early 1970s. The experience of the workers who took part in that migration and of their families provides ample evidence of a significant level of disadvantage in employment (as elsewhere) through disproportionate concentration in jobs where physical conditions are bad, status is low and pay is poor. There is also evidence of various forms of employment discrimination where actions are taken to prevent or limit the entry and movement of individuals within the labour market *because* they are migrants or *because* they are black. Taking the example of workers from the New Commonwealth, the 1971 census showed them to be more heavily engaged in manufacturing industry than was the labour force as a whole (47 per cent to 33 per cent), and in certain sectors of manufacturing the immigrant concentration was greater still. While there has almost certainly been some shift in this pattern subsequently the underlying pattern of disadvantage persists. The workforce in Britain is not as rigidly demarcated as workforces in some of the other labour-importing European countries, but immigrant labour in Britain remains heavily concentrated in less-desirable, non-skilled manual jobs to an extent which caused Smith to conclude (from a survey of 236 employers) that the composition of the minority workforce was 'markedly different', by type of job, from that of the total workforce[1]. It is important for those adversely affected and for society as a whole to extend our knowledge about the extent of such discrimination and disadvantage, about why this occurs, about the impact of immigration on indigenous workers and about what can be done to seek to remedy matters.

These provide some of the underlying themes for this Reader. We concentrate largely on the experience of black workers because of their predominance in the 1950s–1970s immigration and because the evidence shows a greater element of disadvantage and discrimination than that experienced by other immigrant workers in the UK. However we do not entirely turn from the issues faced by workers who are members of other ethnic groups. Apart from its intrinsic significance, their experience, particularly when looked at in the wider European context, adds to understanding of the nature of black disadvantage and discrimination. But subjective response to skin colour does provide an additional dimension of disadvantage which is also more durable. The opportunity for black migrants and their descendants to merge within the population through the adoption of indigenous attitudes, customs etc – not an option migrant groups have necessarily wished to exercise – is less open, being more dependent on attitudes within the native population.

This is becoming clearer as increasing numbers of black workers whose birthplace is the UK and whose education has been entirely within the UK seek to enter the labour market. This emphasizes the importance of examining the profile of black employment as a specific issue in order to establish whether the extent of disadvantage is decreasing or increasing. If it is decreasing, it can be asked whether corrective mechanisms of the labour market will of themselves resolve matters within an acceptable time? Or, is external intervention necessary, and to what ends and in what directions should it be applied? The case for looking specifically at black workers has been strengthened by the long-term rise in levels of unemployment which has been evident since the early 1970s. An increasing body of evidence shows that as unemployment rises, so black workers are disproportionately affected. But much of the existing literature reflects the context of full employment and, indeed, of excess demand for labour, in which black labour was first recruited, and which prevailed till the early 1960s. We have endeavoured in the last article to explore some of the issues raised by prolonged levels of high unemployment.

Having argued that the experience of black and other migrant workers does raise some largely discrete issues, it is important to draw this argument into perspective for this experience can only be adequately understood by reference to a wider social and employment context. Yet such reference emphasizes further omissions in the literature. The issues facing black workers tend either to be effectively ignored or their uniqueness is overemphasized. The presence and circumstances of black workers have generally been subsumed in studies of the more general issues of industrial relations, while there have been no significant attempts to establish whether aspects of industrial relations practices have implications for black and other migrant workers. The limited input from specialists in industrial relations has caused the potential significance for black workers of aspects of workplace behaviour, of custom and practice, of rules governing workplace entry and of the inertia which results from adherence to established practices to be overlooked. These issues of industrial relations policy and practice may contribute powerfully, if inadvertently, to patterns of disadvantage and to so-called institutional discrimination. For example, recruitment to apprenticeships has, in some cases, depended on the existence of strong, family ties. This may serve to limit the entry of the 'second generation' of black workers even where they may have gained the appropriate qualifications. Where issues have arisen which seem inescapably related to the employment of black workers (for example, allegations of the connivance of trade unions in cases of discrimination), these have been generally regarded as being matters for specialists in the study of race relations. Much of the existing literature on black workers and employment concentrates therefore on the extent of deliberate racial discrimination, the attitudes which cause it, and the policies designed to eradicate it. We adopt a wider perspective and take the view that black employment patterns provide an additional dimension of discrimination and disadvantage within the labour market. The economic reasons for the initial recruitment and placement of migrant workers, and for their subsequent deployment, which help to explain patterns of disadvantage, have tended to be overlooked because of too great a concentration on cultural differences, on the attitudes of black and white workers and on discrimination. This contributes to a further problem in that the disadvantages experienced by the black population are often regarded in isolation. The problems of black workers tend to be abstracted from wider problems of inequality and disadvantage in the labour market and in society more generally.

On the other hand, emphasizing the relationship between the discrimination and disadvantage endured by black workers and wider patterns of inequality should not be confused with the approach which explains their problems simply in terms of their recent arrival. It has long been a favoured view that, as with other minorities who migrated to Britain in the past, the position of black immigrants would improve as they adopted British customs and practices. Hence, after a generation or two, the hostility of the indigenous population would diminish and the descendants of the original immigrants would be free to take full advantage of the opportunities provided by an advanced industrial country such as Britain (for example, in the field of education). This perspective, it may be argued, removes from employers, government and trades unionists alike much of the burden of taking action on discrimination and disadvantage except in cases of the most manifest injustice. It has been evident – as in past deliberations of the Trade Union Congress for example – that such a perspective may easily lead to black workers being regarded as the agents of their own misfortune where they are suspected of failing to adopt 'British ways' with the appropriate speed.

In this context, it is important to be aware of the frameworks of reference which underlie policies designed to improve the position of black and other minority workers in Britain. Many of these reflect the recent civil rights experience in the USA, and have been borrowed or adapted wholesale to apply to the circumstances of the United Kingdom. Twenty years ago the phrase equal opportunity was rarely, if ever, used by employers. Since then equal opportunity has become an important goal in society which is backed by legislation. The expanding flow of employee rights now includes protection, in law at least, against unfair treatment on grounds of race, colour, national or ethnic origins and nationality. This is matched by corresponding legislation outlawing discrimination on grounds of sex or married status. But by 1980 neither the Race Relations Act nor for that matter the Sex Discrimination Act appear to have been very successful in eliminating discrimination, and the number of successful cases brought before tribunals each year is insignificant compared with the scale of racial discrimination which research studies have revealed.[2]

The Commission for Racial Equality, and its predecessor the Race Relations Board, have argued strongly in favour of employers adopting formal equal opportunity policies. This followed American experience, which was not surprising as the Race Relations Act 1976 (the third since 1968) was modelled closely on anti-discrimination law in the United States.[3] The main argument in favour of equal opportunity policies is that a positive stance by employers is required if discrimination is to be detected and eliminated. It was recognized that much discrimination is covert, and that indirect discrimination (the racial discrimination that can result from certain institutional practices) could often only be detected by systematic examination of employers' policies and practices. The law in the USA is energetically enforced, and employers can face huge fines; the courts for the most part have been sympathetic to the legislation. Perhaps most important of all, Federal contractors (employing nearly one-third of the American labour force) have to comply with stringent equal opportunity regulations in order to obtain and maintain their contracts. Almost all employers have now developed equal opportunity policies and many have appointed equal opportunity officers, ostensibly to ensure that the policy is effective in practice. In addition, most employers measure the results of their policies to determine whether or not sufficient blacks are being recruited and are moving upwards in the organization into areas previously occupied by whites only, to an extent that, at the least, will avoid prosecution.[4] But the effectiveness of law enforcement varies widely, reflecting variations in State-wide policies and predominant attitudes. The result has been a steady improvement in the opportunities for some blacks but little appears to have changed for the mass of disadvantaged blacks such as those who are concentrated in America's inner cities.

To what extent can equal opportunity policies by employers succeed in creating equality of opportunity for black people in the very different conditions that prevail in Britain? At one level answers may be sought by examining the micro issues of the labour market and in looking at what a specific policy is trying to do. If the aim is merely to avoid discrimination against suitably qualified black applicants, it may suggest the removal of arbitrary barriers in employment. Black people may then be able to obtain jobs they would not otherwise have obtained. But the passive removal of barriers will only have limited impact if black workers are not already employed in a particular occupation or factory and few apply. A more active stance could seek to increase the proportion of blacks employed by what is often referred to as positive action. This might involve action to discriminate in favour of black applicants in occupations where they are under-represented and could include the provision of training solely for black people (which is permitted under the Race Relations Act under prescribed conditions). Such action can be justified on the grounds that discrimination and disadvantages in the past and now have meant that black people have not had opportunities to acquire the skills, experience and qualifications which are essential for the more rewarding and secure jobs.

It is generally accepted that, to be effective, positive action in the sphere of employment needs to be accompanied by action in other areas or, rather, that action to improve the lot of black and other ethnic groups needs to be taken on a broad front. Yet, it is less clear that some of the other, potentially more significant problems are adequately acknowledged. This is indicated by some of the assumptions upon which positive action and other measures are based. The notion of equal opportunity or of action which will secure movement towards some more desirable employment profile presupposes that there is a generally accepted degree of equality of opportunity within society as a whole. This is demonstrably not the case. We have already referred to the significance for individuals of employment and in this area alone a wide range of factors such as sex, age of school leaving, family background, and age, have a persistent influence on the location of individuals in more or less privileged jobs as well as on their prospects of becoming unemployed and of remaining unemployed.

At best, then, equal opportunity within society as it stands is unlikely to mean more than movement, admittedly in a positive direction, towards the more general profile of disadvantage which is evident within the population. This reiterates the importance of viewing the circumstances of black workers as part of a wider and more complex pattern of disadvantage. But when the nature of this wider disadvantage and origins are taken into account there must be doubt about even the achievement of the limited progress referred to above unless inequality is tackled on a wider front. Black workers were certainly recruited to perform less desirable jobs, but these jobs existed before their arrival. They entered a labour market in which disadvantaged forms of employment had been created 'prior, logically and empirically, to acts of racial discrimination perpetrated by individuals'.[5] While facing additional problems black workers became an integral part of the general pattern of disadvantage. To understand the particular problem of black workers it is then necessary to look at both the nature of the underlying and broader basis of disadvantage and at the processes which initially drew black workers into the workforce. In the context of employment we have already referred to the way in which aspects of industrial relations may contribute to disadvantage. The values and practices underlying company recruitment and promotion offer one example while another may be the practices through which workers seek to establish their own forms of market control, evidenced in seniority rules, closed shop provisions and so on. In some circumstances it may be tempting to interpret the effects of these on black workers solely in terms of discriminatory perspectives but more fundamentally they reflect long term experience of the rigours of the labour market and of employers' control from which attempts to limit these effects have gradually developed and extended.

Where the processes of migration are concerned, the experience of the UK is not unique for there are parallels between the position of black workers in Britain and those of immigrant workers in France, West Germany and Switzerland. In each of these countries sustained economic growth in the 1950s and 1960s helped to produce increasing shortages of labour. These shortages were most pronounced in less desirable sectors which had been deserted by those indigenous workers able to take advantage of the job opportunities presented by economic expansion and by a general commitment to full employment. According to the thinking of the time, the easiest way to remedy these shortages (which, if unchecked, threatened to cause severe production bottlenecks) was neither to replace men with machines nor to adjust wage rates in order to attract indigenous workers back into areas of labour shortage, but to import labour. Little thought was given to the long-term social and economic consequences of this option, because the decision – in so far as it was a considered decision – to import immigrant labour was seen as the ideal solution to what was viewed as a temporary problem.

Thus the processes which gave rise to black immigration do much to explain both the present circumstances of the first generation of black workers and the prospects of their children. Immigrant workers were initially spread unevenly throughout the labour force as a whole largely because labour shortages were in the past uneven. They occupied a 'helot' role in the economy; their labour was required primarily to carry out jobs which indigenous labour was unwilling to perform: they were 'suitable' people to do 'unsuitable' jobs. It is reasonable to suppose that: 'As long as coloured people tend to be employed in a limited range of jobs largely at the lowest end of the scale a consistent set of attitudes and prejudices will be attached to them'.[6] Such attitudes will conflict, in particular, with the expectation of the second-generation of black workers, who are largely British-educated, that they ought to be able to avoid the less desirable jobs which their parents were obliged to accept.

We have already referred to the types of factors which are likely to deny these expectations. All or most of these are likely to be intensified in effect by the persistence of economic stagnation and of high unemployment. In this direction also, a perspective which takes account of the effects of migration is important. The wave of migration into Western Europe which took place from the 1950s to the 1970s is but one episode in the wider processes of migration of various factors of production. By the late 1970s, as at times in the past, the movement of labour had been overshadowed by the movement of capital which on this occasion was managed largely through the medium of multi-national companies. This new phase of capital movement has serious implications for all workers in Britain. Many jobs such as those for which black workers were once recruited can now be exported to selected less developed countries. The demand for both black and white labour in Britain may be reduced thus removing some of the fundamental and seemingly durable changes in the social fabric which took place in the period from the 1940s. These issues are taken up in the final reading.

The selection of readings and their arrangement in sections has sought to follow these themes as far as is possible with the available material. Some are considered further in the two Open University course texts which were developed in conjunction with this Reader. In Section 1 we take up the underlying context of migration. Section 2 is concerned with movement into specific areas of the economy including the issues of self-employment and home-working which, with all the attendant disadvantages, have come to provide black and other groups with important alternatives to the inequalities and unfairnesses of organizational employment. Section 3 considers aspects of the union response to migration while Section 4 examines aspects of British and American experience of anti-discrimination measures. We have endeavoured to keep changes to articles to a minimum but where this has been necessary it is indicated by the customary symbol: [. . .].

Finally, we wish to register our appreciation of the advice and assistance received from our colleagues on the course team and in particular to Mrs Sheila Waters for her energy and commitment to the drawing together of this Reader.

## Note

1. Smith, 1974, p. 85.

## References

1. Racial Disadvantage in Employment, PEP. June 1974 Report No. 544.
2. *A Review of the Race Relations Act;* London: the Runnymede Trust, 1979.
3. Macdonald, I. (1977) *Race Relations – the New Law;* London, Butterworth.
4. Equal Employment Opportunity – Programs and Results; PPF Survey No. 112; March 1976, Washington DC; Bureau of National Affairs.
5. Allen, Sheila, Bentley, Stuart, Bronat, Joanna (1977) *Work Race and Immigration;* University of Bradford, School of Studies in Social Sciences.
6. Daniel, W. W. (1968) *Racial Discrimination in England*, Harmondsworth, Penguin.

# SECTION 1

## THE ROLE OF IMMIGRANT LABOUR

# INTRODUCTION

The migration of the 1950s and 1960s was no new phenomenon for the UK. British employers have frequently sought out migrant labour. In a number of industries, workers from other parts of the UK, from the Irish Republic, from continental Europe, and from the New Commonwealth have been successively recruited where suitable local labour has not been forthcoming at the rates of pay the employer was prepared to offer. Nor was the migration of the 1950s and 1960s confined to the UK. Böhning (Chapter 1.1) and Castles and Kosack (Chapter 1.2) examine this phase of migration as one which was common to much of Northern Europe. In all the cases they looked at, the immediate reasons for the migration were the same: the post-1945 economic boom produced labour shortages which it became impossible to meet by the traditional means of drawing from the agricultural labour force. Refugees from central Europe had some impact in England and considerably more in Germany but, as both authors emphasize, governments were then faced with a choice between deflation to reduce demand, acceptance of a high wage policy which would hasten economic restructuring or to draw in labour from new areas. In all cases the latter course was adopted although in varying combinations with the other options. However, as both readings make clear, this was regarded as an essentially short term expedient since the post-War boom was not expected to last. (In both chapters we have excised the supporting statistical material for reasons of space.)

Thus there was a conscious decision to rely on migrant labour but for our purposes this raises two questions to which Böhning and Castles and Kosack provide answers, albeit with rather different emphases: was the British experience identical to that of the other European countries? What were the reasons for this choice of option? The British experience differs from that of Europe in two important ways, both related to the UK's imperial past. First, the migration *to* the UK from the New Common-wealth was matched by a migration *from* the UK to the Old Common-wealth so that the total labour force did not expand to the extent that was evident in Germany, France or Switzerland. As Castles and Kosack point out, this may be one reason explaining why the UK economy performed so poorly in comparison with the other North European countries. Certainly governments in the 1960s took the view that labour shortage was a major factor constraining economic growth but nonetheless they sought to close off the one major supply of mobile labour.

The other major contrast lies in the retention by the UK of the notion of British citizenship for patrials of Commonwealth countries so that entry from the Commonwealth was not restricted in terms of type of work or ability to bring dependants and settle. In other North European countries, particularly West Germany and Switzerland, migration was: by permit only; for specific jobs; for specific periods; and without any right to bring dependants. Thus, at the end of a contract, if not before, migrant workers could be expelled to their own countries, strengthening employer control in the workplace and adding a new tool of economic regulation – reducing unemployment by exporting it. From 1962 the UK began moving towards this system. Yet, as Böhning, Castles and Kosack show, this did not resolve the 'problem'. Notwithstanding permit systems, migration creates a momentum which it is difficult for governments to resist given the context of interstate relations and a desire to maintain the semblance of open, tolerant and democratic societies. Böhning shows how this momentum derives from two factors: that while initially a short term expedient, migrant labour became an indispensable part of the labour force and as migration proceeds so the characteristics of migrants shift from a profile dominated by young, single, mobile and more skilled workers to one that is more representative of the populations of the sending countries.

Böhning's explanation of the process of migration is clearly rooted in a pluralistic framework in which the initial decision to accept migrants is seen as a matter of expediency and subsequent phases develop largely through 'natural' or ad hoc processes. Castles and Kosack, however, view the process in terms of an industrial reserve army which is required to provide a flow of labour to meet demand and, by reducing labour market pressures, to maintain control over pay levels and other aspects of work behaviour. This requires the recruitment of migrant labour when the domestic workforce is no longer able to provide the reserve. At the same time, the drawing in of migrant labour fulfils a further function, that of emphasizing and maintaining divisions within the indigenous workforce. It is these that provide a focus of industrial conflict, diverting attention from more fundamental conflicts between labour and capital. These divisions become particularly important during periods of unemployment when working class unity is likely to be most dangerous.

The concept of members of the native workforce moving up the job hierarchy and rejecting jobs that are in some way unpleasant, low paid or of low status, jobs which have then to be filled by migrant labour, provides a clear explanation for the initial profile of disadvantaged employment. But to what extent does the structure and operation of the employment system, as opposed to acts of discrimination, explain the persistence of a profile of disadvantage? The answer is most likely to be found through examining specific industries and occupations which we undertake in Section 2. However, a general explanatory framework has been advanced by a number of labour economists. Briefly, the hypothesis, derived from American experience, is that the labour market is in effect divided into two sectors, the primary and secondary. The former, composed mainly of large, bureaucratized companies, is relatively advantaged compared with the generally small, low technology companies largely reliant on transient marginal labour which predominate in the secondary sector.

Blackburn and Mann in Chapter 1.4 undertake a critical scrutiny of this initially attractive and persuasive explanation based on research in areas of employment where this hypothesis is most likely to be supported.[1] They show that divisions within the labour market can readily be found such as those between the sexes, or between free labourers and 'bonded labourers' – migrant workers – in Western Europe. Yet dualism in the sense in which it is generally used, is rejected as a central explanation of either disadvantage or discrimination. There is little evidence to demonstrate the validity of such a categorization and, as they suggest, employers in general tend to resist over-segregation. Patterns of disadvantage cut across divisions in terms of organizational size or forms of production technology. They suggest that it is more fruitful to think in terms of primary and secondary *workers*, categories related to age or sex, and skill category as well as ethnicity. The two groups overlap to some extent in terms of occupation of disadvantaged or 'good' jobs, suggesting a pattern of overlap which makes action to combat problems of disadvantage far more difficult than the general dualist theory implies.

Much of the contemporary analysis of the migration of labour is, like Chapters 1.1 and 1.2, rooted in or influenced by the migration of the mid-twentieth century. The development of the dualist theory – or at least its application to the UK – is similarly related to this phase. But since the early 1970s both the pattern of migration and the economic context have changed radically. One explanation of the change, particularly economic change, is that this is a transient phase, ultimately manipulable by traditional methods of economic regulation and in many ways similar to the long depressions of the past. In Chapter 1.3, Sivanandan seeks to develop a more comprehensive explanatory framework which encompasses both the migration to Europe and subsequent changes in employment levels. Fundamental to this are the international divisions of production and of labour interlocked in a constantly changing relationship. The second central element is the relationship between the industrialized, ex-colonialist countries at the centre of the global economy and the countries of the formerly colonialized, less developed periphery. Overall, he perceives the period since 1945 in terms of attempts to establish a new colonialism which would overturn the significance of national boundaries. The first 25 years or so were characterized by the migration of labour from the periphery to the centre. By the 1970s, however, the development of a global economy had been facilitated by innovations in communications and other electronic technology. This process was hastened by the increasing ability of giant corporations to shift capital and work around the globe in accordance with calculations of unit labour and capital costs. Major shifts in the location of production from the centre to the periphery have been accompanied by the emergence of new patterns of migration between the countries of the periphery. This, he suggests, has been particularly apparent in South East Asia where labour has moved into the countries selected for capital investment by virtue of their compatible political philosophies and ready availability of cheap, flexible and subdued labour. While our first two readings did not encompass the significance of migration for the sending countries – the authors undertook that elsewhere – Sivanandan indicates some of the adverse implications which are likely to be only partially offset by the remission of money to dependants. The extension of the skill base, often held to be a home country benefit, is likely to be limited; apart from recruitment of those with existing skills, much of the work is unskilled. He suggests that the transition towards a global economy is likely to be accompanied by shifts towards authoritarianism in prevailing political and economic philosophies and a polarization of the labour force across the globe between a highly skilled elite minority and the largely superfluous unskilled indigent mass.

While aspects of their perception of change may possibly be open to challenge, the picture of the UK's experience that emerges is depressingly familiar. During the first of Sivanandan's two phases, as many have observed, the UK's chosen path was that of labour intensiveness, made possible by labour importing and yielding low pay, low productivity and, ultimately, decline or extinction in many areas of activity. As the UK belatedly sought to move towards the general North European pattern, so there was a retreat from labour importing and calls for repatriation. The article also draws out the significance of technological change for the level and type of unemployment and its implications, as serious for women as for black workers. But, for indigenous workers in the UK and elsewhere, as for migrant workers, it is the ability of companies to shift jobs and unemployment that is most likely to dominate the prospects for security of employment, job progression, and the distribution of rewards during the rest of the century.

## Note

1. In view of our earlier comments about lack of attention to the implications of the functioning of the labour market or the processes of industrial relations it should be noted that 'The Working Class in the Labour Market' provides a valuable exception. It is a general study of labour market processes which does look at the more specific issue.

# CHAPTER 1.1

# THE SELF-FEEDING PROCESS OF ECONOMIC MIGRATION FROM LOW-WAGE TO POST-INDUSTRIAL COUNTRIES WITH A LIBERAL CAPITALIST STRUCTURE*

W. R. Böhning

[. . .] This chapter examines the structural causes of contemporary labour immigration into European countries and the ways in which supposedly temporary migrants turn, on a large scale, into permanent settlers. Migrants who from the outset had the intention of settling abroad permanently need not be considered here. However, they are few and far between on the European scene, with the possible exception of some sections of the coloured immigrant population in Britain. Apart from the trainees and seasonal migrants, almost all economic migrants in Europe are polyannual migrants in intention when they leave their countries of origin, but are not emigrants in the traditional sense (Böhning, 1971). Yet, after a few years a third of the polyannual migrants to Britain settle permanently; 42 per cent of Switzerland's foreign workers with year-round permits are counted as having been continuously resident for over five years (1969 figures); and 57 per cent of Germany's male foreign workers and 39 per cent of the females are shown as having been uninterruptedly resident for over four years (*Erfahrungsbericht 1969*, 1970, p. 49: 1968 figures). Somewhere there must be a mechanism in our post-industrial capitalist societies which makes polyannual migrants change their mind about returning home as quickly as possible.

A post-industrial society is denoted by a relatively small agricultural sector, a large semi-automated industrial sector which tends to decline in relative terms, and an equally large and expanding tertiary sector:

* From *The Migration of Workers in the United Kingdom and the European Community*, OUP, 1972. Reprinted by permission of Oxford University Press.

*If one assumes that such a society:*

*firstly,* has a liberal capitalist structure,

*secondly,* is committed to full employment and high real growth policies, and

*thirdly,* is not a traditional country of immigration and does not experience any significant immigration,

then it follows that:

*fourthly,* this society will run into endemic labour shortages in socially undesirable and low-wage jobs because it is unable to change its traditional job structure, and that,

*fifthly,* it will try to meet these labour shortages by engaging foreign workers from low-wage countries with labour surpluses, thereby,

*sixthly,* rigidifying the social job structure, forestalling an effective solution of the labour shortage problem, and setting in motion a process of migration which, under current trends of technological development, is unending and self-feeding.

This hypothesis can be exemplified by reference to Germany because the relevant data are available. The UK was approaching model conditions in the 50s but has since increasingly deviated from the essential assumption of *high* real growth (entailing a fast rising standard of living). Italy and Spain may provide a future test of the hypothesis, though in the case of Spain this will depend on its degree of liberalism.

Under an increasingly liberal regime of international trade, a society of the kind stipulated generally experiences a fast increase in the standard of living of its working-class population shortly after the transition of its economy from an industrial to a post-industrial one. The rising standard of living is achieved with the traditional social job structure, that is, the structure developed during the first stages of industrialization with socially undesirable and low-wage jobs at the bottom. In a fully employed economy, a noticeable increase in the standard of living has the following two effects. Firstly, it induces a growing gap between the rising expectations that go with an increase in the standard of living and better schooling, on the one side, and the undesirability of given jobs in terms of status, physical hardship, and pecuniary reward, on the other. Secondly, it gives workers the opportunity to leave undesirable jobs for those that are more socially acceptable and better paid, without much difficulty. Consequently workers drift into job openings which are more likely to fulfil their aspirations in respect of status and pay. The result is a partial labour shortage in socially undesirable jobs.

These symptoms of structural maladjustment are commonly overlooked in the beginning or accredited to partial demand situations. However, what *is* overlooked is the *systemic* character of these symptoms and the fact that they are indicative of an impending *general* labour shortage. The partial labour shortages may arise in different parts of the economy in different countries – in mining in Belgium, in tourism and private households in Switzerland, in agriculture in Germany – but they always make themselves felt first and foremost in sectors with a high concentration of undesirable and low wage jobs. Sometimes these high concentrations are to be found in sectors of seasonal employment and low job security; and, at other times, in declining industries (which clouds the issue in the sense that the structural development of the economy and the structural maladjustment of the labour market go hand in hand). However, the signal of structural maladjustment may be given by any sector, including booming industries such as tourism or construction or the steel industry, because it is not the economic sector as such but the incidence of socially undesirable jobs that matters and there is practically no sector where there are no badly paid and undesirable jobs. Thus, the symptom of partial labour shortage is no less than a signal of impending general labour shortage. The speed and intensity of this development may be influenced by such external factors as demographic developments (eg losses of active population resulting from wars), but it is essentially independent of them.

A post-industrial capitalist society facing the first instances of endemic labour shortage has two options open to it. Firstly, it could pursue a revolutionary manpower policy by adapting its social job structure to post-industrial requirements, ie to pay a truly economic wage for undesirable jobs, taking into account the fact that market forces are largely inapplicable on the labour 'market' and that wage structures are determined socio-politically. Secondly, it could fill these jobs with foreign workers admitted not for settlement but for the specific purpose of filling the supposedly temporary shortages on the labour market (the *Konjunkturpuffer* approach). The alternative to the first option, namely, to permit large-scale unemployment and a considerable drop if not reversal in the real growth of the economy in order to stop the flight from undesirable jobs, is not feasible politically because it would catapult the party in power out of government[1] (this alternative would not fit in with the second assumption). The alternative to the *Konjunkturpuffer* option would be to have a settlement immigration related to economic needs. No government in a country which is not traditionally a country of immigration and which deliberately set out to invite aliens to settle inside its borders on purely economic grounds, would survive the onset of this immigration. Permanent settlement migration is usually not even considered because the labour shortage problem is seen as essentially short term.

The first option is one that does not commend itself to the political decision-makers on socio-political grounds. A drastic rearrangement of the social structure of jobs might require, for example, that a dustman be paid as much or more than an accountant or that an agricultural labourer be given the same status as a research assistant. Needless to say, capitalist societies are neither willing nor able to do this on the scale required in view of the social consequences anticipated.[2] Furthermore, under current technological conditions the problem cannot be solved by automation because many of the socially undesirable jobs are not open to automation, particularly in the service sector, and because automation often creates new low paid jobs. The present stage of semi-automation in manufacturing industries has given rise to many boring and frustrating activities which do not attract sufficient indigenous manpower. Hence, the second option seems the only way out. It also seems the easiest way out with the least political friction and the greatest degree of freedom of manoeuvre in relation to both its execution and the alternatives. Governments fall for this solution. They are under the illusion that the labour shortages which make themselves felt are basically temporary in character. Significantly, they usually permit the employment of foreigners in specific jobs long before full employment levels are reached in macro-economic quantitative terms.

Once the political decision has gone in favour of the foreign worker or *Konjunkturpuffer* approach, the self-feeding process of migration from the chosen labour surplus areas into the labour shortage jobs commences and it can only be reversed by a political decision which is incomparably more difficult to take – because of the increased internal and additional international constraints – than a decision to adopt a strongly reformist manpower policy when the first gaps in the labour market appeared.

There are two aspects to this self-feeding process. One, as already implied, relates to the structure of post-industrial societies and the other to the migratory process itself. These will now be examined in turn.

The foreign worker approach does not stop the secular drift of the indigenous labour force from socially undesirable jobs, for it does not deal with the cause of the problem. On the contrary, it actually reinforces the given social structure of jobs and may even accelerate the drift described. An indigenous worker will often feel less inhibited in changing jobs if he finds that he is working side by side with a foreigner and if he suspects that his employer has engaged him to keep wages down. Sentimental attachment is lowered, too, when it is obvious that vacant jobs are filled quickly. The social job structure remains fixed, the drift of the indigenous work force continues, and the problem becomes less and less amenable to a reformist solution. The reshuffle that would have been necessary to meet the original labour shortage problem quickly reaches the proportions of upheaval. As the task becomes more formidable, the resolve to conquer it diminishes, which in turn reinforces the tendency to opt again and again for the import of foreign workers whenever there is a labour shortage.

After about six years of high real growth this process has usually worked its way through the whole of the economy. The initially isolated pockets of structural maladjustment, now filled with foreign workers, extend to all sectors of production. Sectors that are under represented in the beginning attract an increasing share of the foreign work force and the concentrations in sectors of original labour import fade out. This development would be much clearer statistically if other factors could be held constant or if one compared the type of demand for foreign workers over time. For example, in 1956, 95 per cent of the foreigners recruited for employment in Germany were seasonal workers, mainly in agriculture. In 1970 over a third of the recruits were engaged in metal goods and the electricity industry, but less than two per cent were in agriculture. In both years the absolute number of recruits for agriculture was about the same (5,800).

This spreading of the employment of foreigners to all sectors of the economy is basically due to two factors. On the one hand, there is the well-known complementarity of jobs, which means that different grades of labour are dependent upon each other for the performance of one production process. Wherever this holds true and wherever this involves socially undesirable jobs, there is the likelihood that sooner or later foreign workers will have to be engaged if national workers leave the bottom grades.[3] Nurses emptying bedpans and building labourers fetching bricks and cement are cases in point. On the other hand, employers in mass-production processes who have hitherto not resorted to foreign labour realize that its easy availability in conjunction with an appropriate redesign of the production system would enable them to turn out far more goods than would otherwise be the case. They further subdivide many skilled jobs into simple components which can readily be taught to workers who have never before stood at a production line. Thus, the *pattern* of demand for labour *changes* towards the skills available or their lack. It is usually in the large firms in manufacturing industries, which can look further ahead and which can afford to take on a contingent of foreigners on a trial-and-error basis, where foreigners of all grades and levels of literacy are taught in a day or two how to turn a screw or how to operate a lever. Often the production process is already so much subdivided that no further redesigning is required, the car industry being an example. In other cases employers may completely redesign their whole production process to adjust it to the kind of immigrant labour available (Cohen and Jenner, 1968).[4] The general point here is that, apart from the fact that there are undesirable and badly paid jobs in almost all sectors of the economy, the semi-automated manufacturing industries of today can easily adapt their mass-production processes to the kind of skills offered; and if, say, semi-literate farmers from under-developed countries can offer no industrial skills at all, they can still be put into a work place where no more than a repetitive manual movement is required. In manufacturing industries the complementarity of jobs and the adjustability of production processes coincide to a very high degree and the resulting concentration of foreign workers in such jobs is no surprise: over twenty per cent of Switzerland's foreign workers are employed in metal goods and over twenty per cent in other manufacturing industries; over one-third of the foreign workers in both the Netherlands and Germany are employed in metal goods, and manufacturing industries as a whole absorb about two-thirds of the foreign work force in both countries. The complementarity of jobs on its own, ie without the additional factor of adaptable mass-production processes, comes to the fore in the construction industry: one-third of Luxembourg's foreign workers are employed in construction; the proportion is as high as a quarter for Switzerland and stood at that level in Germany during the first half of the 60s, but has now fallen to one-sixth.

A breakdown of the total labour force by economic sectors reveals that the import of foreigners has had a scaling effect. A breakdown by socio-economic status, on the other hand, reveals an increasing differential between the foreign and the indigenous work force.[5] Taking the *total* distribution in terms of socio-economic status as the *structural* requirement of the economy, one finds a growing under-representation of the indigenous worker in the blue-collar sector in general and in unskilled and semi-skilled positions in particular. Between 1961, ie shortly after the large-scale engagement of foreigners had begun, and 1968, half a million German men and 600,000 German women left the broadly manual sector and were partly replaced by over 350,000 foreign men and over 200,000 foreign women. During the same period, 600,000 German men and half a million German women, as well as 20,000 foreign men and the same number of foreign women, entered into broadly white-collar positions. At the latter date, foreign men constituted a quarter of the group of unskilled male wage earners, ten per cent of the semi-skilled, and three per cent of the skilled wage earners (overall 7·9 per cent). Thus, over time, foreign workers become a more and more indispensable part of the labour force of post-industrial societies unless their employment is curtailed by a political act.

The second aspect of the self-feeding process relates to the migratory process itself. It is based upon the notion of chain migration but goes further than this in that it does not see the chain ending in one particular village or region; rather this chain extends to the whole of the labour-sending country. This might be called the 'maturity' of a migration. This aspect represents an autonomous contributory factor to the self-feeding process, ie it is not caused by the incidence of endemic labour shortage. Nevertheless, its momentum can keep the immigrant population growing long after the purposive recruitment of foreign workers has been curtailed politically or ended temporarily during a recession.

Migration is a social process: a migrant leaves one social context for another on the basis of a hierarchically ordered set of values. For economic migrants the socio-economic deprivations at home are often (though not necessarily) a sufficient condition of his out-migration. Lured by the prospects of an El Dorado magnified through hearsay, he sees himself as a *target worker*, that is, someone who goes abroad to earn as much money as possible, as quickly as possible, in order to return home. The target worker notion, of course, coincides perfectly with the *Konjunkturpuffer* approach of most European labour-receiving countries. What these two notions fail to take into account is the fact that migration leads to changes in the interactional system of the polyannual migrant. In the case of polyannual migrants coming from developing to post-industrial countries, this amounts potentially to a complete secondary socialization at the age of twenty or 30 (Böhning, 1971). The secondary socialization is in many cases not very successful, but in almost all cases the migrant absorbs at least superficially some of the norms and values of the host society. In particular, he becomes part of the system of norms, values, and deprivations of a consumer society within a matter of a year or two. After about one year, most polyannual migrants realize that short-term participation in a high-wage economy does not once and for all eliminate their deprivation back home, however spartan their conduct in the country of employment. They decide to extend their stay abroad in the expectation of really amassing the big wage packets they have been hoping for and then returning home and starting a new life. By this time, however, a polyannual migrant has become subject to new deprivations, namely, those of the lower working class in the receiving country. Some of these deprivations are entirely new in the sense that he had never experienced them before entering a consumer society (eg he is made to want cameras, record players, tape recorders, electric shavers, and so on). Others are simply the extension or transference to the new milieu of the deprivations he experienced in his place of origin (eg those related to housing, schooling, and so on). So the migrant slowly becomes socialized in that unsocial game between the standard of living and the cost of living in a post-industrial society.

The polyannual migrant, then, is constantly torn between his desire to overcome his deprivations and his desire to return home to a social context where he must feel the deprivations even more deeply than when he left. The result is that again and again he extends his stay abroad, or he re-emigrates repeatedly after returning home for a short while. Finally this process will lead to a significant number of target workers tending to settle down in the receiving country, if not for ever at least until retirement age. The migrant becomes an immigrant.

This process is applicable to both single and married workers. The young single migrant tends to predominate in the early stages of migration. He is less constrained to take the decision to go abroad and he is also less inhibited when it comes to deciding whether to return 'now' or 'a little later'. Once the apparent success of migration to a particular receiving country makes the round back home, the married worker joins the stream, probably on his own and with the intention of returning home to wife and children as soon as possible. While abroad, he not only has the very human desire to be united again with his family, but he is also most likely to come to that typically lower working-class conclusion that if he wants to improve his lot, and if he is not to return home and admit failure, he will have to send for his wife and older children and will have to send them out to work where he is. He will convince his wife that this is the best solution, and thus over the years the majority of married migrant workers will be joined by their families. However hostile the immigration regulations are towards family reunion, a determined migrant will not be put off by them and will try to satisfy all the provisos: legally if possible, illegally if necessary. Also, in a liberal capitalist society, the inhuman regulations hindering family reunion are coming under increasing pressure from enlightened national and international opinion as well as employers themselves, who find that their foreign workers stay longer and are better workers – that is, more profitable – when they are reunited with their families.

[. . .] It is clear that more and more of the married migrants in Germany were joined by their families during the 60s and that a constant proportion of the shrinking share of separated migrants wished their spouse to come and join them.

Looking at this process in more detail, one can see that a target worker migration stream matures in four stages, which are analytically distinct but historically intertwined in any actual situation and therefore difficult to disentangle empirically. In the *first phase* young single workers, usually male (depending on the social system in the country of origin and the type of labour demand at destination), form the bulk of the migration. They come from the more industrialized and urbanized areas of the sending country, that is, the bigger towns with their more developed networks of internal and international communication, where employment opportunities abroad first become known and information from the emigrants is first relayed; these areas are thus the locus of the 'grapevine' which sets in motion a chain migration. As the first small batch of migrants originates from the more developed part of the sending country, it will comprise a considerably higher level of skills and more industrial skills than the non-migrant population as a whole. If these first migrants come into a country which has only just started to import labour, their duration of stay is likely to be very short, partly because the migration has not yet matured and partly because the first immigrants are likely to be employed in the most marginal positions. Turnover or the ratio of (temporary and permanent) returnees to the size of the foreign work-force is largely a function of the economy of the receiving country and is likely to be very high in marginal jobs. If the first migrants come into a country which is already employing other nationalities, their duration of stay is still likely to be short, but not so much on account of employment in marginal positions as these workers are likely to be employed in a wider variety of jobs.

In the *second phase* the migration stream ages slightly, its sex composition remains basically unchanged, but its composition in terms of marital status resembles more that of the non-migrant population (except that married workers are not necessarily accompanied by spouse and children). Duration of stay increases slightly but perceptibly as both single and married workers tend to extend their stay; turnover decreases accordingly. Looking at the second phase from the viewpoint of the sending country, one can discern the following development. Once the first emigrants return home, they talk in glowing terms to friends and neighbours about their experience, for to do otherwise would imply that their migration was a failure; then newspapers and radios carry reports, and more and more people in the area where the migration started and in neighbouring areas get to know about the luring opportunities. First of all, it is the hitherto hesitant married worker in the area of original emigration who decides to try his hand. The obvious solution is to leave wife and children behind, to go abroad for a definite period of up to one year, to save as much money as possible, and to return and start anew. As married workers are generally somewhat older than single workers, the migration stream shows a slightly higher average age. At the same time the word has gone around in other areas – probably those in close proximity to the area of original migration – that easy money is to be made in a certain labour importing country. Again it is predominantly the single (male) worker who is the first emigrant from the new catchment areas, the pioneer who returns – often only temporarily – to spread the word about high wages and living standards. The geographical extension of the areas of origin from the bigger towns to the surrounding smaller towns and countryside brings with it a greater variety, but lower level, of skill and socio-economic status. Yet it is still true that not only does each new chain of migration show a higher average skill level than its catchment area, but that the migration stream as a whole is more skilled than the general working population of the country from whence it comes.

In the *third phase* the receiving country experiences a continuation of the ageing of the migration stream and a change in the sex composition in favour of the originally under represented sex, as married workers send for their spouses. In this phase the hitherto stable ratio of economically active to inactive immigrants begins to fall: not so much because the wives or husbands of married workers are inactive – they are predominantly taking up employment themselves – but because younger children join their parents abroad. Duration of stay increases further, especially for families, and turnover decreases considerably. Its speed depends on the intensity of the demand for labour in the receiving country and business cycle fluctuations as well as the size of the sending country and possible political interferences there.

In the third phase the married migrant who left the area of original emigration during the second phase begins to realize that he has exchanged one set of deprivations for another and that the desired accumulation of money is taking place at a much slower speed than he had imagined. In the receiving country he finds himself at the bottom of the socio-economic ladder. To return home permanently after only a year abroad would mean that his emigration was not successful in terms of the goals he set for himself when he left his home. Therefore, he decides to go back temporarily and tell his wife that more time is needed for him to achieve his goals. He might possibly suggest, or have indicated in an earlier letter, that two pairs of hands can earn more than one and that his wife should consider accompanying him abroad. This would put an end to their separation and together they could finish the job of earning a great amount of money much more quickly than he could do on his own; it would also eliminate the expense of maintaining two separate households. If the children cannot be cared for by grandparents, they might just as well come along, too. They would surely receive a much better education in the receiving country than at home. Thus, after the first batch of predominantly single migrants and the subsequent wave of unaccompanied married workers one can then detect a wave of family reunion from the original area of emigration. At the same time the areas from which new migrants were first drawn when the receiving country had entered the second phase of maturing, now experience, during the third over-all phase, their second stage of maturing, ie married workers leave from here without their spouses, and so on. And also during the third over-all phase the remaining areas of the sending country that had hitherto not participated in this migration stream will be drawn into its ambit as the message spreads into the more backward and less accessible parts of the country. For them the development repeats itself by starting with young, single workers, and so on. This new and additional part of the migration stream depresses its skill level further and changes its composition more towards the kind of occupations prevalent in the backward areas. But it can still be seen that the skill level of the migrant population is on the balance higher than that of the non-migrant population (Böhning, 1971,

Tables 6 and 7). Whether or not the migration stream from the sending country as a whole finally comes to be dominated by the flows from the more backward areas depends on the size of those areas relative to the intermediate and most developed areas of the country concerned.

Up to the beginning of the third stage the migratory process is not self-feeding in the sense that more migrants are entering the receiving country than are wanted for work there. During the third stage the self-feeding process [. . .] commences, predominantly through the immigration of dependants. Moreover, by this time the immigration population has swollen so much that it induces significant infrastructural demands for housing, schooling, and consumer goods. This means that additional infrastructure and capacity will have to be provided and that additional demand for labour will be exerted, some of which can only be satisfied by importing additional workers.

Finally, longer stays and a significant extent of family reunion lead in the *fourth phase* of maturity to an enlargement of the immigrant population via the entry of employers, secular and religious leaders, and others. As the psychological comfort afforded by the company of their fellow countrymen leads the immigrant workers and families to settle in groups and colonies, there slowly arises a demand for ethnic shops, churches, schools and other facilities. Each of these ethnic institutions will subsequently be staffed predominantly by ethnic workers, which means additional immigration both in terms of additional workers and additional non-workers. For this to materialize there must be present a significant number of ethnic immigrants, that is, a certain concentration over a given space. The threshold for the major European post-industrial societies seems to lie between 100,000 and 200,000 ethnic immigrants. When the fourth phase has begun for the labour-receiving country, the intermediate areas of the sending country only experience their third stage, ie family reunion, and the least developed areas only their second stage, ie the migration of married workers without families.

The picture which I have painted in terms of an ideal type of development is of course less sharp as regards the distinction of developed/ intermediate/backward areas if one has only aggregate data at one's disposal. And the fact that the four-stage development for the receiving country is composed of a staggered four-stage development for various areas of origin in the sending country makes the statistical picture slightly less impressive than if one could follow the maturing of the migration stream from a small controllable area.

It is worthwhile to consider briefly some of the implications for the return movement of target workers deriving from this four-stage model of maturity. There is unmistakable evidence that integration into the host society is largely a function of the level of skills and education: that is, the higher the level of skills and/or education of foreign workers entering the host society, the more quickly and easily they will become integrated into that society.[6] These workers tend to extend their stay repeatedly until they finally settle (Hagmann, 1971; and Böhning, 1971). Therefore, one can expect a disproportionate share of the original migrants from the most developed areas not to return permanently but to settle and possibly marry abroad. Furthermore, the married worker who overcomes the initial adjustment difficulties and who asks his wife and children to join him abroad, consciously or subconsciously opts for at least semi-permanent settlement. With his family he will be able to overcome further adjustment problems more easily and, once some of his children go to school in the receiving country, he begins to realize that they are slowly becoming alienated from their country of origin and that returning home would severely diminish their chances of living the life he wishes for them. Anyway, he himself becomes inextricably enmeshed in the demands and rewards of a consumer society, and after some years of employment abroad he is gradually but noticeably climbing the socio-economic ladder. Migrants from the backward areas of the country of origin have the least favourable educational and skill endowment, and their family structure may also retard the degree of family reunion more than is the case for married workers from the cities and intermediate areas. It is these people, ill equipped to be successful in a post-industrial society, who form a disproportionately large share of the returnees in terms of both permanent returnees and the large number of people who circulate on the European labour market without ever finding a comfortable niche.

A stream of economic migrants into our contemporary post-industrial societies is self-feeding and unending because, on the one side, our job structures are becoming fossilized and the demand for labour can be restructured in low-skilled repetitive jobs to suit the potential supply, and, on the other side, because the repercussions on labour demand and the build-up of ethnic communities during maturation create, autonomously and additionally, demand for workers which was not foreseen when the labour import commenced and which can largely be satisfied only by the import of new workers.

# Notes

1. Witness the fall of Chancellor Erhard at the end of 1966.
2. It was instructive to hear the public outcry in April 1971 following British Leyland's decision to give lavatory attendants at the Longbridge works an annual salary of £1,500.
3. This was well seen by Lutz (1963, note 35, p. 30), but not as being sufficiently forceful to upset her two-sector model.
4. This aspect of the debate on the economic effects of immigration has generally been overlooked. Whether too many marginal firms are kept in business and whether capital widening is preferred to capital deepening, depends more on the nationally prevalent investment policy and on the degree to which firms are sheltered from competition than on the import of labour in the lower wage brackets. The construction industry, for example, has not been known to be particularly exposed to international competition.
5. Jones and Smith (1970) seemed to be somewhat surprised to find that Commonwealth immigration has had a scaling effect in terms of both industrial sectors and occupational groups as early as five or six years after it had commenced. Their analysis with respect to occupations is defective (mainly through lack of data) in so far as it takes account of only one dimension of this two-dimensional problem. One is very much reminded of the bird's-eye view of Paris which found that immigrants are distributed fairly evenly over the whole of the city when every Parisian knows that immigrants are living mainly in lofts and cellars, which you find everywhere in Paris.
6. [Editorial comment] For contrary evidence see Ballard and Holden in this volume.

# References

Böhning, W. R. (1971) 'The Social and Occupational Apprenticeship of Mediterranean Migrant Workers in West Germany' in Livi-Bacci, M. (ed.) *The Demographic and Social Pattern of Emigration from the Southern European Countries*, Firenze, Dipartimento Statistico Matematica.

Cohen, B. G. and Jenner, P. J. (1968) The Employment of Immigrants: A Case Study within the Wool Industry (see this volume).

Hagmann, H. M. (1971) 'Les Pays d'Immigration' in Livi-Bacci, M. & Hagmann, H-M (eds.) *Report on the Demographic and Social Pattern of Migrants in Europe, especially with regard to International Migrations*, Strasbourg, Council of Europe.

Jones, J. and Smith, A. (1970) *The Economic Impact of Migration*, London, CUP for National Institute of Economic & Social Research.

Lutz, V. (1963) 'Foreign Workers and Domestic Wage Levels, with an Illustration from the Swiss case', *Banca Nazionale del Lavoro quarterly review*, Vol.XVI, No.64 pp. 3–68.

# CHAPTER 1.2

## THE FUNCTION OF LABOUR IMMIGRATION IN WESTERN EUROPEAN CAPITALISM[*]
### Stephen Castles and Godula Kosack

The domination of the working masses by a small capitalist ruling class has never been based on violence alone. Capitalist rule is based on a range of mechanisms, some objective products of the economic process, others subjective phenomena arising through manipulation of attitudes. Two such mechanisms, which received considerable attention from the founders of scientific socialism, are the industrial reserve army, which belongs to the first category, and the labour aristocracy, which belongs to the second. These two mechanisms are closely related, as are the objective and subjective factors which give rise to them.

Engels pointed out that 'English manufacture must have, at all times save the brief periods of highest prosperity, an unemployed reserve army of workers, in order to produce the masses of goods required by the market in the liveliest months.'[1] Marx showed that the industrial reserve army or surplus working population is not only the necessary product of capital accumulation and the associated increase in labour productivity, but at the same time 'the lever of capitalist accumulation', 'a condition of existence of the capitalist mode of production'.[2] Only by bringing ever more workers into the production process can the capitalist accumulate capital, which is the precondition for extending production and applying new techniques. These new techniques throw out of work the very men whose labour allowed their application. They are set free to provide a labour reserve which is available to be thrown into other sectors as the interests of the capitalist require. 'The whole form of the movement of modern industry depends, therefore, upon the constant transformation of

[*] New Left Review, 1972, No. 73.

a part of the labouring population into unemployed or half-employed hands.'[3] The pressure of the industrial reserve army forces those workers who are employed to accept long hours and poor conditions. Above all: 'Taking them as a whole, the general movements of wages are exclusively regulated by the expansion and contraction of the industrial reserve army.'[4] If employment grows and the reserve army contracts, workers are in a better position to demand higher wages. When this happens, profits and capital accumulation diminish, investment falls and men are thrown out of work, leading to a growth of the reserve army and a fall in wages. This is the basis of the capitalist economic cycle. Marx mentions the possibility of the workers seeing through the seemingly natural law of relative over-population, and undermining its effectiveness through trade-union activity directed towards co-operation between the employed and the unemployed.[5]

The labour aristocracy is also described by Engels and Marx. By conceding privileges to certain well-organized sectors of labour, above all to craftsmen (who by virtue of their training could not be readily replaced by members of the industrial reserve army), the capitalists were able to undermine class consciousness and secure an opportunist non-revolutionary leadership for these sectors.[6] Special advantages, sometimes taking the form of symbols of higher status (different clothing, salary instead of wages, etc) rather than higher material rewards, were also conferred upon foremen and non-manual workers, with the aim of distinguishing them from other workers and causing them to identify their interests with those of the capitalists. Engels pointed out that the privileges given to some British workers were possible because of the vast profits made by the capitalists through domination of the world market and imperialist exploitation of labour in other countries.[7] Lenin emphasized the effects of imperialism on class consciousness: 'Imperialism . . . makes it economically possible to bribe the upper strata of the proletariat, and thereby fosters, gives shape to, and strengthens opportunism.'[8] '. . . A section of the proletariat allows itself to be led by men bought by, or at least paid by, the bourgeoisie', and the result is a split among the workers and 'temporary decay in the working-class movement'.[9]

The industrial reserve army and the labour aristocracy have not lost their importance as mechanisms of domination in the current phase of organized monopoly capitalism. However, the way in which they function has undergone important changes. In particular the maintenance of an industrial reserve army within the developed capitalist countries of West

Europe has become increasingly difficult. With the growth of the labour movement after the First World War, economic crises and unemployment began to lead to political tensions which threatened the existence of the capitalist system. Capitalism responded by setting up fascist régimes in the areas where it was most threatened, in order to suppress social conflict through violence. The failure of this strategy, culminating in the defeat of fascism in 1945, was accompanied by the reinforcement of the non-capitalist bloc in East Europe and by a further strengthening of the labour movement in West Europe. In order to survive, the capitalist system had to aim for continuous expansion and full employment at any price. But full employment strikes at a basic principle of the capitalist economy: the use of the industrial reserve army to keep wages down and profits up. A substitute for the traditional form of reserve army had to be found, for without it capitalist accumulation is impossible. Moreover, despite Keynsian economics, it is not possible completely to avoid the cyclical development of the capitalist economy. It was therefore necessary to find a way of cushioning the effects of crises, so as to hinder the development of dangerous social tensions.

### Immigrants as the new industrial reserve army

The solution to these problems adopted by West European capitalism has been the employment of immigrant workers from under-developed areas of Southern Europe or from the Third World.[10] Today, the unemployed masses of these areas form a 'latent surplus-population'[11] or reserve army, which can be imported into the developed countries as the interests of the capitalist class dictate. In addition to this economic function, the employment of immigrant workers has an important socio-political function for capitalism: by creating a split between immigrant and indigenous workers along national and racial lines and offering better conditions and status to indigenous workers, it is possible to give large sections of the working class the consciousness of a labour aristocracy.

The employment of immigrant workers in the capitalist production process is not a new phenomenon. The Irish played a vital part in British industrialization. Not only did they provide a special form of labour for heavy work of a temporary nature on railways, canals and roads;[12] their competition also forced down wages and conditions for other workers. Engels described Irish immigration as a 'cause of abasement to which the English worker is exposed, a cause permanently active in forcing the whole class downwards'.[13] Marx described the antagonism between

British and Irish workers, artificially created by the mass media of the ruling class, as 'the secret of the impotence of the English working class, despite their organization'.[14] As industrialization got under way in France, Germany and Switzerland in the latter half of the nineteenth century, these countries too brought in foreign labour: from Poland, Italy and Spain. There were 800,000 foreign workers in the German Reich in 1907. More than a third of the Ruhr miners were Poles. Switzerland had half a million foreigners in 1910 – fifteen per cent of her total population. French heavy industry was highly dependent on immigrant labour right up to the Second World War. According to Lenin, one of the special features of imperialism was 'the decline in emigration from imperialist countries and the increase in immigration into these countries from the more backward countries where lower wages are paid'.[15] This was a main cause of the division of the working class. The fascist form of capitalism also developed its own specific form of exploiting immigrant workers: the use of forced labour. No less than seven and a half million deportees from occupied countries and prisoners of war were working in Germany by 1944, replacing the men recruited for the army. About a quarter of German munitions production was carried out by foreign labour.[16]

Compared with early patterns, immigration of workers to contemporary West Europe has two new features. The first is its character as a permanent part of the economic structure. Previously, immigrant labour was used more or less temporarily when the domestic industrial reserve army was inadequate for some special reason, like war or unusually fast expansion; since 1945, however, large numbers of immigrant workers have taken up key positions in the productive process, so that even in the case of recession their labour cannot be dispensed with. The second is its importance as the basis of the modern industrial reserve army. Other groups which might conceivably fulfil the same function – non-working women, the disabled and the chronic sick, members of the lumpenproletariat whose conditions prevent them from working,[17] have already been integrated into the production process to the extent to which this is profitable for the capitalist system. The use of further reserves of this type would require costly social measures (eg adequate kindergartens). The main traditional form of the industrial reserve army – men thrown out of work by rationalization and cyclical crises – is hardly available today, for reasons already mentioned. Thus immigration is of key importance for the capitalist system. [. . .]

The migratory movements and the government policies which direct them reflect the growing importance and changing function of immigrant labour in West Europe. Immediately after the Second World War, Switzerland, Britain and France recruited foreign workers. Switzerland needed extra labour for the export boom permitted by her intact industry in the middle of war-torn Europe. The 'European Voluntary Workers' in Britain (initially displaced persons, later Italians) were assigned to specific jobs connected with industrial reconstruction. The reconstruction boom was not expected to last. Both Switzerland and Britain imposed severe restrictions on foreign workers, designed to stop them from settling and bringing in their families, so that they could be dismissed and deported at the least sign of recession. France was something of an exception: her immigration policy was concerned not only with labour needs for reconstruction, but also with permanent immigration to counteract the demographic effects of the low birth-rate.

When West German industry got under way again after the 1949 Currency Reform there was at first no need for immigrants from Southern Europe. An excellent industrial reserve army was provided by the seven million expellees from the former Eastern provinces of the Reich and by the three million refugees from East Germany, many of whom were skilled workers. Throughout the 50s, the presence of these reserves kept wage-growth slow and hence provided the basis for the 'economic miracle'. By the mid-50s, however, special labour shortages were appearing, first in agriculture and building. It was then that recruitment of foreign workers (initially on a seasonal basis[18]) was started. Here too, an extremely restrictive policy was followed with regard to family entry and long-term settlement. 'Rotation' of the foreign labour force was encouraged. In this stage, the use of immigrants in the countries mentioned followed the pre-war pattern: they were brought in to satisfy special and, it was thought, temporary labour needs in certain sectors. They were, as an official of the German employers' association put it, 'a mobile labour potential'.[19]

By the 60s, the situation was changing. Despite mild cyclical tendencies it was clear that there was not going to be a sudden return to the pre-war boom-slump pattern. The number of immigrant workers grew extremely rapidly in the late 50s and early 60s. Between 1956 and 1965 nearly one million new workers entered France. The number of foreign workers in West Germany increased from 279,000 in 1960 to over 1·3 million in 1966. In Switzerland there were 326,000 immigrant workers (including seasonals) in 1956, and 721,000 in 1964. This was also the period of mass immigration to Britain from the Commonwealth.[20] The change was not merely quantitative: immigrants were moving into and becoming indispensable in ever more sectors of the economy. They were no longer filling gaps in peripheral branches like agriculture and building but were becoming a vital part of the labour force in key industries like engineering and chemicals. Moreover, there was growing competition between the different countries to obtain the 'most desirable' immigrants, ie, those with the best education and the least cultural distance from the receiving countries. The growing need for labour was forcing the recruiters to go further and further afield: Turkey and Yugoslavia were replacing Italy as Germany's main labour source. Portugal and North Africa were replacing Italy and Spain in the case of France.

As a result, new policies intended to attract and integrate immigrant workers, but also to control them better, were introduced. One such measure was the free labour movement policy of the EEC, designed to increase the availability of the rural proletariat of Sicily and the Mezzogiorno to West European capital.[21] Germany and Switzerland liberalized the conditions for family entry and long-term settlement, while at the same time tightening political control through measures such as the German 1965 Foreigners Law. France tried to increase control over entries, in order to prevent the large-scale clandestine immigration which had taken place throughout the 50s and 60s (and still does, despite the new policy). At the same time restrictions were made on the permanent settlement of non-Europeans – officially because of their 'greater difficulties in integrating'. In Britain, racialist campaigns led to the stopping of unrestricted Commonwealth immigration in 1962. By limiting the labour supply, this measure contradicted the economic interests of the ruling class. The Immigration Act of 1971, which could provide the basis for organized and controlled labour recruitment on the German and French pattern, is a corrective, although its application for this purpose is not at present required, since the ruling class has created an internal industrial reserve army through unemployment.

In view of the stagnant domestic labour force potential and the long-term growth trend of the economy, immigrant labour has become a structural necessity for West European capitalism.[22] It has a dual function today.[23] One section is maintained as a mobile fluctuating labour force, which can be moved from factory to factory or branch to branch as required by the development of the means of production, and which can be thrown out of work and deported as required without causing social tensions. This function was shown clearly by the West German recession of 1966–7, when the foreign labour force dropped by 400,000, although there were never more than 29,000 receiving unemployment benefit. As a United Nations study pointed out, West Germany was able to export unemployment to the home countries of the migrants.[24] The other section is required for permanent employment throughout the economy. They are offered better conditions and the chance of long-term settlement.[25] Despite this they still fulfil the function of an industrial reserve army, for they are given inferior jobs, have no political rights and may be used as a constant threat to the wages and conditions of the local labour force.

## Occupational position

The immigrant percentage of the population in no way reflects the contribution of immigrants to the economy. They are mainly young men, whose dependents are sent for later if at all. Many of them remain only a few years, and are then replaced by others, so that there are hardly any retired immigrants. Immigrants therefore have higher than average rates of economic activity, and make contributions to health, unemployment and pension insurance far in excess of their demands on such schemes.[26] Particularly high rates of activity are to be found among recently arrived groups, or among those who for social and cultural reasons tend not to bring dependents with them: Portuguese and North Africans in France, Turks in Germany and Pakistanis in Britain. Immigrant workers are about 6·5 per cent of the labour force in Britain, seven to eight per cent in France, ten per cent in West Germany and 30 per cent in Switzerland. Even these figures do not show adequately the structural importance of immigrant labour, which is concentrated in certain areas and types of work.

The overwhelming majority of immigrants live in highly industrialized and fast-growing urban area like Paris, the Lyon region, the Ruhr, Baden-Württemberg, London and the West Midlands. For example 31·2 per cent of all immigrants in France live in the Paris region, compared with only 19·2 per cent of the total population. Nine and a half per cent of the inhabitants of the Paris region are immigrants.[27] In Britain more than one third of all immigrants are to be found in Greater London compared with one sixth of the total population. Immigrants make up twelve per cent of London's population.[28]

More important still is the concentration in certain industries. [. . .] In Britain the concentration of immigrants in certain industries is less marked [than in other labour importing countries of North-Western

Europe], and different immigrant groups have varying patterns. The Irish are concentrated in construction, while Commonwealth immigrants are over-represented in metal manufacture and transport. Pakistani men are mainly to be found in the textile industry and Cypriots in clothing and footwear and in distribution. European immigrants are frequently in the services sector. Immigrant women of all nationalities tend to work in services, although some groups (Cypriots, West Indians) also often work in manufacturing.[29]

In general immigrants are concentrated in certain basic industries, where they form a high proportion of the labour force. Together with their geographical concentration this means that immigrant workers are of great importance in the very type of enterprise and area which used to be regarded as the strongholds of the class-conscious proletariat. The real concentration is even greater than the figures show, for within each industry the immigrants tend to have become predominant in certain departments and occupations. There can be hardly a foundry in West Europe in which immigrants do not form a majority, or at least a high proportion, of the labour force. The same applies to monotonous production line work, such as car-assembly. Renault, Citroen, Volkswagen, Ford of Cologne and Opel all have mainly foreign workers on the assembly line (The British motor industry is an exception in this respect).[30] [. . .]

Immigrants form the lowest stratum of the working class carrying out unskilled and semi-skilled work in those industrial sectors with the worst working conditions and/or the lowest pay.[31] The entry of immigrants at the bottom of the labour market has made possible the release of many indigenous workers from such employment, and their promotion to jobs with better conditions and higher status, ie skilled, supervisory or white-collar employment. Apart from the economic effects, this process has a profound impact on the class consciousness of the indigenous workers concerned. This will be discussed in more detail below.

## Social position

The division of the working class within the production process is duplicated by a division in other spheres of society. The poor living conditions of immigrants have attracted too much liberal indignation and welfare zeal to need much description here. Immigrants get the worst types of housing: in Britain slums and run-down lodging houses, in France *bidonvilles* (shanty-towns) and overcrowded hotels, in Germany and Switzerland camps of wooden huts belonging to the employers and attics in the cities. It is rare for immigrants to get council houses.[31A] Immigrants are discriminated against by many landlords, so that those who do specialize in housing them can charge extortionate rents for inadequate facilities. In Germany and France, official programmes have been established to provide hostel accommodation for single immigrant workers. These hostels do provide somewhat better material conditions. On the other hand they increase the segregation of immigrant workers from the rest of the working class, deny them any private life, and above all put them under the control of the employers 24 hours a day.[32] In Germany the employers have repeatedly attempted to use control over immigrants' accommodation to force them to act as strike-breakers.

Language and vocational training courses for immigrant workers are generally provided only when it is absolutely necessary for the production process, as in mines for example. Immigrant children are also at a disadvantage: they tend to live in run-down overcrowded areas where school facilities are poorest. No adequate measures are taken to deal with their special educational problems (eg, language difficulties), so that their educational performance is usually below-average. As a result of their bad working and living conditions, immigrants have serious health problems. For instance they have much higher tuberculosis rates than the rest of the population virtually everywhere.[33] As there are health controls at the borders, it is clear that such illnesses have been contracted in West Europe rather than being brought in by the immigrants.

The inferior work-situation and living conditions of immigrants have caused some bourgeois sociologists to define them as a 'lumpenproletariat' or a 'marginal group'. This is clearly incorrect. A group which makes up ten, twenty or 30 per cent of the industrial labour force cannot be regarded as marginal to society. Others speak of a 'new proletariat' or a 'sub-proletariat'. Such terms are also wrong. The first implies that the indigenous workers have ceased to be proletarians and have been replaced by the immigrants in this social position. The second postulates that immigrant workers have a different relationship to the means of production than that traditionally characteristic of the proletariat. In reality both indigenous and immigrant workers share the same relationship to the means of production: they are excluded from ownership or control; they are forced to sell their labour power in order to survive; they work under the direction and in the interests of others. In the sphere of consumption both categories of workers are subject to the laws of the commodity market, where the supply and price of goods is determined not by their use value but by their profitability for capitalists; both are victims of landlords, retail monopolists and similar bloodsuckers and manipulators of the consumption-terror. These are the characteristics typical of the proletariat ever since the industrial revolution, and on this basis immigrant and indigenous workers must be regarded as members of the same class: the proletariat. But it is a divided class: the marginal privileges conceded to indigenous workers and the particularly intensive exploitation of immigrants combine to create a barrier between the two groups, which appear as distinct strata within the class. The division is deepened by certain legal, political and psychological factors, which will be discussed below.

## Discrimination

Upon arrival in West Europe, immigrants from under-developed areas have little basic education or vocational training, and are usually ignorant of the language. They know nothing of prevailing market conditions or prices. In capitalist society, these characteristics are sufficient to ensure that immigrants get poor jobs and social conditions. After a period of adaptation to industrial work and urban life, the prevailing ideology would lead one to expect many immigrants to obtain better jobs, housing, etc. Special mechanisms ensure that this does not happen in the majority of cases. On the one hand there is institutionalized discrimination in the form of legislation which restricts immigrants' civic and labour market rights. On the other hand there are informal discriminatory practices based on racialism or xenophobia.

In nearly all West European countries, labour market legislation discriminates against foreigners. They are granted labour permits for a specific job in a certain firm for a limited period. They do not have the right to move to better-paid or more highly qualified positions, at least for some years. Workers who change jobs without permission are often deported. Administrative practices in this respect have been liberalized to some extent in Germany and Switzerland in recent years, due to the need for immigrant labour in a wider range of occupations, but the basic restrictiveness of the system remains. In Britain, Commonwealth immigrants (once admitted to the country) and the Irish had equal rights with local workers until the 1971 Immigration Act. Now Commonwealth immigrants have the same labour market situation as aliens. The threat of deportation if an immigrant loses his job is a very powerful weapon for the employer. Immigrants who demand better conditions can be sacked for indiscipline and the police will do the rest.[34] Regulations which restrict family entry and permanent settlement also keep immigrants in inferior positions. If a man may stay only for a few years, it is not worth his while to learn the language and take vocational training courses.

Informal discrimination is well known in Britain, where it takes the form of the colour bar. The PEP study,[35] as well as many other investigations, has shown that coloured immigrants encounter discrimination with regard to employment, housing and provision of services such as mortgages and insurance. The more qualified a coloured man is, the more likely he is to encounter discrimination. This mechanism keeps immigrants in 'their place', ie, doing the dirty, unpleasant jobs. Immigrants in the other European countries also encounter informal discrimination. Immigrants rarely get promotion to supervisory or non-manual jobs, even when they are well-qualified. Discrimination in housing is widespread. In Britain, adverts specifying 'no coloured' are forbidden, but in Germany or Switzerland one still frequently sees 'no foreigners'.

The most serious form of discrimination against immigrant workers is their deprivation of political rights. Foreigners may not vote in local or national elections. Nor may they hold public office, which in France is defined so widely as to include trade-union posts. Foreigners do not generally have the same rights as local workers with regard to eligibility for works councils and similar representative bodies. The main exception to this formal exclusion from political participation concerns Irish and Commonwealth immigrants in Britain, who have the right to vote (the same will not apply to those who enter under the 1971 Act). But the Mangrove case [36] shows the type of repression which may be expected by any immigrants who dare to organize themselves. Close police control over the political activities of immigrants is the rule throughout Europe, and deportations of political and trade-union militants are common. After the May Events in France, hundreds of foreign workers were deported.[37] Foreign language newspapers of the CGT labour federation have been repeatedly forbidden. The German Foreigners Law of 1965 lays down that the political activity of foreigners can be forbidden if 'important interests of the German Federal Republic require this' – a provision so flexible that the police can prevent any activity they choose. Even this is not regarded as sufficient. When Federal Chancellor Willy Brandt visited Iran in March 1972 to do an oil deal, the Shah complained strongly about Iranian students being allowed to criticize him in Germany. The Greek and

Yugoslav ambassadors have also protested about the activiti
citizens. Now the German Government is working on a new ₁₁ᵥ. ₋₋₋₋₋₋₋
would go so far as to make police permission necessary even for private
meetings of foreigners in closed rooms.[38]

## Prejudice and class consciousness

Discrimination against immigrants is a reflection of widespread hostility
towards them. In Britain, this is regarded as 'colour prejudice' or
'racialism', and indeed there can be no doubt that the hostility of large
sections of the population is at present directed against black people. Race
relations theorists attribute the problems connected with immigration
partly to the immigrants' difficulties in adapting to the prevailing norms of
the 'host society', and partly to the indigenous population's inbred distrust
of the newcomers who can be distinguished by their skin colour. The
problems are abstracted from the socio-economic structure and reduced to
the level of attitudes. Solutions are to be sought not through political
action, but through psychological and educational strategies.[39] But a
comparison of surveys carried out in different countries shows that
hostility towards immigrants is everywhere as great as in Britain, even
where the immigrants are white.[40] The Italian who moves to the
neighbouring country of Switzerland is as unpopular as the Asian in
Britain. This indicates that hostility is based on the position of immigrants
in society and not on the colour of their skin.

Racialism and xenophobia are products of the capitalist national state
and of its imperialist expansion.[41] Their principal historical function was
to split the working class on the international level, and to motivate one
section to help exploit another in the interests of the ruling class. Today
such ideologies help to deepen the split within the working class in West
Europe. Many indigenous workers do not perceive that they share a
common class position and class interests with immigrant workers. The
basic fact of having the same relationship to the means of production is
obscured by the local workers' marginal advantages with regard to
material conditions and status. The immigrants are regarded not as class
comrades, but as alien intruders who pose an economic and social threat.
It is feared that they will take away the jobs of local labour, that they will
be used by the employers to force down wages and to break strikes.[42]
Whatever the behaviour of the immigrant workers – and in fact they
almost invariably show solidarity with their indigenous colleagues – such
fears are not without a basis. It is indeed the strategy of the employers to

use immigration to put pressure on wages and to weaken the labour movement.[43] The very social and legal weakness of the immigrants is a weapon in the hands of the employers. Other points of competition are to be found outside work, particularly on the housing market. The presence of immigrants is often regarded as the cause of rising rents and increased overcrowding in the cities. By making immigrants the scapegoats for the insecurity and inadequate conditions which the capitalist system inevitably provides for workers, attention is diverted from the real causes.

Workers often adopt racialism as a defence mechanism against a real or apparent threat to their conditions. It is an incorrect response to a real problem. By preventing working-class unity, racialism assists the capitalists in their strategy of 'divide and rule'. The function of racialism in the capitalist system is often obscured by the fact that racialist campaigns usually have petty-bourgeois leadership and direct their slogans against the big industrialists. The Schwarzenback Initiative in Switzerland – which called for the deportation of a large proportion of the immigrant population – is an example, [44] as are Enoch Powell's campaigns for repatriation. Such demands are opposed by the dominant sections of the ruling class. The reason is clear: a complete acceptance of racialism would prevent the use of immigrants as an industrial reserve army. But despite this, racialist campaigns serve the interest of the ruling class: they increase tension between indigenous and immigrant workers and weaken the labour movement. The large working-class following gained by Powell in his racialist campaigns demonstrates how dangerous they are. Paradoxically, their value for capitalism lies in their very failure to achieve their declared aims.

The presence of immigrant workers is one of the principal factors contributing to the lack of class consciousness among large sections of the working class. The existence of a new lower stratum of immigrants changes the worker's perception of his own position in society. Instead of a dichotomic view of society, in which the working masses confront a small capitalist ruling class, many workers now see themselves as belonging to an intermediate stratum, superior to the unskilled immigrant workers. Such a consciousness is typified by an hierarchical view of society and by orientation towards advancement through individual achievement and competition, rather than through solidarity and collective action. This is the mentality of the labour aristocracy and leads to opportunism and the temporary decay of the working-class movement.

## Immigration and society

The impact of immigration on contemporary West European society may now be summarized.

*Economic effects:* the new industrial reserve army of immigrant workers is a major stabilizing factor of the capitalist economy. By restraining wage increases, immigration is a vital precondition for capital accumulation and hence for growth. In the long run, wages may grow more in a country which has large-scale immigration than in one which does not, because of the dynamic effect of increased capital accumulation on productivity. However, wages are a smaller share, and profits a larger share of national income than would have been the case without immigration.[45] The best illustration of this effect is obtained by comparing the German and the British economies since 1945. Germany has had large and continuous increases in labour force due to immigration. At first wages were held back. The resulting capital accumulation allowed fast growth and continuous rationalization. Britain has had virtually no growth in labour force due to migration (immigration has been cancelled out by emigration of British people to Australia, etc). Every phase of expansion has collapsed rapidly as wages rose due to labour shortages. The long-term effect has been stagnation. By the 60s, German wages overtook those of Britain, while economic growth and rationalization continued at an almost undiminished rate.

*Social effects:* the inferior position of immigrant workers with regard to employment and social conditions has led to a division of the working class into two strata. The split is maintained by various forms of discrimination and is reinforced by racialist and xenophobic ideologies, which the ruling class can disseminate widely through its hegemony over the means of socialization and communication. Large sections of the indigenous workers take the position of a labour aristocracy, which objectively participates in the exploitation of another group of workers.

*Political effects:* the decline of class consciousness weakens the working-class movement. In addition, the denial of political rights to immigrants excludes a large section of the working class from political activity, and hence weakens the class as a whole. The most exploited section of the working class is rendered voiceless and powerless. Special forms of repression are designed to keep it that way. [. . .]

## Notes and references

1. Engels, 'The Condition of the Working Class in England', in Marx and Engels, *On Britain*, Moscow 1962, p. 119.
2. Marx, *Capital*, Vol. I, Moscow 1961, p. 632.
3. Ibid., p. 633.
4. Ibid., p. 637.
5. Ibid, p. 640.
6. Engels, Preface to the English edition of 'The Condition of the Working Class in England', op. cit., p. 28.
7. Engels, 'The English Elections', in *On Britain*, op. cit., p. 505.
8. Lenin, *Imperialism – The Highest Stage of Capitalism*, Moscow 1966, pp. 96–7.
9. Ibid., pp. 99–100.
10. In this article we examine the function of labour migration only for the countries of immigration. Migration also plays an important stabilizing role for the reactionary regimes of the countries of origin – a role which is understood and to some extent planned by the ruling class in West Europe. Although we are concerned only with West Europe in this article, it is important to note that the use of certain special categories of workers, who can be discriminated against without arousing general solidarity from other workers, is a general feature of modern capitalism. The blacks and chicanos are the industrial reserve army of the USA, the Africans of white-dominated Southern Africa. Current attempts by 'liberal' capitalists to relax the colour bar to allow blacks into certain skilled and white-collar jobs, both in the USA and South Africa, however estimable in humanitarian terms, are designed mainly to weaken the unions and put pressure on wages in these sectors.
11. Marx mentions several forms taken by the industrial reserve army. One is the 'latent' surplus-population of agricultural labourers, whose wages and conditions have been depressed to such an extent that they are merely waiting for a favourable opportunity to move into industry and join the urban proletariat. (*Capital*, Vol. I., op. cit., p. 642.) Although these workers are not yet in industry, the possibility that they may at any time join the industrial labour force increases the capitalist's ability to resist wage increases. The latent industrial reserve army has the same effect as the urban unemployed. Unemployed workers in other countries, in so far as they may be brought into the industrial labour force whenever required, clearly form a latent industrial reserve army in the same way as rural unemployed within the country.
12. See E. P. Thompson, *The Making of the English Working Class*, Harmondsworth 1968, pp. 469–85.
13. 'The Condition of the Working Class in England', op. cit., p. 123.
14. Letter to S. Meyer and A. Vogt, 9 April 1870, in *On Britain*, op. cit., p. 552.
15. *Imperialism*, op. cit., p. 98.
16. Hans Pfahlmann, *Fremdarbeiter und Kriegsgefangene in der deutschen Kriegswirlschaft, 1939–1945*, Darmstadt 1968, p. 232.
17. For the role of the lumpenproletariat in the industrial reserve army, see *Capital*, Vol. I, op. cit., p. 643.
18. Many foreign workers are still employed on a seasonal basis in building,

agriculture and catering in France and Switzerland. This is a special form of exploitation. The worker has no income in-the off-season and is therefore forced to work very long hours for the nine to ten months when he does have work. He cannot bring his family with him, he has even more limited civic rights than other immigrants, and he has absolutely no security, for there is no guarantee that his employment will be continued from year to year.

19. Ulrich Freiherr von Gienanth, in *Der Arbeitgeber*, Vol. 18, 20 March 1966, p. 153.

20. For Commonwealth immigration see E. J. B. Rose et al., *Colour and Citizenship*, London 1969.

21. Eurocrats refer to the free movement policy as the beginning of a 'European labour market'. But although EEC citizens have the right to choose which country to be exploited in, they lack any civic or political rights once there. Moreover, the Southern Italian labour reserves are being absorbed by the monopolies of Turin and Milan, so that intra-EEC migration is steadily declining in volume, while migration from outside the EEC increases.

22. Where formalized economic planning exists, this necessity has been publicly formulated. Prognoses on the contribution of immigrants to the labour force were included in the Fourth and Fifth Five-Year Plans in France, and play an even more prominent part in the current Sixth Plan. See *Le VIe plan et les travailleurs étrangers*, Paris 1971.

23. Cf. Ruth Becker, Gerhard Dörr, K. H. Tjaden, 'Fremdarbeiterbeschäftigung im deutschen Kapitalismus', *Das Argument*, December 1971, p. 753.

24. United Nations Economic Commission for Europe, *Economic Survey of Europe 1967*, Geneva 1968, Chapter I, p. 49.

25. The distinction between the two sections of the immigrant labour force is formalized in the new French immigration policy introduced in 1968. There are separate regulations for South Europeans, who are encouraged to bring in their families and settle permanently, and Africans (particularly Algerians) who are meant to come for a limited period only, without dependents.

26. It is estimated that foreign workers in Germany are at present paying about seventeen per cent of all contributions to pension insurance, but that foreigners are receiving only 0·5 per cent of the total benefits. Heinz Salowsky, 'Sozialpolitische Aspekte der Auslanderbeschaftigung', *Berichte des Deutschen Industrie instituts zur Sozialpolitik*, Vol. 6(S), No. 2, February 1972, pp. 16–22.

27. Calculated from: 'Statistiques du Ministère de l'Intérieur', *Hommes et Migrations: Documents*, No. 788, 15 May 1970; and *Annuaire Statistique de la France 1968*.

28. 1966 Census.

29. 1966 Census. For a detailed analysis of immigrants' employment see: K. Jones and A. D. Smith, *The Economic Impact of Commonwealth Immigration*, Cambridge 1970. Also *Immigrant Workers and Class Structure in Western Europe*, op. cit., Ch. III.

30. [Editorial note: This probably remains the case although the 1971 census figures subsequently showed that the employment of migrants in vehicle manufacture – 6·4 per cent all migrants, 3·0 per cent NCW migrants – was

rather higher than for industry as a whole – 5·8 per cent all migrant workers, 2·2 per cent NCW workers].

31. Some employers – particularly small inefficient ones – specialize in the exploitation of immigrants. For instance they employ illegal immigrants, who can be forced to work for very low wages and cannot complain to the authorities for fear of deportation. Such cases often cause much indignation in the liberal and social-democratic press. But, in fact, it is the big efficient firms exploiting immigrants in a legal and relatively humane way which make the biggest profits out of them. The function of immigration in West European capitalism is created not by the malpractices of backward firms (many of whom incidentally could not survive without immigrant labour), but by the most advanced sectors of big industry which plan and utilize the position of immigrant workers to their own advantage.

31A. [Editorial note: It is no longer such a rarity, though people of New Commonwealth origin are still under-represented in such housing.]

32. 'So far as we are concerned, hostel and works represent parts of a single whole. The hostels belong to the mines, so the foreign workers are in our charge from start to finish', stated a representative of the German mining employers proudly. *Magnet Bundesrepublik*, Informationstagung der Bundesvereinigung Deutscher Arbeitgeberverbände, Bonn 1966, p. 81.

33. A group of French doctors found that the TB rate for black Africans in the Paris suburb of Montreuil was 156 times greater than that of the rest of the local population. R. D. Nicoladze, C. Rendu, G. Millet, 'Coupable d'être malades', *Droit et Liberté*, No. 280, March 1969, p. 8. For further examples see *Immigrant Workers and Class Structure in Western Europe*, op. cit., Ch. VIII.

34. For a description of how a strike of Spanish workers in a steel-works was broken by the threat of deportation, see P. Gavi, *Les Ouvriers*, Paris 1970, pp. 225–6.

35. W. W. Daniels, *Racial Discrimination in England*, based on the PEP Report, Penguin, Harmondsworth 1968.

36. [Editorial note: This followed a police raid on the Mangrove, a West Indian owned restaurant in London, carried out in 1971.]

37. See *Review of the International Commission of Jurists*, No. 3, September 1969, and *Migration Today*, No. 13, Autumn 1969.

38. Cf. *Der Spiegel*, No. 7, 7 February 1972.

39. See Mark Abrams' study on prejudice in *Colour and Citizenship*, pp. 551–604. The results of the study are very interesting, but require careful interpretation. The interpretation given by Abrams is extremely misleading. The results of the prejudice study, which was said to indicate a very low level of prejudice in Britain, attracted more public attention than all the other excellent contributions in this book. For a reanalysis of Abrams' material see Christopher Bagley, *Social Structure and Prejudice in five English Boroughs*, London 1970.

40. We have attempted such a comparison in *Immigrant Workers and Class Structure in Western Europe*, op. cit., Chapter IX. Historical comparisons also tend to throw doubt on the importance of race as a cause of prejudice: white

immigrants like the Irish were in the past received just as hostilely as the black immigrants today.

41. Oliver Cromwell Cox, *Caste, Class and Race*, New York 1970, p. 317 ff. This superb work of Marxist scholarship is recommended to anyone interested in racialism.

42. Surveys carried out in Germany in 1966 show a growth of hostility towards immigrants. This was directly related to the impending recession and local labour's fear of unemployment.

43. Historically, the best example of this strategy was the use of successive waves of immigrants to break the nascent labour movement in the USA and to follow with extremely rapid capital accumulation. *The Jungle* by Upton Sinclair gives an excellent account of this. Similar was the use of internal migrants (the 'Okies') in California in the thirties – see John Steinbeck, *The Grapes of Wrath*.

44. Although the Federal Council, the Parliament, the employers, the unions and all the major parties called for rejection of the Schwarzenbach Initiative, it was defeated only by a small majority: 46 per cent of voters supported the Initiative and 54 per cent voted against it.

45. Many bourgeois economists and some *soi-disant* Marxists think that immigration hinders growth because cheap labour reduces the incentive for rationalization. Bourgeois economists may be excused for not knowing (or not admitting) that cheap labour must be the source for the capital which makes rationalization possible. Marxists ought to know it. A good study on the economic impact of immigration is: C. P. Kindleberger, *Europe's Postwar Growth – the Role of Labour Supply*, Cambridge (Mass.) 1967.

# CHAPTER 1.3

# IMPERIALISM AND DISORGANIC DEVELOPMENT IN THE SILICON AGE*

*A. Sivanandan*

One epoch does not lead tidily into another. Each epoch carries with it a burden of the past – an idea perhaps, a set of values, even bits and pieces of an outmoded economic and political system. And the longer and more durable the previous epoch the more halting is the emergence of the new.

The classic centre-periphery relationship as represented by British colonialism – and the inter-imperialist rivalries of that period – had come to an end with the Second World War. A new colonialism was emerging with its centre of gravity in the United States of America; a new economic order was being fashioned at Bretton Woods. Capital, labour, trade were to be unshackled of their past inhibitions – and the world opened up to accumulation on a scale more massive than ever before. The instruments of that expansion – the General Agreement on Tariffs and Trade, the International Monetary Fund and the World Bank – were ready to go into operation.[1] Even so, it took the capitalist nations of western Europe, Japan and the United States some 25 years to rid themselves of the old notions of national boundaries and 'lift the siege against multinational enterprises so that they might be permitted to get on with the unfinished business of developing the world economy' (Rockefeller). The Trilateral Commission was its acknowledgement.

Britain, hung up in its colonial past, was to lag further behind. It continued, long after the war, to seek fresh profit from an old relationship – most notably through the continued exploitation of colonial labour, but this time at the centre. So that when the rest of Europe, particularly

* *Race and Class*, vol. XXI, No. 2, 1979. Institute of Race Relations, London. This is a development and reformulation of a paper originally given at the 'Three Worlds or One?' Conference, Berlin, June 1979.

Germany, was reconstructing its industries and infrastructure with a judicious mix of capital and labour (importing labour as and when required), Britain, with easy access to cheap black labour and easy profit from racial exploitation, resorted to labour-intensive production. And it was in the nature of that colonial relationship that the immigrants should have come as settlers and not as labourers on contract.

The history of British immigration legislation including the present calls for repatriation is the history of Britain's attempt to reverse the colonial trend and to catch up with Europe and the new world order.[2]

That order, having gone through a number of overlapping phases since the war, now begins to emerge with distinctive features. These, on the one hand, reflect changes in the international division of labour and of production, involving the movement of capital to labour (from centre to periphery) which in turn involves the movement of labour as between the differing peripheries. On the other hand, they foreshadow a new industrial revolution based on microelectronics – and a new imperialism, accelerating the 'disorganic' development of the periphery. And it is to these new developments in capitalist imperialism that I want to address myself, moving between centre and periphery – and between peripheries – as the investigation takes me, bearing in mind that these are merely notes for further study.

The early post-war phase of this development need not detain us here, except to note that the industrialization undertaken by the newly independent countries of Asia and Africa (Latin America had begun to industrialize between the wars) put them further in hock to foreign capital, impoverished their agriculture and gave rise to a new bourgeoisie and a bureaucratic elite.[3] The name of the game was import substitution, its end the favourable balance of trade, its economic expression state capitalism, its political raison d'être bourgeois nationalism. Not fortuitously, this period coincided with the export of labour to the centre.

## Capital and labour migration

By the 1960s, however, the tendency of labour to move to capital was beginning to be reversed. The post-war reconstruction of Europe was over, manufacturing industries showed declining profit margins and capital was looking outside for expansion. The increasing subordination of Third World economies to multinational corporations made accessible a cheap and plentiful supply of labour in the periphery, in Asia in particular. Advances in technology – in transport, communications, information and data processing and organization – rendered geographical distances irrelevant and made possible the movement of plant to labour, while ensuring centralized control of production. More importantly, technological development had further fragmented the labour process, so that the most unskilled worker could now perform the most complex operations.

For its part, the periphery, having failed to take off into independent and self sustained growth through import substitution,[4] turned to embrace export-oriented industrialization – the manufacture of textiles, transistors, leather goods, household appliances and numerous consumer items. But capital had first to be assured that it could avail itself of tax incentives, repatriate its profits, obtain low-priced factory sites and, not least, be provided with a labour force that was as docile and undemanding as it was cheap and plentiful. Authoritarian regimes, often set up by American intervention, provided those assurances – and Free Trade Zones provided their viability.[5]

The pattern of imperialist exploitation was changing – and with it, the international division of production and of labour. The centre no longer supplied the manufactured goods and the periphery the raw materials. Instead the former provided the plant and the know-how while the latter supplied primary products and manufactures. Or, as the Japanese Ministry of Trade in its 'Long Term Vision of Industrial Structure' expressed it, Japan would retain 'high-technology and knowledge-intensive industries' which yielded 'high added value' while industries 'such as textiles which involve a low degree of processing and generate low added value [would] be moved to developing countries where labour costs are low.'

Or, as Samir Amin put it in *Imperialism and Unequal Development*, 'the centre of gravity of the exploitation of labour by capital (and in the first place, by monopoly capital which dominates the system as a whole) had been displaced from the centre of the system to the periphery'.

The parameters of that new economic order are best expressed in the purpose and philosophy of the Trilateral Commission. Founded in 1973, under the sponsorship of David Rockefeller of the Chase Manhattan Bank, the Commission brought together representatives of the world's most powerful banks, corporations, communications conglomerates, and international organizations plus top politicians and a few 'free' trade unions and trade union federations (from North America, Europe and Japan) to reconcile the contradictions of transnational capital, while at the same time checking 'the efforts of national governments to seize for their own countries a disproportionate share of the benefits generated by foreign direct investment'.[6] As Richard Falk puts it: 'The vistas of the Trilateral Commission can be understood as the ideological perspective representing the transnational outlook of the multinational corporation' which 'seeks to subordinate territorial politics to non-territorial economic goals'.[7]

And for the purposes of that subordination, it was necessary to distinguish between the differing peripheries: the oil-producing countries and the 'newly-industrializing' countries, and the under-developed countries proper (which the Commission terms the 'Fourth World').

The implications of this new imperial ordinance for labour migration – not, as before, between centre and periphery but as between the peripheries themselves – are profound, the consequences of these countries devastating. The oil-rich Gulf states, for instance, have sucked in whole sections of the working population, skilled and semi-skilled, of South Asia, leaving vast holes in the labour structure of these countries. Moratuwa, a coastal town in Sri Lanka, once boasted some of the finest carpenters in the world. Today there are none – they are all in Kuwait or in Muscat or Abu Dhabi. And there are no welders, masons, electricians, plumbers, mechanics – all gone. And the doctors, teachers, engineers –they have been long gone – in the first wave of post-war migration to Britain, Canada, USA, Australia, in the second to Nigeria, Zambia, Ghana. Today Sri Lanka, which had the first free health service in the Third World and some of the finest physicians and surgeons, imports its doctors from Marcos' Philippines. What that must do to the Filipino people is another matter, but all that we are left with in Sri Lanka is a plentiful supply of unemployed labour, which is now being herded into the colony within the neo-colony, the Free Trade Zone.

Or take the case of Pakistan, which shows a similar pattern of emigration, except that being a Muslim country the pull of the Gulf is even stronger. Besides, the export of manpower – as a foreign exchange earner – is official policy, a Bureau of Emigration having been set up in 1969 to facilitate employment overseas. Consequently Pakistan 'is being progressively converted into a factory producing skilled manpower for its rich neighbours'[8]

But the export of skilled workers is not the only drain on Pakistan's resources. Apart from its traditional export of primary products, its physical proximity to the oil-rich countries has meant also the smuggling out of fresh vegetables, the sale of fish in mid-seas and the export, often illegal, of beef and goat meat. (The Gulf states raise no cattle.) 'The adverse effects of this trade', laments Feroz Ahmed, 'can be judged from the fact that Pakistan has one of the lowest per capita daily consumptions of animal protein in the world: less than 10 grammes.'[9]

The Middle East countries in turn have only invested in those enterprises which are geared to their own needs (textiles, cement, fertilizer, livestock) and rendered Pakistan's economy subservient to their interests. And to make this 'development of underdevelopment' palatable they harked back to a common culture. Iranian cultural centres sprouted in every major town in Pakistan, outdoing the Americans, and the teaching of Arabic and Persian was fostered by official policy. 'We the Pakistanis and our brethren living in Iran', wrote a Pakistani paper, 'are the two Asiatic branches of the Aryan Tree who originally lived in a common country, spoke the same language, followed the same religion, worshipped the same gods and observed the same rites . . . Culturally we were and are a single people.'[10]

But if Pakistan has been relegated, in the pecking order of imperialism, 'to the status of a slave substratum upon which the imperialist master and their privileged clients play out their game of plunder and oppression'[11] the privileged clients themselves exhibit a distorted 'development'. Take Kuwait for instance. In the pre-oil era Kuwait's economy was based on fishing, pearling, pasturing, trade and a little agriculture. Today all these activities, with the exception of fishing, have virtually ceased – and fishing has been taken over by a company run by the ruling family. The oil industry, while providing the government with 99 per cent of its income, affords employment only to a few thousand. Almost three-fourths of the native work force is in the service sector, with little or nothing to do. (A UN survey estimated the Kuwait civil servant works seventeen minutes a day.)[12] But more than 70 per cent of the total work force and over half the total population consists of non-Kuwaiti immigrant labour. And they are subjected to harsh conditions of work, low wages, no trade union rights, wretched housing and arbitrary deportation. Kuwait is, in effect, two societies, but even within the first 'the ruling elite lives in a swamp of consumer commodities and luxuries, while those at the bottom of the Kuwaiti social pyramid are being uprooted from their traditional productive activities and thrown on the market of unproductiveness'.[13]

The pattern of labour migration in South-east Asia is a variation on the same imperial theme, and its consequences no less devastating. The first countries to industrialize in this region were Taiwan in the 1950s and, in the 1960s, South Korea, Singapore and Hong Kong. Taiwan and South Korea were basically offshore operations of the USA and Japan – and, by virtue of their strategic importance to America, were able to develop heavy industry (ship building, steel, vehicles) and chemicals in addition to the usual manufacture of textiles, shoes, electrical goods, etc. And by the middle of the 1970s, these two countries had gone over from being producers of primary products to producers of manufactured goods. Singapore's industrialization includes ship repair (Singapore is the fourth largest port in the world) and the construction industry. Hong Kong, the closest thing to a 'free economy', is shaped by the world market.

What all these countries could offer multinational capital, apart from a 'favourable climate of investment' (repatriation of profit, tax holidays, etc), was authoritarian regimes (Hong Kong is a colony) with a tough line on dissidence in the work force and a basic infrastructure of power and communications. What they did not have was a great pool of unemployed workers. That was provided by the neighbouring countries.

Hong Kong uses all the migrant labour available in the region, including workers from mainland China, and is currently negotiating with the Philippines government for the import of Filipino labour. South Korea's shortage of labour, by the very nature of its development, has been in the area of skilled workers. (Not illogically South Korea has been priced out of its own skilled workers, some 70,000 of them, by the developing oil-rich countries of the Middle East.) But it is Singapore which is the major employer of contract labour – from Malaysia mostly (40 per cent of the industrial work force) but also from Indonesia, the Philippines and Thailand - and that under the most horrendous conditions. For apart from the usual strictures on gastarbeiters that we are familiar with in Europe, such as no right of settlement, no right to change jobs without permission and deportation if jobless, Singapore also forbids these workers to marry, except after five years, on the showing of a 'clean record', and then with the permission of the government – and that on signing a bond that both partners will agree to be sterilized after the second child is born. Lee Kuan Yew, with a nod to Hitler, justifies the policy on the ground that 'a multiple replacement rate right at the bottom' leads to 'a gradual lowering of the general quality of the population'.[14] Their working conditions too are insanitary and dangerous and makeshift shacks on worksites (like the bidonvilles) provide their only housing.

And yet the plight of the indigenous workers of these countries is not much better. The economic miracle is not for them. Their lives contrast glaringly with the luxury apartments, automobiles and swinging discos of the rich. To buy a coffee and sandwich on a thoroughfare of Singapore costs a day's wage, in South Korea twelve and thirteen-year-old girls work eighteen hours a day, seven days a week, for £12 a month, and Hong Kong is notorious for its exploitation of child labour.[15]

How long the repressive regimes of these countries can hold down their work force on behalf of international capital is a moot point – but multinationals do not wait to find out. They do not stay in one place. They gather their surplus while they may and move on to new pastures their miracles to perform.

The candidates for the new expropriation were Indonesia, Thailand, Malaysia and the Philippines whose economies were primarily based on agriculture and on extractive industries such as mining and timber. Like the first group of countries they too could boast of authoritarian regimes – ordained by the White House, fashioned by the Pentagon and installed by the CIA – which could pave the way for international capital. Additionally, they were able to provide the cheap indigenous labour which the other group had lacked – and the Free Trade Zones to go with it. What they did not have, though, was a developed infrastructure.

Multinationals had already moved into these countries by the 1970s and some industrialization was already under way. What accelerated that movement, however, was the tilt to cheap labour, as against a developed infrastructure, brought about by revolutionary changes in the production process.

To that revolution, variously described as the new industrial revolution, the third industrial revolution and the post-industrial age, I must now turn - not so much to look at labour migration as labour polarization –between the periphery and the centre, and within the centre itself, and its social and political implications in both.

## Capital and labour in the silicon age

What has caused the new industrial revolution and brought about a qualitative leap in the level of the productive forces is the silicon chip or, more accurately , the computer-on-a-chip, known as the microprocessor. (You have already seen them at work in your digital watch and your pocket calculator.)

The ancestry of the microprocessor need not concern us here, except to note that it derives from the electronic transistor, invented by American scientists in 1947 – which in turn led to the semiconductor industry in

1952–3 and in 1963, to the integrated circuit industry. Integrated circuits meant that various electronic elements such as transistors, resistors, diodes, etc. could all be combined on a tiny chip of semi-conductor silicon, 'which in the form of sand is the world's most common element next to oxygen'.[16] But if industrially the new technology has been in existence for sixteen years, it is only in the last five that it has really taken off. The periodization of its development is important because it is not unconnected with the postwar changes in the international division of production and of labour and the corresponding movements and operations of the multinational corporations.

The microprocessor is to the new industrial revolution what steam and electricity was to the old — except that where steam and electric power replaced human muscle, microelectronics replaces the brain. That, quite simply, is the measure of its achievement. Consequently, there is virtually no field in manufacturing, the utilities, the service industries or commerce that is not affected by the new technology. Microprocessors are already in use in the control of power stations, textile mills, telephone-switching systems, office-heating and typesetting as well as in repetitive and mechanical tasks such as spraying, welding, etc, in the car industry. Fiat, for instance, has a television commercial which boasts that its cars are 'designed by computers, silenced by lasers and hand-built by robots' – to the strains of Figaro's aria (from Rossini). Volkswagen designs and sells its own robots for spot welding and handling body panels between presses. Robots, besides, can be re-programmed for different tasks more easily than personnel can be re-trained. And because microprocessors can be re-programmed, automated assembly techniques could be introduced into areas hitherto immune to automation, such as batch production (which incidentally constitutes 70 per cent of the production in British manufacturing). From this has grown the idea of linking together a group of machines to form an unmanned manufacturing system, which could produce anything from diesel engines to machine tools and even aeroengines. And 'once the design of the unmanned factory has been standardized, entire factories could be produced on a production line based on a standard design'.[17] The Japanese are close to achieving the 'universal factory'.

A few examples from other areas of life will give you some idea of the pervasiveness of microelectronics. In the retail trade, for instance, the electronic cash register, in addition to performing its normal chores, monitors the stock level by keeping tabs on what has been sold at all the terminals and relays that information to computers in the warehouse which then automatically move the necessary stocks to the shop. A further link-up between computerized check-outs at stores and computerized bank accounts will soon do away with cash transactions, directly debiting the customer's account and crediting the store's. Other refinements such as keeping a check on the speed and efficiency of employees have also grown out of such computerization –in Denmark, for instance (but it has been resisted by the workers).

There are chips in everything you buy – cookers, washing machines, toasters, vacuum cleaners, clocks, toys, sewing machines, motor vehicles – replacing standard parts and facilitating repair: you take out one chip and put in another. One silicon chip in an electronic sewing machine for example replaces 350 standard parts.

But it is in the service sector, particularly in the matter of producing, handling, storing and transmitting information, that silicon technology has had its greatest impact. Up till now automation has not seriously affected office work which, while accounting for 75 per cent of the costs in this sector (and about half the operating costs of corporations), is also the least productive, thereby depressing the overall rate of productivity. One of the chief reasons for this is that office work is divided into several tasks (typing, filing, processing, retrieving, transmitting and so forth) which are really inter-connected. The new technology not only automates these tasks but integrates them. For example, the word processor, consisting of a keyboard, a visual display unit, a storage memory unit and a print-out, enables one typist to do the work of four while at the same time reducing the skill she needs. Different visual display units (VDUs) can then be linked to the company's mainframe computer, to other computers within the country (via computer network systems) and even to those in other countries through satellite communication – all of which makes possible the electronic mail and the electronic funds transfer (EFT) which would dispense with cash completely.

What this link-up between the office, the computer and telecommunications means is the 'convergence' of previously separate industries. 'Convergence' is defined by the Butler Cox Foundation as 'the process by which these three industries are coming to depend on a single technology. They are becoming, to all intents and purposes, three branches of a single industry'.[18] But 'convergence' to you and me spells the convergence of corporations, horizontal (and vertical) integration, monopoly. A 'convergence' of Bell Telephones and IBM computers would take over the world's communication facilities. (Whether the anti-trust laws in America have already been bent to enable such a development I do not know, but it is only a matter of time.)

Underscoring the attributes and applications of the microprocessor is the speed of its advance and the continuing reduction in its costs. Sir Ieuan Maddock, Secretary of the British Association for the Advancement of Science, estimates that 'in terms of the gates it can contain, the performance of a single chip has increased ten thousandfold in a period of fifteen years'. And of its falling cost, he says, 'the price of each unit of performance has reduced one hundred thousandfold since the early 1960s'.[19]

'These are not just marginal effects', continues Sir Ieuan, 'to be absorbed in a few per cent change in the economic indicators – they are deep and widespread and collectively signal a fundamental and irreversible change in the way the industrialized societies will live . . .Changes of such magnitude and speed have never been experienced before.'[20]

The scope of these changes have been dealt with in the growing literature on the subject.[21] But they have mostly been concerned with the prospects of increasing and permanent unemployment, particularly in the service industries and in the field of unskilled manual employment – in both of which blacks and women predominate.[22] A study by Siemens estimates that 40 per cent of all office work in Germany is suitable for automation – which, viewed from the other side, means a 40 per cent lay off of office workers in the next ten years. The Nora report warns that French banking and insurance industries, which are particularly labour intensive, will lose 30 per cent of their work force by 1990. Unemployment in Britain is expected to rise by about three million in that time.[23] Other writers have pointed to a polarization in the work force itself – as between a small technological elite on the one hand and a large number of unskilled, unemployable workers, counting among their number those whose craft has become outmoded. Or, as the Chairman of the British Oil Corporation, Lord Kearton, puts it: 'we have an elite now of a very special kind at the top on which most of mankind depends for its future development and the rest of us are more or less taken along in the direct stream of these elite personnel'.[24]

All the remedies that the British Trades Union Congress has been able to suggest are 'new technology agreements' between government and union, 'continuing payments to redundant workers related to their past earnings' and 'opportunities for linking technological change with a reduction in the working week, working year and working life time'.[25] The Association of Scientific Technical and Managerial Staffs (ASTMS), whose members are more immediately affected by automation, elevates these remedies into a philosophy which encompasses a changed attitude towards work that would 'promote a better balance between working life and personal life', 'recurrent education throughout adult life' and a new system of income distribution which in effect will 'pay people not to work'.[26]

But, in the performance, these are precisely the palliatives that enlightened capitalism (ie multinational capitalism as opposed to the archaic private enterprise capitalism of Margaret Thatcher and her mercantile minions) offers the working class in the silicon age. Translated into the system's terms, 'new technology agreements' mean a continuing social contract between the unions and the government wherein the workers abjure their only power, collective bargaining (and thereby take the politics out of the struggle) and a new culture which divorces work from income (under the guise of life-long education, part-time work, early retirement, etc) and provides the raison d'être for unemployment. Already the protagonists of the establishment have declared that the Protestant work ethic is outdated (what has work got to do with income?), that leisure should become a major occupation (university departments are already investigating its 'potential'), that schooling is not for now but for ever.

I am not arguing here against technology or a life of creative leisure. Anything that improves the lot of man is to be welcomed. But in capitalist society such improvement redounds to the few at cost to the many. That cost has been heavy for the working class in the centre and heavier for the masses in the periphery. What the new industrial revolution predicates is the further degradation of work where, as Braverman so brilliantly predicted, thought itself is eliminated from the labour process,[27] the centralized ownership of the means of production, a culture of reified leisure to mediate discontent and a political system incorporating the state, the multinationals, the trade unions, the bureaucracy and the media, backed by the forces of 'law and order' with microelectronic surveillance at their command. For in as much as liberal democracy was the political expression of the old industrial revolution, the corporate state is the necessary expression of the new. The qualitative leap in the productive forces, ensnared in capitalist economics, demands such an expression. Or, to put it differently, the contradiction between the heightened centralization in the ownership of the means of production – made possible not only by the enormous increase in the level of productivity but also by the technological nature of that increase – and the social nature of production (however attenuated) can no longer be mediated by liberal democracy but by corporativism, with an accompanying corporate culture, and state surveillance to go with it.

But nowhere, in all the chip literature, is there a suggestion of any of this. Nor is there in British writings on the subject,[28] with the exception of the CIS report,[29] any hint of a suggestion that the new industrial revolution, like the old, has taken off on the backs of the workers in the peripheries – that it is they who will provide the 'living dole' for the unemployed of the West. For, the chip, produced in the pleasant environs of 'Silicon Valley' in California, has its circuitry assembled in the toxic factories of Asia. Or, as a Conservative Political Centre publication puts it, 'while the manufacture of the chips requires expensive equipment in a dust-free, air-conditioned environment little capital is necessary to assemble them profitably into saleable devices. And it is the assembly that creates both the wealth and the jobs'.[30]

Initially the industry went to Mexico, but Asia was soon considered the cheaper. (Besides 'Santa Clara was only a telex away'.) And even within Asia the moves were to cheaper and cheaper areas: from Hong Kong, Taiwan, South Korea and Singapore in the 1960s, to Malaysia in 1972, Thailand in 1973, the Philippines and Indonesia in 1974 and soon to Sri Lanka. 'The manager of a plant in Malaysia explained how profitable these moves had been: "one worker working one hour produces enough to pay the wages of ten workers working one shift plus all the costs of materials and transport"'.[31]

But the moves the industry makes are not just from country to country but from one batch of workers to another within the country itself. For, the nature of the work – the bonding under a microscope of tiny hair-thin wires to circuit boards on wafers of silicon chip half the size of a fingernail – shortens working life. 'After three or four years of peering through a microscope', reports Rachael Grossman, 'a worker's vision begins to blur so that she can no longer meet the production quota'.[32] But if the microscope does not get her ('grandma where are your glasses' is how electronic workers over 25 are greeted in Hong Kong), the bonding chemicals do.[33] And why 'her'? Because they are invariably women. For, as a Malaysian brochure has it, 'the manual dexterity of the oriental female is famous the world over. Her hands are small and she works fast with extreme care. Who, therefore, could be better qualified by nature and inheritance to contribute to the efficiency of a bench assembly production line than the oriental girl?'[34]

To make such intense exploitation palatable, however, the multinationals offer the women a global culture – beauty contests, fashion shows, cosmetic displays and disco dancing – which in turn enhances the market for consumer goods and western beauty products. Tourism reinforces the culture and reinforces prostitution (with packaged sex tours for Japanese businessmen), drug selling, child labour. For the woman thrown out of work on the assembly line at an early age, the wage earner for the whole extended family, prostitution is often the only form of livelihood left.[35]

A global culture then, to go with a global economy, serviced by a global office the size of a walkie-talkie held in your hand[36] – a global assembly line run by global corporations that move from one pool of labour to another, discarding them when done – high technology in the centre, low technology in the peripheries – and a polarization of the workforce within the centre itself (as between the highly skilled and unskilled or de-skilled) and as between the centre and the peripheries, with qualitatively different rates of exploitation that allow the one to feed off the other - a corporate state maintained by surveillance for the developed countries, authoritarian regimes and gun law for the developing. That is the size of the new world order.

## Disorganic development

But it is not without its contradictions. Where those contradictions are sharpest, however, are where they exist in the raw – in the peripheries.[37] For what capitalist development has meant to the masses of these countries is increased poverty, the corruption of their cultures, repressive regimes – and all at once. All the GNP they amass for their country through their incessant labour leaves them poorer than before. They produce what is of no real use to them and yet cannot buy what they produce – neither use value nor exchange value – neither the old system nor the new.

And how they produce has no relation to how they used to produce. They have not grown into the one from the other. They have not emerged into capitalist production but been flung into it – into technologies and labour processes that reify them and into social relations that violate their customs and their codes. They work in the factories, in town, to support their families, their extended families, in the village – to contribute to the building of the village temple, to help get a teacher for the school, to sink a well. But the way of their working socializes them into individualism, nuclear families, consumer priorities, artefacts of capitalist culture. They are caught between two modes, two sets, of social relations, characterized by exchange value in the one and use value in the other – and the contradiction disorients them and removes them from the centre of their being.

And not just the workers, but the peasants too – they have not escaped the capitalist mode. And all it has done is to wrench them from their social relations and their relationship with the land. Within a single life-time, they have had to exchange sons for tractors and tractors for petrochemicals. And these things too have taken them from themselves in space and in time.

And what happens to all this production, from the land and from the factories? Where does all the GNP go – except to faceless foreign exploiters in another country and a handful of rich in their own? And who the agents but their own rulers?

In sum, what capitalist development has meant to the masses of these countries is production without purpose, except to stay alive; massive immiseration accompanied by a wholesale attack on the values, relationships, gods that made such immiseration bearable; rulers who rule not for their own people but for someone else – a development that makes no sense, has no bearing on their lives, is disorganic.

To state it at another level. The economic development that capital has super-imposed on the peripheries has been unaccompanied by capitalist culture or capitalist democracy. Whereas, in the centre, the different aspects of capitalism (economic, cultural, political) have evolved gradually, organically, out of the centre's own history, in the periphery the capitalist mode of production has been grafted on to the existing cultural and political order. Peripheral capitalism is not an organized body of connected, interdependent parts sharing a common life – it is not an organism. What these countries exhibit, therefore, is not just 'distorted' or 'disarticulated' development (Samir Amin), but disorganic development: an economic system (itself 'extraverted') at odds with the cultural and political institutions of the people it exploits. The economic system, that is, is not mediated by culture or legitimated by politics, as in the centre. The base and the superstructure do not complement and reinforce each other. (That is not to say that they are in perfect harmony at the centre.) They are in fundamental conflict – and exploitation is naked, crude, unmediated – although softened by artefacts of capitalist culture and capitalist homilies on human rights. And that contradiction is not only general to the social formation but, because of capitalist penetration, runs right through the various modes of production comprising the social formation. At some point, therefore, the political system has to be extrapolated from the superstructure and made to serve as a cohesive – and coercive –force to maintain the economic order of things. The contradiction between superstructure and base now resolves into one between the political regime and the people, with culture as the expression of their resistance. And it is cultural resistance which, in Cabral's magnificent phrase, takes on 'new forms (political, economic, armed) in order fully to contest foreign domination'.[38]

But culture in the periphery is not equally developed in all sectors of society. It differs as between the different modes of production but, again as Cabral says, it does have 'a mass character'. Similarly at the economic level, the different exploitations in the different modes confuse the formal lines of class struggle but the common denominators of political oppression make for a mass movement.

Hence the revolutions in these countries are not necessarily class, socialist, revolutions – they do not begin as such anyway. They are not even nationalist revolutions as we know them. They are mass movements with national and revolutionary components – sometimes religious, sometimes secular, often both, but always against the repressive political state and its imperial backers.

## Notes and references

1. GATT was set up to regulate trade between nations, the IMF to help nations adjust to free trade by providing balance-of-payments financial assistance, the World Bank to facilitate the movement of capital to war-torn Europe and aid to developing countries.
2. See A.Sivanandan, *Race, Class and the State: The Black Experience in Britain*, Race & Class Pamphlet No. 1 (London, 1976). Also see A. Sivanandan, *From Immigration Control to 'Induce Repatriation'*, Race & Class Pamphlet No. 5 (London, 1978).
3. See *Ampo*, Special issue, 'Free Trade Zones and Industrialization of Asia' Vol. 8, no. 4 and Vol. 9, nos. 1–2, 1977.
4. Even in the period of import-substitution – more succinctly described by the Japanese as 'export-substitution investment' – the multinational corporations were able to move in 'behind tariff barriers to produce locally what they had hitherto imported', *Ampo*, Special Issue, 'Free Trade Zones and Industrialisation of Asia', 1977.

5. The first Free Trade Zone was established at Shannon airport in Ireland in 1958 and was followed by Taiwan in 1965. In 1967 the United Nations Industrial Development Organisation was set up to promote industrialization in developing countries and soon embarked on the internationalization of Free Trade Zones into a global system. South Korea established a Free Trade Zone in 1970, the Philippines in 1972 and Malaysia in the same year. By 1974, Egypt, Gambia, Ivory Coast, Kenya, Senegal, Sri Lanka, Jamaica, Liberia, Syria, Trinidad & Tobago and Sudan were asking UNIDO to draw up plans for Free Trade Zones. (Ampo, op. cit.) Sri Lanka set up its Free Trade Zone in 1978 soon after a right-wing government had taken power, albeit through the ballot box.

6. Jeff Frieden, 'The Trilateral Commission: Economics and Politics in the 1970s', *Monthly Review* Vol. 29, no. 7, December 1977.

7. Richard Falk, 'A New Paradigm for International Legal Studies', *The Yale Law Journal* Vol. 84, no. 5, April 1975.

8. Feroz Ahmed, 'Pakistan: The New Dependence', *Race & Class*, Vol. XVIII, no. 1, Summer 1976.

9. Ibid.

10. *Dawn* 13 May 1973, cited in ibid.

11. Ibid.

12. Cited in 'Oil for Underdevelopment and Discrimination: The Case of Kuwait', *Monthly Review* Vol. 30, no. 6, November 1978.

13. Ibid.

14. Selangor Graduates Society, *Plight of the Malaysian workers in Singapore* (Kuala Lumpur, 1978).

15. Walter Easey, 'Notes on Child Labour in Hong Kong', *Race & Class* Vol. XVIII, no. 4, Spring 1977.

16. Jon Stewart and John Markoff, 'The Microprocessor Revolution', *Pacific News Service*, Global Factory (Part II of VI).

17. Association of Scientific Technical and Managerial Staffs, *Technological Change and Collective Bargaining* (London, 1978).

18. D. Butler, abstract, *The Convergence of Technologies*, Report Series no. 5, Butler Cox Foundation, quoted in ASTMS, op. cit.

19. Ieuan Maddock, 'Beyond the Protestant Ethic', *New Scientist* 23 November, 1978.

20. Ibid.

21. See, for instance, I. Barron and R. Curnow, *The Future with Microelectronics* (London, 1979); C. Jenkins and B. Sherman, *The Collapse of Work* (London, 1979); Trades Union Congress, *Employment and Technology* (London, 1979); ASTMS, op. cit.; Colin Hines, *The 'Chips' are down* (London, 1978).

22. Of course there are those (guess who) who suggest that automation will not only release people from dirty, boring jobs and into more interesting work, but even enhance job prospects.

23. Harman *Is a Machine After Your Job?* (London, 1979). Cambridge Economic Policy Group, *Economic Policy Review* March 1978.

24. Introductory address to the British Association for the Advancement of Science Symposium, Automation Friend or Foe?

25. Trades Union Congress, *Employment and Technology* (London, 1979).
26. ASTMS, op. cit.
27. Harry Braverman, *Labor and Monopoly Capital* (New York, 1974).
28. American writers, however, have done better in this regard. See in particular the articles of Jon Stewart and John Markoff in the *Pacific News Service* and Rachael Grossman *et al.* in the Special issue of *Southeast Asia Chronicle*.
29. Counter Information Services, *The New Technology*, Anti-Report no. 23 (London, 1979).
30. Philip Virgo, *Cashing in on the Chips* (London, 1979).
31. Cited in Rachael Grossman, 'Women's Place in the Integrated Circuit', *Southeast Asia Chronicle* no. 66, Jan-Feb 1979.
32. Ibid.
33. 'Workers who must dip components in acids and rub them with solvents frequently experience serious burns, dizziness, nausea, sometimes even losing their fingers in accidents . . . It will be ten or fifteen years before the possible carcinogenic effects begin to show up in the women who work with them now.' *Southeast Asia Chronicle*, no. 66, January-February 1979.
34. Cited in ibid.
35. See A. Lin Neumann, '"Hospitality Girls" in the Philippines', *Southeast Asia Chronicle* no. 66, Jan-Feb 1979.
36. See 'The Day After Tomorrow', by Peter Large, *Guardian* 17 February 1979
37. For the purposes of the general analysis presented here, I make no distinction between periphery and developing periphery.
38. Amilcar Cabral, *Return to the Source* (New York, 1973).

# CHAPTER 1.4

## THE DUAL LABOUR MARKET MODEL*
### Robin Blackburn and Michael Mann

This model arose from the union of two hitherto separated problems, the persistence of discrimination within the labour market, and the internal labour market. Neo-classical [economic] theory had always experienced difficulty with the former. Like any theory which contents itself with analysing existing market forces, it can only take as 'given' the parameters of that market. If discrimination between races and sexes is built into the structure of the market, the theory must content itself with an explanation of rational choice made within that structure. To explain discrimination itself, a wider historical and sociological approach would be necessary. The dual labour market model does not actually provide such an approach, but it does attempt to provide a fuller description of discrimination, and to note its peculiar contemporary links with internal labour markets.

As its title suggests this model asserts that the labour market is increasingly divided into *primary* and *secondary* sectors. Into the primary sector go the monopolies, capital-intensive, highly profitable and technologically advanced firms and industries. Into the secondary sector go small, backward firms located in competitive markets – in retail trade, services and non-durable manufacturing industries such as clothing or food processing.[1] The primary sector is high-wage, highly unionized and contains internal labour markets. In this sector, to quote the major 'dualists'.[2]

> . . . differences between the skills and abilities of the labour force and the requirements of jobs are reconciled through a series of instruments which are controlled within the internal labor market. These instruments – recruitment procedures, training, compensation, and the like – exist because a number of functions conventionally identified with the competitive labor market have been internalized by the enterprise (Doeringer and Piore, 1971: 189–90; see also Kerr, 1954; Mann, 1973).

In the extreme form of the internal labour market, only the lowest manual

* Extract from *The Working Class and the Labour Market*, by permission of Macmillan, London and Basingstoke.

jobs are filled from outside. The remainder are filled by promotion from within, either by seniority, ability or a mixture of the two. More normally, however, at least two levels of 'port of entry' job will exist, at the unskilled and at the skilled levels.

According to the dual theorists two interconnected processes have brought about the development of the internal labour market. Firstly, the growth of economic concentration has given the large corporation an unprecedented degree of control over its product market. As production needs are stable and secure, the employer's need for stability from his workforce becomes even greater. He is less interested in hiring and firing according to fluctuations in the product market, and he wants, above all, to reduce labour turnover and to count upon steady production from his workers. Secondly, technological developments have led to an increase in capital-intensity in this primary sector, and so unsteadiness from any worker will result in greater damage than ever before. Furthermore, the specialized nature of the costly equipment needs, not conventional skills, but *experience*, and so the employer retains his labour force by promoting them through more-and-more specialized jobs. Alongside this, he will increase the 'golden chains' of fringe benefits, and will link sickness pay, holiday pay and pensions to length of service. One of us has described this in previous research as an increase in *mutual dependence* – neither employer nor worker wishes to expose himself to labour market uncertainty (Mann, 1973).

Yet these processes only affect part of the economy. The data on economic concentration show not only an increase in the market shares of the largest companies, but also an increase in the number of very *small* companies (for US data, see various articles in Andreano, 1973). Furthermore, Suzanne Berger (1972) has shown that in the case of Italy, the monopoly sector and the small, competitive sector are now in a symbiotic relationship with each other. The low-wage competitive sector can make technologically-simple products very cheaply, and so the monopolies have hived off simpler aspects of their production to them. Thus, by preserving the competitive sector, they can keep down both wage levels and the level of unionization in the economy as a whole. Thus – at least in Italy – the primary and secondary sectors are now in a stable, functional relationship.

Such a bifurcation has important consequences for the workers. While the primary sector is looking more than ever for the stable worker, the secondary sector needs to use turnover, and redundancy to adjust employment volume to unpredictable product markets. Thus secondary employers abandon the 'queue' and look for *unstable* employees – women, ethnic minorities and other marginal and relatively docile groups. The result is a stratified labour market.

These are the arguments of Doeringer and Piore and their dualist colleagues (Bosanquet and Doeringer, 1973, Doeringer, 1973; Doeringer and Piore, 1971; Piore, 1973a and 1973b). We should note at once that they have produced very little hard data to support their arguments, which are really interesting hypotheses rather than established fact.

Yet they make life difficult for themselves by one methodological error, pointed out by Barron and Norris (1976). The dualist argument depends on demonstrating that there is actual *segregation* in the labour market. Yet the only supporting evidence produced concerns *average differences* between say, the wages paid to men and women, whites and black, and workers in manufacturing and service industry. The evidence needed, however, concerns the degree of overlap between the groups. Social stratification involves two elements, inequality and segregation. It is highly unlikely that stratification within the working class can occur, or that the stratified groups can attain separate consciousnesses, without some degree of segregation. There are two main criteria of labour market stratification readily available to us: segregation in terms of wage levels and segregation of actual jobs.

Though wages data are plentiful, a simple and comprehensive distributional analysis for men and women, blacks and whites, etc. has not yet been undertaken. The clearest analysis is by Barron and Norris (1976), of sex differences in wages in Britain in 1962. They found that the area of overlap between the hourly earnings of men and women is less than a third of the area of the combined distribution. This is an astonishing degree of segregation, apparently unrivalled among the ethnic groups. Most data on the latter came from the United States, and though they reveal the expected differences between whites and blacks, these are only about half of the sex differential (Morgan, 1974) and the distributions are much closer together (Wohlstetter and Coleman, 1972). They have also been decreasing in the period 1950–70 (Freeman, 1973; Szymanski, 1975). There is no good distributional analysis for Britain, though sample surveys have revealed that the average earnings of Commonwealth immigrant groups are only between ten per cent and 30 per cent lower than indigenous averages – probably insufficient for clear segregation (Jones and Smith, 1970: 91–2; Political and Economic Planning, 1976: 84–8).

Much of this difference is actually accounted for by the fact that immigrant job levels are considerably lower than those of native British workers. Comparing immigrants and natives doing similar jobs produces a much lower wage difference, although it ignores that part of discrimination attributable to job rather than wage processes. So let us turn to job segregation.

In investigating the occupational segregation of men and women, Barron and Norris (1976) note that the job categories used in national censuses are too broad to permit reliable conclusions but that they nevertheless indicate considerable segregation. A study like ours is able to use much more precise job categories over a smaller area. In Chapter 2 [of *The Working Class and the Labour Market*. See also Chapter 2.4] we note that in the town of Peterborough occupational segregation is virtually complete – men and women are almost never interchangeable as individuals in the manual labour market. Of course sexual discrimination is too obvious really to need specialized sociological investigation. It is so uniform that *everyone knows* that women are rarely allowed to do men's jobs, that where they are they are paid less, that their shifts are restricted, that they are rarely allowed to supervise men. In both Britain and the United States recent legislation has attempted to remedy the worst abuses, yet discrimination is thoroughly built into the institutional framework of industrial relations, so that, for example, redundancy practices often entail the laying-off of women before men. This points us to the conclusion that effective stratification in the labour market may need a legal or institutional framework, outside of the immediate market, to be effective.

This is a conclusion that is highly relevant to the recent growth of 'bonded labourers' in Western capitalist countries. By this we refer to the use by almost all Western countries of immigrant labour which does not enjoy traditional labour market freedoms. In all European countries, for example, an immigrant worker cannot initially change his employer without permission from the immigration authorities. Restrictions are sometimes removed after a certain period of stay – in Britain, four years (Castles and Kosack, 1973: 98–107). In the United States, Mexican immigrants cannot change employment within the first two years (although thereafter they are free). In Britain, those Commonwealth and Irish citizens who arrived after 1971 do not possess full labour market rights. In all these cases the immigrants are naturally at the mercy of their employer. Furthermore, all these legalized schemes have created an illegal underworld of smuggled immigrants, certainly a majority in the case of

Mexicans in United States, although probably minorities elsewhere. These workers are even more helpless.

This is a dual labour market with a vengeance, separating the working class into free and semi-free legal statuses reminiscent of feudalism rather than capitalism. Yet it is not the kind of dualism posited by Doeringer and Piore, and it does not apply at all to the group that the dual model was really devised for. Blacks in the United States – and Puerto Ricans, too – have full citizen rights and full freedom on the labour market. So, too, do most immigrants to Britain. It is the countries of continental Europe (and the State of California) which most practise this form of dualism. In this system, the discrimination is not merely, or even primarily, in terms of wages, but in terms of the discipline the employer is able to enforce on the worker and of the inability of the worker to negotiate his conditions of employment.

How segregated are both free and semi-free immigrant groups in terms of the occupations they hold? This is where the various Western countries diverge, mainly according to the proportion of immigrant or ethnic group workers in the total employed population. In Switzerland, this proportion is highest, with nearly 40 per cent of all factory workers being foreign-born. This gives rise to high concentration figures among manual workers in a few industries: 63 per cent in clothing, shoes and linen and over 50 per cent in textiles, hotels and catering, and construction. The lowest stratum of occupations in these industries is probably entirely filled by immigrants. Thus Switzerland is the exemplar of the dual labour market. Elsewhere, concentration on this scale is unusual. In France it appears confined to the building industry, where the smaller (low-paying) firms are almost exclusively filled by foreigners (a study quoted by Castles and Kosack, 1973: 107). But immigrant workers have also penetrated the high-paying but extremely unattractive industry of automobile assembly. This happened early in France and Germany, though it is more recent in Britain (Political and Economic Planning, 1976: 69).

In Britain, concentration is lower. Immigrant males did not constitute more than five and a half per cent of the workers in any industry according to the 1966 Sample Census. The proportions among females are even lower. Even using finer occupational classifications we find that immigrant males constitute at most 26 per cent of males in any occupation – the highest being 'winders and reelers' in textiles. Again, the proportions among females are lower: the highest, among hospital orderlies, is only seven per cent. (Jones and Smith, 1970). Again we would undoubtedly find higher concentrations if we were able to use finer occupational categories at the lowest manual levels. Furthermore, national figures conceal regional variations, which are very great in all Western societies because of the residential patterns of immigrants. So, bearing in mind that high concentration at the 'macro-level' of industries is comparatively rare, we will turn to micro-studies for a more realistic view of segregation in employment.

First we will consider micro-studies of internal labour markets. This is the most critical aspect of dual theory. Here we encounter international differences. In the United States internal labour markets are more highly developed than in Europe, probably not because of either immediate economic or technological differences but because of the US tradition of plant-bargaining. Plant unionism tends to privilege present employees *vis-à-vis* other workers in the labour market, and, in particular, to develop formal seniority rules for promotion. In Britain, seniority governs redundancy practices more than it does promotion. A study of three labour markets in the engineering industry found that 'ports of entry' existed at every skill level. Very few semi-skilled workers were upgraded, and although rather more unskilled were promoted, nevertheless internal mobility contributed less than mobility between firms to promotion (Mackay *et al.*, 1971: Chapter 11).

Even the United States is not dominated by internal labour markets. Reynolds noted that steady upward movement, where it occurred, tended to be internal, yet only a minority of workers had moved steadily up. Only 28 per cent said that they had moved to a better job since starting with their present employer, and even among the longest-service group only one-half had moved up. Yet overall, 38 per cent of these who had started in semi-skilled positions had risen to skilled, while 67 per cent of those who had started in unskilled jobs were now in semi-skilled or skilled ones. In fact much upward mobility is irregular, not to say haphazard (1951: 134–151). These data are over 25 years old, of course. The Bay Area Study gives us more recent information on employer policy in the United States and shows that it is quite diverse. About two-thirds of employers in manufacturing industry said that promotion from unskilled to semi-skilled jobs occurred frequently, but all the employers in other industries said it occurred only infrequently (Gordon and Thal-Larsen, 1969: 347–8).[2] In all countries, therefore, the internal labour market normally co-exists with the external market.

This is important, for in the overall market the internal and external elements may cross-cut each other. All firms contain some 'bad' jobs, even if the firm is itself in the primary sector. Thus a high-paying job may be a high job in a low-paying firm, or a medium or high job in a high-paying firm. There is additionally a third determinant of wage-levels, the type of payment system involved. British research shows that unskilled piecework jobs often receive higher wages than skilled timework (Mackay *et al.*, 1971: Chapter 5). One study of part of the Coventry and Glasgow labour markets concluded that internal and external labour markets and payment systems interact in such a confused way that the overall wage structure is chaotic (Robinson, 1970). Some other work rewards are similarly distributed. Fringe benefits are generally granted to all the employees of a company, but the tendency to relate benefit level to length of service may confuse the simple inter-firm hierarchy. Security also incorporates both an inter-firm (expanding or contracting) and an intra-firm ('first in, last out') hierarchy. There is obviously considerable complexity in the distribution of these and other work rewards. No study has yet delineated the precise relationship of internal to external markets for all major rewards. In Chapter 4 [of *The Working Class and the Labour Market*] we attempt this.

Finally, we must consider the supply side of the dual argument, the characteristics of the workers in the supposed primary and secondary sectors. The micro-studies reveal that there are relatively few firms that are composed overwhelmingly of immigrants or ethnic minorities. Indeed, employers often deliberately resist such concentration, fearing trouble from their existing workers if they allow numbers to creep past ten to fifteen per cent (Wright, 1968: 68–6; cf. also Gordon and Thal-Larsen, 1969). Thus discrimination may reduce segregation. Yet one uniformity remains – that immigrants have little opportunity for promotion. Employers in Europe say that they will not generally consider this for fear, again, of alienating native-born workers (Wright, 1968: 81; Castles and Kosack, 1973). And in the United States, Piore found that Puerto Rican workers in Boston had few advancement possibilities (1973: 11–12). It seems probable, however, that current 'Affirmative Action' programmes[3] in the United States are reducing this handicap, at least for blacks. Apart from this possible improvement, however, we confront an odd paradox: promotion may be largely confined to highly segregated industries and firms. It is only there that minorities can supervise minorities. The PEP national study of England and Wales, conducted in 1974, found that only eighteen per cent of Asian and West Indian men were supervising other people, compared to 40 per cent of white men. Even so, however, Asians and West Indians were more likely to be supervised by their compatriots than by white men (PEP, 1976: 98–9). The probable result is that the average level of wages and other work rewards of immigrant groups is less than that of the natives, but overlap between the two groups is considerable.[4]

The explanation would seem to be that the labour market contains not one but several hierarchies that can often cross-cut each other. These are: firstly, the rival internal and external labour markets, where jobs can be desirable in certain respects either because the firm is 'good' (even if the job level is low), or because the job is a high-level one (even if the firm is 'bad'); secondly, there are jobs which offer unusually unbalanced work rewards, such as assembly-line work, foundry work, many kinds of heavy labouring, where secondary workers can earn high wages doing unpleasant work. We note elsewhere that immigrants have penetrated to the automobile industry. Physical strength and youth can generally earn high wages if the worker is prepared to incur other severe costs. Thirdly, piecework systems often escape market forces.

Thus there may be effective segregation only at the extreme of the market: secondary workers will only rarely have jobs which offer high rewards on all dimensions, and primary workers will rarely have generally 'bad jobs', but in the middle there is considerable overlap. This receives some support from Lester's (1952) somewhat impressionistic and now rather old study of hiring practices in manufacturing industry in one US labour market. He observed that differences in wage-rates between firms were only related to differences in 'worker quality' (as seen by management) in the few firms right at the top and at the bottom of the hierarchy.

Thus segregation between ethnic groups within the labour market is far from complete. It is also far less complete than segregation in other spheres of life. The degree of residential and educational concentration of ethnic minorities and immigrants is certainly higher than in employment in most countries. The dual argument in the United States has thus involved considerable discussion of the 'ghetto' (Harrison, 1972 and 1974). And, although Western societies have a rather weak tradition of organizing around urban and educational issues, interracial strife is generally fiercer there than in the sphere of labour relations.

Only segregation between the sexes reaches the proportions envisaged by dual labour market theorists – and this is, of course, traditional. Powerful discriminatory forces have also traditionally existed in the position of ethnic groups. Yet the competitive, and often chaotic, forces of the market and of the firm prevent these from ossifying into dualism. Only two changes in that direction can be observed. The first is the growth of the internal labour market. Yet, as we have seen, this development is uneven, greater in the United States than elsewhere. More importantly, unless industrial structure became simplified to the point where the entire labour force of all primary firms were located within an internal labour market, the internal market must often cross-cut the hierarchy of the external market and reduce dualism. The second change is the highly sinister recent development of unfree immigrant labour, most notably in the European countries, but also involving Central Americans in the American South-west and East Coast. With this main exception, we are sceptical of the extent to which real labour markets, certainly in Britain, approximate to the dual model.

Furthermore, we should remember that some other characteristics of secondary workers are not stable sources of stratification. Both adolescents and older workers disproportionately occupy secondary-type jobs. The former have reasonable chances of primary employment on reaching the age of eighteen or 21, the latter may have already held such employment. The problem of old age is that the extent of demotion, with failing powers, is often unpredictable. Some firms have benign reputations, 'carrying' their workers nearing retirement, others are more ruthless. All older workers are aware that they stand little chance on the external labour market. Thus the older workers hang on to present employment with a grimness and a wariness that often depresses the outside observer (eg Palmer, 1962). This is the more negative side of the internal labour market, indicating that it may not offer a better job to the worker, but rather the *only* job. The powerlessness of old age in the labour market is often added to by ill-health or disability, sometimes predictable from childhood but sometimes incurred in the course of work itself. These are fears which are almost uniform throughout the manual working class – they do not lead to stable social stratification within it.

## Notes

1. Though some food processing now involves highly automated production and capital-intensity – and therefore internal labour markets. For an example of this, see Mann (1973).
2. These data are given somewhat obliquely and it is not possible to give comparable figures for internal promotion from semi-skilled to skilled, except for manufacturing industry, where it occurred in just under half the cases. The apparently large difference between manufacturing and other industries may support a dual theory, of course.

3. See Chapter 4.5 of this book, for a discussion of affirmative action in relation to the UK.
4. We assume that Piore also found this in his study of Puerto Ricans. Though he does not give details, he says that their jobs were broadly in the secondary sector, but the diversity of jobs was large (apart from the low promotion chances). He concludes, in rather puzzled fashion, that this is 'troubling analytically' (Piore, 1973b: 11 2a).

# References

Alexander, A. 'Income, Experience and the Structure of Internal Labour Markets', *Quarterly Journal of Economics*, Vol. 88, 1974.

Andreano, R. L. (ed.), *Superconcentration/Supercorporation*, Andover, Mass.: Warner Modular Publications, 1973.

Barron, R. and Norris, G., 'Sexual Divisions in the Dual Labour Market', in D. L. Barker and S. Allen (eds.), *Dependence and Exploitation in Work and Marriage*, London: Longman, 1976.

Berger, S., 'The Uses of the Traditional Sector: Why the Declining Classes Survive', unpublished paper, M.I.T., November 1972.

Bosanquet, N. and Doeringer, P. B., 'Is There a Dual Labour Market in Great Britain?', *Economic Journal*, Vol. 83. 1973.

Castles, S. and Kosack, G., *Immigrant Workers and the Class Structure in Western Europe*, London: Oxford University Press, 1973.

Doeringer, P. B., 'Low Pay, Labor Market Dualism, and Industrial Relations Systems', *Harvard Institute of Economic Research*, Discussion paper No. 271, April 1973.

Doeringer, P. B. and Piore, M. J., *Internal Labor Markets and Manpower Analysis*, Lexington: D. C. Heath, 1971.

Freeman, R. B., 'Decline of Labor Market Discrimination and Economic Analysis', *American Economic Review*, Vol. 63, Papers and Proceedings of the 85th meeting, 1973.

Gordon, M. S. and Thal-Larsen, M., *Employer Policies in a Changing Labor Market*, Berkeley: Institute of Industrial Relations, 1969.

Harrison, B., *Education, Training and the Urban Ghetto*, Baltimore: Johns Hopkins Press, 1972.

Harrison, B., 'Ghetto Economic Development: A Survey', *Journal of Economic Literature*, Vol. 12, 1974.

Jones, K. and Smith, A. D., *The Economic Impact of Commonwealth Immigration*, Cambridge: National Institute of Economic and Social Research and Cambridge University Press, 1970.

Kerr, C., 'The Balkanization of Labor Markets', in E. W. Bakke *et al.*, *Labor Mobility and Economic Opportunity*, Cambridge, Mass.: M.I.T. Press, 1954.

Lester, R., 'A Range Theory of Wage Differentials', *Industrial and Labor Relations Review*, Vol. 5, 1952.

Mackay, D. I., *et al.*, *Labor Markets Under Different Employment Conditions*, London: Allen & Unwin, 1971.

Mann, M., *Workers on the Move*, London: Cambridge University Press, 1973.

Morgan, J. N., *5,000 American Families – Patterns of Economic Progress,*University of Michigan, Survey Research Centre, Institute for Social Research, 1974.

Palmer, G., (ed.), *The Reluctant Job-Changer,*Philadelphia: University of Pennsylvania Press, 1962.

Piore, M. J., 'On the Technological Foundations of Economic Dualism', *M.I.T. Working Paper*, No. 110, May 1973b.

Piore, M. J., 'The Role of Immigration in Industrial Growth: a Case Study of the Origins and Character of Puerto Rican Migration to Boston'. *M.I.T. Working Paper*, No. 112a, May 1973a.

Political and Economic Planning, 'The Facts of Racial Disadvantage', *P.E.P. Broadsheet No. 560* (by D. J. Smith), February 1976.

Reynolds, L., *The Structure of Labor Markets*, New York: Harper and Row, 1951.

Robinson, D., (ed.), *Local Labour Markets and Wage Structures*, London: Gower Press, 1970.

Szymanski, A., 'Trends in Economic Discrimination against Blacks in the U.S. Working Class', *The Review of Radical Political Economics*, Vol. 7, 1975.

Wohlstetter, A. and Coleman, S., 'Race Differences in Income', in A. H. Pascal, *Racial Discrimination in Economic Life,*Lexington: D. C. Heath, 1972.

Wright, P. L., *The Coloured Worker in British Industry*, London: Institute of Race Relations and Oxford University Press, 1968.

# SECTION 2

# ETHNIC MINORITIES IN THE LABOUR MARKET

# INTRODUCTION

As has been indicated in Section 1 (see Chapters 1.1 and 1.2), the unequal position of black workers on the labour market owes much to the circumstances of their initial recruitment. They were then largely employed as replacement labour in a limited range of jobs where wages and conditions had become unacceptable to the majority of indigenous workers. Cohen and Jenner (Chapter 2.2) investigated this first large-scale recruitment of black labour in the wool-textile industry. Most of their findings are consistent with Böhning's analysis of the need for immigrant labour in the industrialized countries of Western Europe during the post-1945 period (see Chapter 1.1).

Though the industry was labour-intensive, the recruitment of black workers into textiles was, contrary to Cohen and Jenner's expectations, associated with the installation of expensive new capital equipment. This equipment was considered an essential part of the fight against stiff international competition, but if it was to repay the cost of installation it had to be worked intensively. This necessitated the implementation of a two- or even three-shift system, but it was widely believed by employers that the level of wages required to attract local labour into shift-work would have rendered such a pattern of work uneconomic. The recruitment of workers from the New Commonwealth appeared as the easiest solution to the problems faced by many 'labour starved' textile employers, largely because immigrants could be seen as 'mobile' labour, willing to work hard at an economic rate of pay. In retrospect, however, it might be said that this recruitment merely slowed the decline of individual firms, and perhaps of the entire British textile industry, though it might be added that had immigration controls not artificially limited the supply of labour the textile industry's prospects might have been improved. The initial concentration of black workers in certain industries and occupations does much to explain their subsequent employment experience. They have been disproportionately affected both by the general decline in manufacturing output and by the sharp decline in industries such as textiles.

Though the recruitment of black workers may have variously averted production bottlenecks or permitted an industry to remain competitive, their insertion into the labour force cannot be regarded purely as a 'structural adjustment'. Though their arrival may be said to have improved the prospects of a particular industry, it was not always welcomed by their fellow workers. The extract from Brooks' investigation of race and labour in London Transport (Chapter 2.3) is concerned not so much with these structural reasons for the recruitment of immigrant workers, but with the hostility which their arrival precipitated. Brooks concludes that 'colour' was the most frequent objection to the employment of black workers, but he emphasizes that the objections voiced by white workers ought to be seen in the context of a perceived weakening of bargaining power (in terms of wages, conditions and 'standards') as staff shortages were reduced. According to Brooks, there would have been opposition to any identifiable group of outsiders; colour made opposition both more widespread and intense, appearing to confirm the already declining status (compared with the 1930s) of working for London senior
Transport.

The extract from 'Britain's Black Population' (Chapter 2.1), which leans heavily on the findings of the 1971 census (the 1981 census did not provide similar information), is intended to provide an overview of the position of black workers in the labour market. It emphasizes the difference between the pattern of black employment and that of the British population as a whole, and the extent to which black workers remain concentrated in the type of unskilled and semi-skilled jobs for which they were initially recruited in the 1950s and 1960s.

The present position of black workers reflects not only the unequal circumstances of their original entry to the labour market, but also the unequal treatment that they have since encountered. Both these aspects emerge from the survey carried out by Blackburn and Mann in Peterborough (Chapter 2.4), though it applies as they point out, to 'relatively well-placed immigrants, both black and white' and not to the immigrant communities as a whole. Nevertheless, its findings offer a valuable modification to the picture of the position of immigrant workers painted by Castles and Kosack (Chapter 1.2). According to Blackburn and Mann, in periods of high employment, wage discrimination against immigrants was not high. Indeed, they found that differences in earnings between immigrant and non-immigrant men were quite small. But they add the important rider that this near wage-equality (at least for white and

English-speaking immigrants) was achieved only at significant cost to immigrant workers in terms of longer hours, higher incidence of shiftwork, and less pleasant working conditions. Blackburn and Mann also found that the degree of ethnic segregation in the labour market was not very great. However they add the qualification that the considerable occupational overlap between immigrant and native workers owes more to the fact that native workers are found at almost every level than because immigrant workers are similarly dispersed. Moreover, a minority of almost a third of immigrant workers occupied 'clearly segregated, low-level jobs'. Blackburn and Mann conclude that as the immigrant worker's work life lengthens, so differences between his position and that of the native worker widen: the opportunities for advancement are very restricted and higher level jobs are rarely reached.

Blackburn and Mann's survey lends considerable support to the distinction which they draw (see Chapter 1.4) between primary and secondary jobs. Much of the literature on racial discrimination in employment has been devoted to the experiences of manual workers, particularly in unskilled work or in 'secondary jobs'. To some extent the initial concentration of black workers in less-desirable manual employment could have been explained in terms of the level of skills, work experience and qualifications that they brought to the labour market. However this is the case to only a limited extent. Many black and other migrant workers have brought high levels of qualification and skill only to find these undervalued or disregarded. Either their qualifications and experience may gain them jobs only at a level below that normally achieved by white workers with similar backgrounds or they may be affectively disregarded at the stage of promotion or upgrading. The Report of the Royal Commission on the Health Service provided evidence of the way in which migrant doctors are unrepresented in the more senior medical grades and over-represented in unpopular geographical areas of medical specializations such as geriatrics. At the level of skilled manual work, migrant workers often had difficulty in gaining acceptance of their skilled status even where this could be practically demonstrated. Ultimately the consequences and frustrations of such experience can only be adequately expressed by the individual voices of those affected. Given our concern with the wider conceptual issues this is not something we have been able to encompass within this Reader, although Chapters 2.5 and 2.6 give some hint of what lies behind the statistics of disadvantage. Wallace Collins (Chapter 2.5), a skilled Jamaican woodworker migrated to

England in 1954. While he experienced little difficulty in gaining work during the years of labour shortage this did not isolate him from the pressures and consequences of racial hostilities in the workplace. 'Harold Stephens', a Barbadian (Chapter 2.6) came to Britain at a time when the job market had deteriorated (1962 – see Chapter 5.1) and which from 1966 began a progressive decline. As in Collins' case, support came from the arrival of other West Indians in the work groups. But as was the case for the population as a whole, the rigours of unskilled work increasingly had to be faced without much option of going elsewhere. The counterpart of Tommy Robson, the jolly and 'enlightened' foreman at the bagging plant, would probably have been encountered in many workplaces.

Wallace Collins and Harold Stevens were first-generation migrants. It has been argued that the problems and pressures accompanying the arrival of new workers would gradually disappear as they and members of the host-population became more accustomed to each other and culturally 'acclimatized'. Furthermore, as black applicants gained suitable British experience and qualifications, they would be able to secure more-desirable non-manual jobs. Ballard and Holden (Chapter 2.7) sought to discover what employment prospects awaited the children of black immigrants who, having taken advantage of educational opportunities in Britain, had obtained degree-level qualifications. They found that black students met with less success than similarly qualified white students at all stages of seeking a job. They contend that their evidence indicates that, in practice, employers must first consider all suitably qualified white candidates and only when this supply is exhausted will serious consideration be given to black candidates. Moreover, when there is an excess of suitable white applicants, as may be supposed is the case in time of recession, black applicants may rarely reach the front of the queue. Ballard and Holden's argument finds support in the results of the correspondence testing carried out by Smith (Chapter 2.8). This experiment indicated not merely that black candidates faced substantial discrimination in applications for white-collar jobs, but that they would often be unaware that discrimination had taken place.

The extracts from Kosmin (Chapter 2.9) and Shah (Chapter 2.10) parallel the findings of Cohen and Jenner in that they refer to an industry – the clothing industry – which has always been labour intensive and which, because of narrow profit margins and international competition, has had to keep down labour costs. Like textiles, the clothing industry has traditionally relied on immigrant labour in the absence of sufficient indigenous workers. But the extracts from Kosmin and from Shah, along with that from Allen *et al* (Chapter 2.11), have been included to draw attention to forms of economic activity which have been somewhat neglected in the literature on ethnic minorities, namely self-employment and home working. The clothing industry provides great opportunity for those with nominal capital or who are denied access to conventional sources of finance, to set up in business for themselves. Kosmin's view of Jewish involvement in the industry emphasizes that Jews did not see themselves as a permanent part of the working class and that their ideal was to become self-employed.

Such an analysis may have considerable application to elements of the Asian community (especially those who came with an entrepreneurial background from East Africa), and to their prospects for economic advance. But, perhaps more important, the question of minority-owned businesses can be seen as constituting an alternative economic system, which not merely provides employment to many members of ethnic minorities who would otherwise face discrimination, but also offers an environment sheltered from the outside world in which the cultural integrity of the minority group can be more easily maintained. In this context, reference might also be made to the last of Böhning's four phases of migration (Chapter 1.1). In this phase the existence of a distinct ethnic minority numbering, say, between 100,000 and 200,000 generates a demand for specifically ethnic facilities, such as shops, schools and religious institutions. These facilities will be staffed predominantly by members of the ethnic minority concerned. Therefore, a sizeable ethnic presence can be expected to generate its own employment opportunities. However, such an alternative economic system is only likely to provide employment for a minority of the minority: the remainder must continue to seek employment in the 'majority' economy with all that implies.

# CHAPTER 2.1

# A PROFILE OF BLACK EMPLOYMENT*

*The Runnymede Trust and the Radical Statistics Group*

In 1978 the labour force of Britain was 26 million people. According to the last census in 1971 a total of one and a half million of the workforce were born outside the UK or had both parents born outside the UK. Approximately half a million of these people were black. The patterns of employment – and indeed unemployment – amongst this black population differ in important respects from those of the British population as a whole. For example, proportionately more black people than white people have unskilled or semi-skilled jobs and the rate of unemployment for black youths is higher than that of their white peers.

These differences are a result of a number of factors which will be discussed in this chapter. Some are caused by racial discrimination; others are a consequence of some people from the Indian sub-continent having not been resident in the UK long enough to acquire the skills and language needed for work. Another factor is that the average age of the black population is much younger than the population as a whole. As young people are generally more likely to be unemployed (or take longer to enter into jobs), even without racial discrimination, unemployment rates for blacks, all other things being equal, would be higher than those for the population as a whole. For these and other reasons the black population is more susceptible to the effects of economic decline than the population as a whole. When unemployment rates rise, the black population is usually the first to suffer.

* An edited version of Chapter 3, Employment, from *Britain's Black Population*, Heinemann Educational Books, 1980.

## Black people in the working population

Black people form a relatively small but growing proportion of the labour force in Britain. In 1971, people who were born outside the UK or who had both parents born outside the UK accounted for just under six per cent of all economically active persons: 2.2 per cent (555,520) were from the New Commonwealth, 1.7 per cent (421,130) from Ireland, and two per cent from elsewhere. The figures are shown in Fig. 1.

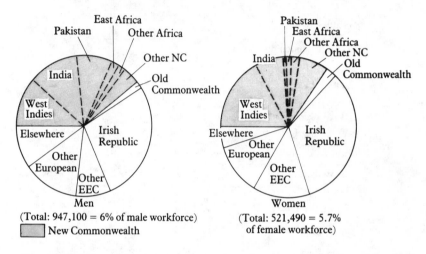

(Total: 947,100 = 6% of male workforce)
(Total: 521,490 = 5.7% of female workforce)

New Commonwealth

*Source:* 1971 *Census of Population*

**Figure 1:** Immigrant contribution to the labour supply, 1971.

The percentage of immigrants in the workforce varies from 1.3 per cent in the North to over fifteen per cent in Greater London (this is shown in Fig. 2). Black people as immigrants settled in the more prosperous conurbations where their labour was in demand. In these conurbations they are often concentrated in inner city areas whose white and total population are declining. In these areas the demand for labour has been relatively high. However, in some cities there has also been a trend of population dispersal into the suburbs.

One study has shown that while the number of employed persons born in the UK fell between 1961 and 1971, the number of employed people born outside the UK rose.[1] The increase in the number of economically

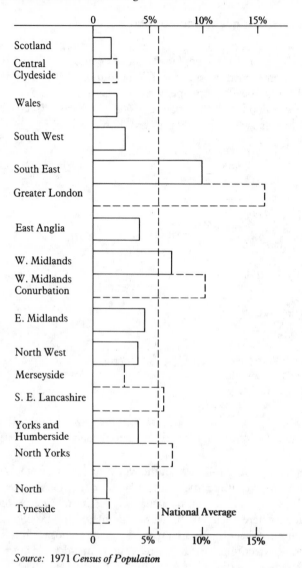

*Source:* 1971 *Census of Population*

**Figure 2:** Geographical distribution of immigrant workers, 1971. Economically active persons born outside the UK with both parents born outside UK as percentage of total economically active in region and conurbation.

active persons born in the New Commonwealth is likely to have continued for at least two reasons. First, children who came here to join their parents will have reached or will be reaching working age. Second, economically active immigrant males from the New Commonwealth have a lower average age than that for economically active males taken as a whole. Comparisons between blacks and whites are strongly influenced by the difference in age profile – a far greater percentage of whites than of blacks are above retiring age. Because of this, a relatively high proportion of men from the black groups are working – 91 per cent of black men in comparison with 77 per cent of white men. In 1971 half the number of black women aged fifteen and over were economically active, compared with 43 per cent of women for the general population.

There were, however, marked differences between activity rates of the different groups that comprise the black population. For example, 67 per cent of West Indian women aged fifteen and over were economically active in contrast to only 39 per cent for Indian women and sixteen per cent for Pakistani women. It is likely that the religious and cultural pressures on women from the Indian sub-continent (especially Pakistani women, who are mainly Moslems) not to seek employment outside the home will relax, to some extent. This is particularly likely if 'ethnic work groups' can be established so that women can work together with no direct contact with men.

Black people work in a wide range of mainly manual industries and occupations but tend to be concentrated in unskilled and semi-skilled jobs for which it is difficult to recruit or retain workers because of 'unsocial' hours, an unpleasant working environment and relatively low earnings. Reasons for this include language difficulties and differences in educational and training standards which are not readily acceptable to British employers. Moreover, it should be remembered that these features characterized those sectors of the economy that were short of labour in the late 1950s and early 1960s, this shortage being the initial stimulus for immigration. Hence, black people work in these industries and occupations partly because these were the ones which were willing to employ them. But it is also the case that movement out of these industries and occupations is retarded by racial discrimination.

The proportion of those in each industry in 1971 who were immigrants are shown in Fig. 3. Of all employed immigrants 36 per cent of all employed immigrants and 47 per cent of those from the New Commonwealth worked in manufacturing industries III to XIX (see

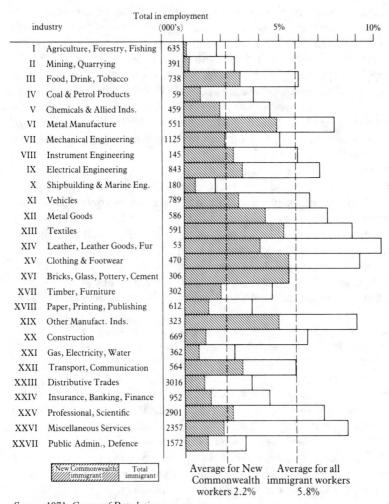

**Figure 3:** Immigrant workers as a percentage of the total workforce by industry.

Fig. 3). The corresponding percentage of all employed persons was 33 per cent. A number of studies have indicated that home-working, often with very low wages, is widespread amongst women from the Indian sub-continent and from Cyprus.[2] West Indian women seem more likely to work outside the home. This difference is explained by the language and cultural barriers which prevent many Asian women from taking a job outside the home.

According to the 1971 Census a much higher proportion of economi-cally active black people than of the population as a whole were labourers and the proportion of black people who were administrators and managers, clerical or sales workers, was well below the corresponding proportion for all economically active persons. In the manufacturing industries, black people generally worked directly in production or related activities such as packing and relatively few in service or maintenance.

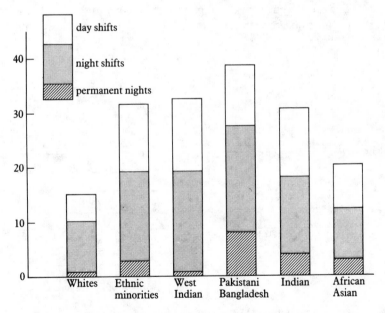

*Source:*  D. Smith *The Facts of Racial Disadvantage* PEP, 1976

**Figure 4:**  Percentage of male working shifts (by country of origin).

Black workers are greatly underrepresented at supervisory levels. According to a recent report, employers largely attributed this to a combination of low turnover among existing supervisors and promotion systems which depend largely on seniority coupled with the presence within the organization of white workers with greater seniority than any black employees.[3]

Black people are more likely to be employed on shifts, particularly night shifts. The PEP study showed that 32 per cent of the plants visited in which members of the ethnic minorities accounted for most of the workforce had permanent night shifts as compared with only 12 per cent of those firms employing only white workers (see Fig. 4).[4]

As is shown in Fig. 5, both manual and non-manual black male workers are likely to earn less than white workers. However, because there are fewer part-time workers in the black female earning group than in the white female earning group, the earnings of black women will tend to be higher than those of their white counterparts although pay rates may be lower. These differences in earnings are attributable to the fact that black workers tend to be concentrated in lower status jobs and those with less responsibility.

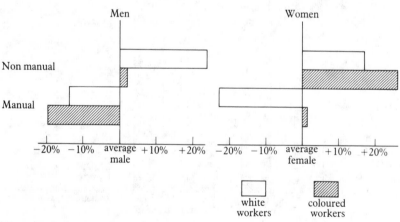

*Source:* OPCS General Household Survey 1975 and 1976

**Figure 5:** Comparison of average earnings for white and coloured workers against overall average for sex.

In London a high proportion of West Indians are in transport and labouring jobs, while in the West Midlands many black people and especially Pakistanis are in labouring jobs. Indians in the West Midlands are disproportionately represented in furnace, forge, foundry and rolling mills. In the London area Cypriots and Pakistanis are concentrated in service occupations and in the clothing trades.

Another study showed that the pattern revealed by PEP at a national level was reflected in a typical West Midlands town.[5] In a sample of firms which together employed some 1800 black people most black employees were shown to be employed in unskilled or semi-skilled jobs. Most firms only recruited black workers because no suitable whites were available, and of the 1800 black workers in the sample only two were foremen.

Although immigrant labour accounts for only about six per cent of all economically active persons in Britain, it forms a sizeable element in the labour force of certain firms and industries. Examples include:

1. Textiles in Lancashire and Yorkshire where nightshifts are often manned almost entirely by Indian and Pakistani workers;[5A]
2. The National Health Service in England and Wales in which over one-third of hospital medical staff, about one-sixth of doctors in general practice and a little over one-fifth of all student and pupil nurses and pupil midwives are born overseas;[6] and
3. Restaurants, cafes and snack bars in which nearly one-quarter of all workers nationally and over one-half in Greater London are immigrants.

## Discrimination in employment

There is evidence from a number of reports and surveys of widespread discrimination against black people in British industry. One report suggests that discrimination is not a question of employers simply displaying prejudice against people with black skins, but that employers appear to have mistaken assumptions about the actual abilities of black people.[7]

A survey of nearly 300 plants, comprising case studies and interviews conducted by PEP, showed that more than half the plants practised some form of discrimination and a black person had to make twice as many applications as a white person before finding a job.[8] A second PEP report[9] in the same year stated that substantial discrimination was found, even at the level of recruitment for unskilled jobs; further, more than 30 per cent of Indian and West Indian applicants were discriminated against at the earliest stage of recruitment – the written application stage – in a broad range of white collar jobs. This research included Greek subjects to test the extent to which discrimination related to 'foreigness' rather than skin colour. Its authors stated that the findings in all the tests strengthened the conclusion that it was skin colour which underlay most of the discrimination shown in these cases.[9]

According to a report published by the Tavistock Institute of Human Relations, black people are considerably less successful than white in applying for jobs and promotion in the Civil Service.[10] The departments studied were the Department of Health and Social Security, the Ministry of Defence and HM Dockyard, Portsmouth. In the London North DHSS Region, out of 317 applications for clerical officer grade jobs between June and November 1976, one-third came from black candidates and two-thirds from white. Only ten black candidates were offered jobs in comparison with 78 whites: this translates to a success rate of eighteen per cent in comparison with 54 per cent for whites. Furthermore, more black than white candidates rejected for interview possessed the minimum educational qualifications. The researchers also found that of 100 clerical officers studied, 30 were 'over-qualified' and of these 23 were black, showing that many black employees accept jobs below their level of qualification.

## Unemployment

In February 1980, according to figures published by the Department of Employment, there were 1,422 thousand persons (or six per cent) of the total workforce) unemployed in Great Britain. Of these, 54.4 thousand were black.[11] Unemployment amongst black people, as a percentage of all those registered as unemployed in the UK, has increased rapidly during the past few years. This is shown in Fig. 6. There is, however, evidence to suggest that this is primarily a result of the rapid rise in unemployment amongst black youths aged from sixteen to 24.

According to both Department of Employment figures and the PEP survey, unemployment among black people increases disproportionately when the general level of unemployment is rising (see Fig. 6). For example, between November 1973 and February 1980 total unemployment doubled, whereas the number of black people on the register quadrupled. Several factors have been suggested to explain why unemployment among black people increases in this way:

1. There are increasing numbers of black young people leaving full-time education and entering the employment field at a time when job prospects for young people generally are adversely affected by the cutbacks in recruitment during the present recession.

2. The shorter average duration in employment of black workers makes them vulnerable to 'last in, first out' rules at times of redundancy.

3. There have been greater percentage increases in unemployment in the regions – for example, the South East and West Midlands – where most black people live.

4. Racial discrimination by individual employers and in recruitment and selection procedures means that, faced with a plentiful supply of labour, employers will hire white in preference to black labour.

5. Lack of appropriate skills and qualifications including knowledge of English on the part of recent immigrants from the Indian sub-continent.

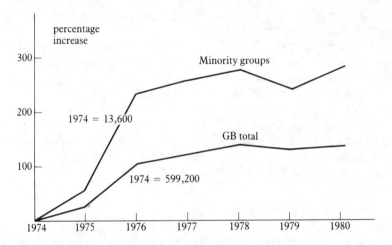

*Source:* Department of Employment *Gazette*, 1980, Vol. 88  No. 3.

**Figure 6:** Percentage increase in unemployment since 1974 of minority groups and total workforce in Great Britain.

How important each of these factors is relative to all the others is difficult to determine. Without doubt, given the evidence on the extent of discrimination which occurs when black people apply for jobs, racial discrimination is a major factor, but it does not necessarily follow that the other factors are of only peripheral importance.[11A]

Statistics published by the Department of Employment showed that between February 1979 and February 1980 registered unemployment among black workers rose by 11.6 per cent compared with 2.5 per cent for the total unemployed for Great Britain.[12] The increase was not evenly spread through the black workforce. Among West Indians, unemployment went up by 13.5 per cent while among Pakistanis it increased by 10.1 per cent. There does not appear to be a single explanation for those discrepancies, and it would seem that differing industrial occupation, area of residence and age structure may all have been contributory factors.

## Youth unemployment

In general, black school-leavers are particularly likely to be unemployed. This is both because of a reduction in the number of jobs available and because the black population is on average younger than the population as a whole, so even without discrimination proportionally more blacks than whites would be unemployed.[13]

Between February 1977 and February 1978 the increase in unemployment in the sixteen to 24 age group accounted for 36 per cent of the total increase in unemployment for Asian workers (excluding those from East Africa). Between February 1979 and February 1980, unemployment amongst black youths increased by the same percentage (eleven per cent) as for the total black unemployed. Allowing for a low level of registration (see below), particularly among young people, these figures are probably a considerable underestimate of unemployment among young black workers.

## Unregistered unemployment

The number of people who are unemployed but have not registered as such at employment offices and job centres is by definition difficult to assess. The Department of Employment estimated that in 1973 there were a total of 100,000 unregistered males and 160,000 unregistered females.[14] The 1971 Census showed that the *majority* of unemployed black people were not registered as unemployed in 1971. This may be for a number of reasons including the fact that some black people may be disenchanted with the kinds of jobs thought to be suitable and therefore offered to them by local employment offices. The fact that just under half of the males born in the West Indies who were not working were not registered as unemployed meant that they were not eligible for benefits. More recent estimates of the extent of non-registration have varied[15] though it is probably true to say the level of non-registration amongst blacks, particularly young West Indians, is considerably higher than amongst the total population even within a similar age range.

According to a survey published in 1978, unemployment among black school-leavers in the borough of Lewisham in London is three times higher than among white school-leavers despite the fact that they try just as hard to find jobs.[16] Those in employment had taken longer to find work and have had to try harder than their white contemporaries. Both the black and white unemployed sample were actively looking for work and two-thirds of the unemployed blacks thought that they had been discriminated against by employers. Although the educational achievement of the black sample was on average lower, it did not seem to be a crucial factor in explaining the different success rates in finding jobs. The survey of 500 school-leavers concluded that 'whether intentional or unintentional' discrimination has been an important factor. [. . .]

The difficulties that black people face in employment are, however, not as much a result of any lack of skills or abilities on their part as much as the circumstances with which they are confronted. A British Youth Council's report made the following comment: 'Although many of the disadvantages suffered by ethnic minorities are the same as those suffered by other young unemployed people, all the available evidence points to racial discrimination as being the major factor in the disproportionately high youth unemployment levels they face.'[17] [. . .]

## Notes

1. Department of Applied Economics, Cambridge University. Referred to in *The Role of Immigrants in the Labour Market*, Runnymede Trust Briefing Paper, 1977.
2. S. Shah, *Immigrants and Employment in the Clothing Industry: The Rag Trade in London's East End*, London: Runnymede Trust, 1975. (This volume, 2.10.)
3. Unit of Manpower Studies, *The Role of Immigrants in the Labour Market*, London: Department of Employment, 1977.
4. D. J. Smith, *Racial Disadvantage in Employment*, London: Political and Economic Planning, 1974.
5. D. Brooks, *Black Employment in the Black Country*, London: Runnymede Trust, 1975.
5A. [Editorial Note: see Cohen and Jenner, this volume.]
6. British Medical Association, 'Medical Manpower, Staffing and Training Requirements', *British Medical Association Journal*, 19 May 1979, pp. 1365–76.

7.  Unit of Manpower Studies, op. cit.
8.  Smith, op. cit.
9.  D. J. Smith and N. McIntosh, *The Extent of Racial Discrimination*, PEP vol. XI, Broadsheet 547, 1974.
10. Tavistock Institute of Human Relations, *Application of Race Relations Policy in the Civil Service*, London: HMSO, 1978.
11. Department of Employment, *Gazette*, March 1980, Vol. 88, no. 3, p.245.
11A. [Editorial Note: see Rhodes and Braham, this volume.]
12. Department of Employment, *Gazette*, 1979, Vol. 87, no. 3, p. 259 and 1980, Vol. 88, no. 3, p. 245.
13. Youthaid, *Study of the Transition from School to Working Life*, London, 1979.
14. Department of Employment, *Gazette;* December 1976, Vol. 84, no. 12.
15. M. Navitt, *Unregistered Unemployment: a background paper*, London: Youthaid, 1979.
16. Commission for Racial Equality, *Looking for Work*, London, 1978.
17. Runnymede Trust, *A Review of the Race Relations Act 1976*, London, 1979.

# CHAPTER 2.2

# THE EMPLOYMENT OF IMMIGRANTS: A CASE STUDY WITHIN THE WOOL INDUSTRY*

*B. G. Cohen and P. J. Jenner*

## Introduction

In order to assess the economic effects of immigration on the economy of this country one is faced with a lack of hard factual information on what happens at the micro-level, that is within a firm, industry or region. In order to rectify this, a small industry case study was carried out to see what actually happened when a flow of immigrants started working in an industry. The companies studied were in the wool textile industry in the West Riding of Yorkshire.

Three general areas of interest were investigated. Firstly, what was the effect of immigrant labour on investment policies? Secondly,[1] what the actions of employers might have been if the immigrants had not been available? Thirdly from the standpoint of management how did immigrant labour compare with local labour?

## Background to area and industry

The study was carried out in and around 'Wooltown', a large West Riding town, where the wool textile industry has been the major employer for over 150 years. In appearance Wooltown is a typical Southerner's view of what a Northern industrial town should look like. Its population has been slowly declining since the early years of this century with movement from the centre to the surrounding countryside and also out of the region. Much of the housing in the centre has been or is being demolished and new housing estates are being built further up the valleys within the borough boundaries.

---

* *Race* vol. 10, 1968–9.

The wool industry is still the most important employer of labour but its pre-eminence has been increasingly challenged by industrial diversification especially since the war. Competition for labour, especially female, has increased with the greater variety of jobs now available in the area. This is reflected by the unemployment figures for Wooltown which have not been above one and a half per cent for the four years previous to the study and have been below one per cent for most of the period.

The number of workers in the wool industry has been steadily declining and the relative size of the wool industry in relation to the national economy has also been falling. The industry can be divided into two major sections, woollen and worsted, and can also be divided vertically into combers, spinners, weavers, etc. Other major activities include dyeing, rag wool manufacture, carpet manufacture, etc. The industry is in the main made up of small units many of which are old family firms well over one hundred years old.[2]

## Method of work and details of sample

As this study was covering new ground it was felt that a fairly unstructured approach would be most effective. It was decided in view of the structure of the industry to interview a senior member of the management of a sample of companies in one sector of the industry. The interviews would be unstructured except insofar as certain points would be raised in each interview.

The sample was selected from a trade directory published by the local Chamber of Commerce. The directory classified companies in each of the many different sections of the wool textile industry and all the companies in one section were selected. Many of the companies, however, were also active in other parts of the wool industry.

The names and addresses of the 26 companies were obtained but this was reduced to 24 as we were informed at the outset that two had gone out of business. A detailed letter was sent explaining the purpose of the study and a request for an interview. Sixteen companies agreed to be interviewed and for one company information was obtained over the telephone (Company Z). During the interviewing it was found that two of the companies on our list were administered as one unit and they were treated as one company (Company O). Of the seventeen companies for which information was obtained twelve were within the borough boundaries of Wooltown and the others were in small towns and large villages nearby.

**TABLE I**    Sample of Companies in Wool Industry Survey
Numbers of Employees, Density of Female and Immigrant Employees

| Company | Total number of employees | Female employees as % of total | Immigrant employees as % of total* |
|---------|------------|------------|------------|
| A | 95 | 72 | 7 |
| B | 85 | 71 | 4 |
| C | 517 | 48 | 15 |
| D | 82 | 67 | 7 |
| E | 397 | 49 | 14 |
| F | 300 | 50 | 33 |
| G | 247 | 54 | 0 |
| H | 180 | 67 | 14 |
| I | 80 | 75 | 1* |
| J | 165 | 73 | 0 |
| K | 38 | 16 | 24 |
| L | 145 | 62 | 6 |
| M | 952 | 58 | 1 |
| N | 70 | 79 | 0 |
| O | 500 | 85 | 5 |
| P | 77 | 32 | 9 |
| Z | 105 | 65 | 15 |
| Total numbers | 17 | 4035 | 2424 | 349 |
| Mean numbers | – | 237 | 143 | 21 (25)† |
| Mean density % | – | | 60.07 | 8.65 (9.82)† |

Notes: Table adapted by the editors from Cohen & Jenner's data. Figures for female and immigrant density rounded up.

* The 1% of employees at company I comprises 1 female West Indian. All remaining immigrants in the Cohen & Jenner study were male.

† Figures in brackets are for mean numbers of immigrant employees and mean immigrant density for the 14 immigrant employing firms only, excluding firms G, J and N.

Data gathered by Cohen & Jenner in April/June 1967, except for companies F and K – data for September 1966, gathered prior to closures of these companies.

Table 1 summarizes the size of the companies, by number of employees and the percentages of female and immigrant employees.[3] The figures for immigrants refer to those from the 'New' or coloured Commonwealth and the vast majority were Pakistanis.[4] The only female immigrant employee was a West Indian at Company I. For the six companies in the original sample not listed in Table 1, it is known that three did not employ immigrants, one did employ them, and no information is available about the other two companies.

## Reasons for employing immigrant labour

It has been pointed out in studies of race relations and employment opportunities for immigrants in industry that there is a reluctance for employers to change from a known, tested labour supply to a new, strange labour supply. For this reason, the companies were asked, 'Why did you first employ immigrants?' on the assumption that there would have to be some special reason for employing immigrants.[6]

Certain themes emerged from employers when answering this question and it is necessary to examine their answers in relation to the labour situation as a whole and the development of the industry. All the companies stressed that the recruitment of good labour was far more difficult than it had been in the past especially in the inter-war period. After World War II they had faced severe labour shortages and nearly all had employed European refugee labour. The situation had eased slightly in the early 1950s but became more severe again and many of the companies had widened the area of their recruitment and had transported workers in from outlying areas. Some of the companies had used Hungarian and West Indian labour in the late 1950s and early 1960s but few stayed and the arrival of the Pakistanis in the early 1960s can be seen as the last of a long stream of immigrant workers to the wool industry. Many respondents were well aware of this as was Mr O (that is, the person interviewed at Company O) who in answer to the question, 'When did the company first employ immigrants?' replied, 'Since the firm was founded 130 years ago.'

The Pakistanis differ from previous immigrant groups in that they are a source of male labour only, and to understand their employment position other factors of change within the industry must be considered. Certain sections of the industry have always used predominantly female labour, and in the past the most pressing employment problems of many firms have been shortages of female labour. The basic machinery used in much of the wool industry has not changed very radically over the past 50 years and most of the companies seen still had a sizeable proportion of pre-1939 machinery. Since the mid-1950s there has been an increasing availability of new machinery with a greater productive capacity utilizing less labour. The draw-back to the newer machinery is its cost especially in relation to the older machinery. Thus for the purchase of new machinery to be an economic proposition it must be very intensively worked which implies some form of shift working. Additionally, much of the older machinery was worked by female labour and there are institutional obstacles to the employment of females on shift work and therefore males must be employed instead to man the new machinery. In some cases females worked day shifts, males nights. Other companies used changing shift systems or had males day and night as the day shift worked very long hours and thus employed only male labour on the new machinery.

A further complication for a company deciding whether to invest in the new machinery is that male labour and shift work are considerably more expensive than female labour. Obviously the decision to invest would depend not only on a company's assessment of the level of demand but also on whether they could obtain the labour necessary to keep its new expensive machinery at near full capacity.

In eight instances the companies stated that the reason they first employed Pakistani workers was closely associated with new capital investment that involved either shift working or very long hours and in one other case it was associated with shift working but not with any new investment. Of the four companies not employing immigrants only one of them, Company G, had made substantial new capital investment in the recent past. The other four companies employing immigrants employed them mainly for labouring jobs and their recent capital investment had generally been lower than that of the first group of companies.

Table 2 summarizes the position in the seventeen companies with regard to capital investment and the intensity of utilization of plant. It should be made clear that the rating of the degree of capital investment in separate categories is of a qualitative nature. Companies C and E had invested more in new machinery than any other companies in the sample. All the companies had either bought new machinery or converted old machinery in the recent past and not all the companies in category I would be considered as being more up to date than those in category III. In two cases (B and D) the only new machinery that had been installed was a ring spinner and it was only to man this machine that Pakistanis were

**TABLE 2** Relationship between new capital investment, employment of male immigrants and utilization of machinery

| Company | Immigrant employees as % of total | Employment of immigrants (1) | Recent capital investment (post 1958) (2) | Number of running hours per week for most intensively used m/c. |
|---------|------|------|------|------|
| A | 7 | L | III | 41½ (59½) |
| B | 4 | 0 | I | 41½ (59½) |
| C | 15 | (0) | I | 168 |
| D | 7 | 0 | I | 120 |
| E | 14 | (0) | I | 168 |
| F | 33 | (0) | I | 115 |
| G | 0 | – | II | 110 |
| H | 14 | (0) | I | 120 |
| I | 1 | F | III | 41½ (+ o/t) |
| J | 0 | – | III | 41½ (+ o/t) |
| K | 24 | 0 | I | 100 |
| L | 6 | 0 | I | 88 |
| M | 1 | L | II | 80 |
| N | 0 | – | III | 41½ (62½) |
| O | 5 | L | II | 41½ (+ o/t) |
| P | 9 | (0) | III | 96½ |
| Z | 15 | 0/L | III | 41½ (+ o/t) |

Notes: **1** 0 = Immigrant labour employed as operatives;
   (0) = Mainly as operatives;
   L = As labourers;
   F = Female employees;

**2** Categories for capital investment were:
   I  Capital investment associated with employment of immigrant labour
   II Capital investment not associated with employment of immigrant labour
   III Little or no new capital investment
   For details of data collection, see Table 1.

employed. The number of hours worked in Table 2 applies in all cases to the most intensively operated parts of these companies and usually to the newest machinery in these companies.

Of the eight companies in category I, only Company B did not have some double shift working of some type. This company worked a standard

41½ hour week, plus an evening shift. Known as the housewives shift this shift is usually four days a week four and a half hours per day and is mainly used to even out production between the different stages in production. It is quite common in the industry. Company B would have liked to employ its new machinery more intensively but it was not considered worthwhile to open the factory for just one unit and thus the Pakistanis employed on the ring spinner worked a 59½ hour week.

It would not be correct to state that the employment of immigrants in these eight companies was solely related to the new machinery that they had purchased. New capital investment is itself often an indicator of other large changes occurring within a company or industry. Company F three years earlier experienced a large rise in orders and this necessitated the working of a night shift on its old machinery together with the installation of new machinery. This meant that the Company had to expand its labour force considerably and the number of Pakistanis employed by the Company rose from fifteen to a hundred in a period of six months. Similarly for other companies a rise in demand meant the introduction of shift working on existing machinery plus new investment. In Company P, rising demand led to more intensive shift working but not to the installation of new machinery, as only one floor of the mill was strong enough to support the newer, heavier machinery.

Company G was the company that had made the most substantial recent capital investments that did not employ immigrant operatives. The mill worked a five-day week partly on a two-shift system (6–2, 2–10, that is, 80 hours per week) and its most modern machinery was on a 22 hours a day system. It was the only company in the sample that had a night shift and did *not* employ immigrant labour. In a letter from Mr G he explained: 'The natural position of these mills, being out in the country and in a valley not connected with (Wooltown), coupled with extensive modernization of both room and plant, has enabled us to attract all the local labour of West Riding ancestry that we require.' When interviewed, Mr G stated that his company had never suffered from serious shortages of male labour and he thought that this was in part due to the fact that several housing estates had been built in nearby villages in the recent past. He was confident that as the number of workers the company employed on shift work increased they would be able to recruit sufficient labour locally.

The three companies (A, M and O) that employed immigrants as labourers only and not as operatives generally worked shorter hours than those companies with immigrant operatives. Both companies M and O were at a transitional stage with regard to new investment and were currently trying to project exactly what their policy would be with regard to the organization of shift working. Mr M stated that his company had taken the opportunity of the credit squeeze and the lull in demand to clear out certain old machinery and to install new machinery where they thought future demand would warrant this. The company wanted to buy more new machinery but this would await an upturn in demand. Mr M felt that it would be necessary at some later date to have full shift working and the company would probably have to employ male immigrant labour to do this. Mr O was also at the stage of having decided to install new machinery, but was not certain exactly how he would organize shift working and whether it would be necessary to recruit immigrants.

Apart from the Pakistanis employed as machine operatives, usually working shifts, the other category of employment was as labourers or on unskilled labouring type jobs. Some of the companies in the sample had them only in this type of occupation, whilst nearly all the companies that employed them as operatives had a few in this type of job as well. The general reason for their employment was the extreme difficulty in obtaining labour to fill jobs that were in the main dead-end and low-paid. The position is well illustrated by the situation at Company A where seven of the ten labourers employed by the company are Pakistani juveniles. Mr A stated that the work was fairly light and thus suitable for juveniles – at the end of the war he had employed refugees and later on school-leavers. For a period during the 1950s West Indians had had these jobs but for the last six years the work had been done mainly by Pakistani juveniles. The job had always had a high turnover rate and he thought Pakistanis used it as a stepping-stone. It was very difficult to obtain local labour as the pay was low and there were no real prospects. Similarly, Mr O stated that the Pakistanis in his firm, mostly juveniles, were mainly employed in dead-end labouring jobs.

Very few Pakistanis were found in jobs other than machine operatives and labouring. The most important exception was in Company E where the quality controller for the mill, a junior executive, was a Pakistani. He was the only Pakistani in the sample who had any position that gave authority over local labour. There were a few Pakistani overlookers who were in charge of shifts but they too were fairly rare.

The other three companies that did not employ male immigrants (I, J and N) all worked only 41½ hour weeks plus overtime. Two of them (I and J) were situated outside the borough boundaries but other companies fairly near them did employ immigrants. Both Mr I and Mr N stated that the newer types of machinery would be uneconomic for them as most of their orders were for lots often too small for the more modern machinery. Mr J stated that the main objection to investing in new plant was lack of supervisory staff to look after extra shift work. Without adequate supervision the quality of the firm's product would fall and the reputation of the company for quality would be lost. In all three companies labouring jobs were either done by pensioners who had formerly worked for the companies or by a few juveniles who were taken on as trainees.

## The alternatives to immigrants

All respondents were asked what would be the alternatives that their companies would have considered, or did consider, and what they would have done if the immigrants they employed had not been available. The answers to this question varied considerably and many were, not surprisingly, extremely vague. Before interviewing started it had been thought that the two most probable alternatives were either a rise in wage rates or increased capital investment. As the enquiry progressed and it was seen that new capital investment was often a reason for rather than an alternative to the employment of immigrants, an attempt was made to see if companies had appreciated beforehand the implications of new invest-ment with reference to the labour force that would man this machinery. Where answers were obtained these often proved to be vague and this was probably in part due to our own inability to pinpoint the crucial steps within the decision-making process.

As noted earlier, the wool industry has always been an employer of immigrant labour. The best example of this comes from the two biggest companies in the sample which due to their size were probably able to be the most active in recruitment policies. Mr C, the managing director of Company C, has often personally gone recruiting. In the immediate post-war years he had recruited DPs (displaced persons, ie refugees) EVWs (European voluntary workers) and many others; he regularly visited Eire and brought over families and young girls to work in his mill (when interviewed he had just returned from one such visit). In 1956 he had gone to camps in the Midlands and the South of England to recruit Hungarian refugees. He had travelled on the Continent to find workers. In the past he has recruited labour in South Wales and from other high unemployment areas. He stated that if Pakistani labour had not been available he would have recruited male labour from wherever available and included in his list of possible areas Eire, Malta, Gibraltar and Cyprus. Mr M, the company secretary of Company M, gave in essence a similar account of his company's efforts to overcome long-standing labour shortages. One of the directors had recently been to Yugoslavia and had recruited 24 females to work at another mill belonging to the company, in Wooltown. Visits had been made to Italy to recruit labour and just after the war the company had employed many Europeans (male and female). This company ran a regular bus from the South Yorkshire coalfields (a distance of about twenty miles) for miners' wives. Whilst Company M did not employ many Pakistani immigrants it was clear that if they needed labour they would obtain it, if necessary, from outside the British Isles.

On a smaller scale other companies had followed similar policies in widening their area of recruitment. Company L had maintained a hostel for 30 European girls for about ten years in the post-war period. Company E which was situated about three miles from Wooltown ran a special coach to the factory for workers. Company O ran a bus from the South Yorkshire coalfields for miners' wives. Mr E said that if the Pakistani immigrants had not been available one of the alternatives that his company would probably have employed would have been to recruit over a geographically larger area. Mr E was very doubtful, however, whether this would have been more than a partial solution to his company's problems.

The method of running bus-loads of workers to a mill has obvious limitations. It is unlikely to attract anyone already in work unless the pay and/or conditions are going to be superior to those they already enjoy. Unless a number of workers are recruited in the same area their recruitment becomes expensive to either company or individuals (and if individuals, they are unlikely to be attracted to the work). Lastly, the method is mainly, in the conditions existent in the West Riding, a source of female labour, which is only a partial substitute in certain sets of circumstances to male labour.

The alternative to using immigrant labour that seemed at the outset to be the most probable was a rise in wage rates that would have attracted more entrants into the industry. It unfortunately proved difficult to make any meaningful comparison between one company and the next as to the pay of their employees. Some companies pay by piece-work, others by the hour, and others with combinations of hourly rates plus bonuses either for personal production or group production. Some respondents felt that they could give a meaningful answer as to what the average rate of pay was, whilst others felt that it varied too much from individual to individual to do this. From the information no discernible pattern emerged, but it must be emphasized that the quality of information was not high. The company that paid the highest rates was Company E which employed a large number of immigrants; Company G which also paid above the average employed no immigrants. Among the lower than average payers was Company N that employed no immigrants and Company P that did employ immigrants. Wage rates in the wool industry generally compare unfavourably with rates in other industries, especially engineering which is a big competitor for labour in the area.

Nearly all the respondents when asked whether they thought a rise in the wage rates would have been a possible alternative to the employment of immigrants doubted whether this was possible. The reasons for this can be seen when one looks at the type of jobs the immigrants did and the economic choices open to employers. In the main immigrants were either shift-workers or held low-paid unskilled labouring-type jobs offering little future. Many employers felt that to overcome local labour's reluctance to work shifts very large rises in the wage rates were needed, and that would make it uneconomic to work such shifts. The pay of labourers was a more marginal issue in view of the smaller numbers concerned, but there was a fear that if one employer put his wages up the others would, and the shortage would still remain. This was coupled with the underlying feeling that the labourers who in the main had fairly light, undemanding jobs, were not worth more, and a rise in wages for them could upset the wage equilibrium of the mill.[7] It is debatable whether these are accurate analyses of the situation or natural rationalizations for keeping down costs.

In a discussion of this nature the position of the industry as a whole must also be examined. The wool industry is highly competitive and it is exposed to very strong competition not only from wool industries in other countries but also from cotton and artificial fibres. As an industry it is fairly labour intensive (over half the firms in the sample attributed 40 per cent or more of their costs to labour) and changes in wage rates will have an effect on prices. The industry is contracting and many companies have gone into liquidation in the recent past. In such a situation the pressures on an employer to keep his costs as low as possible are intense and this must have had some influence on the responses given to this question.

Increased capital investment was not considered a feasible alternative to the employment of immigrants in any company. Mr M stated that his company was buying new productive machinery but systems of material handling for which he felt that there was scope would have to wait due to the general shortage of capital. Many companies complained about being already stretched to their financial limit buying new machinery. Other limitations on new capital investment are delivery delays (up to two years) and the physical structure of some mills. As has already been discussed new capital investment would often mean an increase in the number of male immigrant workers (on shifts) coupled with a decrease of local labour, often female.

Another possibility open to these companies was the setting up of satellite companies in other areas. This would depend on a number of criteria such as the possibility of hiving off one part of the company's activities, expense, and finding a suitable location. Only Company E had considered this possibility, at a time when they had started a policy of large-scale capital investment. They had however thought that sufficient labour would be forthcoming and had decided not to move.

A factor that militates against the setting-up of satellite companies is the extreme geographic concentration of the wool industry in Great Britain. Over three-quarters of the industry is in the West Riding of Yorkshire and there is a reluctance to move out of the area. Amongst the reasons for this are the interdependence of various parts of the industry which buy and sell to each other, and the pool of skilled workers in the area. The setting up of the satellite company in another part of the West Riding would be a possibility, but there would be the danger that in the new locale conditions would not be much better than the present situation.

The final possibility that presented itself to employers was to use commission workers, such as combers, spinners, weavers. Within the industry there are companies that will comb, spin or weave on a commission basis for other companies. These companies are either solely at work on commission orders or they have their own production and use any spare capacity for meeting other companies' requirements. Mr I stated that his Company used commission spinners when it was faced with large rises in the level of orders and some of the other companies had also used them occasionally but factors of price and delivery often meant that they were not regarded as a good alternative solution.

The attempt to differentiate between the decision to install new machinery and the awareness of whether the labour for this machinery would be available was not successful. Most respondents knew that there were difficulties but thought labour would be available. Who this labour would be some companies were unaware of and were surprised when they found that most or all applicants for some jobs were immigrants. The earlier quoted position of companies M and O is worth noting here where both anticipated problems in manning new machinery, and one company thought that it would probably have to use Pakistani labour and the other was unsure of what the position would be.

## Comparability of immigrant and local labour

All respondents who had experience of immigrant labour were asked how immigrants compared with local labour. They were asked if the quality and quantity of their work was comparable, how long they took to train and whether there were any additional costs in employing immigrants. Twelve of the fourteen companies that were asked this questions found immigrant workers generally comparable in all respects to local labour. In some cases Pakistani labour was said to be superior to other labour that could be recruited for these particular jobs. Mr A had employed a group of English school-leavers three or four years earlier, at a time when there were plenty on the labour market (probably the winter of 1962–3) and he had had to sack them all as they had been so bad. He had never had any troubles with the Pakistani juveniles he employed. Company D had installed, six months earlier, a new machine which it was decided to work in two twelve-hour shifts a day, five days a week. Mr D had originally engaged a Pakistani day shift (three men) and an English night shift (three men). Mr D had sacked the night shift for unreliability and had taken on a Pakistani night shift. Productivity had doubled since the engagement of the Pakistanis. Mr D felt that the doubling of output was due among other factors to the fact that the Pakistanis are better, more reliable labour. Mr P explained that it was impossible for him to recruit good local labour and that he preferred to select the better type of coloured labour. Mr B said that his Pakistani labour was as good as other labour and certainly better than Irish labour. One or two other employers also made unfavourable comparisons of the suitability of Irish labour as compared to Pakistani labour in the wool industry.

Most respondents when asked about the comparability of immigrant labour stressed that the standard of labour applying for jobs had generally fallen since the war and was continuing to fall. Thus the long-term employees were often of higher calibre than recent recruits. It follows that the local labour which the industry was able to recruit was often of a fairly low standard (these remarks are much more applicable to male labour). Also immigrant labour was as mixed as any other labour – some good, some bad. It was further stated that it was much harder to identify at the recruiting stage a good immigrant worker mainly because of the difficulty in communication. Many respondents said that they were lucky and/or skilful and only employed good immigrant workers but they knew of other employers who had not been so fortunate. [. . .]

## Summary and conclusions

In summarizing this study and drawing any conclusions it must be emphasized that we have only looked at a small sample of companies mainly concentrated in one section of the wool industry. The results of this study therefore should be treated with caution and are not necessarily applicable to the whole wool industry or even that part of it concentrated in the West Riding of Yorkshire. It would also be unwise to draw too many conclusions as to the degree to which results can be extended to other industries, although certain aspects may well be applicable.

Possibly the most interesting finding of the study is that relating to capital investment. The degree to which new capital investment and the employment of immigrants go together is surprising and it would be fair to conclude that the employment of immigrants has facilitated new capital investment in the sample of firms under study. This is because new machinery is too expensive to be worked only 40 or 48 hours a week and it must be employed as intensively as possible thus necessitating shift work. This is a trend not confined to the wool industry and may well, in the future, make headway into more white-collar occupations. It is well recognized that there is a general disinclination to work nights or changing shifts and higher rates of pay are the general rule. The immigrant (Pakistani) worker is usually more willing to take this work than local labour for a variety of reasons. Firstly, the undoubted discrimination in employment against the immigrant restricts his choice of jobs severely. Secondly, his lack of suitable qualifications and language problems further restrict opportunities. Thirdly, one can hypothesize that the immigrant newly established in this country is much nearer the economist's ideal of economic man. The majority of immigrants are single adult males less constrained than the English worker by non-economic factors such as socially awkward hours of work, and are willing to work as long hours as possible to earn as much as possible.[8]

The alternatives to the employment of immigrants are more varied and more difficult to define than any other aspect of this study. One alternative that is not really an alternative would be the employment of another type of immigrant, from other parts of the UK, Ireland, Europe, or elsewhere. The major alternative to immigrant labour would have been a rise in wage rates to attract more labour into the industry. It is probable that in the absence of Pakistani immigrants there would have been a rise in the wage level of the industry but the degree of this rise is problematical and its scope would have been limited probably by the ability of employers to pass on higher costs to consumers. Within the context of the wool industry the room for manoeuvre of any individual employer to raise prices is very small and the current contraction of the industry would probably have been much swifter but for the presence of immigrant labour.[9] Thus some of the less efficient firms in the industry have been allowed time to become more efficient and modernize and extremely painful and over-rapid contraction of the industry has been avoided. This slowing down of the possible decline of certain firms may have relevance to those companies which used immigrants mainly as labourers and had embarked on a process of modernization but did not have sufficient resources to do the job in one go. It can also be argued that a rise in wage rates, especially for shift work, would have had an inhibiting effect on the rate of new capital investment and it would have remained cheaper to use older machinery. Other alternatives to the immigrant include the setting up of satellite companies and a wider recruitment area for labour but these would seem to be only limited solutions for the problems affecting most companies in the sample.

Generally the immigrant was considered by his employer to be as good as any other labour that could be employed. With the exception of two companies, the immigrant (Pakistani) worker was said to be as productive as his local equivalent and in some cases was considered preferable to the indigenous labour that could be recruited. In general no extra costs were associated with the employment of immigrants and no company found it necessary to provide extra facilities for them such as separate toilets. The training of immigrants was the same as for other labour. The reasons why two companies found immigrant labour worse than local labour could be for a variety of reasons or a combination of them. The immigrant labour could have been worse, or it lacked good supervision, or the companies failed to select and train their staff properly, or the companies were incapable of attracting better immigrant workers, etc. All the companies, with the exception of the two that found immigrants were inferior workers, stated that they were more mobile than local labour.

This study can only be treated as a starting point for the building up of a body of knowledge of what actually happens when a flow of immigrants start working in an industry and there is an obvious need for further studies of this kind in this and other industries. However, despite the limitations of such a study certain general ideas suggest themselves. Both the industry and the immigrant were in a transitional stage. The industry has to change to survive; the immigrant poised between two cultures is probably more willing to adapt to change. The resistance against change in work routine which local labour has built up through a long history of institutional factors is less relevant for the immigrant. But the flexibility of the immigrant is probably only a short run process and over time institutional constraints will become more important.

## Notes and references

1. Ceri Peach in *West Indian Migration to Britain: A Social Geography* (London, OUP for the Institute of Race Relations, 1968), has suggested that it is the pull factor of labour shortages in Britain rather than the push factor in the migrant's home country that determines the level of immigration. If Peach is correct then the question of the 'non-immigrant solution' is crucial in trying to assess any balance sheet of immigration.
2. See, *The Woollen and Worsted Industry: An Economic Analysis* edited by G. F. Rainnie (Oxford, Clarendon Press, 1965); and a P.E.P. Report, *Thrusters and Sleepers: A Study of Attitudes* in Industrial Management (London, Allen and Unwin, 1965), re-published in paperback under the title of *Attitudes in British Management* (Harmondsworth, Penguin Books, 1966), for a more detailed description of the industry.
3. Information was only obtained in relation to addresses listed in the directory and did not include any associated companies except for Company P. The address listed was head office which was mainly office staff and the Chairman of Company P suggested a visit to one of their mills in an area to which all references in the tables and text refer.
4. An attempt was made to gather details of other immigrant workers but many of those interviewed were very unsure of numbers. Nearly all the companies had employed European immigrants and many still retained them.
5. See for example, Sheila Patterson, *Dark Strangers* (Tavistock Publications, 1963; Harmondsworth, Penguin Books, 1965).
6. It was thought that this approach of asking employers to explain why they had employed immigrants rather than asking them to justify their position from a discrimination/non-discrimination stance would allow for freer discussion. No direct questions were asked about discrimination but a few respondents commented on the general subject especially vis-à-vis the reaction of their other workers.
7. The question of wage equilibrium of differentials highlights the point that an employer may be faced with constraints on raising wages for particular jobs by a whole series of non-economic reasons.

8. See chapter by Peter Jenner 'Some Speculations on the Economics of Immigration' in *Immigration, Medical and Social Aspects: A Ciba Foundation Report* (London, Churchill, 1966), which discusses some of the points raised here.

9. It can be argued that the arrival of immigrants has allowed inefficient firms to continue to operate when it would be better for the economy if these companies closed down. This argument does not allow for possible social pressures that may have forced Government to intervene and prop up the industry if the rate of contraction of the industry has been too rapid. Thus it could be postulated that immigration has allowed a contracting industry to modernize without Government intervention.

# CHAPTER 2.3

# RACE AND LABOUR IN LONDON TRANSPORT: SOME CONCLUSIONS*
*Dennis Brooks*

## Relationships at work: a summary and discussion

In all three departments [of London Transport] white native workers voiced their opposition to and resentment of the initial employment of coloured immigrants. The passage of time has all but precluded any accurate comparison of the reported reactions of native staff in the three departments, but opposition appears to have been least in Permanent Way. Between Central Buses and Railway Operating it is difficult to say whether opposition was more widespread or intense in one than the other, but only in Central Buses was strike action threatened. This was, though, confined to one or two garages.

Colour was the most frequently mentioned reason for objections to the employment of coloured staff, followed by fears that wages, conditions, and standards would be threatened. Most of the evidence of the social significance of colour – particularly on likely reactions to coloured supervisory staff – suggests that a dark skin is associated with low status. To that extent, the data support the colour-class hypothesis.

It is probable that there would have been an adverse reaction to the employment of any *identifiable* non-traditional group, though it appears that colour made this reaction both more widespread and more intense. In Central Buses, though, the employment of women conductors is far from completely accepted by their male colleagues, and the employment of women drivers has, up to the time of writing, been successfully opposed.

* Extract from Chapter 17 of *Race and Labour in London Transport*, OUP for the Institute of Race Relations and the Action Society Trust, 1975, pp. 328–39. Reprinted by permission of Oxford University Press.

In the years prior to the Second World War, employment with London Transport was seen as desirable for a number of reasons. With a relatively high level of unemployment prevailing, *any* employment was sought-after. London Transport offered a high degree of job security at a time when insecurity was the norm. It offered pay and conditions which compared favourably with those found in many other occupations and industries. These factors appear to have given employment with London Transport a relatively high status – certainly in the eyes of its employees. Some long service workers compared their situation with those of others whom they thought were at a similar status level in the pre-war era: postmen, firemen, and policemen.[1]

In the immediate post-war years, the favourable wages position of London Transport workers had been eroded somewhat, but it still offered job security – an incentive for a number who joined – when a return to pre-war levels of unemployment was apparently widely expected. By the early 50s a relatively low level of unemployment had prevailed for ten years or so, and an economic depression was not obviously just over the horizon. It was at this time that London Transport employment began to appear less attractive, and staff shortages became prevalent. The relative earnings position of London Transport workers had declined. Whilst this might have been acceptable to some as the price to be paid for job security had unemployment been high, this security probably appeared less of an advantage now that it was apparently becoming more common in the wider labour market. Security, is, though, far from unimportant now. Given this decline in the relative advantages of London Transport employment, it may be hypothesized that its status would similarly decline, and this appears to have happened. The opposition to the employment of coloured immigrant workers is, then, partly explicable in terms of the weakening of bargaining power which was seen to result from a reduction in the staff shortage and from the employment of a group perceived as possibly unreliable in the event of organized industrial conflict. Moreover – and this was the most important consideration – the newcomers were coloured. Apart from other antipathies arising from this fact, the already declining status of London Transport employment was seen to be further threatened.

That there was apparently least opposition in Permanent Way is consistent with the colour-class viewpoint: Permanent Way men appeared to have been least concerned with the question of status.[2] Market considerations appear to have been most important for the busmen:

conflict over wages has been fairly constant in Central Buses and from time to time the question of *recruitment* overseas has been brought into this conflict. That London busmen form a discrete bargaining unit is obviously relevant here, too: the likely effects of a reduction in the staff shortage on bargaining power could most immediately be perceived. Considerations of status and, related to this, of tradition appear to have been most salient for the trainmen. The Railway Operating Department was in most respects the most tradition-bound; its beliefs and values stressed continuity and long service; its culture was one likely to be inhospitable to newcomers who were both strange and perceived as low in the status hierarchy. Whilst there were these differences between the two operating departments in the opposition to the newcomers, they are relatively small compared with the over-all common pattern.

It is not suggested that the colour-class hypothesis is the complete explanation for the widespread white British aversion to dark-skinned people. Feelings on this are obviously deeply held, and there is clearly scope for much more detailed research on the social significance of colour. Certainly, I was impressed by the *strength* of feeling of many on the question of colour. This aversion came out most strongly in the answers on the possibility of coloured supervisors. Yet a marked antipathy towards coloured people in general was at times combined with complete or near-complete acceptance of individuals.

The numbers of women in our samples were relatively small, and any conclusions on over-all differences between the sexes must thus be treated with caution. With this reservation, there were indications that the native women were both more hostile towards the immigrants than were their male colleagues, and also that they perceived a deeper and more widespread hostility amongst the natives than did the men. This hostility appeared to be directed more against coloured men than women, so the situation was complicated by sex differences.

To return to my theme, I concluded that given the existing market and status situations, there would probably have been opposition to any *identifiable* group of outsiders. That the outsiders were coloured served to make any opposition aroused both more widespread and – more importantly – more intense. In part, then, the situation was one of immigration and in part one of race relations. To state with any degree of accuracy which of these was uppermost in the native British response is difficult. Certainly, it was reported to us more in terms of colour than of any other factor, and to that extent it may be seen as a race relations response. The *ease* of identification was an important factor in relationships between white and coloured workers, particularly between bus crews on the road.[3]

It is, perhaps, useful at this point to ask how realistic the opposition of the native British workers was, in the sense of how accurately their fears were fulfilled. On the question of the relative status enjoyed by public transport workers, I can say little, since these workers were our only source of data. It appeared to be fairly widely assumed that their status had declined, but the employment of coloured workers was seen as only one of the factors contributing to this decline: market and other considerations were also important.

The fear that coloured immigrants would be unreliable in organized conflict proved to be groundless, and their reliability in this respect has been important in their acceptance by native workers.

It is not obvious that an absence of coloured recruits would have improved the pay and conditions of the existing staff: more rapid technical change or a more marked reduction of services were possible alternative reactions to a staff shortage. Certainly, it is most unlikely that a large publicly owned organization operating in the capital could have avoided employing numbers of coloured immigrants, had it wished to.[4] More important, though, it is far from self-evident that the employment of coloured immigrants has significantly reduced the staff shortage over the past fifteen years or so. I return to this topic in more detail below.[5]

One other fear reported was that standards of performance would be lowered. There was nothing to suggest that the work performance of the immigrants as a group was at all different from that of the native workers.

Whilst there were these objections to the employment of coloured immigrants, the work performance and personal characteristics of the early recruits to both Central Buses and Railway Operating encouraged their acceptance. They were good ambassadors, and to that extent allayed somewhat the fears and hostility of the native workers and smoothed the way for later coloured recruits. Possibly, the recruitment staff were more selective in the early stages of recruitment and engagement of immigrant workers, and these early recruits may have accorded more closely with the ideal type than did those engaged later. Job discrimination elsewhere was probably more widespread in the early fifties than in later years, and possibly these early recruits were more proficient or adaptable.[6] Certainly, the very first coloured workers were regarded as something of a novelty, and to that extent, had an attraction for some.

Numbers were important in that with very few coloured workers employed at any location, they had to fit in and conform to the natives' norms. The development of separate immigrant groups, in canteens, messrooms, and so on, possible when a number were employed, appears to have been the occasion of increased hostility and resentment from the native workers. To that extent, numbers were important. However, hostility between native and immigrant workers had passed its peak and was declining. This decline was in the context of a growth in the relative numbers of coloured immigrants, and in this respect numbers were unimportant.

The native workforce has, of course, changed considerably over the past few years. Those who joined before the early 1950s were accustomed to an all-white or almost all-white workforce. Many have since resigned, retired, or died. Few who have joined in more recent years can have been unaware that they would in all probability be working with numbers of coloured men and women. This continual change in the native workforce has quite likely had an impact on its predominant attitudes and behavioural norms. It is unlikely, though, that this was the only or even the major variable in the decline in overt hostility reported.

The following conclusions can be drawn on the size and speed of build-up of an immigrant workforce. When *very* few are employed, they *have* to fit in and conform. That a fairly continuous growth of the immigrant workforce was accompanied by an increase and then a decline in hostile attitudes and behaviour from the natives, strongly indicates that once the numbers of coloured immigrants have passed a low figure it is the *rate* of build-up which is the important variable conditioning the native response. I cannot say how small this low figure will be. It will differ according to a number of variables, the most important of which are the technical and social organization of work. There is in all probablility an optimum rate for the build-up of coloured immigrants in a workforce or, rather, there is a maximum rate which, if exceeded, will cause an increase in hostile attitudes and behaviour on the part of the native workers. Again, it is not possible to say what this maximum rate is; again, it will vary between establishments. The important variables here appear to be the traditions and culture of the organization, the skills and other attributes of the immigrants, the tasks to be learned and performed, and again, the technical and social organization for these tasks. The data strongly indicate that in the London Transport situation this optimum rate was exceeded: the build-up was too rapid for smooth acceptance. In general, it would appear that, from the point of view of smooth absorption, in the sense of minimizing hostile reactions from the native workforce – including managers and supervisors – and of gaining acceptance, a slow rate is preferable to a fast one.[7]

At the time of the fieldwork,[8] the extent of hostile behaviour was declining and the incidence of hostile actions was lessening. Moreover, *very* hostile attitudes were confined to a relatively small number of the natives. The manifestations of this hostility appeared to be largely confined to writing on the walls to some natives ostracizing the coloured staff, to 'a rough word' now and again, and to some conflict both between and within crews. I concluded that the vast majority of the natives accepted that the coloured staff constituted a permanent part of the workforce, that they were not a temporary expedient which would be replaced when more 'normal' times returned. There were a few who did not accept this, some whose hostility was unremitting and who it is reasonable to assume were prejudiced.[9]

Beyond this, one must proceed with caution: a lack of hostile behaviour is not to be equated with full acceptance. It was *individuals* who were accepted, rather than the immigrants as a group or a number of groups. Task performance and other aspects of behaviour were the key variables in acceptance, task performance probably being the most important of all.

Similarly with other aspects of behaviour: the more closely the immigrants accorded with the natives' behavioural norms, the more likely they were to be accepted. One important exception here concerned acceptance of coloured immigrants in the minor supervisory roles they occupied at the time of the fieldwork. A condition of acceptance of immigrants made by some natives was that they did not fully exercise the authority content of such roles. In one respect some of the immigrants appeared to go beyond the natives' norms, as it were, in that they were seen to be 'real gentlemen' – a designation which indicated a rather Old World courtesy, and behaviour which is not widespread amongst natives in the work situation, such as handshaking.[10]

Whilst there was this acceptance of individuals as *individuals*, there was between groups a considerable extent of pluralism. This applied most markedly in situations associated with work, but not task performance: there was a tendency for mixed crews to separate for meal breaks, there were ethnically based card or domino 'schools', there was some separation in the Permanent Way cabins.[11] Outside the work situation pluralism was the norm.

I concluded that the industrial absorption of immigrants is a slow process. The majority of natives accepted that the immigrants were a permanent part of the workforce, but this acceptance was often grudging, a recognition of reality as it was perceived. Many probably wished it were otherwise. Beyond this minimal acceptance, individuals were accepted more or less as equals. Given that this was an organization which had employed coloured immigrants longer than most in Britain, that its policies and tasks were in most respects favourable for the absorption of minority groups, this may appear a pessimistic conclusion, in that I emphasize the slowness of the process. It is, though, the conclusion that all the data point to.

Comparing the acceptance which the natives accorded the various immigrant groups, I can only comment on the West Indians and the Asians: the other groups were too small in number. The West Indians were the groups most fully accepted, and at the same time they were the object of most antagonism. The Indians and Pakistanis appeared to provoke relatively little antagonism: they fitted in in the sense that they were thought to be unobtrusive. The pluralistic model applied most to relationships between native British and the Indians and Pakistanis. There was little antagonism and only minimal acceptance. Other commentators have noted that Indians and Pakistanis seek only limited acceptance, but in this respect those in our samples were atypical. They all spoke good English, otherwise they would not have been engaged. Certainly, they were concerned to emphasize how well *they* were accepted and most reluctant to discuss the hostility they had encountered. Moreover, they *wanted* to be accepted: from many of their comments one might have concluded that only the West Indians experienced difficulties. Yet the Asians were less *fully* accepted by their native workmates than were *some* West Indians.

On the other hand, the West Indians were the object of most antagonism. Colour was a variable here, and it was a handicap which those who were accepted had overcome: 'we don't think of him as coloured'. Acceptance of individual West Indians was often accompanied by marked antipathy towards others. Some natives resented the exuberant gregariousness of the West Indians, and their outward enthusiasm and gusto when playing cards or dominoes, for example. Certainly, their behaviour here was some way removed from that of the more staid, reserved natives.

In so far as native workers distinguished between the West Indian groups – which was relatively rarely – it was the Jamaicans who were regarded with most disfavour. Individual Jamaicans were, though, accepted as much as were members of other groups.

Comparing the three departments, the pattern of answers to a number of questions was often very similar. Yet over-all acceptance was greatest and overt hostility least in Permanent Way; acceptance was least and overt hostility greatest in Central Buses. Railway Operating occupied a middle position on this axis, and here I differentiate between trainmen and station staff. A number of factors lead to these conclusions.

There was far more conflict built into the organization of bus work than in either of the railway departments. Particularly important here was conflict between crews over the allocation of the workload: there was the *actual* fiddling and the *belief* that fiddling was commonplace. I have shown, too, the possibilities of conflict between driver and conductor which arise from different expectations of performance. Relationships between crews and supervisors were a further area of conflict. Whilst the reported patterns of relationships between both bus and train crews and inspectors were fairly similar, the bus inspector was far more likely than his rail counterpart to take arbitrary actions, and hence to be accused of unfairness or favouritism.

The absence of coloured bus inspectors [at the time the research was carried out], coupled with a belief that this did not result from chance, legitimated the views of the native busmen who were antipathetic towards the coloured immigrants. The immigrants, on the other hand, resented, often bitterly, the fact that none had been promoted to the inspector grade. Recruitment overseas had from time to time been a live issue in Central Buses and whatever the intentions of the Central Bus Committee may have been, there is no doubt that many, both white and coloured, interpreted its actions as aimed against the employment of coloured staff *as such*. The presence of immigrants was resented by some natives because it was seen to reduce both the staff shortage – and hence weaken the case for wage increases – and the amount of overtime and rest-day work. Some drew a parallel here between the coloured immigrants and women conductors.

In the Railway Operating Department, the traditions of railway work, particularly the emphasis on long service, experience, and so on, may be seen as contributing to a culture inhospitable to outsiders, particularly coloured immigrants. There was, though, far less conflict built into the organization of train crews' work as compared with that of busmen.

That role allocation in the Railway Operating Department was largely by seniority was important: promotion was automatic and impersonal; the opportunity for discrimination inherent in a merit system was thus largely absent. It is likely that by this time the promotion of coloured immigrants to supervisory posts *by seniority* will have increased their acceptance by white staff. Promotions on this basis are far more likely to be seen as legitimate than are those made on the largely subjective basis of merit.

Conflict between coloured immigrant and white native staff was more apparent among station staff than among trainmen. Station staff interacted in face-to-face situations for a far longer part of the shift; within the relatively close confines of a station, individuals made a considerable impact on the quality of immigrant-native relationships. Conflict with passengers often intruded into these relationships.

A number of factors contributed to the greater acceptance of coloured immigrants in Permanent Way and the relative lack of overt conflict. Considerations of status were less important than in the operating departments. The task performance of individual platelayers was important to their workmates in every respect. The organization of the workforce in relatively small groups, too, was important: familiarity was more likely to be an element in the relationships between members of a small work group. Finally, numbers of coloured immigrants had been promoted, and had been *seen* to have been promoted, to minor supervisory roles in the Department. The promotion structure of Permanent Way, with its gradual 'steps', facilitated these upgradings and probably reduced the likelihood of native resentment. Compared with Central Buses, each promotion step was small.

## The acculturation of attitudes

One of my hypotheses was that the less the immigrant stands out in his new society, the more fully he is absorbed into it. This is relevant both for behaviour and attitudes. In our interviews of native and immigrant workers, we explored a number of attitudes. We were interested here in seeing how far the immigrants had acquired the attitudes of the

In most of the attitudes revealed it was the similarity between the native and immigrant groups which was most striking, rather than the reverse. In Central Buses and Railway Operating there was some indication that the immigrants were more conscious of the various time constraints, and it is likely that they had not fully internalized the time values.

In their expectations of the good supervisor, there was a broad measure of agreement between the immigrants and natives, though there were one or two differences. Across the three departments there was no consistent difference between the immigrants and the natives, and again the patterns of answers must be related as much to the specific situation as to some more general cultural factor. For example, the immigrant platelayers' greater emphasis on fairness as a quality of the good supervisor is explicable in terms of the belief of some that certain supervisors were not fair.

The immigrants' difficulty over time came out again in their expectations of reciprocity from supervisors over late bookings on, though they appeared to recognize that there were limits, set by the requirements of the task, to the amount of lateness possible.

In both the Railway Operating and Permanent Way departments, the natives showed a greater positive orientation towards various aspects of the task, and I suggested that this reflected a greater extent of self-selection amongst the natives as compared with the immigrants. The immigrant trainmen's greater stress on freedom from supervision was explained in terms of a marked reduction in the possibility of discriminatory actions from first line supervisors, as compared with other occupations, that is. That London Transport was seen as a good or fair employer by the immigrant platelayers was explained largely in terms of the formal procedures, which again reduced the likelihood of discrimination.

The pattern of dislikes was broadly similar between the native and immigrant samples, but the immigrants' difficulty over accepting some of the formal requirements of the organization was in evidence. Particularly important here was the requirement that absences from duties should be explained. Some objected to being called upon to give an explanation when this involved personal or private matters. Others reasoned that as they were not paid for a day off, they should not have to give any explanation. The contractual obligations of their employment, in other words, were seen to cover only the hours worked. There appeared to be also some resentment against having to give a *written* explanation.

It was in their expressed promotion aspirations that the natives and immigrants differed most markedly. In all the male samples, the immigrants were far more likely to say that they wished to be promoted than were the natives. There were differences between the samples that go some way towards explaining the different patterns of promotion aspirations, but they do not appear to be the complete explanation.

One variable here may have been the fact that the interviewers were white: esteem was involved and it may have been that the coloured immigrants wished to appear confident of their own abilities. The fact of colour may be important in another way, too: studies of coloured immigrant children in Britain[13] and Negro children in the United States[14] have both shown that these children had higher aspirations than their white fellow-pupils. In so far as these children mirror their parents' aspirations for them, this may 'reflect an understanding by the Negro that in a 'white world' he must aim higher and be better to get as far as his white counterpart'.[15] Similar considerations may be relevant here. A number of the immigrants appeared to be imbued with what in another context has been termed the 'American dream'; an optimism that opportunities are wide open to those who 'have what it takes'.[16] Yet this apparent confidence and optimism were held against a background of known discrimination: in employment and in housing, for example. Only in Central Buses was there widespread conviction that internal promotion was influenced by considerations of colour, and this as I have shown, was well founded.[17]

It may, of course, be that some self-deception was present here: it is reassuring to be able to look forward to a better tomorrow, whatever the problems of today. I do not know how realistic these aspirations were, in the sense of being attainable, regardless of ethnic origins. The socialization which moulds aspirations is a subtle and complex process. It may be that the natives were unduly modest in their aspirations. Alternatively, they may have made a realistic assessment of their likely chances of rising in the occupational hierarchy.

## Notes

1. Some policemen apparently joined London Transport's predecessors after the 1919 police strike.
2. This does not mean that they necessarily accepted the low status ascribed them.
3. See Brooks Chapter 5.
4. In the United States urban transit industry, public ownership has also been conducive to the recruitment of black workers. See Jeffress, 1970, pp. 49 and 93.

5. See Brooks, pp. 353–4.
6. Probably, too, their behaviour conformed more closely to the Englishman's expectation of the deferential black man than did that of later recruits: the 'Uncle Tom' image. There were changes in this respect over the years: some were less prepared to play this deferential role.
7. The relative size of the immigrant part of the workforce as a variable in acceptance is further discussed in Brooks pp. 349–52.
8. The fieldwork was carried out from mid-1965 to mid-1967.
9. Defined by Brooks as 'a hostile attitude which is not amenable to modification as a result of learning . . . The cause of prejudice is seen as lying in the individual. It is an essentially psychological, irrational phenomenon, originating in individual inadequacies.' This is contrasted with antipathy: ' "as an attitude it is . . . arrived at in a rational way, and the cause lies in the object of aggression or in the subject's image of the object; attitudes of this kind are culturally and socially transmitted, whereas prejudice . . . is not" (Banton, 1959) . . . the behavioural manifestations of prejudice and antipathy can be very similar, . . . the difference between the two lies solely in their origins and in the possibility of modification by experience. Antipathy can be so modified; prejudice cannot.' (Brooks p. 14)
10. This is not to suggest that natives did not regard some of their fellow-workers as gentlemen, but the behaviour of West Indians in particular in respect of these gentlemanly aspects was favourably commented on, and it was behaviour that was not seen to be widespread amongst the natives.
11. It is possible that between the white groups, eg the English and the Irish, there was a considerable extent of pluralism, but it was not evident.
12. I do not wish to imply that attitudes should change in a one-way direction, only that this appears to aid acceptance and reduce conflict.
13. See David Beetham, 1967.
14. See Martin Deutsch, 1967, quoted in Nandy, 1969, pp. 9–11.
15. Ibid.
16. See Ely Chinoy, 1955, p. 1.
17. See Brooks, Chapter 6.

# References

Beetham, David (1967) *Immigrant School Leavers and the Youth Employment Service in Birmingham*, London, Institute of Race Relations, Special Series.

Banton, Michael (1959) *White and Coloured: The Behaviour of British People towards Coloured Immigrants*, London, Cape.

Chinoy, Ely (1955) *Automobile Workers and the American Dream*, New York, Doubleday.

Deutsch, Martin (ed.) (1967) *The Disadvantaged Child*, New York.

Jeffress, Philip W. (1970) *The negro in the Urban Transit Industry*, Philadelphia, Pennsylvania, Industrial Research Unit, Dept. of Industry, Wharton School of Finance and Commerce, University of Pennsylvania.

Nandy, Dipak (1969) 'Unrealistic Aspirations', *Race Today*, Vol. 1, No. 1, pp. 9–11.

# CHAPTER 2.4

# ETHNIC STRATIFICATION IN AN INDUSTRIAL CITY*
*Robin Blackburn and Michael Mann*

## Ethnic stratification

Our sample of 951 respondents in Peterborough contains 199 persons (21 per cent) born outside the British Isles. Rather unusually for British labour markets, the majority of these are not from the British Commonwealth but from Europe. The only large single national group are Italians. The others are more conveniently grouped by region: central and eastern Europeans (Poles, Czechs, Germans, Ukrainians and other Soviet minorities), and workers from the Indian sub-continent (Indians and Pakistanis – remembering that we interviewed before Bangladesh broke away). There are only two West Indians and no Africans in the sample.

Obviously this is an unusual collection of immigrants, contributed principally by the brick industry, which (as in its other main centre, Bedford) recruited extensively among prisoners-of-war and European Voluntary Workers at the end of the Second World War. When this source of labour dried up, the brick companies, especially London Brick, started recruiting directly in Italy and the tradition, although declining since 1960, has continued. We find Italians and other Europeans in seven of our nine companies, although 89 out of the 146 are at London Brick and almost all have worked there at some time in the past. The Indians and Pakistanis are more widely dispersed, again in seven of our companies, but with no company contributing more than the 30 per cent of Farrow's. So in this case 'immigration' is not co-terminous with 'colour'. We are dealing more with ethnic than racial divisions, as these terms are conventionally

* An extract from *The Working Class and the Labour Market*, Macmillan, 1979, by permission of Macmillan, London and Basingstoke.

understood. We believe, however, that these are rather similar phenomena within the labour market. The recruiting activities of London Brick among Italians are parallel to those of major textile and rubber firms among Pakistanis. And all the groups in our sample share one problem, usually absent with West Indians in Britain, a linguistic barrier between themselves and the host-nation. Furthermore, we could find few relevant differences between the main immigrant groups in our sample. The Asians were slightly younger than the Europeans, and in terms of the job characteristics we discuss in this chapter, we will mention the few differences as we go along. As we found few significant differences within the British Isles group, ie no difference between English, Welsh, Scots, Irish (of whom we have very few, however), our analysis will proceed by simply contrasting British (ie British-Isles born) with immigrants.[1]

We will present data on wages, hours and various intrinsic job aspects.[2] Are the conditions of employment of immigrants significantly different from those of natives? However, the answer to this question is on its own insufficient to test the dualist hypothesis. Even if we demonstrate that the conditions of immigrants do differ, this might be due not to their essential 'foreign-ness' but to some other, coincidental feature of the immigrant group. This is especially likely in the case of the manual labour market. The importance of the internal labour market, and of seniority as a criterion of promotion within it, ensure that better jobs are often filled by older workers. We will examine this in detail later in the chapter. But as immigrants are usually relatively young, they may have worse jobs for this reason alone. Thus we have controlled for age, and also for length of service and works status, in this analysis. First, then, we examine whether the immigrants do differ on these characteristics.

Table 1A shows the expected. Immigrants are slightly younger, of slightly less seniority, and of lower works status. But the details of the table are worth close examination. It is not that the immigrants are especially youthful, but rather that they contain more of the middle-aged and fewer of the oldest workers. Only ten per cent of them are 52+, compared to 30 per cent of the British-born. Perhaps as a consequence, their seniority 1B is similarly concentrated in the middle ranges, and none has worked with their present employer for 24 years or more, compared to seventeen per cent of the British. But this pattern is not carried over to works status 1C, where the difference is now at the extremes: only four per cent of immigrants, compared to eighteen per cent of the British, are in the highest status level, while far more are in the two lowest levels

**TABLE 1**   British-born and immigrants by age, length of service and works status

A

| age group | –25 | 25–35 | 36–43 | 44–51 | 52–59 | 60+ | Total | N. |
|---|---|---|---|---|---|---|---|---|
| Percentage in group | | | | | | | | |
| British | 10 | 23 | 22 | 16 | 15 | 15 | 100 | 746 |
| Immigrant | 6 | 24 | 26 | 34 | 8 | 3 | 100 | 198 |

B

| Length of service | –1 yr | 1-3 yrs | 3-6 yrs | 6-12 yrs | 12-24 yrs | 24+ yrs | | |
|---|---|---|---|---|---|---|---|---|
| Percentage in group | | | | | | | | |
| British | 16 | 16 | 15 | 18 | 18 | 17 | 100 | 743 |
| Immigrant | 15 | 15 | 25 | 17 | 28 | 0 | 100 | 196 |

| Works status | Lowest | Level 2 | Level 3 | Level 4 | Highest | | |
|---|---|---|---|---|---|---|---|
| C | | | | | | | |
| Percentage in group | | | | | | | |
| British | 10 | 15 | 36 | 22 | 18 | 100 | 746 |
| Immigrant | 16 | 22 | 35 | 23 | 4 | 100 | 198 |

(38 per cent compared to 24 per cent). Here, indeed, we have the first sign of actual ethnic difference. The low attainment of immigrants – which we can, perhaps safely, predict – is not merely a question of lack of seniority. Even when they possess seniority, it does not apparently transfer into promotion. Let us now turn to the details and mechanisms of discrimination.

First we examine the most obvious job characteristic, wages. The first three columns of Table 2 contain details of wages per week, hours, and wages per hour (ie wages per week/hours).

**TABLE 2**   British-born and immigrants – work rewards by works status level

| All Workers | Mean wage per week (£) | Mean hours per week | Wage per hour (pence) | Mental abilities | Skill | Autonomy | Effort | Working conditions |
|---|---|---|---|---|---|---|---|---|
| | | | | | | Mean job factor scores* | | |
| A British-born | 27.9 | 48.7 | 58.2 | 0.25 | 0.10 | -0.00 | -0.03 | 0.18 |
| B Immigrants | 30.9 | 53.8 | 58.3 | -0.60 | -0.31 | -0.40 | -0.30 | -0.13 |
| C Difference expressed in standardized units† | 0.61 | 0.72 | 0.02 | 0.80 | 0.42 | 0.37 | 0.31 | 0.40 |
| D Eta value | 0.25 | 0.29 | 0.00 | 0.33 | 0.19 | 0.15 | 0.12 | 0.20 |
| E Differences – by status levels between British and immigrants‡ | | | | | | | | |
| Within lowest level | -4.3 | 3.4 | -4.9 | 0.16 | 0.05 | 0.63 | -0.21 | 0.42 |
| Level 2 | -5.7 | 4.8 | -5.9 | 0.29 | -0.02 | 0.23 | 0.00 | 0.01 |
| Level 3 | -3.6 | 4.1 | -2.8 | 0.53 | 0.22 | 0.37 | 0.27 | 0.29 |
| Level 4 | -2.7 | 6.0 | 1.5 | 1.28 | 0.38 | 0.33 | 0.52 | 0.45 |
| Highest level | -2.6 | 4.4 | 0.9 | 0.73 | 0.30 | 0.71 | 0.70 | 0.90 |

\* For Job Factor Scores see Appendix III. The mean of these scores approximates to zero, and one standard deviation to 1.00. A positive score indicates a relatively desirable level of reward on that factor, a negative score a relatively undesirable one. This assumes consensus about the characteristics of a 'desirable' job. The workers in Blackburn and Mann's sample considered the high expenditure of physical effort to be undesirable – as is low opportunity to use mental abilities, skills, autonomy, and as are noisy, dirty or dangerous working conditions.

† As a decimal proportion of 1 standard deviation from the mean of each item.

‡ A minus score indicates that British workers do less well than immigrants.
Only eight immigrant workers are in this category, making comparisons rather risky.

We cannot pretend to have expected such results! The immigrants receive higher weekly wages than British-born workers. Nor is the difference trivial: the immigrant figure of £30.9 per week is eleven per cent higher than the £27.9 of the British. Controlling for age, length of service and status does not alter this, for the differences persist within almost all the sub-groups. There is a slight decline in the difference if we control for age – for the fact that more immigrants are prime-age males earning higher wages – but it is still there. There is, however, a very simple explanation, which the rest of the table reveals. It is that the immigrants work longer hours, eleven per cent longer to be exact, and so the wages per hour of the two groups are almost identical. Of course, as their wages contain substantial overtime premiums, their basic rate of pay. must be lower than that of the natives. Within the immigrant group we find a difference here, as the non-Europeans work significantly longer hours than the Europeans. Indeed 47 per cent of them actually work 60 hours or more per week, compared to thirteen per cent of the Europeans and only five per cent of the British. These are very large differences. But the Europeans make them up somewhat on another aspect of the wage-effort bargain: more work on piecework (55 per cent of the Europeans, 47 per cent of non-Europeans, and 40 per cent of British). These findings make clear our overall interpretation: that immigrants must work harder, either for longer hours or on piecework, in order to reach the same wage. Elsewhere we noted that immigrants from Europe, but not from Asia, were rather more 'economistic' than the native-born. Thus they, at least, are highly motivated to work harder for these wages. Actually, the wages can be looked at in two ways: we can choose to emphasize the higher weekly wages of the immigrants, or we can stress the fact that immigrants must work harder for the same wage-rate. The first emphasis minimizes discrimination (indeed, it reverses it), the latter maximizes it. Of course, if longer hours are not available – as they would not be during a period of recession – the immigrants will do relatively less well. Nevertheless, at least in a period of high employment, wage discrimination is not high.

How do these surprising results fit in with those of other surveys? The presupposition is surely that they do not, for discrimination against immigrants is generally believed to be widespread. Indeed, several pieces of careful research conducted by PEP have thoroughly documented a high level of discrimination, although the latest study showed a welcome decline in such practices (1976: Chapter 10). However, such difficulties are experienced by immigrants in job selection, not in wages. Wages *per se* do not seem to differ as much as might be expected.

Average differences in the wages of native and immigrant workers are in the region of 10–30 per cent [see Blackburn and Mann, Section 1.]. Before interpreting this, however, two controls are necessary, for job level and for age. Controlling for job level – ie for the depressing effect on immigrants' wages that their predominantly low-skill level produces – can sometimes *reverse* the difference. The most comprehensive recent study is that conducted in 1974 by PEP, to which we have just referred. That also found that the wages of the Asian and West Indian semi-skilled and unskilled men were actually *higher* than those of white men in these categories, while those of the skilled Asians and West Indians were only about four per cent lower than those of their white counterparts. Our results are not out of line with these. However, when PEP introduced the second control and looked only at prime-age males aged 25–54, the differences at the semi- and unskilled levels disappeared entirely, and at the skilled level the white men now earned rather more (eleven per cent more) than the Asians and West Indians. There were not additional differences in hours worked, but the Asians and West Indians were considerably more likely to be working on shifts, as they were also in the Department of Employment study (1977: 44–9). On both these specific points our own findings diverge from that of the PEP study, but the more general point remains: that near wage-equality may be the product of greater *effort* on the part of immigrants, through longer hours, piecework or shiftwork.[3] Yet even if we take note of this, the data of the PEP study do not really support the conclusion of its author, that for men 'there are substantial inequalities of earnings between the minorities and whites' (1976: 84–8). The differences among manual workers are actually quite small and disappear altogether at the lower strata.

So our findings, although slightly inflating immigrants' wages, are not very atypical of the British employment scene. Also, the slight deviation is readily explicable in terms of the biases of our sample. We have not sampled thoroughly what dualists term the secondary sector of the economy. True, we have three firms located in *secondary* industries, ie these termed secondary by American dual theorists: Bettles, in the building industry, Combex, in low-quality plastics and chemicals, and Farrow's, in simple food-processing. But in Britain, in general, immigrants, apart from West Indians, do not work in building firms (unless one counts the Irish as immigrants). As for Farrow's, this is the main firm at which extremely long hours push up wage-rates. But excluded from our sample are the two sectors which in Britain probably pay the lowest wages (outside agriculture) and which employ large numbers of immigrants: personal services (restaurants, shops, etc.), and textiles and similar industries organized into domestic out-work and 'back-street sweat shops'. Compared to their comrades in these industries, our immigrants are undoubtedly privileged. Secondly, our immigrant sample is biased towards those who speak adequate English – with the exception of Italians, whom we interviewed in their own language but who are white. This naturally gave us relatively privileged immigrants. PEP discovered that earnings level was strongly and positively related to fluency in English (1976: 86–7). Wherever we went we could not fail to notice that among the Asians it was the fettlers and not the foundry labourers, the machinists and not the sweepers-up, who made the language grade and were interviewed. This helps to explain the wage level of our immigrants. The rather more surprising results that now follow should be regarded as appertaining to relatively well-placed immigrants and not to the immigrant communities as a whole.

Our main contribution to the debate about immigrants in the labour market lies in our analysis not of wages – which have been documented in earlier studies – but of the intrinsic nature of the job. Here we can use our job scores, and the factors derived therefrom, to give a detailed picture of the jobs which this immigrant élite is asked to perform. The last five columns of Table 2 present these data, broken down by *works status*, one of our job scores measures, which divides each firm's jobs into five hierarchical levels.

We should note, therefore, that jobs of equivalent status level in different firms are *only* similar in this single aspect – their ranking *within* their firms. They may be very differently ranked in terms of overall wages and conditions. Thus this table enables us to separate two aspects of occupational achievement: the works status measure gives us relative achievement within the internal labour market, the job factor scores measure achievement within the labour market as a whole. Separating these two aspects produces rather remarkable results.

The overall finding of this table is absolutely clear: that immigrants have worse jobs: they expend more effort but use fewer manual and mental skills, they are less autonomous in their work, and their working conditions are more unpleasant. The largest difference concerns the opportunity to use mental abilities, as can be seen in Table 2 from row C which standardizes the differences. The next largest differential is in terms of hours, followed by wages. All the differences are significant. The difference in effort was already prefigured by our wages and hours data, and confirms that to obtain equivalent wages immigrants must work harder or longer, or both. We should note that the mental abilities factor does include ability to read instructions in English, which might be thought to have a significant effect on the overall result. However, almost all the non-Italian immigrants in the sample were able to read basic English, and as there was no overall difference between the scores of the Italians and the other immigrants, we can discount this objection. The mental abilities scores are also backed up by the results for skill and autonomy. Finally, the working conditions of the immigrants are significantly worse.

So we arrive at a rather interesting finding. White and English-speaking immigrants can rival the wages of native British workers – but only at very significant costs in terms of the intrinsic nature of the job. The most frequent working-class trade-off – wages in return for unpleasant effort – is worsened even for relatively privileged immigrants.

So far, we have examined average differences between immigrants and native-born workers. But arguments about 'dual' and 'segmented' labour markets should centre on actual *segregation* between the jobs and job rewards of the two groups. (See Blackburn and Mann: The Dual Labour Market Model, this volume.) In a moment we shall look at job segregation itself – whether immigrants are working side-by-side with the natives. But first we can see whether the job rewards are segregated. This we have done with an analysis of variance, calculating the eta values in Table 2.

Eta may be taken as a measure of association between ethnicity and work rewards. As there are only two ethnic groups in question, it is analogous to a dichotomous correlation coefficient. As can be seen, except for wages per hour, the correlations are all clear, and all are significant at the 0.001 level. Now, if we square these correlations, we obtain the proportion of total variance attributable to differences between native and immigrant workers. As the correlations are not high, the values of $E^2$ are not very impressive. Mental abilities produces the highest figure for $E^2$ of 0.11, which means that ethnicity accounts for eleven per cent of the differences in the use of mental abilities within the Peterborough labour market. Hours is next with nine per cent followed by wages – six per cent. This means that the degree of *segregation* between the ethnic groups is not great. Although immigrants receive less on average, their conditions overlap very considerably with those of native British workers. As we have already remarked, our sample of immigrants is to be regarded as relatively privileged, and the degree of overlap between immigrant and native workforces in Britain as a whole is perhaps a little less than this. However, the situation would have to be extraordinarily different to produce actual segregation.

Now let us see what happens in Table 2 when we control for works status. With one or two small exceptions, the results are uniform. Immigrants have worse jobs partly because their status is lower. But controlling for this still leaves differences which widen with higher status. This means that 'status' is for immigrants somewhat deceptive, applying only to the internal labour market and not to the market as a whole. They may rise up a firm's hierarchy but this does not lead to a good job. Controlling for length of service produces almost identical results (not shown here). Thus the relative position of immigrants worsens with years of experience. As this is also true of their wages, we can see that it is a general feature of their market position. They do not seem to benefit from the internal labour market. We have two possible interpretations: either the immigrants are in the worse firms, or they are more subtly discriminated against within the higher status levels of each firm. Let us examine which.

The immigrants tend to be concentrated in a few of the firms. Almost half are in London Brick and 86 per cent are in four of the nine firms (London Brick, Baker-Perkins, British Rail and Farrow's). Our sample understates the degree of concentration. In no firm did immigrants compose more than 52 per cent of the sample (the London Brick figure). Yet we should also take account of the number of immigrants whom we could not interview because of language difficulties. If we return to the original sampling frame, then around three-quarters of the labour force of three firms (London Brick, Combex and Farrow's) is composed of immigrants. Are these the firms that also provide the worst jobs? A negative answer is suggested by the lack of significant correlation between a firm's overall ranking on the job factor scores and the ranking of the firms according to the proportion of immigrants in their labour forces (details not given here). However, this could be because of the crudity of the comparison. In the case of the worse firms we need to know whether immigrants are doing its worst jobs. So we will look in a little more detail at the jobs being done by immigrants, and see whether they are also performed by natives. This is also the best measure of actual job segregation.

Our basic data here are the detailed job titles used by the companies and further sub-divided by us so as to enumerate separately every job whose tasks differed significantly from those of other jobs. For example our list of job titles enumerates separately among the engine testers at Perkins 'Marine Engines Tester, Rate 1', 'Quality Control Tester, Rate 1', 'Other Rate 1 Tester', 'Long Tester, Rate 2' 'No. 1 Tester, Rate 3', and 'No. 2 Tester, Rate 5', while machine operators usually have such specific titles as 'Machine Operator, Base Trays: Farrow's, Preserves Department'. This wealth of detail gives us much finer classification than do census data concerning ethnic segregation in the labour market. Perhaps the classification is too fine, because we are left with a number of jobs performed by only one man! If we exclude these cases, then we find that 28 per cent of the remaining immigrants do not share a job with a native British worker (25 per cent among the European immigrants and 38 per cent among the Asians). These figures are significantly higher than random allocation would produce, and so there is a measure of ethnic segregation in the labour market, but nevertheless the majority of immigrants are sharing jobs with the native-born. Except for quite trivial merit bonuses paid to the individual in one of the firms, the conditions of employment are identical within these job titles. Therefore the majority of immigrants are enjoying equality of formal treatment with at least one native-born worker. We cannot quite say that they are also working *alongside* a native-born worker, because we have no data on the physical proximity of co-workers of different ethnic groups. But workers in most of these jobs are indeed working relatively close to each other. Thus the level of occupational segregation is not high by this measure.

The next step is to examine the characteristics of those jobs which are performed by immigrants. Are they the worst of jobs? By and large the answer is positive. Virtually all the exclusively immigrant jobs (excluding the solitaries) are in the lowest two of the five status levels of their firms. Even the exceptions on the higher status levels are distinctively 'immigrant jobs' in some way – they are either jobs as chargehands in command of other immigrants, or jobs involving quite complex machinery in unpleasant working conditions (eg as furnace operators). The distinctively immigrant jobs are spread throughout the labour market – they are in five of our nine firms – but they are at the lower level. By contrast, the jobs shared by immigrants and native-born tend to occur at all status levels, as indeed do the all-native jobs.

Thus, among our relatively privileged working-class immigrants we find that, although the majority are integrated in formal ways into the native job structure, a minority of just under a third (and just over a third in the case of the coloured Asians) are occupying clearly segregated, low-level jobs.

These are obviously 'intermediate' results in terms of the theories of the labour market we are examining. Both in terms of the jobs they do and in terms of the work rewards they receive, immigrants are not homogeneous. The degree of overlap between them and native British workers is considerable, although that is more because we find the natives at every level and in almost every job than because immigrants are similarly dispersed. As the immigrant's work life lengthens, the differences between himself and native workers widen. This parallels the findings of Parnes (1970, Vol 1: 116–28) that occupational differences between US blacks and whites are greater in their current jobs than in their first jobs. The opportunities for advancement for immigrants and ethnic minorities are extremely restricted, and there can be no doubt on our data that illegitimate discrimination against them occurs. Our Asians and most of our Europeans can speak and understand English. Our immigrants as a whole are slightly healthier than our UK workers. Thus most higher-level jobs in our sample are objectively within their competence, as they are within the competence of almost all workers. Yet they rarely reach them. On the other hand, there are not such obstacles to wage-earning capacity. The cross-cutting effects of these three processes – little wage discrimination, substantial discrimination in terms of other work rewards, and only partial segregation – produce a mixed situation to which immigrant organizations will have difficulty responding. Across-the-board discrimination and segregation would obviously call forth a strong anti-racist reaction of protest. But when the employment situation of immigrants is not homogeneous, industrial and political action is likely to be muted by the satisfaction of many with their wages and by the satisfaction of a few with their employment in general. Now that Britain's apparatus of immigration legislation adds only a trickle of new immigrants, we would not expect nationally any very dramatic occurrences in the sphere of race relations in industry. Overt race conflict is more likely to be found in the housing and educational spheres, where segregation is considerably greater, than in industry.

## Notes

1. We ought perhaps to add that we have no cases of white and obviously 'British' workers born abroad, or of black or brown British-born workers. Either might have confused this dichotomy.
2. This is based on data presented in Blackburn, R. and Mann, M., *The Working Class and the Labour Market*, Macmillan, 1979, Chapter 3.
3. The notion that long hours and shiftwork might be inter-changeable aspects of the immigrant's employment situation receives support from Cohen and Jenner's (1968–69) study of textile employment in a Yorkshire town in which the decision to employ immigrants was related to their supposed willingness to work shifts or long hours.

## References

Cohen, B. G. and Jenner P. J., 'The Employment of Immigrants: a Case Study within the Wool Industry' (This volume p. 109.)

Department of Employment, Project Report by the Unit for Manpower Studies, *The Role of Immigrants in the Labour Market*, London: 1977.

Parnes, H. S., (ed.), *The Pre-Retirement Years: a longitudinal study of the labor market experience of men*, U.S. Department of Labor, Manpower Administration Research Monograph No. 15,Washington: U.S. Government Printing Office, 3 vols., 1970.

Political and Economic Planning: The Facts of Racial Disadvantage PEP Broadsheet No. 560 (by D. J. Smith) February, 1976.

# CHAPTER 2.5

# JAMAICAN MIGRANT*
## *Wallace Collins*

I packed up my underpressing job in the East End of London and went to work on the railways, where I earned up to fifteen pounds a week. This made me independent so I left my cousin's house and rented a back room in Kentish Town. I was comfortable and decided to sever all my acquaintances and drop my pub habits; so for a few months I lived like a hermit; that is from home to work and work to home. By this time I was equipping myself generally and bought a smart radiogram. I was getting myself set as the saying goes in Jamaica.

One day while walking down Highgate Road in Kentish Town, I passed a woodworking shop. I turned back and went inside; there I met the foreman, a sprightly, tight-lipped sedate gentleman who looked at me thoughtfully and immediately identified himself with the church. I was more eager to get the job so I said, 'I have a reference here,' and as I handed it to him I said, 'The name is Collins.' He looked over the top of his spectacles and repeated almost icily, stressing *the*, '*The* name is Collins!' He folded the bit of paper and said, 'When can you start?' I told him Monday and he said rather courteously, 'All right, Wallace, we are expecting you on Monday.'

Four months in Britain and two jobs behind me, I was now making furniture; and how! I had not realized how famous this firm was in England, and when people asked me where I worked and I told them they were surprised and in fact doubted me. That job really put me on the British spot, where I was confronted with the echelons of colonialism. First of all my co-workers (men who were old enough to be my father), were astonished that I, a little black boy, barely older than any of the apprentices in the shop, and coming from one of 'our' backward colonies,

* Extract from *Jamaican Migrant*, Routledge and Kegan Paul, London, 1965.

a banana jungle as it were, was able to work alongside them without asking questions. They implored me to tell them all about how I learned my trade; was I taught by a Christian father or was it by my own colour? And what part of Africa is Jamaica. At first I thought they were genuinely ignorant, but later on I found out that they did not want to know about me or my country, they were satisfied with their textbook definitions and when-I-was-in-India experiences during the first world war.

Nevertheless, they accepted me as a cabinet maker. I was pleased. It gave me confidence, made me realise the value of my skill and observe the seriousness attached to it in England; a seriousness which inspired me to attend a furniture design school in Holborn; but the novelty of London exhausted me and I dropped out.

Though my earnings had dropped to eight pounds a week, I was happy and my co-workers were the most decent Englishmen I have worked with. The shop was like an institution. You were cared for. Some of the men had worked for the firm since 1914 and were as enthusiastic as I, a newcomer. They were extremely conservative and very proud to uphold and prolong the tradition of cabinet making at that establishment, which I soon grew to admire and respect.

Their tools were as old as half a century, and their usefulness long outmoded by machine; yet these wooden tools were referred to, as the old adage. They would be used patiently on every section of a job in such a way that when each section was fitted together the result was absolutely right. Time did not matter, only skill. They were proud of the skill they could manipulate on wood.

The foreman wore a pinhead grey suit, white shirt with well starched collar that creased his thin neck. His men wore arm garters, over lily-white shirts with worsted trousers and herringbone tweed jackets, and black shoes always. Their aprons reached below their knees and were as white as their shirts. But what puzzled me was their humour. It was so dry and terse that at first I did not think they were funny. I thought they were stupid, and suspected it was a prelude to liberty taking, mainly because of the double meaning that it carried. I soon found out that if you are ignorant of the English and their humour you will suffer among them, and be looked upon as an outsider.

You know, there is a shrewdness in Jamaicans which I found very valuable in England, mainly because it enabled me to grasp English humour and in turn understand the English as a people [. . .]

[*Collins left this job and sought work elsewhere.*]

For the first time in my two years in Britain, I went to the Labour Exchange for a job. After the usual palaver, (I soon got accustomed to it), I was sent to a job in Holborn. I started my new job with an apprehension that made me nervous through the day. This was mostly hardwood joinery, and though I could read the drawings I was not sure I would be able to do the work. To my surprise, at the end of the day I felt completely refreshed, and within a few days had settled down nicely in my new job. The shop was huge, with about eighty men employed, and there I was in the centre of this arena, with all eyes watching me wrestle with the most difficult jobs I'd yet done.

Everything was documented, besides the drawings were in full scale and were pretty easy to read, so all I did was concentrate and I won. So much so, that it was not long before another Jamaican was employed there, and then another until there were five of us. The foreman gave me a raise of pay and I was now in charge of the other four fellows. We were watched and ogled at, and I could see the surprised expression on some of the men's faces disbelieving the efficiency with which we executed difficult jobs with comparative ease and speed. The shop steward (Union Steward) told me that I was favoured by the foreman, and that the men were grumbling, but not to worry for we were doing a good job.

Soon their grumblings became open discontent, and no amount of encouragement from the foreman or shop steward could quench the open hostility of the men around us; in fact, I was forced to retaliate verbally. During which time I found out that at the worst all Englishmen stuck together in regard to the West Indians. One day the foreman said to me, 'I don't care what they say about your fucking black race, you're all the same to me; Wallace you're making a good job here and you know it, you will be the last to leave if there is a slacking off of work.' And with that he walked off. But it was like a thorn in my heels, to know that I was working in an atmosphere of hostility. It gave me an unwelcome feeling and a 'you're not wanted here, get out' complex, from which I became utterly pessimistic and a trifle hostile. In the end I lost interest in my job, and the work at hand, and fell down on my efficiency and aptitude as a skilled man. Meanwhile, my fellow West Indians drew into their shells. This passivity overawed me, and I gave out only to find that I was holding the dirty end of the stick. They resented my advice on how to do the job, and were complaining to the foreman of my methods of dealing with them including swearing. But what I wanted to convey to them was, that we should have a singleness of action; that is, since we were being maliced by the men then malice them also, and not turn the other cheek and fawn on them, because we would only be despised. I tried to get them to unite with me into a solid group of men, who did our work properly, and didn't give a damn what the other men in the shop thought of us. For a while I had them going strong, and the Englishmen were baffled at the effectiveness of this strategy. Then they reverted to a well known strategy of the coloniser, that is, to divide and rule. They sought out the weak among us, who they knew relied on my instruction and could not do a job on their own. They became bosom friends with these cowards, and deliberately ignored me. Thereupon I found myself on an island, in a sea of spiteful indifference and treachery. I was too young and inexperienced to understand and fight back, so I wilted under the pressure.

I became agitated and nervous, and lost my temper at everybody. It went so far that one of the fellows threatened to smash my face in, and I told him that I would push his chest in if he came around my bench, seeking a fight. In the end I was given the sack, as the foreman put it 'for not co-operating with him'.

I felt used and discarded, as I lugged my tool box out of the shop that Friday evening, and in fact was oozing with bitterness against the white man and black man as such.

Yet in spite of bitterness, I felt a certain sympathy for the foreman, for I knew that he meant good at the outset, which was even commented on by one of my co-workers who said, 'Wallace, if you were white you would be foreman in this shop.' But I could see plainly that he was a victim of pressure from his colour, and I could not forgive him for the way he succumbed to such injustice. There was a gesture which momentarily lifted the load of bitterness off my shoulders. As I left the shop, a very old man who worked near my bench came out the door with me and shook my hand and said to me, 'It's not your fault, Wallace, you did a good job here, but you didn't have a chance, all the best.' He turned away quickly and went into the shop.

The lessons I learnt in that job were, it doesn't pay to be too interested in the white man's work, lest you be accused of being geared to do him out of his job; and it is wise to make yourself as inconspicuous as possible, which was brought home to me when one of my fellow Jamaicans said 'You talk to the foreman, you're the bright boy' and when audible whispers reached my ear from a nearby bench, 'Oh, they are only tear-arses' (fast workers, a most ungainly accusation in England). In order to work unnoticed in that shop, or get ahead with the men, I would have had to arrest my individualism, work within the confines of the myth they perpetuated about West Indians, and become a black senseless robot, an illiterate migrant from the land of banana and sugar cane from an isle a former British Prime Minister described as 'The British Empire's slum'.

But I am from a new generation of Jamaicans, whose determination is to escape poverty and the lack of opportunities which exist in Jamaica, and in the West Indies for that matter, and which seem to have an umbilical connection to our race. Yet as we try to unshackle these miseries and strive to better ourselves as men, we are counteracted by all manner of prejudices and suffer the most polite and bare-faced indignities in tightly populated Britain; geographically squashed in by the Atlantic in the west and North Sea in the east, yet sitting disdainfully on a slim cushion of water in the south, the English Channel. Even without myth having its sway, we penniless and uneducated migrants have nothing to lose except our pride (we give our lives for it), and all to gain (barring the throne); so with only the one force we know, harsh words and violence, we clobber politics at its fountain head and demand our rights, if not through democracy, then as Christian human beings (which we are), to live and work in antique Britain even as an historical debt. For surely the days are gone when peasants hanker and beg, carping and cringing at their master's gate for a bowl of broth.

## CHAPTER 2.6

## BLACK WORKER, WHITE FOREMAN*
*Theo Nichols and Huw Beynon*

Harold Stevens was born in Barbados in 1941. His father owned a small farm and he arranged for Harold to be trained as a stone mason – 'what do you call it here? Bricklaying and things like that?' Increasingly, though, he found it difficult to get work in his trade, or any work at all. He worked in factories and on building sites – and he cut sugar cane. 'You'll be in a job today, tomorrow you go home. You see what I mean? That was the trouble in the West Indies.' Finally, in 1962, he got what he describes as 'the travelling urge'. By that time most of his friends and the relatives of his generation had emigrated – mostly to Britain but some to the USA as well – and he had a brother and a cousin living in Provincial. He decided to follow them.

'I wanted to do a bit of travelling like. To see different things and different ways of living. I think it's necessary. But when I decided to come over here, my old man said, "Don't go." You know he has worked hard, got a good position, and I had learned my trade. So he wanted me to stay – to stick it out there like. But I said: "Everybody's going over there. Why can't I go and have a try and see how it goes." Well he said, "You'll be back soon. It is cold over there" and all that you know. But I told him that I wanted to have a good go at it.'

So in 1962 he had a go. The Barbados government operated a scheme which assisted emigration to Britain, so with the help of that and the encouragement of letters from his brother he moved to Provincial. He was amazed by the factories, the houses, the lights – by the whole fabric of metropolitan urban life. His clearest memories of that time are of the difficulties he found surviving as a single man in a big city.

'You won't believe this but when I first came over here I couldn't cook an egg. I couldn't do anything. You know my old lady and my sisters

* An extract from *Living with Capitalism: Class Relations and the Modern Factory*, Routledge and Kegan Paul, 1977.

they'd done everything for me. . . . I go to work, I come home, I get my dinner. Just like that. I finish my dinner and I have a drink. Everything is put on the table there. It was great . . . but you travel, and you do more things for yourself. I don't regret it.'

He learned to cook – if mostly from tins – and he learned what it meant to be black in a white man's world.

'When you go on a bus I used to find it. I would sit on a bus in a seat by myself and nobody would sit next to me. No white man would sit down by the side of me. Not until the bus was really full up and sometimes then people would prefer to stand up rather than sit by the black man.'

But his biggest problem was finding a job. He searched the town for work but it took him four weeks to get a job. He remembers the experience as being 'really miserable'.

'When I first came, I had a hard time getting a job. I try a few places but, you know, they say they always have no vacancies. I tried to get on the buses first. I went to the Labour Exchange and they said there was a vacancy in the buses and they gave me a letter to send me up. And when I go up there, the chap said, "Well, there is a vacancy but the trouble is, you got to put your name on the list and then when we get to your name, we'll call you up." '

He waited and heard nothing. (The local bus company was later found to have been operating a colour bar on certain of its jobs. Faced by criticism the local TGWU officer defended himself in the local press: 'Because we are trying to run a responsible union without interfering in policy matters we are accused of discrimination.') Meanwhile his cousin had started work at ChemCo. He told Harold and got him fixed up with the opening of the Zap plant. He started as the only 'coloured bloke' on the shift.

'I was the only coloured down here at the time. There wasn't no coloured blokes around and I had a hell of a lot of trouble because the blokes used to be really awkward, you know. They'd try to pick fights and things but there was two blokes on my side which is what I can say, Alf in the control room [the shop steward], and another bloke on D shift. Well they said to me, "don't care" like. I was so hurt first like, I decide to pack it in. I did hand in my notice and there was an assistant foreman on our shift, he's gone now. He said to me, "Oh, care for no man." And the manager came in and said, "Well, I'll have a word with them." Well, it was getting used to it I suppose. After a bit it changed but it was rough for about the first two years. It was a bit rough but I think you got to get nerve really.'

He got his nerve. He ignored a lot of the 'nigger jokes' and the taunting; and he turned his back on men who wanted 'to pick fights'. In this he was helped by white men like Alf but more so by the arrival of other black men from the West Indies. (When we talked with Harold in 1970 a third of the men employed on the Zap and Zap X packing areas were black.) Over the past years they had stuck together, helped each other, returned jibe with jibe and developed some 'jokes' of their own. In all this they were helped by the idea of an international black movement; by the presence of Mohammed Ali and the West Indian cricket team. In 1971 the tour of Garfield Sobers' West Indian team was followed with avid interest and with wild jubilation as the colonialists were defeated at their own game.

By 1970 Harold was finding his life in Britain much more pleasant. He had married a Jamaican three years earlier. They had managed to save enough money to put a deposit down for a house. Harold had saved by working doublers:

'When I first started working down here I did a lot of overtime. I did too much in fact – we were saving for a house then you know. I really done too much. I was really sick – I was dying so I decided to pack it in. I was getting trouble with my stomach and everything. Ear ache, head ache, back ache, I tell you I was dying here. Cos you know I was single then and I was still living on my own. When I'd done a doubler, I'd go home and I had to have a rest. You know, I never had time to cook a meal or anything like that. It was terrible.'

But he managed to save the money and get a house. Only for the Corporation to purchase compulsorily and knock it down to build a road. 'One year we lived in that house. Now we live in a flat. My wife wants to buy another house. But something like that – it makes it hard the second time.' The compensation money was soon gone.

At ChemCo in 1970 there was no black manager or foreman. Neither was there a black control room operator or co-ordinator. Harold had worked on the Zap plant longer than anyone else, and few workers at Riverside had been with ChemCo longer than him. But he still worked on the packing line; and he still disliked it. He feels that 'it nearly drives me mad sometimes'. He talks a lot about seeing green bags for hours after leaving the plant. He describes his job there as 'boring', 'routine', 'useless', and 'bloody hard work'. What he would really like to be is a control room operator. He had spent some time in the control room with Alf and he'd learned how to run the plant – certainly to Alf's satisfaction. He'd quite like to do the job permanently but he knows that to do that – to become a control room operator – he needs to be put on the formalized training scheme. The blokes on the shift have put it to him that he should approach the foreman, ask him for more time training, ask about the possibility of an operator's job somewhere, ask about being made into a co-ordinator. But he won't *ask*.

'Not for that type of favour, I don't like that type of favour at all. Other types of favours, I don't mind. Like asking for a day off or something. But where the job is concerned I don't think I'll ever do it. I've been seven years and never asked yet. I mean, a bloke said to me, "Oh, you've been down here so long you should be co-ordinator, or something like that. Blokes come here after you and they're made co-ordinator." I said, "That's the way it goes. If the foreman don't think I'm good enough, then that's up to him. I'm not gonna beg him." And this is it, see.'

Harold sees the foremen as 'firm's men'.

'Well you see I come to work and do a day's work and get paid. They come to work to do a day's work too, but it's just not the same with them. They're not prepared just to let things go along like. They're always pushing. Production – that is their interest more than anything else. They try to tell you about safety and things like that. Well they might be interested in safety. Nobody likes to see a bloke get into an accident. But, I think if they get their production going and things like that and the job going all right, that's their interest. As far as the blokes are concerned, I don't think they care much about you really. This is my feeling, I might be wrong. But I've been here this long and you see things. For instance, say we on sixty tons an hour, something happen, one of those bags break. None of these foremen, none, none of them, like to drop the rates, none of them. When you are on that rate and the band's stopped for a minute you get a bollocking off the foremen. Even if you miss a bag on a spout, they're shouting. Things like this. Ah, it's never right. And this is why you get these accidents because on this rate blokes, you know, they're rushing. This is it, see. And I think as long as everybody's going in there smooth, and their production's going up, I don't really think they give a damn.'

And production favours the rich:

'The rich man always get the most benefit. What I reckon – what I feel is that everything should be shared equally. And I think a lot of blokes feel like that too. I just don't think the workers get enough of it. I think we're worth a lot more for what we do down here. I reckon we're underpaid. Everything should be shared out equally.'

Frequently he compared the shift work, the pressure for production, the pressure of living in Britain, with his earlier life in Barbados. If he misses anything it is the sense of enjoyment; the loss that comes with working day and night for 'The Man'.

'I think it's more work here you know. It's all work in this country and then when you're at home it's boring – because on these shifts everybody else is at work. You don't see anyone to chat to. You just drive around and get fed up. But in Barbados you stay at home ten months and it doesn't bother you. You know, you chat with some, you go on the beach . . . anything.'

He thinks a lot about Barbados. About leaving. About who he is, where he belongs and if he'll ever go back for good.

'We think about that. You know about when you get older. You say, "we will go back to our country and relax and enjoy ourselves" because, you know, you come here, you work hard and I suppose most of us have it in mind. But sometimes I think it's just a dream, because you might not be able to save enough money to go back there and live over there. You'd still have to get another job. So I suppose it is a dream. It's like thinking about winning the pools or something like that.'

In 1971 he and his wife took a holiday to visit their families in the West Indies. They saved up and took presents back for everyone. 'It cost a fortune you know. Because when you go home – you go to a different country and return – everyone thinks "he's rich now". They don't know, see. But that is what they've got in their head. And everyone expects something.'

Everyone was pleased to see them but what left a lasting impression on Harold and his wife was the high level of prices in the West Indies – that and the poverty and the unemployment. This experience had chilled their hopes of retiring in their country.

'When people ask you, "why did you leave your country?" I just think now that it was necessary. It was just necessary to leave. That's my opinion. Because over there you haven't got a decent job. You can't even earn money to buy shoes and clothes. It was just necessary. It's given me experience and things like that too. I've learned a lot about places that I would never have learned if I'd stayed. And that's it. I haven't any regrets. You know I'd like to see my parents again before they die – or before I die. But apart from that I'm happy. I suppose.' [. . .]

*[One of the foremen on the bagging plant was Tommy Robson.]*

Tommy is a big man and his white coat makes him look even bigger. He stands in his boots, his white coat billowing open, hands in trouser pockets, helmet on the back of his head and all shift long – 'he's *murder* on Nights' – he shouts abuse or laughs. He tells many drinking tales, of drinking seven pints in twenty minutes after the 'two till ten' afternoon shift, of how 'no weekend passes without a piss-up in our house', of how his little lad likes a Guinness with his Sunday dinner. Everyone rates him 'a character'. 'Have you seen Tommy yet?' managers would ask us. 'The salt of the earth, Tommy.'

Born into a family of coalminers in 1921, he spent his youth in a northern pit village: 'thirty-six families and thirty of them related. We knew everybody, everybody knew us.' His father died in the pits when Tommy was ten. He went straight from elementary school down the pits himself. After the war he joined ChemCo as a process worker. 'Up there ChemCo was *the* firm.' But sixteen years later Tommy was still on the shop floor: 'Up there you had to wait for someone to die to get a white coat.' So when his boss asked him if he'd mind going south he says he replied, 'I'll go where I'm bloody well told to go. . . . I was only here seven months and they made me foreman.' [. . .]

As a foreman Tommy doesn't hold back on the shouts and bluffs and threats. But he likes to 'do right by the lads'. He'd be hurt if at a fundamental level he didn't have their respect – even though they are southern, 'don't know what hard work is', and 'haven't seen children go bare-foot'. 'I've not seen a site like this one for thieving', he says, 'Mind', he adds, 'I could leave a pound note on my desk – yes, with bloody door open – and it wouldn't move.' When occasion arises –which is not very often at Riverside since there's no company club with a bar and people rarely meet off the site – he enjoys buying the blokes a pint. In spite of all the comradeship though, he thinks they're all bad workers, and bad trade unionists to boot. He complains that they don't do the job properly, they don't go to Branch meetings, they lack solidarity. Not like 'up north'. 'Up north, if anything happened the others would support you – that's unionism.' However, this doesn't mean that Tommy wants his workers to go militant.

As he sees it, 'a good shop steward should look at every problem in two ways. He hasn't got to be one-sided. He works for ChemCo, ChemCo doesn't work for him.' He doesn't want unions that 'go too far'. No 'reds'. He thought the 1971 Industrial Relations Act 'essential' because 'We've just got to stop having so many strikes.' 'People have just got to pull their bloody socks up *and work.*' The north, the past, the working class and hardship are all one to him. So, he celebrates the rigours of 1926; has a real soft spot for miners; evaluates all current struggles against the *real* struggles of the past – or 'up north'. But feeling that current industrial actions fall short of the tragic dimensions which characterized those of the past, he rejects them. He sees them as 'stupid', or 'bloody minded' – nothing to do with *real* trade unionism.

He's a mixture, is Tommy. 'The working-class man is a bloody fool to himself', he tells you, 'and that includes me.' Watching the blokes hump bags he tells you that 'bandwork is archaic in this day and age' – only to go on and on about how the southerners have got it 'soft'. One day, talking about the 1930s and his Dad and uncles in the pits, he'll be telling you 'unemployment is a great evil'. Next day, complaining about spillage in his plant or absenteeism or lateness he'll rage: 'these buggers need a bout of unemployment'. But given the severe contrast between his childhood and the 'affluence' of the south of England in the early 1970s there's a sort of sense in all this. Because things have changed. Not just in terms of 'affluence' either. For although it is important to him that 'in the old days the difference between the staff and payroll was tremendous', other things have changed as well. There's the workers' 'different attitude of mind' – there's also the blacks, who are 'going to take us over'.

Tommy doesn't put things in official Company language but the nuances of ChemCo's recruitment policy are not lost on him.

'I don't want a fucking industrial psychologist to set me an exam to find the men I'm after. They've got to be physically capable of carrying one hundredweight and mentally capable of normal straightforward arithmetic. I want them wanting to settle down, married, wanting regular work, not just six months. I wouldn't take a single bloke, I can tell you that. You have a job to get the bastards to work. Their time keeping is bad. They regularly have one off for the Queen. If they've got a bit of stuff they're off. A married man may have a bit of stuff on the side, mind. But he's still got to come to work, his wife kicks him out.'

But ask Tommy what sort of workers he gets and he's likely to give you a one word answer – 'Niggers!' 'I'm not colour prejudiced, mind', he tells you, and 'there's no trouble down here. But you find with these Jamaicans that they spend their time sleeping, or hiding. They'll do anything to get out of work.'

We were talking to Tommy one morning in the company of one of his mates, another foreman who had come south, and a fellow fancier of budgies. ('I go round to see his budgie now and then', Tommy told us, 'like a fucking eagle it is.') 'There's coloureds everywhere', his pal said,

'I'd never seen a coloured before I came down here – down here I'm more like a bloody Colonial Chief.' 'Like Powell says. Forty per cent coloured, there are', Tommy chimed in. 'No', we said, 'not even four.' 'Look out that bloody window', they said. We did. In ten minutes seven West Indians passed by and one white. At this Tommy was off – on to 'young kids with more money than sense', 'beer like piss', and workers who 'don't know what work is. Not like up north.'

# CHAPTER 2.7

# THE EMPLOYMENT OF COLOURED GRADUATES IN BRITAIN*
*Roger Ballard and Bronwen Holden*

## Introduction

The majority of the original generation of coloured immigrants to this country were manual workers, although many had craft skills which they sought to utilize. A small minority had higher educational qualifications and professional skills, and although some, such as the doctors, were able to find professional appointments, even they have usually been found in the more junior positions or in jobs with a lower status. Whether coloured immigrants were manual workers or professionals, it remains generally true to say that they have taken the jobs for which no white Britons could be found, and that these jobs are, by definition, the ones which are less well paid, less pleasant, or less prestigious. It has always been possible to argue that coloured immigrants occupy low status jobs because of their lack of knowledge of the English language, and of the social conventions of British society, or that their qualifications were of questionable value since they were acquired abroad. Despite the fact that many members of the first generation would rightly challenge the validity of such arguments, and insist that racial discrimination is at the root of their difficulties, it is nevertheless true to say that the first generation have been prepared to take whatever jobs they could find, however unsatisfactory, without a great deal of public protest.

Their children, on the other hand, the first generation of 'black Britons', are now beginning to emerge from the educational system, and are looking for jobs.[1] Their experiences on the employment market and

*New Community*, vol. IV, No. 3, Autumn, 1975. This is an edited version of the original.

their reactions to these experiences, may well be crucial for the future of race relations in this country. Much official concern has concentrated on educational deprivation and unemployment among young black Britons, and upon racial discrimination in manual employment – on the 'problem' of the young, black and unskilled;[2] nevertheless many children of coloured immigrants are making their way through the educational system, and gaining excellent qualifications.[3]

This generation is British; its members were born and brought up here, and they expect educational success to lead to well-paid professional jobs. As more young people of Asian and West Indian origin have obtained British qualifications, however, there has been a growing feeling of disillusionment. Anthropological field-work[4] revealed frequent examples of qualified people who took months to find suitable jobs, or who were finally forced to take semi-skilled jobs on the production line. One Asian student studying for his 'A' levels was already looking apprehensively ahead: 'There are no difficulties in going to university or college, but the prospects of finding a good job after qualifying are not bright.'

Although the anthropologist's informants indicated growing apprehension and disillusionment, and there were a number of cases where individuals had failed to find suitable employment, it was impossible to know how far this reflected the general experience of young qualified black people. We therefore decided to undertake a survey to find out how a whole group of qualified young black students fared while applying for their first jobs, as compared with a matched group of white students. [. . .]

## Mobility and motivations

Before we embarked on the survey, several careers officers had pointed out that students might fare worse in seeking employment if they were reluctant to move away from home in pursuit of a job, and suggested that this, rather than racial discrimination, might account for their difficulties. We therefore asked our respondents both where they would *consider* taking a job, and where they would *prefer* to take a job. In fact no very clear differences emerged between the two samples. The vast majority in both would consider taking a job anywhere, while whites showed some preference for home region, as against a slight coloured preference for home town. Coloured students in our sample were prepared to move away for jobs at least as much as the whites, and we concluded that

...ns to these experiences, may well be crucial for the future of
...s in this country. Much official concern has concentrated on
...deprivation and unemployment among young black Britons,
...ial discrimination in manual employment – on the 'problem'
...g, black and unskilled;[2] nevertheless many children of
...migrants are making their way through the educational
...gaining excellent qualifications.[3]

...ation is British; its members were born and brought up here,
...ct educational success to lead to well-paid professional jobs.
...ng people of Asian and West Indian origin have obtained
...ications, however, there has been a growing feeling of
...at. Anthropological field-work[4] revealed frequent examples
...eople who took months to find suitable jobs, or who were
...o take semi-skilled jobs on the production line. One Asian
...ng for his 'A' levels was already looking apprehensively
...are no difficulties in going to university or college, but the
...ding a good job after qualifying are not bright.'

...e anthropologist's informants indicated growing apprehen-
...usionment, and there were a number of cases where
... failed to find suitable employment, it was impossible to
...is reflected the general experience of young qualified black
...refore decided to undertake a survey to find out how a
...qualified young black students fared while applying for
...as compared with a matched group of white students.

### ...otivations

...ked on the survey, several careers officers had pointed out
...ight fare worse in seeking employment if they were
...away from home in pursuit of a job, and suggested that
...racial discrimination, might account for their difficulties.
...ked our respondents both where they would *consider*
...where they would *prefer* to take a job. In fact no very
...emerged between the two samples. The vast majority in
...der taking a job anywhere, while whites showed some
...me region, as against a slight coloured preference for
...red students in our sample were prepared to move away
...as much as the whites, and we concluded that

soft spot for miners; evaluates all current struggles against the *real*
struggles of the past – or 'up north'. But feeling that current industrial
actions fall short of the tragic dimensions which characterized those of the
past, he rejects them. He sees them as 'stupid', or 'bloody minded' –
nothing to do with *real* trade unionism.

He's a mixture, is Tommy. 'The working-class man is a bloody fool to
himself', he tells you, 'and that includes me.' Watching the blokes hump
bags he tells you that 'bandwork is archaic in this day and age' – only to go
on and on about how the southerners have got it 'soft'. One day, talking
about the 1930s and his Dad and uncles in the pits, he'll be telling you
'unemployment is a great evil'. Next day, complaining about spillage in
his plant or absenteeism or lateness he'll rage: 'these buggers need a bout
of unemployment'. But given the severe contrast between his childhood
and the 'affluence' of the south of England in the early 1970s there's a sort
of sense in all this. Because things have changed. Not just in terms of
'affluence' either. For although it is important to him that 'in the old days
the difference between the staff and payroll was tremendous', other things
have changed as well. There's the workers' 'different attitude of mind' –
there's also the blacks, who are 'going to take us over'.

Tommy doesn't put things in official Company language but the
nuances of ChemCo's recruitment policy are not lost on him.

'I don't want a fucking industrial psychologist to set me an exam to find
the men I'm after. They've got to be physically capable of carrying one
hundredweight and mentally capable of normal straightforward arithmetic. I want them wanting to settle down, married, wanting regular work,
not just six months. I wouldn't take a single bloke, I can tell you that. You
have a job to get the bastards to work. Their time keeping is bad. They
regularly have one off for the Queen. If they've got a bit of stuff they're
off. A married man may have a bit of stuff on the side, mind. But he's still
got to come to work, his wife kicks him out.'

But ask Tommy what sort of workers he gets and he's likely to give you
a one word answer – 'Niggers!' 'I'm not colour prejudiced, mind', he tells
you, and 'there's no trouble down here. But you find with these Jamaicans
that they spend their time sleeping, or hiding. They'll do anything to get
out of work.'

We were talking to Tommy one morning in the company of one of his
mates, another foreman who had come south, and a fellow fancier of
budgies. ('I go round to see his budgie now and then', Tommy told us,
'like a fucking eagle it is.') 'There's coloureds everywhere', his pal said,

'I'd never seen a coloured before I came down here – down here I'm more like a bloody Colonial Chief.' 'Like Powell says. Forty per cent coloured, there are', Tommy chimed in. 'No', we said, 'not even four.' 'Look out that bloody window', they said. We did. In ten minutes seven West Indians passed by and one white. At this Tommy was off – on to 'young kids with more money than sense', 'beer like piss', and workers who 'don't know what work is. Not like up north.'

CHAPT

## THE EMPLOYMENT OF (
## IN BRI

*Roger Ballard an*

### Introduction

The majority of the original gene
country were manual workers, alth
sought to utilize. A small minorit
and professional skills, and althou
to find professional appointments
the more junior positions or in jol
immigrants were manual worke
true to say that they have taken t
be found, and that these jobs a
well paid, less pleasant, or less
argue that coloured immigrant
lack of knowledge of the English
British society, or that their qua
they were acquired abroad. D
first generation would rightly
and insist that racial discrimin
nevertheless true to say that th
whatever jobs they could fin
deal of public protest.

   Their children, on the
Britons', are now beginning
are looking for jobs.[1] Their

*New Community*, vol. IV, No
original.

their reactic
race relation
educational
and upon ra
of the you
coloured in
system, and
   This gene
and they exp
   As more yo
British quali
disillusionme
of qualified p
finally forced
student study
ahead: 'There
prospects of f
   Although th
sion and disi
individuals ha
know how far
people. We th
whole group o
their first jobs
[. . .]

### Mobility and

   Before we emba
that students r
reluctant to mov
this, rather than
We therefore a
taking a job, an
clear differences
both would cons
preference for h
home town. Colo
for jobs at leas

unwillingness to move could not explain any difference between coloured and white students' success in finding employment.

Questions on respondents' reasons for going to university or polytechnic revealed some interesting differences between coloured and white. Nearly half the coloured students saw higher education primarily as the road to a good job; and while over a third of the whites also saw it in this light, more white students said they had gone to university for non-vocational reasons. These attitudes emerged again in informal interviews, where Asian students in particular talked about 'respectable jobs' or 'a job with good money', while many white students saw themselves, in retrospect, on a kind of educational conveyor belt.

Students were asked whether they were considering taking a further full-time course of study when they had completed their present course, and it became apparent that significantly more coloured students than whites were keeping this option open (54 per cent as opposed to 31 per cent) and that women were more likely than men to have postgraduate study in mind (67 per cent of coloured women, 55 per cent of white women).

Students were also asked for their reasons for considering going on to further study, and it is clear that for many coloured students this alternative was second best. While the same proportion of white and coloured students preferred to do research, significantly more coloured than white (38 per cent as opposed to fourteen per cent) who were considering further study would have preferred to have taken a job. It is clear that these students anticipated difficulty in getting suitable employment (many mentioned this on the questionnaire) and hoped that by continuing their education and studying for higher qualifications they could put off the evil day. One coloured respondent who had made twelve unsuccessful job applications before deciding to accept a place on an MSc course (he gained a II i degree) told us 'I hope the MSc will improve my prospects of getting a job – otherwise I'll end up on Social Security!'

Comparing our coloured and white samples overall, we found very few differences between them. They obtained much the same class of degree, they had similar backgrounds in terms of social class, and they were equally prepared to move in order to obtain a job. The coloured students were rather older, and many seem to have anticipated difficulties in finding employment, and so were considering post-graduate courses more seriously. We were, however, satisfied that the two samples were similar in more important respects when they came to apply for jobs.

## Birthplace and length of residence in UK

Where the two samples did differ, of course, was in colour and in the fact that only three coloured students had actually been born in Britain, although most had arrived by the time they were sixteen years old.

About three-quarters of our respondents were of South Asian origin: apart from the 25 born in India and Pakistan, eight were Asians from East Africa, one was born in Britain and one in the Near East. There were clearly many fewer West Indians in our sample than might have been expected given the numbers of young West Indians in Britain.

It is widely believed that length of residence in England improves a coloured person's chances of good employment, so that as his fluency in English and familiarity with British culture improve, his experience of discrimination should decrease. Well over a quarter of the sample were in Britain by the age of eleven, and had therefore received all or some of their primary education, as well as the whole of their secondary education, in Britain. Nearly 80 per cent of the sample had arrived in Britain by the age of eighteen, and so had obtained at least some of their secondary education in this country. Twenty-one per cent were over the age of eighteen when they arrived in Britain, and most of these would have taken 'A' levels at Colleges of Further Education. Only a minority of coloured students in our sample had received the whole of their education in Britain, but most of them had a substantial part of it here. In fact, in our analysis of job applications we found that length of residence in Britain appeared to make little difference to chances of finding employment among the coloured sample.

## Job applications

Not all the students in the survey planned to apply for jobs (Table 1). Of the 137 respondents in the survey as a whole, 28, including ten coloured students, told us that they planned to go on to take postgraduate courses of some kind, and would not be applying for jobs. Of the remaining students, 54 whites and 22 blacks sent us details of the applications they made up to the point where they had obtained a job or until the point where we ceased to collect data, that is, in September 1974. Thirteen students, only two of them coloured, did not have to look for jobs as they had been sponsored for their courses by their employers. Four coloured students informed us that they would be going abroad after qualifying: three were returning to their countries of origin, and one was to join relatives in Canada. Two of these students told us directly that one of their main reasons for going abroad was their expectation that it would be exceedingly difficult to find a good job in Britain, and we know from conversations with other coloured students that a substantial number were considering re-emigration for the same reason. Finally, for sixteen students, four of them coloured, we have no information other than the fact that they were looking for jobs at the time that they completed our initial questionnaire.

TABLE 1   Future intentions of students in the sample

|  | White | | Coloured | |
|---|---|---|---|---|
|  | No. | Per cent | No. | Per cent |
| Postgraduate course, no job applications | 18 | 19 | 10 | 24 |
| Not seeking job in UK | 0 | 0 | 4 | 10 |
| No details of applications made | 12 | 13 | 4 | 10 |
| Details of applications available | 54 | 57 | 22 | 52 |
| Sponsored by employer | 11 | 12 | 2 | 5 |

In all we had available for analysis details of over 550 job applications made by 76 students, 22 of them coloured. The data on job applications is rather complex, because applications may originate in different kinds of ways, and different students can make different numbers of applications. In addition the application may be turned down, or the candidate may withdraw, at different stages. It is not easy to make sense of such complex data, but perhaps the best way of doing so is by using the analogy of a race-course. Students may set out for the final goal, a job, from two different points, and to reach their goal they have to overcome a number of obstacles, including interviews. The use of such an analogy enables one to examine the ways in which different groups of students set out on this obstacle course, and whether they fare differently in surmounting various obstacles.

There are two main starting points in the search for jobs. A student may attend a 'milk round' interview at his university or college, or he may write directly to an employer. To attend a milk round interview a student only has to sign his name on a list and he is automatically interviewed. The crucial question is whether he is invited to attend a second interview at the company's premises or not. Thus the milk round interview may be seen as a hurdle at which a student may be rejected, or at which he is successful, in that he is offered another interview. For those who apply directly, on the other hand, the question is whether or not the student is invited to attend an interview. Following these initial stages, we can imagine the course coming together for the final hurdle – the final interview at which he is offered a job, or turned down. There are therefore three major hurdles on our racecourse, and we can label them the Milk Round Interview, the Direct Application and the Final Interview. Our analysis will consist of looking at the differential performance of various categories of candidates at different stages.

Let us take Direct Applications first. In all, 172 Direct Applications were made by whites and 110 by coloured students, giving a mean number of applications per applicant of 3.9 for whites and five for coloured. Thus coloured students made, on average, rather more Direct Applications than whites, a difference which would appear to be largely the outcome of greater difficulty experienced by coloureds in finding jobs: they kept on applying, while whites did not need to. Only eighteen per cent of all the applications made by whites were rejected at this stage, while 75, or 68 per cent of the applications by coloureds were rejected outright. No white applicant received more than four rejections at this stage while nine coloured applicants received five or more and three coloured applicants received nine rejections each. The difference is striking.

Checking the statistical significance of the difference is a little complex, because we are taking the application as a case rather than the individual, and the variable numbers of applications made by each individual must be taken into account. We therefore used Student's $t$ to test the difference between the mean rejection rates in each sample, the rejection rate being defined as the ratio between the number of Direct Applications resulting in rejection and the total number of Direct Applications made by each student.[5] Using this method, we established that the difference between the mean rejection rates for coloured and white students is highly significant ($p < 0.1$). (See Table 2.)

Looking at the other route into the job market, we recorded 172 Milk Round Applications made by whites and 99 by coloured students. Thirty-six per cent of those made by whites were rejected after the first interview, as opposed to 81 per cent of those made by coloured. We tested the difference in the mean rejection rate for coloured and whites in the same way as we did for Direct Applications, and once again the difference was highly significant ($p < 0.1$).

**TABLE 2** Applications and rejections of coloured and white students at different stages of the job application process

|  | Direct applications | | Milk round interview | | Final interview | |
|---|---|---|---|---|---|---|
|  | Coloured | White | Coloured | White | Coloured | White |
| No. of applicants involved | 22 | 54 | 18 | 38 | 16 | 49 |
| No. of applications at this stage | 110 | 172 | 99 | 172 | 41 | 144 |
| No. of rejections | 75 | 30 | 80 | 62 | 27 | 47 |
| Mean rejection rate | ·30 | ·08 | ·74 | ·35 | ·52 | ·28 |
| $p$, for student's $t$ | $p < 0.1$ | | $p < 0.1$ | | $p < 2$ | |

We recorded 144 applications made by white students which reached the last hurdle, the final interview (42 per cent of the total), while only 41 applications made by coloured students (20 per cent) got this far. These figures themselves indicate very clearly how many applications by coloured students had been eliminated earlier in the process. At the final interview itself, a third of the white applications were rejected, while 27 or 66 per cent of the black applications suffered this fate. We found that the difference between the mean rejection rates was statistically significant at this stage as well.

At the 'finishing line', 45 white applicants were offered a total of 97 jobs, while 11 coloured applicants were offered a total of 14 jobs. In other words, many white applicants were in a position to choose which job to take, having had several different offers, while only three coloured applicants had any alternative but to accept the single job that they had been offered. Eight-four per cent of the white students had at least one offer, while only 50 per cent of the coloured students had offers, despite the fact that they had made more applications per student. It is also worth mentioning that a number of white applicants were withdrawn midway 'down the course'. Twenty-two white applicants did not bother to attend 33 interviews to which they had been invited, while only three coloured applicants were in a position to turn down a total of four offers of interviews.

These figures point to the general conclusion that coloured students meet with far less success than white students at all stages of seeking a job. The coloured students had fewer offers and almost half had none at all, while in contrast the majority of white students had a number of job offers, and were able to choose which job to take.

Although these figures seemed to point fairly clearly to the operation of racial discrimination, we could not come to any definite conclusions, without making some further checks. It could be, for instance, that our coloured sample differed from the white sample in terms of such factors as age, degree result and social class of parents, and that it was a combination of these factors, rather than race, which was at the root of the difference.

In setting up our control sample we matched for sex and course studied, and concluded that there was no significant difference between the two samples in terms of sex, degree result and social class of parents. As a further check on the impact of these factors, we made the same tests as we did for race, but divided the whole sample successively by sex, by social class of parents (manual or non-manual) and by age (25 years or under, over 25 years). In no case did we find consistently significant differences. We also tested for the effect of degree result, using the Variance Ratio test which allows the comparison of more than two categories, but in the same way as the $t$ test.[6] Once again we did not detect any consistently significant difference.

Taking the data overall, our analysis showed that the effect of factors other than race was never sufficiently large to have a consistent impact of any significance on application success rates, given the size of our sample. We are not in a position to say that these factors have no impact whatsoever on success rates, for we might have been able to identify significant differences had our sample been larger. We can, however, say with confidence that the race of the candidate had an overwhelmingly greater impact on the success rate than did factors such as sex, social class and degree result, and that the small variations produced by these factors could not begin to explain the differences between the experiences of coloured and white applicants.

We turned to the coloured sample alone, and considered whether the two main sets of factors, other than racial identity, which distinguished them from white students, ie their average age, which was slightly higher, and their length of residence in Britain, had any effect on the success rate. Our conclusion was that, while there might be some difference, it was not large enough to be statistically significant given the size of our sample, and that it did not explain the massive difference between coloured and white students which we had identified. Having made all these various checks, we have no alternative but to conclude that it is the colour of the black students in our sample which lies at the root of their difficulties in gaining employment.

## Impressions of the students

For many coloured students the experience of repeated lack of success in applying for jobs, and the failure to obtain a job before the examination period, or even for long after graduating, is disillusioning and extremely depressing. Most interviews with coloured students in the sample were conducted during this time, and many students we talked to were cynical about the way they had been treated. Many were surprised and increasingly depressed by their failure to obtain a job, and were beginning to reassess their plans and expectations. Some were considering turning to the possibility of postgraduate study rather than employment as an immediate solution, and this is reflected in the relatively high proportion of coloured students opting for postgraduate study. We suspect that for many this will not do more than put off the evil day, and that many coloured students with postgraduate qualifications may eventually find that they are rejected by employers on the grounds that they are 'over-qualified'. Other students mentioned the possibility of re-emigrating if they could not find a job which matched their qualifications.

We found that many coloured students were not at all prepared for their experiences. While the path through school and university had been relatively smooth, the employment market presented a very different prospect. Up until this point they had been prepared to give British society the benefit of the doubt or, if they were aware of discrimination, they had believed, or tried to believe, that it would not happen to *them*. Several students reported instances where they felt racial hostility or discrimination had been present during interviews: 'No-one made remarks like "we don't employ coloured people", but some obviously want to get rid of you as soon as they see you . . .' and 'I passed the preselections, it was when they *saw* me that they changed their minds.' The students may sometimes have been wrong in their assumptions, but our survey results indicate that they were probably right on most occasions. Furthermore, these impressions contributed to the disillusionment of the coloured students and their friends.

## Employability, selection and discrimination

Since our survey consisted of an investigation of students and their applications, rather than of employers, our concrete findings are limited to the differences which we discovered between the success rates of our white and coloured sample in seeking jobs. We are not in a position to provide definite explanations of why employers acted in the way in which they did, so that coloured students suffered such a great disadvantage. We have been able to dismiss the arguments that the difference was due to such factors as sex, age, class of degree and social class, but we can only suggest plausible but speculative explanations as to why employers acted as they did.

The most plausible explanation is that straightforward racial discrimination is the main factor involved. What we imagine generally happens is that an employer will initially consider all the suitably qualified white candidates, and that it is only when the supply of suitable white candidates is exhausted that serious consideration will be given to coloured applicants. We believe that our evidence indicates that employers consistently select along these lines and that this is the main explanation why the members of our coloured sample had such great difficulty in obtaining jobs.

In addition, all the careers officers to whom we spoke emphasized that formal academic qualifications are often of less importance in getting a job than such factors as personality, style and an ability to get on with others. Many used the term 'employability' to cover an amalgam of these factors. We have no doubt that careers officers were correct in emphasizing the importance of such factors, but it seems to us that two elements within the concept need to be distinguished – individual personality on the one hand, and social and cultural style on the other. We take it as given that varieties of personality type will be scattered at random through the population, but could it be that the poor results of our coloured graduates are the outcome of their being representatives of a different social or cultural group, something which may automatically relegate them to the back of the queue? One careers officer argues this explicitly. Having stressed that 'getting a job depends on assimilating a culture', he went on to say: 'It is important to discover the extent to which any minority group . . . wishes this absorption to take place. Any member of a minority who wishes to retain a separate culture may be making it considerably more difficult for himself to get the kind of job which requires the sinking of cultural differences.'

Again when we were examining some record cards shown us by a careers officer, we noticed on one coloured student's card the comment 'he does not seem to have a chip on his shoulder', and in the context this seemed a cause for some surprise on the part of the careers officer. Although we had little success in discussing with the careers officer concerned what he meant by the comment, a person described as having 'a chip on the shoulder' in this situation is probably best defined as one who constantly refers to the racial slights that he believes himself to be suffering, the label being applied by another person who believes the first's beliefs about slights to be quite unfounded, or at least unreasonably exaggerated. To avoid the label of 'chip on the shoulder', a coloured student must be ignorant of racial discrimination, or must at least pretend to be ignorant of it, and must certainly never express any of the feelings he may have about the treatment he has received. It seems to us that a student with 'a chip on the shoulder' about race would have greater difficulty in getting a job – but the evidence of our survey indicates that the beliefs on which his behaviour was based would by no means be unfounded.

We were told by one coloured applicant that an employer's representative had advised him, after an interview, to play down the fact that he had been President of the University West Indian Association in any subsequent interviews. It seems unlikely to us that the President of the Hibernian Association, for instance, would have received the same advice, and we can only conclude that the objection arose because of an implied commitment to the ethnic and political interests of *black* West Indians.

It seems clear that in the eyes of careers officers and employers, the best way for a coloured graduate to increase his 'employability' is to be, or rather present himself as if he were, indistinguishable from his white peers. Above all, he should not make an issue of his identity, or his awareness of racial discrimination. This leads us to ask two further questions. Firstly, is the lack of success of our coloured respondents due to their failure to match up to this image and, secondly, how far is it reasonable that they should try to do so?

It is probable that the culture argument has some validity, but the evidence of our survey indicates that it cannot provide a satisfactory explanation of the vast difference between coloured and white students' success rates in our results. If the coloured students were doing poorly solely because of their cultural difference, we would expect them to do much less badly at the Direct Application stage than at any other, for an employer could not assess the cultural and social behaviour of a candidate on the basis of a written application alone. Members of our coloured sample were, however, no more successful at the Direct Applications stage than they were when they had interviews with their prospective employers. Length of residence in Britain also made no difference to a coloured student's chances of getting a job.

A strategy of 'passing', that is of acting as if he was not coloured, also has a number of disadvantages for a coloured student. It demands that the student should deny the reality of himself, for he must pretend that he is not really a non-European. He must deny the reality of his experience, for he must pretend that racial discrimination does not exist. He must deny the reality of his ethnicity, for he must pretend that his family does not come from India, the West Indies, or wherever. Finally he can do nothing to challenge the disabilities from which he suffers, for the strategy demands that he should present himself as if these disabilities did not exist. The 'culture' argument neither explains our results, nor solves the problem.

## Conclusion

We believe that the results of our survey have very disturbing implications for the future. Many young black and coloured Britons have expectations of achieving advanced educational qualifications, and, of course, commensurate employment. These expectations are not infrequently dubbed 'unrealistic', but substantial numbers of coloured students *are* already reaching university and much larger numbers will be receiving higher education in the near future. While carrying out our survey we were struck by the fact that many of the university officials to whom we spoke were unaware of the existence of black British students; the assumption tended to be that anyone with a coloured face must be an overseas student, a much more familiar category. We believe that this is probably symptomatic, and that there is widespread ignorance of the fact that many children of coloured immigrant parents are now gaining a higher education. It is alarming to find such ignorance among the administrators.

Of course some of the coloured students in our survey had found jobs by the time we ceased collecting data, and almost all will eventually find employment of one kind or another. What we cannot say is whether the jobs they got were of the same quality as those obtained by whites, and whether they have the same chances of promotion. To answer these questions would take more research, but it seems obvious that the probability is that coloured graduates will be disadvantaged throughout their careers. Our results do not leave any room for complacency, and furthermore, it seems likely that the situation will tend to deteriorate rather than improve; the numbers of professionally qualified black Britons emerging from the universities is likely to rise sharply in the coming years, and they may well find even greater difficulty in securing suitable jobs.

It seems likely that the more senior and prestigious a job, the more competition there will be for it. Our results indicate that in such a competitive situation it is the suitably qualified white candidates who are considered first, while coloured candidates wait at the back of the queue; where there is an excess of suitable applicants for the job, coloured candidates may never reach the front. The career prospects of coloured job-seekers, however well qualified, look bleak, and will remain so without a radical change of attitudes on the part of employers.

While the older generation of coloured people, who came to Britain as immigrants, have generally accepted the inferior status to which they were assigned without much protest, it is most unlikely that their children will do the same. They will not accept second-class citizenship. Yet while carrying out the survey it was clear to us that few white people in positions of power were conscious of the implications of their actions and assumptions: it is the quiet preference for white over coloured, expressed in a multitude of situations, which perpetuates and reinforces the fundamental racialism of British society.

## Notes and references

1. Some parts of this article have already been published in an article entitled 'Racial Discrimination: No Room at the Top' in *New Society*, 17 April, 1975.
2. Community Relations Commission, *Unemployment and Homelessness*, HMSO 1974.
3. J. H. Taylor, 'Newcastle upon Tyne: Asian Pupils Do Better than Whites', *British Journal of Sociology*, Vol. 54, No. 4, 1973.
4. The survey on which this article is based was carried out as a separate project while one of the authors, R. Ballard, was engaged on an anthropological study of the Sikh community in Leeds.

5. Student's $t$ is a standard statistical test used to investigate the difference between the means of two samples. The more widely known $\chi^2$ test could not be used on our data for mathematical reasons. For details of these tests see M. J. Moroney, *Facts from Figures*, Penguin, 1956.

6. The Variance Ratio Test is a more general expansion of Student's $t$, which allows analysis of a sample divided into more than two categories. This was necessary with the figures for degree results, because they could not readily be reduced to a simple pair of categories, as could be done with sex and social class for instance.

# CHAPTER 2.8

## DISCRIMINATION AGAINST APPLICANTS FOR WHITE-COLLAR JOBS*
*David Smith*

### Correspondence testing

Correspondence testing is a tightly controlled method of assessing the level of discrimination against applicants for white-collar jobs. Written or typed letters of application are sent for a sample of advertised jobs. Two applications are made for each job, one in the name of a white British applicant and the other in the name of an immigrant. Where both applicants are invited to an interview this is treated as a case of 'no discrimination', but where one applicant is invited to an interview and the other is not, this is treated as a case of discrimination. The advantage of the method is that all features of the application can be carefully controlled. The disadvantage is that it only tests for discrimination at the first 'screening' stage of the recruitment process. As we have already argued in the case of telephone testing, this means that *minimum* estimates of the level of discrimination are produced.

One of the two applicants was always white British. The other was Italian, West Indian, Indian or Pakistani. The inclusion of the Italian allows us to assess the effect of race as opposed to foreign origin. The immigrant applicants always stated in their letters: 'I came to England in 1956 from Jamaica/India/Pakistan/Italy after completing my primary schooling. I have been permanently resident in the UK since that time.' The white British applicants always mentioned the town where they went to school; the employer would naturally assume that they were white and were born in England. The names of the applicants helped to establish the country of origin. For example Pakistani applicants were called 'Asif Mirza', while the surname of Italian applicants was 'Binelli'.

---

* An extract from *Racial Disadvantage in Britain*, The PEP Report, Penguin Books, 1976.

The tests covered a range of white-collar jobs, as follows:
Salesman (male)
Accountant (male)
Management trainee (male)
Junior clerical (male)
Junior clerical (female)
Secretary (female)

This list shows the sex of our *applicants*; this does not necessarily imply that sex was specified in the advertisement.

The testing was carried out in the following towns: London, Slough/Windsor, Nottingham, Birmingham, Leeds, Manchester.

Since identical letters could not be sent for the same job, two different letters had to be devised. The substance of each pair of letters was the same, but to ensure that no bias was introduced through the different styles of the two letters, each version was allocated to the white applicant for half of the tests and to the immigrant applicant for the other half. The letters were also varied for each type of job, since the applicant had to have the relevant qualifications and experience. The results show that the two versions of the letters for each job achieved about the same success rates.

The level of qualifications and experience of the two applicants were always the same. Applications for secretarial jobs were typed while the other applications were handwritten.

The letters from immigrant applicants always stated that they had had their primary schooling in the country of origin and their secondary schooling in England. Therefore both applicants had similar promtly to British qualifications. This implied that the immigrant applicants were fluent in spoken and written English, and the standard of the letter itself also made this clear.

Each pair of letters was posted on the same day from the town in which the job was advertised. Altogether 305 pairs of letters were sent evenly in such a way that the success rates could be compared between the six regions, the six job types, the four ethnic groups and the two versions of the letter. Tests which gave no indication of whether there had been discrimination were discarded and are not included in the 305 tests analyzed. Examples of these inconclusive tests are those where both applicants were refused or both received no reply.

## Results of the correspondence testing

Asian and West Indian applicants for white-collar jobs faced discrimination in 30 per cent of cases, compared with only ten per cent for Italian applicants. (These are 'net' figures which take account of cases where the minority applicant was favoured in the same way as before.) Bearing in mind that the method identifies discrimination only at the screening stage, a level of 30 per cent is very substantial. If nearly one third of Asian and West Indian applicants fail to get to an interview because of discrimination, we can expect a still higher proportion to fall by the wayside because of unfair treatment by the time the selection is finally made. The very much lower figure for the Italian applicants [. . .] shows, [. . .] that the discrimination is mainly based on colour prejudice.

There were altogether twenty cases where the minority applicant was favoured, which are allowed for in the figures given. However, in only two of these cases was there an actual refusal of the white British applicant. In the remaining eighteen cases, the white applicant was invited to an interview. It is most unlikely that in these cases the immigrant applicant was actually preferred. What is much more likley is that an employer who has received a large number of replies may choose to consider only the first twenty that come to his notice. Of course, this implies that a similar number of the apparent cases of discrimination against the immigrant arise for the same reason, and this is allowed for in calculating net discrimination.

Levels of discrimination against the three minority groups were closely similar (West Indians 33 per cent, Indians 27 per cent, Pakistanis 30 per cent). This confirms the conclusion drawn in the case of manual jobs, that discrimination is based on a generalized colour prejudice which makes little distinction between black and brown people belonging to different ethnic groups. The levels of discrimination were also much the same for each of the six different towns. People will often admit that discrimination happens in some places, but not in their own town. Our findings demonstrate, on the contrary, that local differences are insignificant.

There were, however, some differences between jobs in the levels of discrimination found. Discrimination was highest for male junior clerical jobs (48 per cent), management trainees (42 per cent) and accountants (35 per cent). The lowest levels of discrimination were found for female applicants – junior clerical 22 per cent, secretary 17 per cent. Although these differences are only just significant from the statistical point of view, they probably are genuine ones, because they seem to make sense. Women seem to face less discrimination than men in the more junior jobs in which they have traditionally worked. This conclusion fits closely with the actual pattern of employment, for the gap in terms of job levels and earnings between the minorities and whites is much greater among men than among women. The explanation is probably that women are already discriminated against as women, and this tends to restrict them to more junior and less well paid jobs; they are therefore not regarded as a threat, and there is less need for employers to discriminate against them on the ground of colour as well, in order to keep them in a subordinate position.

It is highly significant that management trainee applicants face a high level of discrimination, because this is one of the main routes by which young people can set off towards really senior positions. From the findings on job levels, we might expect to find that discrimination was higher for the more senior non-manual jobs. In fact, the situation seems to be more complicated than this, since the highest level of discrimination was found for male applicants for junior clerical jobs. A large number of different jobs would have to be tested in order to arrive at a final conclusion on this point.

## Examples of the replies received

In cases where there was discrimination, this would never have been apparent to the applicants concerned. Five pairs of letters demonstrating discrimination are reproduced in the following pages. In the first example, the employer gives a phoney reason for refusing the West Indian applicant – that, because of the fuel crisis, the management have decided not to increase the sales force after all. On the same day, the white applicant is invited to an interview. In the second example, the employer bluntly tells the Pakistani applicant that he has not been shortlisted, but on the same day he writes to the similarly qualified white applicant asking him to attend an interview. In the third example, the employer pretends to the Pakistani applicant for a position as secretary that it is company policy not to employ married women (this would, if genuine, now be discriminatory under the sex discrimination act); on the same day he writes enthusiastically to the white applicant, also a married woman, asking her to telephone 'as soon as ever possible' to arrange an interview. By the fact that he addresses her as 'Mrs X' he shows that he is fully aware of her married status. In the fourth example, sex discrimination is again used as an excuse for what is really racial discrimination. The fifth pair of letters vividly illustrates how wide the gap between the treatment of the two applicants can be. The Indian applicant is sent a badly reproduced circular letter, containing an obvious spelling mistake, curtly turning him down and claiming that it is impossible to answer each applicant individually. The white applicant is sent a long and carefully composed letter which is calculated to arouse his enthusiasm at the prospect of working for the company as a salesman and which invites him to an exciting meeting at the Midland Hotel. These are five of the 77 examples which the testing produced in all.

10.12.73.

Dear Sir,
    Many thanks for your advert in the Y.E. Post. Unfortunately, since placing the advert. the fuel situation has worsened and the management have decided against increasing the sales force at this present time. We will of course keep your name and address for future reference when the fuel crisis eases.

Yours faithfully,

10.12.73.

Dear Mr. Hayes,
    Many thanks for your reply to our advert. in the Y.E. Post. Basically the work would entail calling on Working Mens Clubs and pubs in Yorks. selling Electric Lamps and tubes.
If you think this is the type of work you are looking for, please would you be good enough to phone me at home any evening after 6.0 pm. I can then arrange a suitable time for an interview.

Yours faithfully,

26th September, 1973

Dear Mr. Mirja,
Thank you for your application in reply to my recent advertisement.
A list of candidates has now been compiled for interview, and I regret to tell you that your name does not appear on the list.
May I take this opportunity to thank you for your interest in the position, and wish you every success for the future.

Yours sincerely

26th September, 1973

Dear Mr. Hayes,

Thank you for your application, in reply to my recent advertisement.

I have read your letter with interest, and would now like you to attend a preliminary interview at:  The Walsall Crest Motel,

Birmingham Road,

Walsall, Staffs.

If you will arrange to be present at 09.15 hrs. on Friday October 5th, 1973 we will take your application a stage further.

If, for any reason, you are unable to attend this interview, I would appreciate advice of this.

Yours sincerely,


12th February, 1974

Dear Mrs. Mirza,

Thank you very much for your letter of the 9th February replying to our advertisement in The Manchester Evening News for a Secretary.

Unfortunately, we have a policy in the office not to employ married women as we unfortunately, had a bad experience recently.

I am sorry that I am unable to help you in this instance.

Yours sincerely,


12th February, 1974

Dear Mrs. Hayes,
Position of Secretary

Thank you very much for your letter of the 8th February applying for the position of Secretary.

Perhaps you would be kind enough to telephone the office as soon as ever possible to arrange a mutually convenient time for you to come in to see us.

I look forward to hearing from you.

Yours sincerely,


13th December 1973

Dear Sir,

Thank you for your letter in response to our advertisement for an Accounts Clerk. Whilst we did not stress this in the advertisement we would prefer to fill the situation with a female and as we have had a number of suitable applicants we shall not be asking you to attend an interview.

Yours faithfully,

13th December 1973

Dear Sir,

With reference to your letter dated 10th December 1973, the position in our Accounts Department, as advertised, unfortunately is no longer available. However, we do have a vacancy within our Fire Department and if you are interested perhaps you would kindly telephone me or in my absence my secretary Mrs. Stead, to arrange a suitable time for interview.

Yours faithfully,

17.1.74

Dear Mr. Hayes,

I was very pleased and interested to receive your reply to our recent advertisement for Salesmen.

I am sure we would both agree that it is extremely important for you to be given every opportunity of finding out as much as possible about our activities as a Company, exactly what is involved in selling for us, and naturally, what rewards success as a Salesman would bring.

The vital question is, of course – how to achieve these objectives. We believe we have the best answer through a very informal meeting of no more than ten or twelve people, all interested in discovering as much as possible about a Sales career with us. The meeting lasts for about two-and-a-half hours and at least half of that time is given over to an open discussion on the Company and the job.

I would emphasize that nothing is raised or discussed which might be considered personal or private to anyone present. The complete informality for which we aim relieves the tensions so often associated with interviews, and, almost without exception, everyone feels the results achieved have been well worth the time spent.

It is with pleasure that I invite you to attend such a meeting at the Midland Hotel, Peter Street, Manchester, on Friday, 1st February 1974, commencing at 10.30 a.m., and I certainly hope that you will want to accept this invitation.

I am enclosing an Application Form which I would like you to complete and bring with you. If, for any reason, you are unable to come but would like me to arrange an alternative appointment for you, please send the completed form to me through the post.

Yours sincerely,

17.1.74

Dear Sir,

I thank you for your reply to our recent advertisement for Salesmen.

I very much appreciate your interest, and it is with regret, therefore, that I have to tell you that we shall not be asking you to attend for interview.

I would also like to apologise for the lack of the "personal touch" in this letter. You will understand, of course, that in trying to reply promtly to everyone who has written to us, it is impossible to answer each applicant individually.

Yours faithfully,

# CHAPTER 2.9

# EXCLUSION AND OPPORTUNITY: TRADITIONS OF WORK AMONGST BRITISH JEWS*
*Barry Kosmin*

The work orientation and behaviour of any social group reflects both the experience, goals and values of that group, and the constraints and opportunities of a particular setting. Jewish ethnicity as a dependent variable in work situations in Britain can be considered in two parts. First, the specific cultural traits which can be generalized for the group and which distinguish its members from the majority of the host population. This distinctive social philosophy, the Jewish *Weltanschaung,* may be termed *the expressive factor.* Second, the using of this common culture as a focus for solidarity and identity in actual social situations. This may be termed the *utility factor.*

We are concerned with both aspects of ethnicity in relation to occupation and economic activity among British Jews: their philosophical and cultural inheritance, and their use of ethnicity as a tool or resource (cf. Wallman, 1975). We are dealing with a concept that is time, area and situation specific, and the two aspects of the concept are themselves differently affected by the immediate environment. [. . . .]

Jewish attitudes towards occupations and economic life have been formed over a long period, but the present cultural inheritance of British Jews has evolved from three main sources. The first is the body of religious and philosophical literature embodied in the Talmud and Torah. The second is the distinctive Jewish culture which arose in central and eastern Europe as a result of oppression and discrimination there. This experience formed the background to perceptions and attitudes of Jewish immigrants into Britain from the eighteenth to the twentieth centuries.

* This edited extract is from *Ethnicity at Work* Wallman, S. (ed.), Macmillan, 1979. By permission of Macmillan, London and Basingstoke.

The third influence has been the environment in Britain: its economy, its social structure and the general attitude towards immigrant and minority group participation in society. [. . . .]

## Immigrants to Britain

The cultural baggage of the majority of Jewish immigrants into Britain after 1850 included various inclinations and aptitudes, technical knowledge and skills. Its importance in this discussion stems from the fact that these immigrants were the ancestors of more than two-thirds of present-day British Jewry, and that they, like most immigrants, clung tenaciously to their cultural heritage, particularly to the religious element, and attempted to transmit it to future generations. Compared to many immigrants, however, they were extraordinarily adaptable. They came from a pre-capitalist agricultural society into the strange environment of urban and industrial Britain, but brought with them energetic habits of work and an orientation to the future which was almost universally positive.

In effect, they were willing to throw off their past and all ties with their homeland except family ones. This capacity for adaptation was crucial. Though they undoubtedly appreciated the freedom from oppression and the increased opportunity for economic betterment which Britain offered, these poverty-stricken Jewish immigrants were not free to choose their occupations without regard to constraints of the current labour market, or of their own lack of capital resources and facility in the English language. Moreover, they did not enter a virgin territory. There was already a small resident Jewish community with an established niche in British society and the British economy, and there were as a result established attitudes and stereotypes among the indigenous inhabitants of jobs and work appropriate to Jews. This situation can be better understood against an outline of the occupational history of the Jews in Britain.

The wave pattern of Jewish immigration into Britain since the Resettlement in 1656 has gradually transformed the Jewish occupational experience from that of impoverished aliens in marginal jobs, which could be classed as 'immigrant occupations' rather than 'Jewish occupations', into higher status positions. The sole exceptions to this trend were the earliest seventeenth-century immigrants from Holland who entered originally as merchants or financiers. In terms of status these would not fall into the 'immigrant' class of peripheral jobs, but their occupations follow the immigrant pattern in the way they made use of skills acquired in their old environment. The Jews in Holland had had a traditional association with finance and trade. Their success in Britain depended on this expertise and on their maintaining contacts with and access to European markets.

During the eighteenth century, as a result of expulsions of Jewish populations and other political upheavals in Germany and eastern Europe, a larger-scale immigration of Jews from these areas began. At about the same time there was a small drift of Jews from Mediterranean countries seeking their fortunes in London. Many of these immigrants depended on the charity of their wealthy predecessors. Some scratched a living selling old clothes or peddling small goods such as spices and slippers – all occupations which required neither capital nor skill.

In the late eighteenth century, Jewish pedlars and tinkers began to move out of London and to sell their goods and services up and down the country. Of those who stayed in London, some rose in status from hawkers to stallholders. Any progression to shop-owning was closed to them by virtue of the fact that they were, until 1831, denied the necessary qualification of Freedom of the City of London. This barrier had two consequences for the pattern of Jewish activity: newcomers unable to find jobs in London were forced to seek them in the provinces; and, within London, Jews made an attempt to widen their occupational options. The Jewish charities associated with the Neve Zedek Orphan Asylum and the Great Synagogue tried to teach poorer Jews a trade, establishing apprenticeships in shoemaking, tailoring, pencil-making and glass-cutting. Those who had engraving skills turned their hands to watch- and jewellery-making.

In the first half of the nineteenth century there was another influx from Holland, this time predominantly of poor urban Jews who had been involved in the tobacco and entertainment industries. The latter applied their skills to setting up pleasure gardens and public houses while the influence of Dutch Jews in tobacco manufacture in London became so great that it soon had the reputation of being a Jewish trade. Those who were not absorbed into legitimate activities turned to the 'informal' economy, including crime: the Jewish element in London's criminal sub-culture was epitomised by the character Fagin in Dickens' *Oliver Twist*.

The immigrants of the period 1881–1914 came in as a mass migration of some 200,000 persons. In such numbers they overwhelmed the existing community which, in 1880, totalled around 70,000. These newcomers fleeing the Tsarist pogroms were alien in outlook and manner to the resident community. The latter had become anglicised and was beginning to enter the respectable middle class, progressing through the economy into the manufacturing sector. Moreover, there were few existing social or family ties between the newcomers and British Jewry. The resident community was unable and often unwilling to absorb the new arrivals into existing commercial firms, nor was there a large number of available places for them in the informal economy. Irish immigrants had now taken over jobs such as peddling and slop-selling, done earlier by Jews. In addition, existing industries such as agriculture, mining, textile manufacture, iron and steel, transport and construction, and bureaucratic service occupations already had established labour forces with traditional recruitment practices. Jewish immigrants to London, for instance, stood no chance of being employed at the docks or in the London produce markets: the indigenous labour force was violently hostile to foreign competitors.

Unable to find work in basic or traditional industries, the new immigrants had to seek openings in areas which did not compete with native workmen. These they found in producing consumer or luxury goods. Such peripheral consumer-oriented industries were arising as a result of higher living standards in Britain and the growing spending power of the masses. The only existing Jewish industrial niche capable of absorbing labour in this sphere was the 76 Jewish East End tobacco factories, mainly producing cigars. Openings here were rapidly filled since there were good wages and strong unions. The new fashion in ostrich feathers supported an industry able to absorb limited numbers of willing workers, but it was clothing which became the main immigrant niche.

The upward progression of Anglo-Jewry in the clothing industry had taken many of the descendants of eighteenth-century immigrants from peddling to market-stall owning and on to ownership of outfitting shops. Clothing merchants such as Montagu Burton were now anxious to move into the manufacture, through mass production, of ready-made clothing such as suits, overcoats and caps, and saw an opportunity for this in the surplus labour of their co-religionists. The advantage of this particular labour pool was that it could be more easily organized to accept the seasonal nature of the work, long hours, job fragmentation, new processes and poor working conditions. The results were the sweat shops of the needle trades and the formation of a Jewish industrial proletariat in the overcrowded London slums of Whitechapel and Stepney, and in similar areas such as Cheetham in Manchester or the Leylands in Leeds. This situation renewed the association between Jews and the 'rag' or *Schmutter* trade. Similar patterns of motivation and development occurred in the furniture trade of Shoreditch and in the footwear industry. In the boot and shoe trade 'skilled Jewish home lasters and finishers took unskilled 'greeners' as assistants and made of their homes . . . workshops' (Gartner, 1973).

In London in 1901, approximately 40 per cent of male Jewish immigrants of Russian and Polish origin were employed as tailors, about twelve per cent were in footwear and ten per cent in furniture. Surveys done between 1895 and 1908 on 9000 recent immigrants showed that, even before emigration, 29 per cent had been making clothes, nine per cent had worked in boot and shoe trades, and seven per cent had been carpenters, suggesting a certain amount of continuity of occupation from their original homeland. It was, therefore, for both economic and social reasons that Jewish immigrants settled in areas of established Jewish communities, predominantly in the cities of London, Manchester, Leeds and Glasgow, where with few financial resources of their own they applied the skills they knew from their home countries, or took jobs in workshops already established by Jews.

New immigrants facing new customs, a new language and a certain amount of hostility from the local population, usually look to their fellows for assistance. The denial of access to other job opportunities was not the only incentive to work for a Jewish employer. The east European Jews' distrust of gentiles was such that they automatically turned to their co-religionists for aid and comfort. Moreover, a Jewish employer was more likely to be able to communicate with them and was usually more amenable to accommodating the sabbath, religious festivals and food taboos.

The gap between immigrant and indigenous workers and the segregation of Jews at work was very evident at the time. Immigrants established trade unions separately from the English workers. There were 22 Jewish trade unions in Edwardian London, both because of the social and cultural gulf between Jewish and English workers and the separateness of the Jewish sectors in the main immigrant trades of garment and boot and shoe making.

## Aspirations

The lack of working interaction with the locals was not the only barrier. The Jewish workers had more bourgeois cultural aspirations and in their leisure activities tended to shun the 'pubs'. Neither did the majority of Jews share a conception of themselves as permanent members of the working class. Thus Jewish workers' horizons and strategies were different: the greatest ambition of most of them was to move from the status of employee to that of self-employed worker or employer. This feature is present in all the types of work to which Jews gravitated from their first arrival in Britain as well as in their occupations before migration. It was reinforced by experience of the sweat shops of London's East End which were the scandal of late-Victorian Britain. The folk memory of this episode undoubtedly had far-reaching effects on the Jewish occupational and economic profile: it fostered a general distrust of industrial labour and its associated hierarchies, and a desire for independent economic activity.

But while the most cherished ambition of the immigrant generation was to save their children from their own predicament, movement out of the clothing and associated trades was difficult. Economic pressures were such that young people, like their parents, had to take jobs where they could find them in the established Jewish community, using skills which they already or which they could easily learn. [. . .]

The sweat-shop experience increased the Jewish bias towards self-employment. It introduced qualitative as well as economic reasons for seeking independent status. At the first opportunity, the London Jewish worker would move over to running a home workshop, doing occasional contract work for a large manufacturer. In the provinces, particularly in Leeds where the clothing industry was on a larger scale, it was more difficult to escape the factory. It often surprised observers to find that among Jews the greatest ambition was not to earn higher wages, but to become a master. What these observers overlooked was the question of autonomy. A worker cannot control his working environment. He has the very real problem that he earns only as long as he is employed. [. . .]

## Specialization

Jewish businesses are still concentrated in clothing, footwear, timber and furniture, leather and furs. German–Jewish immigrants provide two-thirds of the last-mentioned firms. After the centre of this Jewish speciality was destroyed along with the Jewish community in its traditional home of Leipzig, the world centre for the dyeing, dressing and manufacture of furs moved to London in the late 1930s. In 1945 it was estimated, on the basis of examination of trade directories, that Jews participated in only 24 per cent of the 1040 trades practised in

Manchester, 13 per cent of Liverpool's and 8 per cent of Glasgow's. Jewish firms were then still most prominent in textiles, drapery and fashion trades, and it was claimed they owned one-seventh of all furniture manufacturing firms (Barou, 1945). Another popular field which has potentially glamorous contacts with entertainment is the radio, television, hi-fi and electrical industry. Jewish over-representation in the Royal Air Force in both world wars and the fact that electronics was a new growth industry together account for much of this involvement. In London, Jewish firms dominate Tottenham Court Road as much as they do the 'gown' district of Great Portland Street or the market stalls of Petticoat Lane. Despite the growth in the number of manufacturers, the highest proportion of Jewish businesses are today found in wholesaling. Under pressure from multiples, department stores and supermarkets, the independent retailer is a vanishing species and, in the Jewish case, the reluctance of the younger generation to continue in any but the larger firms has quickened the process.

Despite such trends, one can still discern a movement of Jews to occupations in which the intelligent use of small capital makes rapid improvement possible. The most obvious sphere has been that of new or expanding services such as estate and employment agencies, laundromats, hairdressing and beauty parlours, betting shops and small property deals. If a new businessman's personal and family resources were not sufficient to set up a new venture, he had the possibility of calling on communal aid. In the years 1951–5, for example, the loan department of the Jewish Board of Guardians granted 675 interest-free loans to enable small businessmen, handicapped by lack of capital, to carry on or develop businesses in cases where financial help could not be obtained from other sources. Many of these people had trouble with traditional financial institutions because of their progressive approach, new innovations and methods. It is they who have never really lost the outlook of the informal economy, the eye for opportunities and the lack of respect for traditional roles or practices. [. . .]

## The integration of work

[. . .] Where post-war businesses have expanded into regional or national chains, or have become public companies, the owners have had to go beyond their in-group for financing, marketing and associated services. This has led to new forms of integration with non-Jewish society since it is at this stage that gentile business partners and associates enter the scene.

Many large Jewish-owned concerns now have socially desirable gentile directors or managers who are there to provide the 'image' or even 'a touch of class' as often as an injection of enterprise, skill or capital.

This strategy is the end product of a long process of acculturation to British norms and another example of the adaptability of British Jews. Until this point the dominant trait of the successful Jewish entrepreneur has been a great belief in himself, his ideas and his abilities, and in the service he is performing. Moreover, he usually shows, by British standards, a surprising lack of status concern at work. He has a holistic approach to the running of the business, believes in a do-it-yourself policy, and is quite prepared to *Schlap* – that is, to do physical work – if a job needs to be done. Application of these tenets can be seen in the management training at Marks & Spencer's: every candidate, of whatever social or kinship status in relation to the firm, starts at the bottom of the hierarchy – unloading vans. The Jewish businessman, typically, has no patience with the fragmentation of roles, closed-shop practices, demarcation disputes and people who are too proud to do ordinary work. These attitudes show a distrust of specialization and expertise and an impatience with hierarchies. They also entail an empathy for employees, a tendency to be on mutual first-name terms with them and an appreciation of worker initiatives and involvement. The Jewish preference for seeing the whole field of operation may be linked to a philosophical belief in free will and man's domination and comprehension of work. There is an evident desire for autonomy and a willingness to take on the burdens of personal responsibility which reflect an essentially optimistic and positive outlook. A favourite Hebrew and Israeli expression in the face of an apparently overwhelming problem is *hiyé-tov*: 'it will be good – it will come right'.

In Britain and the United States, Jews have been proportionately under-represented in large corporations and state bureaucracies. This is no longer due to discrimination and a fear of hierarchies, but involves also a rejection of the fragmentation of work roles. It is a realization that the techniques of 'scientific management' used by the large corporations have increased the splitting and specialization of work and have diminished individual comprehension of the whole field of operation. Jews prefer jobs in which they can comprehend and control the whole process and in which an individual controls his environment and is the central actor: where there is a chance for *Yikhus* or personal standing, and one can be a *Mensch* – a real person and not a caricature, number or cog in a wheel. As a result, they are over-represented in careers where these possibilities are open – in medicine, law, entrepreneurship, academia, the arts, research and theoretical science. The traditional dislike for a faceless bureaucracy, the need to know who one is dealing with and the desire for social interaction in the working environment are all evident. [. . .]

## Ethnicity, change and achievement

After the externally enhanced solidarity of the 1930s and wartime years, there is now evidence of incipient class differentiation occurring among British Jews. This evidence is, however, complicated by the fact that most Jews of whatever socio-economic background see themselves as middle class and subscribe to supposedly middle-class norms and values. [. . .]

The post-war years have seen the Jewish quest for middle-class acceptance come to fruition. The gradual movement of Jews from the immigrant fringes to a position of integration in the centre of society has come to rest with the large-scale entry of Jews into the professional ranks. Over the whole country in 1961, ten per cent of the male Jewish working population was found to be in professions, and certain area studies such as Edgware (1963) and Sheffield (1975) have found proportions of sixteen and 29 per cent respectively.

This has come about primarily as a result of the traditional respect for learning being re-directed towards secular education, and in a climate of tolerance which has allowed Jews to contribute more fully to the society in which they live. Modern technological society increasingly values higher education and has produced a labour market which demands high educational qualifications. Jews have been especially quick to recognize that education and formal qualifications are the secret of occupational success and social mobility in the twentieth century. The shading of class divisions achieved by individual Jews constitutes an important Jewish contribution to British occupational life. They have been pacesetters in the opening up of the professions –traditionally an area of inherited privilege and conservative social outlook – to a new meritocracy. The post-war expansion of the professions coincided with the Jewish community's post-war readiness to exploit any new opportunities.

With a background of respect for learning and desire for self-improvement, Jews have entered this new competition of 'worth not birth' on a better than equal footing with the English middle and working classes. New national policies of free and open access to education through formal examinations enable Jews to use their traditions of work to compete in the professional market. While they were, in the past, prepared to make economic sacrifices to send their children to grammar or private schools and universities and may have even made this a measure of their own financial achievements, little headway could be made in the professions as long as they were discriminated against either positively or negatively. It has taken over 100 years since the first Jewish university graduate in 1836, the first Jewish barrister in 1849, for Jews to enter the professions in large numbers. What has been required and, to a large extent, achieved, is not just the lifting of quotas in education institutions such as medical schools, but also the acceptance by the education authorities and fellow students of different customs and beliefs. These range from the recognition of peculiar needs in school assembly, meals and religion classes, to allowing non-attendance on festivals and special arrangements for examinations set on these days. All of these were once a very real barrier to the professional advancement of Orthodox Jews.

The post-war commitment to national 'equal opportunity' and meritocracy has, coupled with the improved economic standing of Jews, favoured the general Jewish ideal of self-improvement. The results were first seen in university attendance. In the 1950s, the proportion of Jewish students at universities was four times greater than that of the population as a whole, though it is unlikely that this gross over-representation survived the general university expansion of the 1960s.

Specific professional and vocational ambitions are still typical. In 1954, it was found that 46 per cent of Jewish males taking up university places did so with the intention of adopting careers in medicine, dentistry, law and accountancy – the so-called 'Jewish professions'. These are all prestigious jobs, with possibilities of high income without sacrificing independence in the establishment of small private practices. The popular career of pharmacist offers the dual advantages of being a professional *and* a businessman. Tradition is evident still in this choice of professions: in those historical periods in which Jews were free to take up high positions in European and Islamic courts, they functioned as physicians, court advisers and financiers, posts which more or less correspond to today's doctors, lawyers and accountants. Possibly the same status and financial motives prevailed then as in modern times. There have been practical considerations too. Until recently, professions in Britain had two kinds of entry barriers: those such as architecture, pharmacy, medicine and dentistry, for which a university degree had long been necessary, and those such as law, accountancy and surveying which, until the late 1960s, one could enter with a school certificate or five ordinary level passes in

GCE, serving articles of apprenticeship on a small stipend for five years. The far longer period of economic support necessary for university training precluded poorer families sending their children into professions requiring it, however much they may have aspired to do so.

## Doctors

The archetypal aspiration of the Jewish parent, the 'my son the doctor' syndrome, can be traced to the high status and mystique of the medical profession as much as the career and financial advantages it offers. Ordinary people are more aware of the work of a doctor than, for instance, an architect, and are of the opinion that a doctor can never be out of work. Medicine attracted the most promising of the upwardly mobile Jews for many years since it epitomized the Jewish theory of human capital. A medical qualification was considered a self-evident guarantee of the ability to earn a living anywhere in the world – an ability which was a primary attraction for an insecure people. This does not, however, detract from the sense of idealism and the humanitarian outlook which motivates most Jewish medical students; nor from the fact that medicine is a totally absorbing career which can dominate one's life and so has much appeal to the Jewish mind. There are material and social benefits to be gained from engaging in worthwhile and respected work, and it is undoubtedly hard for the prejudiced to deny skills necessary to them. But even these considerations were often secondary to the sense of vocation.

Before 1939, the average Jewish doctor was more likely to be in an unfashionable general practice than in a hospital. The extra training that was necessary for specialization and the extra years of deferred income were a barrier to many. The hospital, however, was the ladder for professional promotion to consultant status. At this level it was necessary to have a personal introduction to a well-known consultant for whom one could work. Yet it was common knowledge that some consultants were prejudiced against Jews and supported the unofficial quotas operated by the teaching hospitals. The results were made more severe by Jewish habits of self-protective avoidance: many Jews were not willing to expose themselves to a potentially discriminatory hierarchy. Since the war this situation has changed and the National Health Service now includes a significant number of Jewish consultants.

State grants and scholarships have made postgraduate medical studies more accessible for the economically disadvantaged. However, the distribution of Jewish specialization still bears signs of the legacy of the pre-war situation. There is over-representation, for instance, in gynaecology and paediatrics, and Jews are under-represented in specialities such as neurology and orthopaedics. The breakthrough was earlier in the first case and relatively late in the second. Jewish interest in pure research has meant that a very high proportion of Jewish specialists can now be found lecturing in university medical schools. In fact, medical staff today comprise about 30 per cent of the total Jewish faculty membership in Britain. [. . . .]

## . . . and taxi-drivers

A brewery advertisement recently prominent on London underground trains suggests a package of excuses that a (beer-drinking) husband might use to explain his late arrival home: 'Raining. No taxis. Jewish holiday.' This symbolizes a situation well known among Londoners: the Jewish representation in taxi-driving is estimated at around 30 per cent of the capital's 15,700 licensed drivers. There are also significant numbers in provincial cities with large Jewish populations. Given the trends towards the professions and other high-status spheres and industries, the very large Jewish participation in this service industry might seem anomalous. But certain elements of the history and structure of the trade are in keeping with our general observations of occupational demands.

The hackney carriage trade burgeoned with the economic expansion of the mid-eighteenth century, which brought the growth of towns and a consequent increased demand for public urban transport. The introduction and large-scale use of the motorized cab occurred in the first decade of the twentieth century. This was also a period of Jewish immigration and Jews were able to take advantage of the demand for labour in new fields in which they could compete on equal terms with the indigenous population.

Not only were they able to apply their own skills in open competition but, as newcomers, they had a distinct advantage. London's taxi trade had been officially organized much earlier. A rigorous and controlled examination established by the Metropolitan Police's Public Carriage Office in 1853 tested not only physical fitness and knowledge of routes, but also enquired into the candidate's background and character. Since immigrants did not have police records and their backgrounds were unknown they were accepted on the basis of their good conduct in England. Furthermore, a large proportion of applicants were refused licences on the grounds of convictions for alcoholism – and here the reputation of Jews for sobriety and the fact that few of them have had records of drunkenness must have stood them in good stead. [. . . .]

It is, however, in the structure and day-to-day working of the trade that we can see why, when Jews have branched into new occupations and have adapted traditional ones, they still continue to provide such a large proportion of taxi-drivers. The historical connections still obtain in part. Among Jews and gentiles, taxi-driving is often an inherited taste, like medicine or the sea, where an individual is influenced by father, grandfather or uncles to follow the same career. Several Jewish families are known to have been in the trade for over 100 years. A large part of the attraction, now as a century and more ago, must be the opportunities offered for independence, freedom from routine and supervision. There are also the possibilities (albeit remote) of high earnings in a respectable, honest trade in which one can take pride in having command of a body of knowledge and in which initiative is rewarded. The training is still rigorous and a prospective driver has to find means of support during the twelve to eighteen months it now takes. But once in possession of a licence the driver can choose whether to become a journeyman and work for someone else, hiring a cab on weekly or mileage rates, part-time or full-time, or to 'go mush' and become an owner-driver. There is little to choose between the two, for even a journeyman may select his own working hours and routes and may even keep the cab at home when not in use. There is no questioning of reasons for taking time off, an obvious advantage to the observing Jew. All drivers are classed as self-employed and are responsible for their own income-tax returns and national insurance. Most will 'go mush' at some period in their working lives, buying a cab on their own or in partnership and then forsaking this for the fewer responsibilities attached to working for someone else. This accords well with the Jewish ideal of democratic working arrangements: there is little status difference between being 'boss' or being 'worker'.

A disadvantage of self-employment is the complete lack of security in sickness and old age. Some drivers, therefore, work in the trade only part-time, having a more secure job either at night or daytime. A currently popular second string is a GPO overseas telephonist. On the other hand, taxi-drivers are not subject to any enforceable retirement age as long as fitness can be proved. In 1972, one driver, Jack Cohen, was known to be working at the age of 77. The chances of acquiring great wealth are slight, but taxi-drivers are free to choose whether to work long hours or to sacrifice earnings for the sake of leisure time. The number of taxis parked outside houses in the popular 'Jewish' middle-distance suburbs, such as Wembley or Ilford, testify to the economic potential realized by some 'cabbies'.

The trade itself bears some characteristics of Jewish work patterns, whether because of the large Jewish influence or as factors contributory to its compatibility with the Jewish attitude to work. Taxi-driving in London affords opportunities for gaining status through charitable work, for the mixing of work and social activities, and for the expression of traditional attitudes towards social class. [. . .]

In summary, taxi-driving is the Jewish trade *par excellence*. It offers a wide variety of working relations, relatively easy entry and complete independence. It is democratically organized. It demands initial perseverance to obtain a licence, but then has great scope for initiative and gives maximum financial return for work invested. It can be a full- or part-time occupation, allowing those who seek improvement in material status to use their skills to their own advantage and at their own convenience. From first entry into the trade, the driver has the self-employed status sought by so many Jews. Taxi-drivers are socially classless: earning capacity is open, patterns of residence and consumption can vary accordingly, and the occupation itself encourages social mixing.

## Conclusion

The work attitudes of British Jews continue to reflect the world view and moral values of traditional Jewish culture. Generations of oppression and exclusion have nurtured habits of self-help and mutual support and have maintained boundaries of Jewishness all over the world. The occupational patterns characteristic of Jews have, however, altered according to the opportunities and constraints of different contexts of time and place. Against the general background of social changes in Britain, we have seen the particular move of Jews into and through certain professions and have noted their persistent association with the London taxi trade. [. . .]

## References

Barou, N., *The Jews in Work and Trade*, London, Trades Advisory Council, 1945.
Gartner, L. P., *The Jewish Immigrant in England* 2 ed., London, Simon Publications, 1933.
Wallman, S., 'Kinship, a-Kinship, anti-Kinship: Variations in the Logic of Kinship situations', *Journal of Human Evolution*, No. 4, 1975.

# CHAPTER 2.10

# IMMIGRANTS AND EMPLOYMENT IN THE CLOTHING INDUSTRY – THE RAG TRADE IN LONDON'S EAST END*
### Samir Shah

This study is an attempt to describe and explain the factors affecting homeworking in the clothing industry and the people involved in this kind of work in London's East End. 'Homeworking', producing goods at home for sale outside, is a firmly established method of production in certain trades and goes back to the cottage industry of pre-industrial society. The context of homeworking in the East End is complicated and profoundly affected by the interaction of the 'immigrant factor' with the internal problems of the situation itself. However, the immigrant and the clothing industry are by no means strangers to each other; a complex mixture of tradition, distribution, urban location and formal structure has meant that the industry has had a unique relationship with various immigrant groups as it has grown and developed.

## Homeworking in the clothing industry

The industry has always been labour intensive: its central equipment the sewing machine, and the machinist the major worker. This is as true for firms [. . . .] as for the minor sub-contractor in the East End. For this reason, labour costs are of vital importance to the firm's profits and are therefore very susceptible to the competition from sources of low-cost labour. Much competition is from newly independent countries with vast resources of labour (eg, India, Hong Kong). This labour is utilized in the textile and clothing industries – being labour intensive, they are ideal 'starting' industries for countries with low capital – and the relative low

* The Runnymede Trust, London, September 1975. This is an edited version of the original.

cost of the labour provides serious competition to firms in countries such as Britain. One of the main consequences is pressure to use cheap labour sources within the affected country; and one of the major sources of such labour in Western countries is its immigrant population.

Homeworking as a means of production in the clothing trades has existed since the very beginning of the industry itself. It was a means of supplementing the family income well before the effects of the Industrial Revolution. As early as 1810 dockers' wives had been used for making up clothes for the sailor market. Homeworking was not restricted to the clothing trade; it was used extensively in many of the other East End trades – boot and shoe stitching, match-box making, umbrella covering, sack-making, making of chains, nails, boxes and clay pipes and other things.

It was at this time – the early nineteenth century – that the economic foundations that led to the extensive use of homeworking and the development of the sweating system, were laid. It was at this time that a combination of factors based essentially on the seasonal nature of many jobs, and the decline of certain trades, generated a large unemployed and under-employed male labour pool. This enabled the development of a sweating system. In the clothing trade, this system disintegrated the manufacturing process vertically to a series of relatively unskilled processes to be performed by a captive pool of female labour – forced to work due to the poverty of the job situation for their menfolk.

It was not till the technological innovations of the mid-nineteenth century that the system reached its most extensive and iniquitous form. By the 1860s the trade was feeling significant competition from the cheap, factory production of the provincial towns. These towns could take advantage of local power sources, raw material and – of great importance –had space for development, to take full advantage of internal economies of scale. Homeworking, on the face of it, should logically have diminished as horizontal and vertical integration followed the innovations. Instead, it was consolidated and enhanced, as was the use of sub-contracted labour. Two factors affected the use of space in the East End. Firstly, the growth and rise of London as a centre of a world market for commerce and finance produced a tremendous competition for inner urban space, resulting in high land costs and rents. Secondly, LCC regulation, Building Acts and factory inspection all militated against the development of large factories. The result was that those trades which were suited to mechanization and factory production, and which did not have to be physically close to their markets, tended to move out.

## The special case of the East End clothing industry

The fashion industry differed from other manufacturing processes not only in its need to be physically close to its market, but in one other vital aspect as well. The actual hardware was relatively cheap. Only the band-saw was expensive and needed skilled hands to operate it. Thus it was eminently logical for the wholesaler to cut material and let the rest of the work be done in small workshops and at home. Working at home was particularly advantageous since it cut overheads – rent, lighting, heating, power. The employer could further cut costs by paying homeworkers very low wages, by expanding and contracting his production to suit his demand without having to bear the costs. Homeworking in this form is eminently viable where there is an extensive source of captive (female) labour; and this was indeed the case for the East End of London during the nineteenth century. The decline of some traditional trades (silk-weaving, ship building and associated activity – rope makers, riggers), the growing inward migration from the provinces as well as the chronic surplus of dockers and casual labourers, combined to generate a situation where wives were forced, out of necessity, to work. The East End lacked the regular sources of factory employment for females such as existed in the textile mills of Lancashire and West Riding. The labour force was also immobile: a result of the lack of cheap transport facilities, the lack of information about opportunities elsewhere, the need to maintain personal contacts to obtain employment as and when it was available.

This vast captive female labour force was ideal for the development of homeworking. This was the situation of the East End as the Jewish migration of the 1880s began, adding vast numbers of male and female labour to an already strained economic situation. The homeworking housewife was now in an even worse situation, making homeworking as an economic proposition for employers even more viable. The Jews may have entrenched and reinforced the sweating system but they were not responsible for the start of homeworking, or for the inception of sweated labour. This is a vital point, worth bearing in mind when the present day situation is analyzed.

During the years around the turn of the century a great deal of publicity was given to the scandalous conditions of homeworkers. Although publicity has died down, homeworkers did not die out: the economic viability of the system has maintained itself. Economic conditions may have changed, competition may be from elsewhere, but homeworking is still favoured by employers as an effective means of cutting costs. [. . .]

## Homeworking – extent and scope

It is impossible to estimate exactly how many people are involved in this kind of work. As well as its 'behind closed doors' nature, the seasonal nature of employment, and the high labour turnover, mean that any published figure is of doubtful reliability.

The 'comprehensive' survey by the Clothing NEDC in 1972 estimated a total figure of 13,000 homeworkers (three per cent of the labour force). The report of the Commission on Industrial Relations (CIR) (1974) comes to the conclusion that this figure is low. Over 70 per cent of the employers interviewed by them (who employed homeworkers) did not know of the registration procedure. Added to this was the inadequacy of the definition of homeworker that was used. Their survey indicated some 18,500 homeworkers. The present estimate by the Clothing NEDC is of 28,000 homeworkers (now ten per cent of the total labour force). Even this is likely to be an under-estimate: any official inquiry may only guess at the inaccessible unregistered work that is done. The Low Pay Unit's Report of 1974 (December) quoted a figure from a study by Peter Townsend of poverty in the United Kingdom of up to a quarter of a million people engaged in homework. However this figure includes all types of homeworkers, not just those in the clothing trades.

Although overall the proportion of homeworkers in the clothing industry may be around ten per cent, the regional variations are great. The highest concentration is in the East End. Possibly the best estimation is from firms involved in the trade itself. These interviewed during this enquiry suggested that between 30–50 per cent of all production was through homeworkers. At present homeworkers in the rag trade can be only estimated to number a few thousand, accounting for about 40 per cent of the total production in the East End.

## Jewish migration and the East End

A relationship between these three factors of industry, human group, and physical place was formed during the nineteenth century. [. . .] Suffice it to say that the 'fashion trades' (for it is this sector of the industry which is of major importance in the East End) need to be close to the market. This need is not readily measurable in simple cost terms: fashion by definition is forever changing, and it is vital for the survival of the firms in the area to be sensitive to these changes. It is also a well known sociological phenomenon that immigrants tend to arrive and settle in inner city areas, the so-called 'zone of transition'.

With the arrival of the Jews into the trade, questions of 'sweating' systems were raised. As Stewart and Hunter point out, 'the Jews were made the scapegoat, and were subject to outrageous attacks, even in union journals and by union officials.' James MacDonald, secretary of the London West End Tailors, and secretary of the London Trades Council (1896–1907) is quoted as saying, 'They (the Jews) are certainly responsible for its rapid development. Their fellow Gentiles are not slow to follow the lead, but the Jew can always beat them.' Despite the fact that social historians now accept that the arrival of the Jews was not responsible but coincidental with the worsening of sweating, we can again quote from today's papers: 'a conference . . . as a first step to clear up the Indo-Pakistani sweatshop system which is infuriating East London's tailoring industry.' (*East London Advertiser*, 8 June 1973.) [. . .]

## Asian migration

Although many people in the East End are immigrants by one definition or another, it is the recently arrived Asian community that is most clearly identified with the clothing industry. These communities include enclaves of Punjabis, Gujeratis, South Indians, Pakistanis, Bangladeshis, Ugandan and Kenyan Asians. They form small spatial concentrations throughout the East End – the Bangladeshis and Pakistanis in areas of Tower Hamlets such as Whitechapel, Spitalfields, the Indians further east and north into areas of Newham and Hackney, Islington. [. . .]

1971 Census figures for the East End showed some concentrations of Pakistanis (and Bangladeshis) in areas of Tower Hamlets – Whitechapel, Spitalfields, etc – of Indians in Newham and of both communities in areas of Hackney. The population by birthplace for the three main East End boroughs was:

[. . . .] The elements that constitute the background for the present characteristics of homeworking in the trade can now be clearly articulated:

1. There are now substantial and more attractive alternative forms of employment for the indigenous labour force to homework;
2. As a result of a tight labour market the return is slightly higher;
3. Asian workers are particularly immobile and unaware, and are therefore obvious sources of labour for the fashion trade;
3. Until recently there has been no decline in the fashion trade;
4. The possibilities for budding entrepreneurs to launch themselves with only a small capital are such as exist nowhere else. [. . .]

**TABLE 1**   Population of Three East End Boroughs, 1971

|  | Hackney | Tower Hamlets | Newham | Total 3 Boroughs |
|---|---|---|---|---|
| Total population | 220,280 | 165,775 | 237,390 | 623,445 |
| Of which: |  |  |  |  |
| Total New Commonwealth-born | 25,455 | 11,805 | 20,135 | 57,395 |
| As % of total population | 11.6 | 7.1 | 8.5 | 9.2 |
| **Born in India** |  |  |  |  |
| Males | 1,350 | 1,035 | 3,355 | 5,740 |
| Females | 1,090 | 680 | 2,545 | 4,315 |
| Total | 2,440 | 1,715 | 5,900 | 10,055 |
| **Born in Pakistan** |  |  |  |  |
| Males | 415 | 3,090 | 1,340 | 4,845 |
| Females | 220 | 470 | 685 | 1,375 |
| Total | 635 | 3,560 | 2,025 | 6,220 |
| Indian and Pakistani-born population as % of total New Commonwealth-born | 12.1 | 44.7 | 39.4 | 28.4 |

(Source: *Census of Population, 1971*)

Immigrants are not generally associated with two of the major economic activities of the East End – those of the breweries and docklands. They are found to an extent in the service sector: small grocery shops, greengrocers, etc, as well as catering, restaurants, cafes and so on. By far the strongest association is with the clothing industry. To walk through the East End now, it is apparent that many of the small firms and businesses catering for the 'fashion sector' are owned by Asians. The reason for the present association is again one of immigrant labour responding to an ailing industry.

Overseas competition has been a major problem for the industry but not the only one. It also found a lack of workers from the home labour market to enter the trade. The statistics for October 1973[1] show that there was an acute shortage of labour in the industry as a whole (2,902 unemployed females, with 16,886 unfilled vacancies). The deteriorating conditions of the East End, the higher aspirations of English girls, the raising of the school leaving age have meant that not only is there a shortage of home labour but that the industry no longer attracts the native population.

Although many, of course, do still work in factories the relative disadvantages of the clothing industry are beginning to tell: the poor conditions of work, the piece-rate system of pay, the low level of the pay itself. There appears to be a movement away from factory work itself: as one English machinist who had been in trade for fifteen years said of her daughter, 'she don't want to work in no factory'. The pull of secretarial jobs, of clean offices, is much stronger. Eighty-five per cent of the labour in the industry is female, and the job of machining is seen by white British men as women's work. Thus the home male population, as well as having alternative sources of employment, do not take the jobs of machining (as opposed to cutting, tailoring, etc.).

The immigrant, on the other hand, neither has the luxury of a choice of employment, nor, indeed, is in a position to worry about the 'image' of an industry. She/he has merely entered a trade where there was a demand for labour, and because of the nature of the work, people of low skills and language difficulties could be easily accepted. Since the industry has a unique capacity in enabling people to quickly reach an employer or self-employed status, it has meant that alternative systems of employment (eg based on kinship) have been set up. In this way many of the problems and difficulties faced by immigrants in obtaining jobs through 'normal' channels can be avoided.

Undoubtedly, immigrant workers are prepared to tolerate poor working conditions more because they have to than because they have any particular affinity for them. These conditions are part of the urban fabric of the East End, and the industry needs to be located here. To suggest that the immigrants have generated these conditions is as fallacious now as it was when it was applied to the Jews of the nineteenth century. What is almost certainly the case however is that it is only the arrival of recent immigrants with low expectations and a limited frame of social reference which made it possible to revive the industry, resolve the problems of the East End, and turn the industry into a booming business. [. . .]

## The significance of geographical distribution

The spatial patterning of the immigrants in the East End is of particular relevance to the clothing industry. By their very propinquity the communities strengthen their own cultural norms, which indirectly affects their work behaviour; and by this self-identification and the consequent generation of a closed system, the development of sub-employment structures is strengthened and maintained.

The vital aspect of the cultures of the Asian people is the behaviour and role of women in the broader society. It is neither possible nor relevant to expand on the reasons behind the norms and the many diverse results of it. What is relevant to the industry is that because of it, there is an overall restriction on the mobility of Asian women. The effect of this is that the broad pattern based on stage in life cycle is in some cases totally reversed, while in others the validity of the general relationship is diminished. Thus, for example, with what is the most mobile group in the host society – the young unmarried – the situation is totally reversed in the Indian community (the Pakistani and Bangladeshi communities are heavily male dominated and this group is of insignificant size). As a whole young girls are expected to remain at home, and consequently this group is much more associated with homeworking than factory working. The general effect on the other life cycle groups is one of constant pressure to work at home. It is still an accepted norm for most Asian families that women remain at home whilst the husband is the actual breadwinner. However, in a situation such as the East End, the impoverishment of most immigrant families makes it essential for the wife to work and make a substantial financial contribution to the home. To work at home, then, is in many ways a compromise between cultural factors and economic necessity.

[. . .] The basic reasons behind the current heavy involvement of the Asian community in the clothing industry thus boil down, basically, to a limited choice of job alternatives. An immigrant is restricted in choice by two factors – that of colour and language. Thus the West Indian is restricted by white employers' antipathy to colour, the Cypriot by language difficulty. The Asian suffers from both these factors and consequently finds himself with the least choice in employment. This lack of choice is resolved in two ways. One is by working in 'poor quality' jobs which have been, on the whole, rejected by the host society. The second way is to set up an alternative employment structure within the framework of an existing industry and have recruiting patterns within their own community.

This second approach is only manifest in situations where the industry is sufficiently disintegrated to enable individuals with limited capital but with access to sources of labour to start an economically viable business. The rag trade is the classical example of such an industry. Indeed, it is possible to start a business with nominal capital, needing only to know a few machinists prepared to take up some work and a manufacturer able to supply material. One further advantage of the industry is that the basic skills required for low class work are easily learnt. To the Asian immigrant himself, setting up a business is almost second nature since many of them were small businessmen in their country of origin – this is particularly true of the Gujeratis and the East African Indians. The success of their entry into the industry has been the result of their ability to respond to certain problems facing the East End trade, and by efficiently solving them, they have consolidated and strengthened their position. The major problem was the need to cut costs of manufacture due to severe competition of low priced goods from overseas. Not hampered by vested capital interest, the Asian communities have been capable of generating an economic system with low overheads to produce goods at competitive prices. Their prodigious development in recent years attests not only to their high degree of efficiency and work potential but also to their successful setting up of an alternative employment system based on kinship and community networks. The very success of this alternative system emphasizes the failure of the 'normal' employment structure to cater for the immigrant population. It is a sad indictment of the inefficacy of social change with regard to minority groups that the reasons why this latest group of immigrants are involved in the rag trade are essentially similar to those which apply to the nineteenth century Jewish groups; and equally sad to note that the reaction of the host society (which now, ironically, includes the descendants of those Jews) is one of similar intolerance and spurious accusations.

One final point needs to be made about homeworking and the Asian immigrants. It is fortunate that the work situation in the East End is such that homeworking is a necessary and major means of production, since at the moment it is complemented by the cultural requirements of the immigrant community. However, as assimilation occurs and attitudes change, especially those of the younger generation, the lack of alternative forms of work will create antagonism and conflict.

## Note

1. Leila Maw: *Immigrants and Employment in the Clothing Industry – The Rochdale Case*, Runnymede Trust, 1974.

# CHAPTER 2.11

# BUSINESS ACTIVITY AND THE SELF-EMPLOYED*
### Sheila Allen, Stuart Bentley and Joanna Bornat

The importance of self-employment within the general employment structure of Bradford's coloured community was recognized at the time of drawing up the sample of interviews with workers. As our analysis of data progressed the significance of self-employment grew in our estimation. Many of those interviewed saw self-employment as a highly desirable goal and although for most of these the ownership of a business would necessarily remain a dream, others were obviously preparing by saving money to launch themselves into some type of business activity. The existence of Asian businesses in Bradford provides a wider perspective to employment since it indicates an independent social and economic structure which has developed with the arrival of Indian and Pakistani workers and their families in Bradford. In addition, as has already been pointed out, these provide a source of employment, not only for those newly arrived whose inadequate knowledge of English may provide an obstacle to securing a job, but also for the second generation and for those women who seek office or retail jobs which are denied them by white owned business.

At the time of the interviews there were no West Indian owned businesses in Bradford. One or two were known to have been started, but these had not survived. No West Indian businesses existed in Bradford in 1969. One factor may be the relatively small size of Bradford's West Indian population of approximately 2,000. However Bradford's 5–6000 Ukranians, Poles and other Eastern Europeans are

* An edited version of Chapter 8 of *Work, Race and Immigration* (Allen, S., Bentley, S. & Bornat, J.) University of Bradford School of Studies in Social Sciences, 1977.

able to support a wide variety of businesses including clubs, hairdressers, tailors and foodstores.

The greater similarity between West Indian and English consumer cultures may preclude the development of a separate market. Food remains an important exception, however, and many Asian owned shops now stock imported foodstuffs basic to West Indian cooking.

More significant may be an explanation based on the social composition of immigrants from the various countries. Most West Indians are of working class or peasant origin without access to the capital necessary for the establishing of a business. By contrast many Indian and Pakistani businessmen operating in the United Kingdom had previously owned businesses in their home countries. These traders came in fairly distinctive numbers at least until the Labour Government restrictions of 1965 were brought into operation. Thus a network of capital sources had been set up within the Asian communities. In addition the trader class is dominated in the West Indies by people of European and Chinese origin. There is no such ethnic differentiation in India, Pakistan and Bangladesh.

These arguments must all be treated with some care for although West Indians do not seem to have emerged as businessmen in the British Isles they did so in Harlem where they became well known for their success. [. . .]

Physically, the location of Asian businesses in Bradford has certain characteristics. The vast majority are situated in the areas of densest settlement, that is, in the areas of oldest working class housing and of decaying nineteenth century upper class housing within a mile of the city centre. There are three main areas of such settlement, in each of which a particular group from the home areas tends to predominate. For example those living in the Leeds Road area are predominantly Sikhs from the Punjab. In the Little Horton and Great Horton Road area West Pakistanis and Indians from Gujerat predominate. The area between Lumb Lane and Manningham Lane is mixed with people from many parts of the Commonwealth living together; however, in one area within these boundaries Bangladeshis have mainly settled. The owners of the businesses in these areas naturally follow these distinctions since they provide, as grocers, butchers, barbers, travel agents and publicans, the services required by those who have settled in Bradford. Not only are the businesses related to the needs of the citizens in these areas, they are also closely dependent in other ways. For example, sources of finance and sites for businesses in many cases are provided entirely from within the community and independent of any white resources. The range and evident viability of the businesses reflects the extent to which this community has rooted itself as a separate almost self-sufficient entity within Bradford. The reasons for this separation are many. Some businesses quite obviously provide services which white equivalents may not provide, for example in clothing and foodstuffs. However, the development of a separate business community in many ways reflects the real social and economic separation of coloured people in Bradford as a result of discriminatory practices in the providing of such services as entertainment, car-hire, laundries and mortgages. This is not to suggest that Asian businessmen are any more or less altruistic than their white counterparts. Several of those interviewed who are self-employed and, indeed, many of the would-be businessmen in the workers' sample, mentioned that the existence of a coloured community offered good prospects for profit making.

Twenty-nine businessmen from India and Pakistan were interviewed. These businesses were divided into seven groups according to the type of business pursued. (See Table 1.)

**TABLE 1**

| Types of business | Number in each group |
|---|---|
| Public houses | 2 |
| Restaurants and cafes | 5 (3 cafes; 2 restaurants) |
| Personal services | 6 (1 launderette)<br>(1 tailor)<br>(4 hairdressers) |
| General services | 5 (3 travel agents)<br>(1 estate agent)<br>(1 school of motoring) |
| Food | 7 (3 grocers)<br>(3 grocers and butchers)<br>(1 grocer and wines and spirits) |
| Entertainment | 1 (Film and social club) |
| Electrical goods | 3 (including televisions, radios and photographic equipment) |

These divisions are approximate since there is a certain degree of over-lapping. For example, two of the travel agents also sold electrical goods as side lines.

## Occupational experience of the respondents

[. . .] Taking occupations before arrival in England, it is interesting to note that of the 29 respondents, five were in agriculture and of these, two were also traders. The largest group, twelve, had been businessmen trading in transport services, hairdressing and general goods. In addition, two were managers, one had been a bank manager and the other a hotel manager. Two other respondents gave their occupations at home as 'dyer' and 'weaver'. It is possible that these also could have been self-employed since it is not uncommon in the Indian sub-continent for dyeing and weaving to be carried out on a self-employed basis. In all, of the 29 businessmen in the sample, at least sixteen, including the two managers and the two former traders, were already involved in business activity of some type before their arrival in England. This is over half and suggests that the decision to enter self-employment is not determined only by experiences in England. Four of the remaining eight entrepreneurs had been in some form of white collar or professional employment previously. Two had been teachers, one a reader in court and the other a clerk with the Revenue Board. The remaining four comprised a merchant seaman, a soldier, a student, and a respondent who did not give his occupation at home.

In general it appears that in contrast to the major sample of workers relatively few of the self-employed sample were engaged in agriculture before coming to England, fewer still were industrial workers.

## Arrival in England: first employment

Looking at occupations in England before self-employment a completely different picture emerges. Of the sixteen in business occupations in India or Pakistan eleven were self-employed from the beginning, seven of these within a matter of days or weeks. Eleven worked in mills, factories and in transport, and four more in transport alone, that is, as bus conductors or for British Rail. Of the remaining three, one gave his occupation as teacher, one as a sales representative and another gave no indication at all. Thus fifteen of the men on arrival in England took up employment as industrial workers in contrast to both their occupation at home and at the time of interviewing. For these there was a complete break in employment experience varying in length from a matter of months to a decade. Of the eleven who were self-employed from the beginning no less than six continued in the same line of business as they had pursued at home. Apart from the cafe proprietor the others, a tailor and four hairdressers carried on business activities which call for a specific skill and can be started relatively easily because of the low overheads involved. They are also, it should be noted, personal services for which there is likely to be a constantly high demand from within the community not only because of language difficulties but in order to provide insulation against discrimination. [. . .]

Seventy-nine per cent of the businessmen interviewed arrived in Bradford before or during 1962. Although arrival in Bradford need not necessarily have followed immediately after entry into Britain, there does appear to be a distinct tailing off after 1962, the year of the Commonwealth Immigration Act. However, although a majority of the would-be businessmen arrived in England before 1962, the period of highest immigration to Britain from India and Pakistan, more actually began business activities after 1962.

Seventeen of the 29 businessmen started up after 1962 and twelve before 1962. This may have been due to the growing population but was probably accentuated by the 1962 Act of Parliament which restricted entry and movement between Britain and the Commonwealth. This Act led to increased entry figures in the year immediately preceding it as many anticipated the restrictions. It also meant that many migrants considered a longer, more settled stay, with families joining them rather than the more mobile conditions of pre-Act days. The more certain growth of separate institutions in which business plays a definite part must be seen in relation to the beginnings of legal separatism through the creation of distinctive entry categories for Commonwealth migrants.

Other factors, apart from the size of the potential market in demographic terms determine the time at which a business is set up.

Although as many as nine businessmen were able to begin activities within a year of arriving in Bradford, for the remaining twenty, some time had to elapse first. Of the nine early beginners, five were of the personal service type. It has already been suggested that this type of business may not require an expensive outlay initially, this is particularly the case with hairdressing and tailoring. Otherwise no very great difference between the types of self-employment is discernible except for electrical goods which appear to have required one to two years of preparation and in addition did not feature early on in the self-employment structure.

**TABLE 2**   Sources of Finance

| | Number of businesses (n = 29) | Self-financed: savings | Friends and relatives | Personal business contacts | English bank | Home country bank | other |
|---|---|---|---|---|---|---|---|
| Restaurants and cafes | 5 | 4 | 4 | 1 | | | |
| Public houses | 2 | 2 | 1 | | | | |
| Personal services | 6 | 3 | 5 | | | | 1 |
| General services | 5 | 2 | 3 | 2 | 1 | 2 | 2 |
| Food | 7 | 7 | 5 | 2 | 1 | | 1 |
| Entertainment | 1 | | 1 | 1 | | | |
| Electrical goods | 3 | 3 | 2 | 1 | 1 | | 1 |
| TOTAL in each category | 29 | 21 | 21 | 7 | 3 | 2 | 5* |

* of which 3 were hire purchase terms

## Financing business activity and acquiring sites

Capital is a basic requirement for self-employment and therefore the question of finance is obviously central to any business undertaking, however small. The sources of finance are set out in Table 2. The categories are not exclusive of one another since any one respondent may have had more than one source of finance available to him and the total number for each category is given. What is immediately apparent is the extent to which businesses were financed from within the community itself. Self financed savings were mentioned 21 times by respondents. The only respondent not to have relied on this source at all was the businessman in the entertainment industry. Friends and relatives appear to be equally important as sources of finance for business activity. These first two together, which may be termed personal as opposed to institutional, were thus the most frequently used sources of finance. In contrast, banks, both English and Pakistani appear to have played a relatively small part in that they were used only five times as against the 42 'personal' sources. The establishment of branches of Commonwealth banks is related to some extent to the development of the Asian business community itself. The first branch was not opened in Bradford until 1965[1] and this may account for the small part they played in the initial financing of businesses. Of the three respondents who obtained help from an English bank, two were Indians. They were less likely to approach the Pakistani banks and no Indian banks existed in Bradford.

There appears to be little relationship between the type of business and the source of finance enlisted. The sources internal to the community (cols. 1–3) were used for all types of business activity but there is a slight tendency for those in general services (including estate agents, travel agents and driving schools), food and electrical goods to rely less exclusively on this form of finance. The one business concerned with personal services which used external finance was a launderette. This type of activity requires a substantial initial outlay and sufficient financial support may not be possible from within the community itself. Moreover the possibilities of increasing the scale of all the business enterprises are obviously related to the potential for attracting capital from sources outside the immediate community. The business activity, marked as it is by internal financing, at the time of our survey, may be expected to remain on a fairly small scale unless external capital is sought and available.[2] [. . .]

Of equal importance to any would-be businessman is the possibility of finding and securing a suitable site from which to pursue his business activities. The geographical distribution of Asian businesses in Bradford has already been discussed. This tendency to concentrate does not adversely affect would-be businessmen since in general their clientele lies within these areas. In addition it is likely that within these areas property which is owned by fellow-countrymen may be easier to buy or rent. Outside these areas, where white ownership predominates, problems can and do arise. Valerie Karin discusses the difficulties faced by would-be house-owners from India and Pakistan in a town similar to Bradford.[3] In doing so she highlights features which businessmen must equally have to face. She finds that within the areas of densest black settlement demand for property was very high but that opportunities were restricted by '. . . income, racial prejudice and the desire to avoid its expression, ignorance of the market and preference for a close community life. . . .'[4] Only six of the 29 interviewees said that they had had any problem in finding a site for their business.

Most criticism was levelled against estate agents, both for their alleged discriminatory attitudes and for their exclusion of these businessmen from one particular type of property, namely newly constructed developments in the city. A cafe owner remarked, 'I have noticed that immigrants are not encouraged when they apply for premises in newly constructed buildings. Sometimes very high rates are quoted to discourage us. Colour is considered a shortcoming to get good premises'.

Another cafe proprietor felt that there was 'planned discrimination' in the allocation of newly constructed lettings. Much of the criticism of estate agents was direct and bitter. One grocer and butcher felt that 'We are extremely and obviously discouraged when we go to English estate agencies; it is the same case with loan advancing bodies. Had there been any encouragement from such people we should have been in a better position today. In business we come across several types of discrimination, which are not covered by any government regulations.'[5]

A hairdresser was also quite explicit in the direction of his criticisms: 'It is still very difficult for us to get proper places in the city to expand our business. The English landlords come out with lame excuses and hypocritical attitudes. Various estate agents do not consider us suitable for the property they sell.' [. . .]

These were all minority views within our sample although forcefully put. In addition no particular type of business appears to have faced more difficulties than any other in finding a site.

Property was obtained in a number of ways but the majority bought their properties from English owners. For ten of the thirteen who had done this there had been no problems. Those starting up in their own or friends' houses were the next largest category and these cannot strictly be considered as having been in the market for property. They, not unexpectedly, said that they had found no obstacles. Only two had bought from a fellow countryman with a third buying from a West Indian owner. This does not bear out the popular conception that in areas of greatest coloured settlement the ownership, particularly of the most suitable properties for business activities, is already in the hands of members of that community.

Various forms of opposition had been encountered apart from those of the estate agents, but the great majority of the 29 businessmen met with few problems when establishing their businesses. Only four respondents had encountered opposition from other traders and three from English businesses.

The only type of business to meet more opposition than other types was the general service category.

## Customers

The extent to which Asian businesses are patronized by members of different communities is a matter of some interest to those concerned with the developing patterns of social interaction. When they are used mainly or exclusively by coloured groups they indicate an increasing separation from the white society. Moreover where such separation exists the proposition that cultural differences account for it assumes that such businesses serve only their own ethnic group. It is worth examining this in order to clarify how far such differences affect the situation. In explaining the development of separate institutions the factors of colour and culture need to be separately treated. As was mentioned above, the explanation may be partly cultural in those cases where a specific good or service is provided only within a culturally homogeneous group. However it may be the result of discrimination where the same goods and services are available in the white community; that is, either coloured customers prefer to use non-white shops or they are discouraged from seeking goods and services in the wider community. Or again it may indicate a more enterprising attitude on the part of Asian businessmen to the potentiality of new markets as when, for instance, Asian businessmen cater for West Indian food habits.

Our data was collected only from businessmen and we do not have evidence from the customers of their experiences and preferences. This limits the conclusions we are able to reach on the extent to which the various communities rely on their own businesses to supply their needs for different goods and services and the contribution made by any one of the particular factors outlined above.

Each respondent was asked to estimate the proportion of his customers who were coloured and, of these, what percentage were from his own home area. Only one businessman who owned a launderette estimated that he had about 50 per cent coloured and 50 per cent white customers. All the other businesses had, in the estimate of their owners, a majority of coloured customers. Seventeen thought that all their custom was with them and the remaining eleven put the percentage at 71 or more. Estimates of the percentage of these customers who were from their own home areas reveals a much less uniform pattern. Only three respondents, each with a different type of business, thought that their customers came exclusively from their own home areas. Nine more thought that their customers were mainly from their home areas. The largest single group of respondents, twelve, had only a minority from their own home areas.

The evidence shows clearly that the businesses cater mainly for coloured customers but not on the whole drawn exclusively from their own group. In this sense they can be seen to be serving whole communities rather than catering predominantly for specific cultural needs.

There does appear to be some distinction on this point between different types of business. Thus the two service categories appear to have more customers from the home areas than the other types of business although two of these provide mainly for other groups. Nevertheless in personal services it is to be expected that a heavier concentration would be found particularly where different languages are involved.

The interviewees had relatively little to say on the subject of customers. Only two, both the publicans, indicated that a lack of English customers was a problem. For many businessmen English custom may not be missed, while for others again this absence may be something which they do not care to admit. One publican said, 'Some English people come in and when they find me at the counter they just go out.' The other said, 'English customers don't like to come into an immigrants' public bar.'

## Employees

The businessmen interviewed either worked on their own, had help from their wives, or employed a small number of paid employees. The majority had not encountered difficulties in getting people to work for them but, of those who had, two mentioned specifically that skin colour was a factor. A publican who needed a barmaid said that people he contacted declined when it became know he was Indian. A butcher-grocer who wished to extend his business activity found that he 'still could not get English people to work as shop assistants, so that I cannot expand my business in the English population.' A hairdresser who worked on his own said that he had difficulty in finding people to work for him because, 'very few Pakistanis . . . know this trade.' This problem of skill was also mentioned by the fourth respondent who had difficulties, but he was not looking for a member of any particular ethnic group. He was the joint owner of a driving school and said 'I could not get a qualified driver. I taught them first and they qualified . . . and now work for me.' There is thus some indication that when attempts are made to go outside the coloured community difficulties are met, but as yet the situation has not arisen for most of the businessmen who are running small businesses.

Two businessmen, a restaurant owner and a hairdresser, while not indicating specific difficulties, mentioned the general problem of staff shortages. They had each hoped to bring a brother to this country. In both cases permission had been refused by the authorities. The hairdresser could not understand why he had not been allowed to bring his younger brother to work in his shop since he was in real need of assistance, and in this way he would have been responsible for him and, 'he won't be any burden on the government'. The previous year when he had been home to Pakistan for six months his shop had to be closed. He estimated that this had entailed a net loss of £800.

For the 25 businessmen the average number of employees was just over two per enterprise. The largest employer, a restaurant owner, had seven people working for him. Most of the employees were men, 54 as against nine women. Six of the women were white, one a West Indian and two Asian. No white men were employed. The majority of employees were male relatives, or other men from the same ethnic group. The tendency to employ their own kin or people known personally is a situation commonly found in very small scale business enterprises in any community.

All the respondents were married but only ten had the help of their wives in their businesses. Thirteen of the 29 wives were still in India or Pakistan and the remaining six did not work. In addition, therefore, to the two Asian women employees few other women were engaged in an unpaid capacity to work in the family business.

All but one of the respondents had children and most of these were in England. Given the age range of the sample the majority of the children were of or below school-age. Altogether, of the 69 sons and daughters in England only twelve helped their father and this was largely on a part-time basis.

## Conclusion

Since these interviews took place the development of an Asian business community in Bradford has proceeded rapidly. Not only has the number of businesses increased in any particular group or type of business, but also business ventures of a wide variety of types have been launched. The insurance and banking side has developed independently of white companies of this nature. In addition estate agents have become firmly established in the community. One business section not dealt with in this chapter is the wholesale trade. For many retailers the wholesaler is a nationally based business concern. It would be an almost impossible task to discover the extent of Bradford's Asian business community's wider and more international activity. This study has, of necessity, confined itself to the most public and small-scale enterprises. However, they represent a section which plays a vital part in Bradford's non-white social structure.

Advice to would-be businessmen and a suggested means of development was proffered by the oldest interviewee in the sample. A grocer and butcher, originally from Pakistan, he was 57, had come to Bradford in 1948 and worked in a foundry for eight years, finally setting-up in business in 1956. From his lengthy experience he observed: 'We should not start business unless we are financially secure, with clean premises and a team of good shop assistants. We should try to establish businesses in city centres and on a large co-operative basis to compete with English fellow businessmen.'

## Notes

1. This does not mean of course that such banks were not already represented by agents working individually.
2. An item in the local press is an indication of the possible links. The Lord Mayor welcomed the Indian High Commissioner's proposal that Indian-owned and financed manufacturing enterprises should be set up in Bradford, *Telegraph and Argus*, 30th January 1970.
3. Valerie Karin, 'Property values among Indians and Pakistanis in a Yorkshire Town', *Race*, 1969, vol. 10, pp. 269–284.
4. *Ibid.*
5. This was in the days before the Race Relations Act. However it is unlikely that the institutionalized discrimination described by our repondents could have been checked by this Act to any great degree.

# SECTION 3

# BLACK WORKERS AND THE TRADE UNIONS

# INTRODUCTION

In Chapter 2.3, Brooks refers to the initial apprehensions of London Transport workers that the incoming black workers would be neither good trade unionists nor supportive if industrial action were taken. These apprehensions were stilled by experience of industrial action to which black and white workers devoted indistinguishable levels of effort and support. This experience appears, for want of contrary evidence, to have been general, but by the early 1970s a number of well publicized strikes had led to the raising of the question of whether the presence of black workers brought an additional dimension to the nature of industrial conflict. Were relations between black and white workers likely to be a significant and separate source of disputes and a complicating element within disputes about wider issues, either of which might increase the extent of strike activity and of social conflict more generally?

Stuart Bentley (Chapter 3.1) sets out to establish whether race – or colour – is a central issue within a significant number of disputes but concentrates on the difficulties that face attempts to provide a conclusive answer. Industrial conflict is manifested in a variety of forms and along many dimensions. It would be surprising not to find at least some conflicts, expressed through strikes or otherwise, that were not articulated in terms of conflict between groups of black and of white workers, just as one encounters disputes between groups of workers divided in other ways such as by occupational boundaries or by the divisions of functional responsibility which may result in conflicts between managers. But are conflicts between ethnic or racial groups in some way different? At one level the answer lies in the way in which the nature of industrial conflict is viewed. It tends to be seen either in terms of discrete unrelated issues of conflict or as issues which have a common origin in the conflict between the owners and producers of wealth. If the latter view is taken then racial conflicts, to the extent they occur, are part of the underlying pattern of conflict. The former view, however, places emphasis on establishing the causes of disputes to identify the extent to which race is an issue.

The problems facing accomplishment of this are several and consider-able. Researchers have great difficulty in gaining access to all parties and of achieving an understanding of the real meanings attached to events by the participants. The published statistics, whether prepared by the Department of Employment or the Commission for Racial Equality (the Race Relations Board when Bentley wrote) either do not collect appropri-ate information or are incomplete. The only form of conflict on which the Department of Employment collects data is strikes – atypical of industrial action – and the listed possible causes for strikes do not extend to the possibility of race related issues. The Race Relations Board figures, like those of the Commission for Racial Equality show only reported cases of discrimination, generally held to under-represent the extent of discrimina-tion. The most significant problem however is probably the way in which disputes are reported in the media. This is dominated by perception of what is 'newsworthy' and by the values brought by reporters to define the issues. The interest of journalists is often in the short-term issues and, since race is held to be newsworthy, this aspect, as Bentley shows, has at times been drawn out even where it is of no relevance to the underlying issues around which a dispute has developed.

An example illustrating the latter point is provided in Chapter 3.3 where Miles and Phizacklea consider the issues raised by the strike at the Grunwick Film Processing Laboratories in 1976. The company was close to the model of the secondary firm developed by the dual labour market theorists. The strikers were doubly disadvantaged in that most were female and 80 per cent were Asians, mainly from East Africa. Miles and Phizacklea find the factors of sex and ethnicity to be irrelevant both in terms of the immediate issues of pay and recognition and in traceable longer term causes. The dispute was related to central areas of trade union concern yet the issue of race was nonetheless drawn out, not significantly by the press on this occasion, but by some of the external activists.

The Grunwick article also draws out a rather different emphasis on the issue of colour by Apex, the union organizing the strikers who saw the dispute as an opportunity to advance a more positive policy towards black workers. This reflected a significant shift in the policies of the TUC towards black workers which took place in the period before the Grunwick dispute. The nature of this change is examined by Miles and Phizacklea in a further article (Chapter 3.2). Before the mid 1970s, the General Council of the TUC and Congress itself had been firm and consistent in their opposition to racialism but had otherwise scrupulously avoided involvement in most of the issues raised by the arrival of black workers. As Miles and Phizacklea describe elsewhere[1] the perspective which prevailed in the TUC up to 1974 was that black workers did not face special problems. Their problems were essentially those of the workforce as a whole. There was a rejection of the notion that British born workers might hold racially prejudiced views or be prepared to discriminate against black workers. To the extent that black workers were acknowledged to face difficulties these, with the exception of language, were regarded as resulting from different customs and practices. Once 'British ways' became widely adopted by black workers and they then became integrated into the workforce, any difficulties would disappear.

The view that any difficulties were the result of incomplete integration was in effect to oppose tolerance of diversity in culture, an approach with uncomfortable parallels to the goal of racial homogeneity. It also provided a justification for support of immigration control since integration was being retarded or reversed by too great an inflow of minority workers.[2] Clearly the issues were incompletely thought through. While adopting an anti-racialist stance there was a downplaying of evidence that discrimination in employment did occur, such as was provided in the 1966 PEP studies.[3] In addition to accept immigration control which was discriminatory in its implications, was, as in the wider political system, to concede to and legitimate pressures which encompassed a racialist element. Why, given the formal stance, was this path taken? The answer may lie, as Miles and Phizacklea suggest, in the fear of a white backlash if more positive action were undertaken and in the hope that racism might go away if left undisturbed.

One of the dangers of examining the TUC is of course that its policies are not those of individual unions or of groups of unions nor can TUC policies be enforced. But the TUC is not a monolithic body and there was a consistent body of criticism within the TUC during the period up to 1974. Miles and Phizacklea explore the basis of opposition and see this as one of three factors producing the shift in policy between 1974 and 1976. The other factors they identify are the inescapable evidence of racial issues as significant in the Imperial Typewriter and Mansfield Hosiery disputes – also discussed by Bentley; and the effects of National Front activism within trade unions as well as in national and local politics.

During the 1974–76 period the TUC shifted from its passive integrationist policy towards recognition that trades unionists and union officers might support, implicitly or otherwise, discriminatory policies, acknowledged the extent and significance of black disadvantage and accepted that there was a need for active policies to combat the problems. The response, predictably, was partly organizational – establishing new sub-committees – but extended into collective bargaining and drew the TUC into active campaigning against racialism nationally and on a wider scale than the operations of individual trades councils prior to 1976. It also encompassed a fresh look at the implications of immigration policy – but did not prevent the TUC lobbying successfully in 1976 to exclude shop stewards from liability to prosecution under the 1976 Race Relations Act. It is difficult to evaluate the significance of the changes in TUC policy – for the reasons outlined by Bentley – although clearly they are significant. The changes discussed in Chapter 3.2 are further amplified in Chapter 3.4 in which the reasoning behind TUC policy is set out in a special conference document.

## Notes and references

1. The TUC, Black Workers and New Commonwealth Immigration, 1954–73, R. Miles & A. Phizacklea. SSRC Working Papers on Ethnic Relations no. 6, 1975.
2. Miles and Phizacklea (op cit.) They also point out that this concern for integration and fear of the establishment of culturally self sufficient groups did not extend to groups such as the Irish.
3. PEP: *Racial Discrimination*, 1967.

# CHAPTER 3.1

## INDUSTRIAL CONFLICT, STRIKES AND BLACK WORKERS: PROBLEMS OF RESEARCH METHODOLOGY*
### Stuart Bentley

'The increasing number of coloured immigrant employees in Britain has brought a growing number of instances of industrial conflict which are apparently complicated by a racial element.' (George Bain, Hugh Clegg, Allan Flanders.[1])

Strikes involving black and immigrant workers are an undeniable feature of the contemporary British industrial scene. At first sight it would appear that the lobbyists who successfully argued for restricting black immigration to Britain in the late 1950s and throughout the 1960s are being vindicated, at least in the very important sphere of industrial relations. Their argument was, it will be recalled, based partly on the grounds that the alien culture of the newcomers constituted an unassimilable wedge within the (relatively) homogeneous native culture; instability and social conflict would inevitably follow.

In this article and elsewhere, on the other hand, my aim is to challenge the view that the explanation for black and immigrant groups' involvement in conflict in industry is to be sought in the clash of cultures and the incompatibility of disparate normative orders. On the contrary, the initial assumption is that the reasons for this type of conflict in industry, like others, are to be sought in the structural configurations of the workplace, and, at a societal level, in the class formations within the structure of capitalist society. One does not assume *a priori* that the role of group norms, the ideas and values of different groups in conflict situations is that of a determinant in structuring conflict. Here, I shall approach these

* An edited version of an article from *New Community*, vol. V, 1–2, 1976.

questions by raising some of the methodological difficulties which are encountered in conducting research in this area of sociology, and which call into question the assertion by Bain, Clegg and Flanders at the head of this article.

## Methodological issues

Methodological issues in sociological texts are usually consigned to an appendix and that position seems accurately to reflect the importance which is accorded to the issues themselves: if methodological issues are not an afterthought then it appears that they are of minor importance. I suggest, on the other hand, that the links between methodology and conceptual frameworks used in analysis are more intimate than their separate and differential emphasis and treatment in the literature suggest. Particularly, I would argue that structural constraints on the researcher's role reinforce two tendencies already present in the theoretical models. Firstly, there is the tendency to conceptualize strikes and by extension, industrial conflict, as discrete and aberrant events, which have a beginning, a middle and an end. Moreover, a single, or, rarely, a set of causes can be identified and catalogued. There are a number of consequences of such a historical conceptualization of strikes and their causes, and of industrial conflict in general, of which the identification of the outside agitator as the cause of strikes is but one, albeit the most well-worn of single-cause explanations.

Secondly, there has been a tendency for analysis of black workers in industry to take as a starting point those features of the newcomers which are socially visible and apparent, such as dietary and religious taboos, language, colour, and systems of kinship. By simply measuring these 'items' against 'items' from the majority group, it has been thought possible to describe the extent of the dissimilarities and to suggest that the divergence provides potential points of conflict. In contrast I would argue quite a different case but first it is necessary to elaborate the structural constraints affecting the researcher and his methods.

## The researcher as outsider

Typically the researcher is an outsider to the industrial workplace. Some strikes, the so-called 'downers' or 'demonstration' strikes, may last only a few minutes or a few hours; indeed the workforce may not even leave the workplace. As a result the outsider would be unaware of the existence of such strikes. There would be no outward sign of conflict: no picket lines, no leaflets, no coming and going of trade union officials, no newspaper men or cameramen, in short, nothing to indicate to the outsider that any interruption was taking place to the normal running of the enterprise. Typically also the researcher is not involved in those informal social networks centred in the pub, the working men's club, and the neighbourhood, where news of such strikes would be brought to his attention. Wellisz, writing of strikes in Lancashire coal mining, regarded the local pub as the most important centre of strike talk; they were also the places where 'most of the problems affecting work conditions are talked over in an informal way'.[2]

If this holds true for demonstration strikes where white workers are the labour force involved, it applies with even greater force where the work force is made up exclusively or mainly of black and immigrant workers, since those groups' culturally and spatially distinct social networks are rarely, if ever, penetrated by white researchers. Not only is this the case outside the workplace, but the researcher as an outsider misses all the other myriad manifestations of industrial conflict which occur in the workplace and which never develop into strikes of even a few minutes or hours duration and hence are masked from the observer's gaze. Individual and collective expressions of resistance to management are as varied as man's imaginative powers can devise. As Clark Kerr puts it:

> The strike is the most common and most visible expression (of conflict). But conflict with the employer may also take the form of peaceful bargaining and grievance handling of boycotts of political action, of restriction of output, of sabotage, or absenteeism, or of personnel turnover.[3]

Similarly with inter-ethnic group conflict on the shop floor, the continuing complaints registered by the Race Relations Board, especially under section 3(b) of the Race Relations Act 1968 referring to alleged discrimination in the terms and conditions of employment, indicate to the outsider the existence of the unseen, and often generally unperceived, effects of men's imaginative powers to place black workers in disadvantaged positions. Where the allocation of tasks and hiring and firing prerogatives are effectively in the control of lower-level management – eg chargehands, timesetters, and foremen – one would have to widen the scope of Kerr's point to include, along with 'the employer', other grades of workers.

## The researcher as partial insider

One solution to these structurally-based problems is for the researcher to become an insider, to adopt, in other words, the role of participant observer by occupying some workaday role in the workplace. Clearly to sustain total identification with one's 'working' role is extremely difficult but to arrange for an extensive period of participant observation in a workplace *prior* to strike is almost impossible and would probably be prohibitive in terms of expense and research personnel. Assuming that such an exercise was possible, however, perhaps as a fortuitous by-product of some other research project for which a participant role had been already established *in situ*, including ethnic matching where appropriate to the 'work' role, the researcher nevertheless remains an outsider in one important, perhaps crucial respect. He is still, in terms of his own experience, removed from the rest of the workforce. He *knows* his workplace role is temporary; he can escape from it and in the meantime he is sustained by a set of values and a professional ideology which perforce distance him from the rest of the workforce for whom neither permanent escape into another occupation nor ideology are realistic alternatives. The point can be illustrated forcefully by asking the question: to what extent would a researcher identify with the slogan 'We will not go back like dogs. This is a fight for our dignity', carried on a banner by striking Asian workers from Mansfield Hosiery Mills? I would hypothesize that it would be a less than total identification.

Given these problems facing the researcher as a participant observer, it is the case that, almost without exception, the researcher arrives on the scene after the beginning, and frequently some considerable time after the beginning, of a strike. This is always assuming of course that the researcher makes an appearance on the scene at all during the life-span of the strike: he may choose instead to place emphasis upon other methods of data collection. Assuming that he does attend during the course of a strike, knowing little or nothing of the detailed internal organization of the enterprise, its productive process, the formal and informal authority relations, the ethnic structure of the work force and so forth, establishing rapport and gaining access to information via one, or more preferably a number, of the various interest groups involved is the initial task. In this endeavour, each of the interest groups – strikers, perhaps non-strikers, management, trade union officials and outside bodies (eg local community relations councils, political groups, ethnic voluntary associations, and High Commission representatives) – presents its own problems. Establishing the legitimacy of one's research role with one group may entail automatic exclusion by others in the sensitive atmosphere of a strike situation. Two studies illustrate these difficulties encountered in gaining access to information.

In Peter Marsh's[4] study of the Woolf's strike, the problem of communicating with strikers performing key roles, namely the shop stewards leading the strike, was solved; but in the process the problem for Marsh became one of getting information from two other important interest groups in the situation, namely the employer and, to a lesser extent, the full-time union officials.

By contrast, Rimmer's study on the effect of ethnic work groups on conflict in industry, illustrates how effectively the monoglot researcher can be excluded by yet another group, in this case the strikers. The researcher relied upon data derived from every interested party – management, white shop stewards, full-time officials of the union and Department of Employment officials – every group that is, except the Punjabi ethnic work-gangs involved in the stoppages![5] For some purposes this method would be perfectly appropriate; determining the various outsiders' definitions of the situation for example. This was not, however, the purpose of the study, which was rather, as Rimmer says, 'to examine some of the effects that ethnic work-units can have upon industrial relations'. This in turn required that the 'growth of normative disorder' and 'the nature of conflict relationships in industry between coloured immigrants, white workers and management'[6] be examined.

To exclude from consideration the meanings which the Punjabi actors placed upon these issues is, I suggest, not to provide sociological explanation of the issues at stake, it is on the contrary to accept every other interest group's definition of the situation as a valid one at the level of explanation. We cannot tell from the study whether or not the Punjabi strikers agreed with the other parties' definitions of the situation: independently one has indications to suggest that in fact they did not. The problem of communication was cited as the reason why it was impracticable to contact the Punjabi workers and, while one would not wish to minimize the relevance of this factor, there are ways around this obstacle as Marsh and others have found.

### Inter-group conflict and the media

The researcher in such a situation is often forced back upon at least partial reliance on inference, hearsay, media reports and other sources of information, all of which of course have an intrinsic, though strictly delimited, validity for one's analysis. If one takes a specific case of the media's handling of one aspect of one strike it will give a glimpse of the pitfalls which yawn before the unwary researcher. During an unofficial strike by Indian and Pakistani textile workers in Bradford in 1967, the figures given in the press for the total number of workers on strike fluctuated widely over time, as Table 1 shows.

**TABLE**   Figures given by newspapers of striking workforce at Robinson and Peel Ltd., Bradford, September 1967

Days in September, 1967

| NEWSPAPERS | 13th | 14th | 15th | 16th | 18th | 19th | 20th | 21st | 22nd | 23rd | 25th | 26th | 27th |
|---|---|---|---|---|---|---|---|---|---|---|---|---|---|
| Bradford Telegraph & Argus | 150 | 70 | 70 | 70 | 70 | 88 | 54 | 54 | 54 | 54 | 54 | 54 | 54 |
| Guardian | | 150 | 70 | | | 80 | 54 | 70 | 54 | * | 88 | 88 | 54 |
| Yorkshire Evening Post | | | | | | 88 | 54 | 54 | 54 | 54 | | | |
| Yorkshire Post | | | | | | 80 | 88 | 54 | | 54 | 54 | 54 | |
| Daily Mirror | | | | | | | 54 | 88 | | * | | 54 | |
| Daily Telegraph | | | | | | 80+ | 60 | 54 | | 88 | | | |
| The Times | | | | | | | 54 | 54 | | | | | |
| Daily Mail | | | | | | | | 54 | | * | | | |
| Sun | | | | | | | | 89 | | 88 | | | |
| Daily Express | | | | | | | | 54 | | 88 | | | |

* figure not stated in the report.

It is only possible to explain some of the discrepancies in these figures in terms of the mechanics of newsgathering, rather than in terms of the progress of the strike. For example, the figure of 150 strikers given on 13 September in the Bradford evening paper, the *Telegraph & Argus* was picked up and used in the following day's *Guardian*. By the evening of that day, however, the *Telegraph & Argus* produced a corrected figure of 70 strikers from information supplied by the employers and this new figure was duly reported in the following day's *Guardian*. Likewise on the morning of 20 September, the Leeds-based *Yorkshire Post* used the total of 88 for the number of strikers, a figure used on the previous evening by the *Telegraph & Argus*. But by that same evening the *Yorkshire Post's* sister paper, the *Evening Post*, was able to report accurately that dismissal notices had been sent out by the employer to the remaining 54 strikers. The *Yorkshire Post* duly followed next morning with this up-to-date figure. Such an explanation cannot however account for the figures quoted in papers which actually showed an increase as the strike progressed (eg the

*Daily Express*) or swung erratically up and down (eg the *Daily Telegraph* and the *Guardian*.) In the latter case the higher figures were produced by reporters sent to replace the shorter and more modest pieces supplied by locally-based free-lance agency reporters. The national newspapers' reporters were not surprisingly confused by the figures of the number of strikers which were being mentioned in connexion with different phases of the strike. The figure of 54, which gained some permanency in most papers, referred to the number of strikers to whom dismissal notices were sent on 19 September; although this figure was used by the various papers up to the 26th as if it referred to the number of workers still on strike, it is certainly an overestimate, as some workers dodged the pickets and went back to work at the same mill or sought jobs elsewhere. Such a development was of minor importance, as the press required a figure to give their readers as a quick, easily understandable reference point.

The figures given by the newspapers, then, reveal as much about the process of news-gathering and the organization of reporting as they reveal about the size of the striking workforce. No such organizational rationale can be found in the way in which reporters handled the reporting of the ethnicity of the strikers. Reports on this score ranged over a wide field, from the neutral 'about 70 men employed' (*Telegraph & Argus*) through '80 Indians and Pakistanis' (*Guardian*) to the more charged '54 coloured textile workers' (*Daily Mail*). Occasionally a single report would contain a selection from this range, but in no case was the reader left in any doubt that the strikers were not white. Thus reports which opened with a neutral description of the strikers, describing them as 'men' or 'employees', continued with the information that the men on strike were 'Pakistanis and Indians'.

It is important here to note that in the early days of the stoppage the strikers' ethnicity was of decidedly minor importance and it was mentioned almost incidentally, especially in the case of the *Telegraph & Argus* reports. But this treatment of the question was not to remain constant and, as the strike continued, and as the mass circulation national newspapers were attracted, the strikers' ethnic identity became the peg on which day-to-day developments were hung. This finding raises the very important question: to what extent may one's perception of industrial conflict in relation to ethnic minorities be said to be affected by reports in the media?

## Media-led bias?

There is the distinct possibility that the media *do* influence one's perception towards a belief that there are in fact 'a growing number of instances of industrial conflict which are apparently complicated by racial elements', to quote Bain *et al.* The explanation both in journalism, as in academic studies, is to be sought in terms of the prevailing socio-cultural beliefs in white society about black and coloured groups. Hugo Young puts this point succinctly.

> Racial stories are news, fundamentally, because they are thought to reflect a general *problem*. Many events are felt to be newsworthy which, if they did not ostensibly have a racial dimension, would simply not be news. Street brawls, overcrowding, rowdy behaviour, employment disputes, housing difficulties – these are among the stories commonly to be found in this category. They would not be in the papers, certainly not in national papers, if they did not contain a racial aspect.[7]

To follow Hugo Young's point, perhaps the reason why a dispute involving immigrant workers in Stornoway made so little impact on the media is to be sought in the ambiguity which surrounded the ethnicity of some of the workforce.[8] They just did not fall neatly into existing categories and the 'racial aspect' was difficult to point up in the story, even though it appeared to fulfil all the other requirements of a news story. This dispute was a bizarre example of the industrial relations problem in British industry, involving a stitch-in at a Harris tweed factory in the remote Outer Hebrides. The shop steward held two degrees, and six of the approximately 40 strikers were Persians: they all belonged to the Baha'i religious sect, and there were rumours that they were proselytizing amongst the local Christians. Immigrants they most certainly were, but were they coloured? The stitch-in collapsed shortly afterwards, and the problem of identifying the colour of this group of immigrant workers and thereby resolving the ambiguity one way or the other, was unnecessary. No such problem, however, existed in the two big and prolonged stoppages in the East Midlands in 1973. At both Mansfield Hosiery Mills Ltd., Loughborough, and Imperial Typewriters, Leicester, the striking labour force was coloured. I suggest that this fact, and the consequent political activity of right-wing groups, more than the strike's duration or the number of workers involved, contributed to its newsworthiness and the attention of the mass media.

That the media seize on this ethnic aspect of a conflict situation as the most significant one for public consumption is borne out by the comments of the general secretary of a trade union in the textile industry. The Managers' and Over-lookers' Society's annual report for the year 1969 contained a paragraph which pointed out that several assault cases had been taken to court by the society where the assailants were '*mainly* immigrants' (my emphasis), and members were 'urged to be very careful when issuing unpopular instructions to immigrants and, if the order is obviously likely to cause resentment, try and arrange for a foreman or manager to be there, or failing that another overlooker'. As the General Secretary commented later in correspondence:

> I would point out that the reference to attacks by immigrant workers forms a very small part of the report, but this was the main item reported in the press. The number of attacks in a year is small but only two or three a year are too many. The main reason for my reference to attacks in the report was to make my members aware of the dangers that exist when dealing with all male labour and to use some tact in a delicate situation.[9]

## Industrial disputes and racial disputes

The views of a trade union official on press reports of the celebrated Woolf's Rubber Company dispute in Southall in 1966 are even more pertinent, since the conflict was expressed collectively in a strike and the strike is still popularly known, in *academic circles no less than in others,* as the 'racial dispute' or the 'Sikhs' strike'; one newspaper at the time even claimed in its headline 'Race riots feared in Southall.'[10]

Writing in the union journal, the National Officer of the General Workers Group of the strikers' union, the Transport and General Workers Union, gave this dispute a different emphasis and at the same time exposed the role of the media in turning an industrial dispute into a racial one:

> There are necessarily disputes which arise in the life of our movement which, due to conflicting press reports, are completely misunderstood by members who are not directly involved. Even those concerned are sometimes in difficulty, in relating various reports with the actual causes.
>
> This statement is more particularly true, when we are dealing with our brothers from other countries and the recent Woolf's Rubber Company dispute was a perfect example of this position.
>
> ### A 'Difficult' Company
>
> We have as a union had quite some difficulty with this company in the past few years, to such an extent that it was necessary for a new disputes procedure to be negotiated.
>
> In view of the language problem it was agreed that workers due to be punished for 'industrial misconduct' should be suspended *on full pay*

pending an enquiry by higher management. When the company suspended a worker for three days *without* pay our members decided to stop work. (emphasis added).[11]

A further source of bias which may enter one's perception of developments in this field is to be found in the type of paper one reads. Whatever type one draws upon, it is almost certainly not one of the dozen or so papers aimed at black and immigrant readers in this country and this fact will further reinforce the researcher's structural isolation mentioned earlier.

One would expect a professional researcher to take precautions against bias from media sources and to apply standard tests to this problem. But, I suggest, only researchers or academics with a specialist interest in this field of inter-ethnic group relations would take such steps, and then only once a project has begun. Academics, no less than the general reader, are subject to receiving the distortions originating in the majority group's prevailing socio-cultural beliefs about black and immigrant groups. Specifically applied to the workplace these beliefs include items such as the belief that the groups are clannish; they are touchy and sensitive about their colour (especially West Indians); or religion (especially Pakistanis); they are unreasonable/ignorant of rules and norms, and as a result are prone to fly off the handle and strike. In short, they are a problem.

But what safeguards can be used to ensure that every dispute in which black and immigrant workers are involved in some, even a marginal way, does not become a 'racial dispute' and hence contribute to the widespread belief that racial disruption in industry is a well-documented fact and also that as a phenomenon it is increasing in incidence? Such conceptualizations, it seems to me, are a shorthand which tells us more about the group that uses it than about the events under discussion.

## Statistical problems

If one turns to published statistical data hoping to find a relatively straightforward resolution to some of the problems of perception and distortion which one has met as an observer on the picket line or as a participant in the workplace or, at the very least, hoping to find an uncomplicated statistical base-line of data from which to work, one's hopes are disappointed. One merely finds that a different set of problems arise instead.

## The Department of Employment

The major authoritative sources of statistical evidence to which one turns are the Department of Employment's monthly statistics on 'Stoppages of work due to industrial disputes'. The problems presented by these statistics will already be familiar ground to researchers who have no particular interest in the role of ethnicity in industrial conflict and one must deal with them first of all, since they are inherent in the data, quite apart from the question of ethnicity and its attendant problems. It goes without saying that, as the heading of the DE's statistics makes clear, the more general issue of conflict in the workplace is unrecorded; indeed by its nature it is unrecordable: and only stoppages of work are counted. By definition, the Department's strike series:

> refers to stoppages which result from disputes connected with terms and conditions of employment and which are of a certain magnitude: those involving fewer than ten workers, or lasting less than one day, are excluded, except where the aggregate of working days lost exceeds 100.[12]

For the Department's purposes, therefore, some stoppages may occur and yet not be included in the monthly count. Thus nine workers on strike for eleven days, or 99 workers on a demonstration strike for less than a full day, would not be caught in the Department's statistical net.

Furthermore, no distinction is made in the statistics between strikes and lock-outs, and it was not until 1972 that information was included in published sources about those stoppages *known* to have trade union official backing. The main classification of stoppages is concerned with cause(s) of stoppages: each stoppage is further classified according to industry, duration of stoppage, workers directly and indirectly affected, and type of workers involved (labourers, production workers, etc.). As the Department recognizes, the analysis of a dispute for a glimpse of its 'main cause' is a tantalizing job, in which not only must a statistically sound system of classification be prepared (eg mutually exclusive categories, comparability of data through time), but it must simultaneously be sufficiently sensitive to capture complex social reality in such a way that no violence is done to the recording of the stoppage's character. The Department argues that the majority of stoppages pose no difficulties, being quite straightforward and having a single, easily identifiable cause: for example 'protest over the inefficiency of heating installations'. In yet other cases, the stoppage may have a 'multi-facet' cause, as in the example of a stoppage resulting from 'dismissal of a union official for refusing transfer to another department'.

In such cases the Department seeks to ensure that a standard set of procedures are followed to ensure that similar cases are consistently dealt with. It is, however, in the relatively small number of cases of the third and last type, the 'multiple cause' type, that the Department's procedures appear to be most open to idiosyncratic distortion. For such cases, the Department retains the final authority to 'decide which is the principal cause and classifies accordingly'[13]

## Classifying the unclassifiable

Inevitably there will be disagreement in the ranks of the parties to any given stoppage about 'the principal cause': the statistician tries to resolve the irresolvable in the light of his experience, the systematic application of standard procedures and so on. It is important to recognize here that the possibility exists that in the definition of the situation, especially a strike situation involving ethnic minorities, with its complex issues of motivation and consciousness, there is likely to be a wide divergence between that given by the Department's officials and that given by the strikers. In short, the officials quite simply are unable to comprehend the issues at stake. The question then is, do these definitions diverge so widely that the statistics are rendered useless?

A further dilemma arises when one considers that the classification exercise is completed *after* stoppage has been concluded, in the light of the complete case material. The initial cause, the precipitating factor, may diminish in significance in the strikers' eyes as other issues emerge. How one assesses these possibly competing factors and weighs them in importance remains problematic. For the purposes of the Department's statistics, perhaps, it is not a significant problem. For the workers with a sense of the history of industrial relations in a given workplace, however, the grievances collected *during* a stoppage may be an important contribution to their consciousness and experiences; hence they may play a role in precipitating the next stoppage, or the next but one. These data, then, have a part to play in the culture of a particular workplace and consequently in the researcher's analysis. But if these are problems facing anyone working with these statistics, then the researcher with a special interest in ethnic group relations faces additional ones.

The first major one is that the ethnic composition of the workforce in a stoppage is not mentioned in published sources. Secondly, one has no way of isolating the factor of ethnicity in the published statistics and thereby assessing its relevance to the cause of a dispute. For example, in the present revised system of classification, introduced with effect from 1 January 1973, the following selected headings *may* relate to disputes where ethnicity is significant to the interested parties, but any ethnic factor is, as it were, buried under other information:

1. Pay-wage rates and earning levels
   - pay increases concerned with differentials within some plant;
   - feared or alleged reductions in earnings whatever the reason;
4. Redundancy questions
   - guarantees against redundancy;
   - 'first-to-go' problems.[14]

This is by no means an exhaustive list of headings from the classificatory system under which ethnicity as a significant factor may become subsumed and rendered invisible, but it is perhaps sufficient to make the point. On the other hand, when the present system of classification for causes of stoppages at work was introduced, one result of the changes was that one, and only one, type of dispute *explicitly* involving ethnicity could be isolated in the statistics. A new code was added to those in class 7 dealing with stoppages caused by disputes about manning and allocation of work. It reads:

> - allocation of jobs to particular individuals, including degree of consultation, *various forms of alleged discrimination* (*other than against a union*), suitability of qualifications or experience, transfer problems, refusals to accept task alloted (except where this leads to dismissal or disciplinary action, which is Section 8) etc. (Emphasis added)[15]

## The invisible ethnic component

The whole question of what we might call stoppages with a statistically invisible ethnic component is not simply an abstract one; this may be gauged by referring to three recent cases of disputes and stoppages and seeing how the DE dealt with them. I do not intend to suggest that ethnicity 'caused' the disputes, merely that the ethnicity of the workers may have been a factor in precipitating the dispute and shaping the course and content of it. The DE statistics are not concerned with this factor and hence ignore it. My examples have been deliberately chosen to illustrate the statistical difficulties mentioned above as they bear upon the main subject of this article. They also enable one to ask other questions of relevance to research in this area.

In May 1974 nurses in the health service took part in a number of restrictive actions, working to rule and so forth, action which fell short of all-out stoppage of work. In the subsequent weeks they followed this up by staging walk-outs and demonstrations throughout the country.

Since the health service is a major employer of black and immigrant workers we assume, and there is no evidence to the contrary, that they took part in the actions alongside their white workmates. Neither type of action is included in the Department's monthly returns: in the first case because they fell outside the Department's definition of a stoppage and in the second, as the Department confessed, because it simply proved impossible to include the walk-outs etc, for statistical purposes.

Alongside these data, one must also take into account the fact that in the mid-1950s hospital branches of the Confederation of Health Service Employees passed resolutions objecting to the recruitment of coloured nurses.[16] All three manifestations of conflict in which ethnic minorities figured, albeit in very different roles – the union resolutions, working to rule, demonstration stoppages – are excluded from the statistical data.

The second example is of a prominent stoppage in 1973 whose cause or object was recorded by the Department as being 'in support of a demand for the reinstatement of a worker, dismissed for alleged attempted assault on a foreman.'[17] The dismissed worker in question was black and he was employed in the frame shop at Ford's, Dagenham. Two weeks before the alleged attempted assault on the foreman took place, the work quota had been raised by 75 per cent. In an effort to meet the new targets, to quote one account, the foreman 'really went after Winston Williams, constantly harassing him to meet the company's target of 714 pieces per shift'.[18] The worker broke down and received treatment in the medical room. He was later sacked and this led to an immediate strike by 180 workers on the same shift. Other workers were then laid off and, since they were not paid for stoppages caused by internal company disputes, the strike assumed a new dimension, at least for some workers, as they argued for lay-off pay along with the reinstatement of the sacked worker. The issue of lay-off pay had arisen earlier in the month when 'workers in the body plant stormed the personnel manager's offices over the same issue and locked him in'.[19] Ultimately 10,000 workers were affected in an official strike which lasted twelve days, during which time 37,000 working days were lost.

A number of questions arise from the two accounts of this dispute. Was the exercise of management authority in this case affected in any way by the ethnicity of the dismissed worker and its assumed relevance for the anticipated actions of other workers and, in particular, of the actions of the union in calling out its members? Was the cause of the strike as recorded by the DE a sufficient explanation of the action of the strikers? Did the issue of lay-off payment, already a source of conflict, play any significant part?

The third case concerns the stoppage at Mansfield Hosiery Mills Ltd, Loughborough. This stoppage received extensive coverage in the media and almost without exception the cause was attributed to the resistance on the part of white workers and the union to the training and promotion of Asian workers. The DE's published statistics simply give the cause of the strike, during which 23,500 working days were lost, as 'for an increase in pay and dissatisfaction over promotion arrangements.'[20] No indication there that the resistance was ethnically based. The DE's specialists in this area firmly quashed the idea that official statistics could be used to infer a connection between discrimination and disputes, recommending that one should rely on direct observation of this issue in stoppages instead.

## The Race Relations Board

One proceeds on the assumption that complaints of racial discrimination, real or imagined, represent incidents of inter-ethnic conflict arising out of competition between groups over the allocation and disposal of highly valued resources. The mechanisms for resolving the conflict within the normal procedures and processes in the workplace having been ineffective, the Board as an impartial third party is called in to arbitrate under the terms of externally devised 'impersonal' legislation.

The published statistics and case studies presented by the Race Relations Board are valuable data for the researcher in this area. What does the Board's evidence say about the inter-ethnic conflict in industry, its characteristics, its incidence and scale?

The Board's information on employment issues is currently drawn from complaints and/or investigations, made under four sections of the Race Relations Act. 1968. They are, firstly, section 3 dealing with various aspects of employment (recruitment, terms, conditions, training, promotion and dismissal); secondly, section 4, dealing with membership and services provided by trade unions and employers' organizations; thirdly, section 17, which gives the Board powers to initiate an investigation where there is reason to suspect that an unlawful act has been committed, even though no individual has complained of a specific act of discrimination; and finally, section 12, dealing with aiding, inducing or inciting a person to discriminate in breach of the Act. This completes the four sections which concern us most.

For the purpose of this discussion, I exclude complaints made under section 6, the clause dealing with allegations of discriminatory advertisements. In the contemporary period, these are not the means typically used to exclude black people from jobs, houses, etc. Since the complaints and investigations made under the Act deal explicitly with discrimination 'on the grounds of colour, race or ethnic or national origin', it would at first sight appear that the rate of complaints, and the number of opinions of discrimination formed by the Board's conciliation committees, would *a priori* be *a* measure of the level of inter-ethnic conflict in employment, the precise reliability of the measure not being clear at this stage. It would seem that the Board's data avoid one problem encountered in the DE's statistics in that only inter-ethnic conflict, real or imagined, is the subject. Nevertheless, a number of factors have limited the usefulness of the Board's statistical data as a measure of ethnic conflict in employment and they require brief elaboration.

## Exemptions from the Act

There are a number of areas of employment expressly excluded from the terms of the Act. Small employers of labour have constituted one such area. During the first two years of the Act's existence (that is until 26 November 1970), employers of not more than 25 workers were unaffected; in the next two years, employers of not more than ten workers were outside the scope of the Act. Lester and Bindman quote[21] a House of Commons Standing Committee showing that twenty per cent of the working population was initially excluded from the protection of the Act (and fourteen per cent from 1970–1972). A study focussing upon the effects of the 1968 Act over a period would obviously have to take such exemptions into account. The same considerations apply to the racial balance clauses, sections 8(2) to 8(5), which, above all other exemptions to the Act, have stood out as a serious loophole through which much conflict might be filtered, and hence pass unrecorded by the Board.

## The complaints procedure

The Board has mainly relied upon an individual making a complaint and there is the strong probability that the level of reported acts of alleged discrimination underestimates the actual level of discrimination. The reasons for this are familiar: the victim may be unaware of discrimination; he may be unaware of the existence of the Board and its machinery; he may show deference to authority; he may be unwilling to recall his humiliation. It seems, moreover, that the location of the Board's offices has affected the level of complaints *vis-à-vis* other towns in the area. In 1969–70, the Board noted:

> A disproportionate number of complaints in our East Midland area come from Nottingham where our office is situated. Relatively few complaints come from Derby, which has a higher proportion of immigrants.[22]

Another consideration affecting the level of complaints dealt with by the Board is the fact that a special procedure has applied to employment complaints. They are all sent to the Secretary of State for Employment and Productivity, who must first decide whether suitable non-statutory machinery exists within the particular industry to deal with the complaint; only if there is none, is the complaint referred by the Secretary of State to the Board for investigation. One may have no means of telling the number and character of such complaints. For example, one reads that between 1 April 1969 and 31 March 1970, 'industry machinery dealt with just under 25 per cent of all employment complaints under the Act . . .';[23] but even this imprecise figure is missing from the 1973 Annual Report and we are told only that '30 appeals from complainants aggrieved by decisions of industry machinery' were made to the Board.[24]

Under another clause in the Act, section 17, the Board has powers to circumvent the blockage caused by the reluctance of individuals to make complaints. This has often had the result of broadening the scope of the Board's enquiries. As the Board noted in its review of the experience of section 17 between 1968 and 1970:

> Virtually all the cases concerned the treatment of groups of employees rather than a single individual, and therefore generally allowed a broader consideration of employers' policies and practices than is normally possible in investigations arising from a complaint.[25]

In 1973, the 'success rate' of employment cases investigated under section 17, that is, of cases where the committee formed the opinion of discrimination, was almost half (eg 58 of 127), whereas when the committee relied upon individual complaints, the 'success rate' of *all employment* cases (other than those wholly dealt with by industry machinery) ie under sections 3, 4, and 12, was a fraction of that (eg 35 of 358).

The stoppage by coloured workers at Imperial Typewriters, Leicester, affords an illustration of failure by the 1968 Act and its procedures to identify ethnic group conflict in employment. The Board investigated the situation under section 17 of the Act and reported that, after devoting 'a significant proportion of our time in recent months to investigation of allegations of unlawful discrimination at this company', the evidence obtained by the East Midlands Conciliation Committee of the Board '*did not support* allegations made by the strikers' (my emphasis). Nevertheless, it seems reasonable to assume that the strikers had a justifiable grievance: for only two weeks after the three-month-long strike of approximately 400 black workers, the company appointed two equal opportunity counsellors.

This dispute may indeed be a pointer to the future, with coloured workers taking collective action to support a group demand rather than limiting action to the pursuit of a particular individual complaint.

## Conclusion

In conclusion, then, one asks what is the evidence for asserting that there are 'a growing number of instances of industrial conflict which are apparently complicated by racial elements?' as Bain and others have asserted? It cannot be the DE's published statistics; they do not, they cannot, record this. Nor can it be the DE's statistics of stoppages at work; they do not classify their statistics in such a way as to permit one to distinguish 'racial' from 'non-racial' elements in stoppages. Nor can it be based on evidence from the Race Relations Board's statistics, which are, as the Board acknowledges, sketchy, top-of-the-iceberg figures derived usually from individual complainants. On the other hand, if one's impressions are derived from the media, then serious discussion which seeks to establish objectively determined rates of incidence of conflict is at an end.

All this is not to say that coloured workers are not engaged in disputes and that the incidence of them is not likely to increase. It is, however, to doubt the 'racial' content of those disputes and the part it plays in structuring conflict, including especially conflict manifested as stoppages of work.

## Notes and references

1. Malcolm Rimmer, *Race and Industrial Conflict*, London, Heinemann, 1972, Editor's Preface.
2. Stanislaus Wellisz, 'Strikes in Coalmining', *British Journal of Sociology* Vol. V 1953, p. 364.

3. Clark Kerr, 'Industrial Conflict and its Mediation', *American Journal of Sociology* Vol. 59 1954, p. 171.
4. Peter Marsh, *The Anatomy of a Strike: Unions, Employers and Punjabi Workers in a Southall Factory*, London, Institute of Race Relations, 1967.
5. Rimmer, *op. cit.* pp. 7–8.
6. Rimmer, ibid. p. 1.
7. Clement Jones *et al.*, *Race and the Press*, London, Runnymede Trust, 1971 p. 31.
8. See *The Sunday Times, Business News*, 13.3.1974; *The Guardian* 17.3.1974.
9. Personal Communication (March 1970).
10. Paul Foot, 'Who Brought Race into the Southall Strike?', *Tribune*14.1.1966.
11. H. A. Ray, 'Woolf Rubber Dispute – the Facts', *T & GW Record*, March, 1966.
12. Stoppages at work', *Department of Employment Gazette*. Monthly.
13. Stoppages at work due to industrial disputes. Revised classification for cause', *Department of Employment Gazette* Vol. LXXI, No. 2, February 1973, p. 117.
14. *Department of Employment Gazette*, ibid., p.118.
15. *Department of Employment Gazette*, ibid., p. 119.
16. J. A. G. Griffiths *et al.*, *Coloured Immigrants in Britain*, OUP for IRR, 1960, p. 225.
17. Stoppages at work due to industrial disputes in 1973', *Department of Employment Gazette*, Vol. LXXXII, No. 6, June 1974, pp. 505–517. Interestingly the initial report in the monthly issue of the *Gazette* recorded at the time that the dismissal of the worker was for the less serious offence of 'allegedly *threatening* to strike a foreman' (my emphasis). (See the *Department of Employment Gazette*, Vol. LXXXI, No. 10. October 1973, p. 1030).
18. Ford: Sacked Man is Victim of Big Production Drive', *Socialist Worker*, No. 342, 24 September 1973, p. 16.
19. *Socialist Worker*, ibid.
20. *Department of Employment Gazette*, LXXXI, No. 6, June 1973, p. 562.
21. Anthony Lester and Geoffrey Bindman, *Race and Law* (Harmondsworth, Penguin 1972), p. 180.
22. Race Relations Board, *Annual Report* 1969–70, HMSO, p. 23.
23. Ibid., p. 8.
24. Race Relations Board, *Annual Report* 1973, London, HMSO, p. 8.
25. Ibid., p. 35.

# CHAPTER 3.2

# THE TUC AND BLACK WORKERS 1974–1976*
*R. Miles and A. Phizacklea*

## Introduction

Over the past three years or so the trade union movement has begun to demonstrate a more positive policy towards the issues raised by the presence of black workers from the New Commonwealth in Britain. The TUC has reorganized itself internally to deal with 'race relations' issues and, jointly with the Labour Party, has organized an anti-racism campaign in the autumn of 1976 which culminated in a demonstration in London attended by more than 30,000 people. Some individual unions, notably the General and Municipal Workers' Union (GMWU) and the National Union of Public Employees (NUPE), have publicly emphasized their opposition to racism and have issued leaflets to their officials and shop stewards, explaining their policy on discrimination and racism.

These developments have to be seen in contrast to policy and practice prior to 1974. Our examination of TUC policy and practice between 1954 and 1973 has shown that the TUC's failure to act positively followed from the way in which it chose to define the situation in Britain. Although it had a general policy of opposition to all forms of racial discrimination, it did not believe it necessary to take any direct action to deal with discrimination in Britain. For the General Council, the more serious problem was what they saw as the unwillingness of black immigrants to 'integrate', thus transferring the onus for action to black workers. Additionally, the largest unions representing manual workers, and thereby a large proportion of black workers, did not contribute to debates on the 'race issue' and failed to speak in relation to anti-discrimination motions. Finally, the General Council was, with varying degrees of emphasis, concerned with immigration or, more precisely, with immigration from the New Commonwealth

* *The British Journal of Industrial Relations*, vol. XVI, No. 2, 1978, pp. 195–207.

and although it regularly declared itself opposed to any form of immigration control that was racially biased, it nevertheless failed to oppose the 1971 Immigration Act on these grounds until 1973.[1]

It is our intention in this paper to outline and explain the emergence of the new TUC policy and initiatives since 1974. Our argument will be that the TUC has been forced by events, both internal and external to the trade union movement, to re-evaluate past policy and practice: it has now come to recognize the weaknesses and inconsistencies of its policy as a result of isolated reflection and a change of political heart. The coincidence of three developments forced this re-evaluation. First, there occurred in the early 1970s a number of industrial disputes which were distinguished by, amongst other things, complaints by black workers of discrimination made against trade union officials. These disputes received media attention and, as a consequence, there was public criticism of trade union and TUC policy and practice. Secondly, since the 1950s, there has been a current of internal trade union criticism, voiced regularly at the annual congress, and this increased following these disputes. Thirdly, there has been increasing trade union concern about the apparent growth of the National Front which is regarded as a neo-fascist organization. The analysis will, in part, draw upon interviews conducted with senior trade union officials in late 1976 and early 1977.[2]

## TUC policy 1974–1976

The General Council reported to the 1974 Congress[3] that they had submitted a memorandum and oral evidence to the Select Committee on Race Relations and Immigration which was then considering employment. The memorandum made reference to the 1955 Conference resolution and argued that this embodied the TUC's policy on race relations. It went on to state that the TUC believed that certain 'groups of workpeople' had special problems which were directly or indirectly associated with 'colour, race or origin', although it did not clarify what they might be. Without explanation, it was then argued that 'in the nature of the case remedial action has to be taken in the context of the main body of workers, and the General Council seeks remedies by means which will combat alienation and promote equality of opportunity in the widest sense . . .' To this end the General Council recorded its willingness to recommend that its affiliated unions should pursue equal opportunity policies, but commented that this would be a substantial task over a number of years and would require the support of the Government and the Department of Employment.

Also with regard to the promotion of equal opportunity, the General Council argued that this would be more successfully pursued if the Race Relations Board had the right of investigation in the absence of an allegation of discriminatory practice. With regard to complaints procedures, the memorandum indicated that most grievances of black workers seemed to be settled through the operation of ordinary grievance procedures. The General Council was also in favour of an ongoing joint review of the operation of the Race Relations Act. Finally, the General Council said that it was not in favour of classifying or recording individuals as members of 'racial groups' because this would be potentially damaging to the individual, would nourish stereotypes and would prevent the long-term integration of individuals within the workforce.[4]

The memorandum suggested a change in direction only in so far as it indicated the General Council's willingness to recommend the pursuit of an equal opportunity policy. The preceding 25 years had been marked by a refusal to take any active initiative whatsoever with regard to the position of black workers in Britain, but now the General Council was not only finally openly admitting that black workers faced special and particular problems but was also accepting that it had a responsibility to act in relation to these problems. However the action being recommended was unlikely to satisfy those elements within the TUC which had been pressing (erratically) for a positive initiative on the part of the General Council since 1958. The General Council was not calling for immediate and specific action to deal with racial disadvantage and discrimination (such phenomena having been deftly avoided in the memorandum by not stating what special problems faced black workers) but for the pursuit of a long-term equal opportunity programme 'in the widest sense'. Indeed, there was no recognition that trade unionists themselves might be prejudiced and might be involved in discriminatory practice. The suggested equal opportunities programme was no doubt a valid aim of the trade union movement but it could have little or no relevance to or impact on the current-day realities such as were raised by the strike at Imperial Typewriters in the same year.[5]

The picture presented by the TUC memorandum should be considered in the context of the oral evidence presented to the Select Committee by the General Council's representatives.[6] Two themes emerged in their replies to questions from members of the Select Committee which suggest either discrepancy between their views and those expressed in the memorandum, or a development of views after preparing the memorandum. First, in response to a specific question, the TUC representative said that, although white shop-floor workers might refuse to work with black workers, national and regional union officials never sanction such action.[7] In other words it was recognized that white trade unionists do engage in discriminatory practice. Secondly, in responding to a question about the TUC's view about the need for an equal opportunity policy in union agreements, the TUC representative stated that this indicated that they believed the situation to be serious. He was asked why he viewed the situation in this way and his answer distinguished between the first generation immigrant who was faced with all the difficulties of settling in a new country and the children born in Britain to these families and who were educated in Britain. In his view these children would expect equality of treatment with white British, with the consequence that discrimination would become the flashpoint for conflict. In other words, the existence of discrimination is not only an issue for the present but has even greater consequences for the future.[8]

It is not clear whether these were personal views or the opinions of the General Council, but the Select Committee was not impressed with the evidence of the TUC as a whole. The Committee reported that 'The record of the TUC is similar to that of the CBI, in that both organizations have declared their opposition to racial discrimination but have taken wholly inadequate steps to ensure that their members work effectively to eradicate it'.[9] It also commented on the contrast between the 'lack of urgency' reflected in the TUC's written evidence and the representative's awareness of the need for greater action. Additionally, it criticized the organization of the TUC's 'race relations policy' and was clearly not satisfied with the view expressed orally that the TUC was not considering establishing a separate body within its framework to deal with the problems faced by black workers because such a move may not assist 'integration'.

This report by the Select Committee marks a watershed in the history of the TUC's policy and practice with regard to black workers. An official House of Commons committee was now echoing some of the arguments that had been raised by trade unionists on the floor of Congress since 1958. Indeed, these very arguments were raised yet again at the 1974 Congress by a delegate from the Association of Scientific, Technical and Managerial Staffs (ASTMS) responding to the General Council's report on its memorandum to the Select Committee. The delegate welcomed what he described as an important shift in the General Council's opposition to racial discrimination but he believed that the statement did not go far enough:

> What is needed is a determined attack by the trade union movement on racial discrimination, the development of anti-discrimination trade union education and the development of specialist trade union services to the section of our black and immigrant membership who have problems such as language difficulties.[10]

In his view, this policy should be co-ordinated by a new TUC committee which would advise and encourage the various levels of the TUC organization to face up to the issues. And concern was expressed at the same Congress about the General Council's attitude to the 1971 Immigration Act. A delegate from TASS argued that the General Council had not seriously pressed the Government to remove the Act from the Statute Book and expressed the view that it should do so on the grounds that it was both 'racist and anti-union'.[11]

The Report to the 1975 Congress gave little indication of any further consideration of policy with regard to black workers.[12] It was reported that a model clause on equal opportunities had been drawn up and circulated to union officials and representatives involved in negotiations at all levels, with the request that they should try to ensure that the clause was included in subsequent agreements. The General Council undertook to monitor developments. Thus the action promised to the Select Committee was under way. However, the General Council acted less positively to a suggestion from the Chairman of the Race Relations Board that the Board might circularize trade unions about the need to avoid discrimination in redundancy situations and about the relevant legislation on discrimination. The General Council opposed this suggestion, pointing out that there was no evidence to show discrimination in redundancy situations, that redundancy was governed by union agreements and rules which made discrimination unlikely and that, anyway, the General Council had recently given much publicity to the need for equal opportunities. As far as the TUC was concerned there was no problem and, hence, action was not required. But, by way of contrast again, the General Council did respond to the House of Lords' decision in October 1974 that Preston Docker's Labour Club was not guilty of unlawful discrimination. A letter was sent to the Home Secretary asking him to take account of their opposition to discrimination in working men's clubs on grounds of colour, race or origin in reviewing the Race Relations Act, and in addition a meeting was held with the Executive Committee of the Club and Institute Union to discuss ways of ensuring that discrimination was not practised in clubs.

Soon after the 1975 Congress had met, the General Council announced in October a new development which was identified by some journalists who had prior knowledge as 'a major initiative'.[13] Responsibility for 'race relations' and discrimination was to be moved from the International Committee and was to be integrated into the Organizational and Industrial Relations Department, thus placing it in the mainstream of the TUC's work. In addition, a new subcommittee of the General Council, the Equal Rights Committee (ERC), was to be appointed. Two reasons for this were put forward. First, there was a desire to bring together all the work on discrimination and equal opportunity, as they affect both women and minority groups. Secondly, there was specific concern with race relations policies as they relate to employment, industrial relations and the work of trade unions.

The Equal Rights Committee produced its own terms of reference in December 1975 which the General Council ratified. The General Council stated that the Committee's work was to be concentrated upon '. . . those fields where special and cumulative disadvantage exists, for particular groups linked with discrimination on arbitrary grounds (such as race, sex, or religion)'. The overall aim was to develop 'positive policies to promote equal opportunity' and to this end it was agreed that the ERC would be pressing the government to legislate against arbitrary discrimination and would monitor the results of that legislation. In addition, the Committee would examine the policies of the TUC and affiliated unions with respect to equal opportunity, and would ask government and other relevant bodies to take account of and act in relation to the special needs of disadvantaged groups.

The General Council set out a specific set of tasks for the ERC. The first was to monitor legislation as it applied to women and ethnic groups; and the second concerned equal opportunity policies. The Committee was asked to prepare union recruitment literature in ethnic minority languages, to encourage language training in English, to examine the barriers to equal opportunity, to encourage equal opportunity modules in trade union education courses, to review the operation of the equal opportunities model clause, to examine union rule books, to review Government social policies as they affect women and ethnic minorities and to review immigration legislation and policy.

Acknowledging the need for special consideration being given to 'race relations' the General Council additionally decided in December 1975 to establish a Race Relations advisory Committee (RRAC). It was envisaged that there would be a two-way flow between the ERC and the RRAC, with the ERC both referring certain matters to the RRAC for consideration and considering proposals suggested by the RRAC. The RRAC is composed of four General Council members and nine trade union representatives, the latter being chosen from nominations received from affiliated unions, some of whom are also members of minority ethnic groups. Currently the Chairman of both the ERC and the RRAC is Mr Tom Jackson, General Secretary of the Union of Post Office Workers.

In the light of the deliberations of these two committees, the General Council issued a press release in July 1976 which indicated its endorsement of their work. The General Council stated 'Much needs to be done to eliminate the discrimination and disadvantage facing ethnic minorities and for their part the General Council are advising affiliated unions about steps they should take to strengthen trade union organization among immigrant and black workers and unity between work people'. The press release went on to refer to, and deplore, the racialist activities of the National Front in particular, and attempts to blame the high level of unemployment on black workers. Additionally, it made the first mention of a proposed campaign against racialism to be conducted in association with the Labour Party.

This press release foreshadowed what was to happen at the 1976 Congress. The combination of silence and soft-pedalling of the 'race issue' at previous Congresses was forgotten and, instead, there was a clear-cut denunciation of racialism and the activities of what were defined as racist organizations such as the National Front and National Party. A motion on racialism, moved by Mr Bill Keys, General Secretary of the Society of Graphical and Allied Trades (SOGAT), expressed this condemnation and called upon the Government to ban the National Front and the National Party. Additionally it called upon all affiliated unions both to warn their members of the danger to working class unity of racialism and to ensure equal opportunities for black and white workers and upon the General Council to organize and initiate a national campaign against racialism.[14] Mr Keys argued that the National Front was engaged on a programme of infiltration of the trade union movement: 'These people who peddle race hatred are no different from the people who peddled the hatred in Germany in the 1920s and 1930s which led to the last war'.

Mr Maurice Styles (UPW) argued that the roots of racialism were buried in everyone and derived from Britain's imperial past, and said that it should now be recognized that the earlier immigrants were becoming today's British citizens. Mr David Basnett (GMWU) stated that racialism was abhorrent on moral, ethical and trade union grounds. His argument was that racialists attempt to divide the working class by blaming coloured immigrants for unemployment and bad housing which were really caused by the worldwide depression and years of neglect. Mr Louis Mahoney (British Actors' Equity Association), one of the handful of black delegates at Congress and the only one to speak in this debate, called for immediate action because of the threats posed by unemployment and the alienation of black youth, and argued in favour of integrated acting in the media. There were also speeches from delegates from the National Union of Journalists (NUJ) and the National Association of Local Government Officers (NALGO), the former demanding that unions should positively discriminate in favour of ethnic minority members for full-time and elected union posts. Following the debate, the resolution was passed unanimously.[15]

Thus, in the twelve months following the 1975 Congress, the policy and practice of the General Council and the TUC changed in a number of important respects. First, the General Council openly admitted not only that black workers faced disadvantage and discrimination, but also that racialism constituted a serious problem and should be strenuously opposed. Secondly, it was explicitly recognized that the trade unions should actively oppose racialism within their own ranks and should openly argue against racialist and fascist organizations. In other words the problem was not only the presence and activity of the NF and NP but also racialism within the British workforce. Therefore, and thirdly, the stated issues requiring attention and action were not the 'integration' of the immigrants and immigration but racialism and the activities of the National Front and National Party. Fourthly, the General Council declared itself in favour of giving special attention to 'race relations' by means of new internal organization arrangements, and by actively pressing for a policy of equal opportunity. Fifthly, the General Council was not only willing to speak openly about the problems and dangers of racialism, but was also concerned to initiate a campaign with the Labour movement against it. The General Council had therefore moved a long way since its memorandum to the Select Committee in 1974 and, even more dramatically, since its policy and debates in the 1950s and 1960s. We go on to argue that this change occurred as a consequence of the coincidence of three developments.

## Black workers and industrial conflict

During the early 1970s there was a substantial number of industrial disputes involving black workers in which allegations of discrimination by white trade unionists were made,[16] the most notable of which were at Mansfield Hosiery Mills Ltd and Imperial Typewriters Ltd.[17] As we have argued elsewhere[18] the General Council was, at least up until 1973, unwilling to accept publicly that white trade unionists would engage in discriminatory practice, a position that was flatly contradicted by these two disputes, amongst others. The weakness of the TUC's policy was therefore made manifest and criticism was voiced by not only black workers and that group of trade unionists who had opposed the General Council's position, but also by official bodies.

The industrial dispute at Mansfield Hosiery Mills Ltd followed a reference to the East Midland Conciliation Committee (EMCC) of the Race Relations Board (RRB) in May 1972 by an Asian employee alleging discrimination in promotion procedures. In July the EMCC found that the company had unlawfully discriminated and announced that it would then examine the unlawful discrimination by white workers and the National Union of Hosiery and Knitwear Workers (NUHKW) at the factory. In November they reported that both had unlawfully discriminated against Asian employees, following which both company and union announced that they would not discriminate in future. While the EMCC was deliberating, industrial action involving only Asian workers occurred at the company's factories over a wage claim and promotion opportunities. Although the NUHKW had submitted the wage claim and was attempting to negotiate improved promotion opportunities, it only made the strike official when the strikers occupied the local union branch office. Moreover, even after declaring the dispute official, the union did not require the white workers to withdraw their labour, presumably because it was well aware of their hostility to the advancement of the Asian workers.[19]

The dispute was considered to be sufficiently serious for the Conservative Secretary of State for Employment to appoint a Committee of Inquiry to attempt to draw up terms for a settlement. When the dispute was finally resolved, the Commission on Industrial Relations (CIR) was asked to prepare a report. The CIR was particularly critical of the NUHKW, arguing that it had failed to ensure that black workers were adequately represented in the shop-floor organization and that their interests were adequately represented, and predicted: 'Failure to do these things could result in the alienation of immigrant members to such an extent that they might feel the need to enlist the support of alternative organizations or break away completely and form a trade union exclusively for immigrant workers'.[20] The responsibility, it argued, lay with the union leadership who should have an active and positive policy on these issues. That this was still lacking among the leadership of the NUHKW after the findings of the EMCC and the final resolution of the dispute was shown by the NUHKW's President who said, 'We helped the Asians more than our own people. This is what stuck in my craw all the time we were trying to get a settlement'.[21]

Similarly the dispute at Imperial Typewriters Ltd involved Asian workers and allegations of discrimination against union officials, and attracted considerable publicity. Although the strike arose out of a dispute between the Asian workers at the factory and management about the speed of the production line and the payment of bonuses, the strikers were also concerned about the representativeness of the shop stewards committee. The first workers to come out on strike all came from the same department and were concerned that there was only one Asian member of the shop stewards committee (1,100 of the factory's 1,600 employees were Asian); they therefore additionally demanded the right to elect their own shop steward. Thus the dispute was, from the start, three-cornered with the Asian workers in conflict with both employer and union, the Transport and General Workers Union (TGWU). During the course of the dispute the TGWU convenor in the factory refused to speak to the strike leaders on the grounds that union members were only eligible for election as shop stewards after two years' membership. Moreover the TGWU never made the strike official. Concern about the role the local TGWU officers played in the dispute led to an internal TGWU inquiry, but its findings were never made public.[22]

Thus both disputes involved not only conflict between (Asian) employees and management but also between (Asian) union members and union officials. Such three-cornered disputes occur regularly in industrial relations situations but in these two cases, there was an additional element, that of allegations of racial discrimination against both employer and union by the Asian strikers. Thus, although we share Bentley's reservations about defining industrial disputes as having been complicated by 'racial' elements because of 'media-led bias', [23] we argue that these two disputes clearly showed that trade unionists and trade union officials could be guilty of discriminatory practice. Moreover it was not only the media that publicly aired criticism of the union's practice: the CIR, a government-sponsored body, was, as has already been shown, worried about the trade union's role regarding black workers. There was therefore public evidence to dispute the General Council's view that the problem was one of integration ('them' adopting 'our' ways) and immigration and not that of the extent of discriminatory practice amongst white workers. Significantly neither dispute was explicitly referred to at the annual Congress, although one critic of the General Council's policy did comment in 1974 that 'There have been too many instances recently when black workers have had to struggle alone. They must be given the support of the whole trade union movement'.[24]

In order to assess the effect of these disputes on the trade union movement and the TUC in particular, the senior trade union leaders interviewed were asked about them. The replies showed a consensus on two points. First, the disputes had no immediate or direct effect on the General Council of the TUC. However, and secondly, they did have a significant effect on the national leadership of the unions involved and particularly the TGWU. It was argued that union officials are extremely busy people and in the absence of specific events jolting their consciousness, there was little reason for considering the position and problems of black workers. As far as the TGWU national leadership was concerned, the Imperial Typewriters strike forced the 'race issue' into their consciousness and the belief that there was little cause for concern was jolted; as one official said, 'Imperial was a necessary lesson'. Doubts were expressed about the lasting effect on the NUHKW of the Mansfield Hosiery strike, but it was felt, particularly by one of Mr Jack Jones' colleagues on the TUC International Committee[25] that the Imperial dispute, in so far as it had caught the attention of the General Secretary of the TGWU had thereby contributed to the process of reassessment of policy by national trade union leaders and the TUC. It is relevant to recall that the TGWU is the largest trade union in Britain and, as a consequence, its General Secretary has a major voice on the General Council of the TUC. In sum, the strikes at Mansfield Hosiery Ltd and Imperial Typewriters Ltd did not suddenly bring about an immediate reassessment of policy by the General

Council but they did force certain trade union leaders to consider the issues, the necessary initial stage for any reassessment of policy.

## The General Council critics

It is misleading to regard the TUC as a monolithic institution with a single view on any issue, including that of the position and problems of black workers. The General Council has had a consistent if internally contradictory policy since the mid-1950s but it is one that has been regularly challenged by delegates on the floor of Congress. The most significant challenge was at the 1967 Congress when a motion was moved by the Association of Cinematograph, Television and Allied Technicians in response to the General Council's report on its opposition to the Government's intention of extending the legislative control of racial discrimination to the field of employment. The motion, in addition to reaffirming the TUC's condemnation of racial discrimination, expressed concern about the extent of racial discrimination as revealed by the 1967 PEP study, called for trade unions to take action to prevent discrimination, and endorsed the Government's intentions to make racial discrimination in employment an offence.[26] In other words the motion was attempting to reverse the General Council's policy.

The General Council member who opened the debate indicated that the issue was to find the best way of 'integrating' the immigrants into the workforce, while for the mover of the motion the issue was the extent of discrimination by whites against blacks. The motion was supported by delegates from five different unions and opposed by only one. The General Council member, in summing up, said that they opposed the motion because it would 'tie our hands completely' and because the law would create special groups of workers, which would not assist 'integration'. Despite the clear majority of delegates speaking in favour of the motion, the President of Congress asked Congress whether it was in favour of the motion being remitted to the General Council (which was opposed to the policy laid down in the motion!) and then ruled, on the basis of vocal evidence, that it was. This manoeuvre raised a protest from the floor of Congress which was then overruled by the President, with the result that the General Council was able to survive the challenge to its policy.[27] Although this was the most significant challenge to the General Council's policy, it was not the only one, but it does serve to indicate that a substantial proportion of trade unionists were of the view that the TUC should act positively to deal with racial discrimination.

Further evidence for the existence of an opposition to the General Council policy is to be found in a memorandum submitted to the Select Committee in 1974 by the Midland Region Trade Union Conference to Combat Racial Discrimination. The memorandum argued that the average white worker is prejudiced against black workers and because this prejudice is based on colour, it will continue to exist in future generations. It noted that discrimination is widespread and is encouraged by the passive role adopted by Parliament, employers and trade unions and pointed out that no employer or trade union had established a special department to assist the black worker to overcome disadvantage in employment.[28] This Committee had organized a conference, attended by over a hundred delegates from the Midlands in January 1974, which passed a lengthy resolution calling for an active campaign against racist ideology and racial discrimination and for the TUC to appoint a full-time officer to be responsible for 'advising affiliated unions on all aspects of race relations'.[29]

Although they did not present memoranda to the Select Committee, other locally based committees were set up by trade unionists in London, the midlands and the north of England in the 1970s to combat discrimination and to attempt to change their respective unions' and the TUC's policy. In addition. Trades Councils organized conferences and campaigns, expressing concern about racist ideology and racial discrimination within the Labour Movement. For instance, the Black Country Trades Council Conference of 1974 passed a resolution which, amongst other things, committed its participants to press union District Committees to appoint a delegate to deal specifically with 'racialist problems', to initiate recruiting campaigns directed towards immigrant workers (using literature which was printed in their own languages), to demanding an end of police harassment of black workers and to ensure that known racialists do not hold trade union office.[30]

In early 1975, following a trade union conference on the problems of racialism, a delegation from Warley Trades Council met local councillors, following which Warley Council agreed, among other things, to employ a person of 'immigrant origin' to deal with immigrants' language, form filling and other problems relating to the Council', and to call upon constituency bodies to discuss the repeal of the 1971 Immigration Act on the grounds that the 'partial' clauses were racial in intent and effect. A TGWU shop steward and member of Warley Trades Council was quoted as commenting on these decisions: 'We feel we have shown to a growing number in the Black Country Labour Movement the need for solidarity against racists and the danger of the National Front'[31]

It is not easy to assess the meaning or effect of the resolutions passed by, and actions of, these locally based committees and conferences in the early 1970s. Some of the trade unionists who initiated or took part in them were members of political organizations to the left of the Labour Party, but far from all participants were politically committed in this way. Nevertheless these committees and conferences did indicate a current of opposition at the local level to the official TUC policy and were able to pose as representing the trade union principles on racism and discrimination in their areas of influence.

Opposition to the TUC policy has not been confined to the floor of Congress or the grass-roots level. Interviews with trade union officials have revealed that a proportion of full-time officials have worked within the union structures to develop a more positive policy. The various industrial disputes during the early 1970s were evidence to them of the weakness of the TUC policy and the correctness of their own position and they were even more concerned to press for a change in policy. These officials have therefore argued for their position in their own unions as and when the situation has permitted and have, as a consequence, added their voice to the various other currents of opposition to the TUC policy within the trade union movement.

Thus the situation in the mid-1970s within the TUC was one in which certain trade union leaders were, as a consequence of particular events, re-evaluating TUC policy; while within the trade union movement there existed a small but concerned minority of trade unionists who were concerned to see a more positive policy from the TUC. What was additionally necessary was a broadening of the concern on the General Council and within the TUC and this was produced by the apparent growth and increasing public awareness of the National Front.

## The National Front

The two General Elections of 1974 marked an attempt by the National Front to establish itself as a reputable national political party with the aim of achieving political power through the electoral process.[32] In the February election it had 54 candidates and was the fifth largest party as measured by number of candidates, while in the October election it put up 90 candidates, making it the fourth largest party, When compared with its previously rather disorganized and scrappy activity in both local and parliamentary elections, the National Front's 1974 intervention suggested that it was from then on a political force to be reckoned with. Certainly it was able to gain considerable national publicity from contesting a large number of Parliamentary seats, a result which the leadership of the National Front set out to achieve. But the National Front has placed itself in the public arena and in the public consciousness not only by electoral intervention but also by responding to and taking up issues by means of public demonstrations. If their vocal objections to the arrival of the Ugandan Asians in 1972 did not make a mark, their demonstration in London in June 1973, the subsequent violence and the death of a student on the counter-demonstration certainly did. Beginning in 1973–4 the National Front (in common with the National Socialist Party in Germany in the late 1920s and 1930s) has pursued this dual strategy of electoral intervention and organized public demonstration which, in the context of the 1973 violence, serves to achieve further publicity and hence public consciousness of its existence. Thus it was no coincidence that the National Front organized a march and demonstration through Hackney, London on 23 April 1977 and contested all but one of the seats in the GLC elections on 5 May 1977.

Le Lohé argues that the 1974 General Election results indicate that the National Front made little political progress and was not very well organized and hence, '. . . their threat is a minor one which should not be over-emphasized'.[33] That may or may not be true but it should be recognized that, in a society with an extensive and immediate system of mass communication, the influence of a political organization can be out of all proportion to its actual membership and financial resources. This, we argue, is relevant to the re-evaluation of TUC policy on 'race relations' which was beginning in the middle of 1975.[34] The substantial electoral intervention, particularly in constituencies which were subsequently won by Labour,[35] the street demonstrations, and the consequent publicity had by then established the National Front as a real threat in the eyes of trade union leaders. The National Front emphasis upon electoral intervention in Labour-held seats combined with deep-rooted fears of fascism therefore finally forced a re-evaluation of policy.

All the union officials interviewed were asked about the reasons for the re-evaluation of TUC policy and about National Front activity amongst their own members. All of them said that the National Front was active and had some support amongst their members, and four of them specifically referred to it as a fascist organization; two officials drew a parallel between the National Front and the rise of National Socialism in Germany, pointing to the current economic crisis and high level of unemployment. Although two officials also pointed out that the current influence of the National Front should not be over-estimated, there was concern about its activity and future potential amongst all union officials interviewed. Three of the five officials, including a member of the TUC General Council, also stated that the 'rise' of the National Front had necessitated a new policy from the TUC. The General Council member, Mr Tom Jackson, referred to the 'casual attitude of the TUC to the "race question" prior to 1975,' saying that the members of the General Council either believed that there was no real cause for concern or felt that they 'did not want to lift the stone'. However, when the National Front intervened in 'a big way' by putting up candidates on a large scale, he and one or two other Council members began to press for action. The other members included Mr Jack Jones (TGWU) and Mr David Basnett (GMWU). Mr Jackson concluded that '. . . it is unfortunate that the National Front had to stimulate the action because we could have dealt with it more rationally and could perhaps have prevented the rise of the National Front'. Mr Jackson's claim may or may not be accurate, but it does serve to show that the General Council's refusal to 'lift the stone' covering working-class racism did not prevent it being pushed aside by other forces, and once this had been done, the General Council was forced into a positive response.

There is, however, a further dimension to this. Mr Jackson also claimed that the National Front intervention of 1974 gave the Left in the trade union movement a good reason to act on the 'race issue'. To interpret this we would argue that trade unionists who have wanted a more positive policy towards the issues posed by black immigrant workers have had to contend with the racism of fellow (white) unionists, but it became possible after 1974 for them to argue that the National Front, as a neo-fascist party, was the enemy of the trade union movement. By identifying an external 'enemy', the National Front, they could, simultaneously, openly demand support for a policy of opposition to racialism.

It would therefore seem that the National Front has done more to force the General Council and the TUC to act in relation to the 'race issue' in the last three years than the combined activities of the internal critics at the annual Congresses and the left-wing organizations and rank-and-file trade union groupings over the past 25 years. The latter have served to needle the General Council continually but, with the exception of the motion passed at the 1973 Congress opposing the 1971 Immigration Act, they have not been able to have a fundamental and decisive impact. What remains for speculation is whether the General Council have been reacting to the 'rise' of the National Front or to a media-led construction that the National Front substantially increased their influence after 1974.

## Conclusion

We have argued that the change in TUC policy has been forced by the coincidence of the three developments as described. The focus of TUC action and speeches by General Council members since 1974 has therefore been upon combating racism and racialist practices within the white working class. If, however, Maurice Styles was correct in arguing that the roots of racialism are buried in everyone and are derived from Britain's imperial past, then, in the absence of evidence to the contrary, one must doubt whether a propaganda campaign lasting a few months, and of very uneven intensity, was adequate to the task. Certainly, some of the trade union officials interviewed were cynical about the extent of the influence of the campaign on shop floor practice, although all believed that union representatives at all levels were now fully aware of union policy and were unlikely to act in opposition to it.

The General Council has, in comparison, placed less public emphasis upon dealing with the material disadvantage of black workers.[36] The stated policy has been, first, to press all affiliated unions to negotiate acceptance by employers of equal opportunity clauses, and secondly, to press both Government and CBI to pursue equal opportunity policies. Whether the former has any real effect on employers' recruitment and promotion policies is a matter for investigation, not least because the signing of an equal opportunity policy by an employer need be nothing more than a public relations exercise.

The second strategy is even more amorphous but follows logically from the way in which the General Council has increasingly conducted its affairs, particularly since the mid-1960s. The General Council aims to persuade Government to take specific action through persuasion and argument, expressed on the numerous committees upon which both are represented along with employers' organizations, and its policy of enforcing equal opportunity is no exception. As in many other areas the 'success' of the General Council's approach will be measured by the extent of government action, in this instance, to correct the disadvantaged position of black workers. If past evidence of government practice regarding black workers is anything to go by, they have good reason to be concerned about the advantages to be gained from such a strategy.

Nevertheless, when compared with earlier policy and practice, the change in TUC policy since 1974 is both significant and substantial. The explicit concern is no longer with 'integration' and immigration but with racial discrimination, and to a lesser extent with disadvantage and the possibility of the growth of a neo-fascist political organization feeding upon working-class racism. The General Council has shown itself willing to face openly the reality of racism amongst trade union members and has campaigned against it in conjunction with the Labour Party, whereas it played down or was silent on this issue in the past. While the policy developments since 1974 constitute an advance, there are still no grounds for complacency: however, the ice once melted, it is possible for the critics to press for further positive action.

## Notes and references

1. R. Miles and A. Phizacklea, 'The TUC, Black Workers and Immigration 1954–1973', *RUER Working Papers in Ethnic Relations* 1977, No. 6.
2. Senior trade union officials from the following unions were interviewed: Amalgamated Union of Engineering Workers, General and Municipal Workers' Union, National Union of Railwaymen, Transport and General Workers' Union, and the Union of Post Office Workers. These unions were selected because: (a) they include the largest unions in Britain and have, as a consequence, considerable influence on the General Council of the TUC; (b) they are the unions with the highest proportion of black members (see D. Smith, *The Facts of Racial Disadvantage*, PEP 1976, p. 231).
3. Trades Union Congress, *Report of Proceedings of the 106th Annual Trades Union Congress*, London, 1974, p. 106 (thereafter abbreviated as Report of 106th Congress, Report of 107th Congress etc.)
4. Select Committee on Race Relations and Employment, *Employment Vol. II, Evidence and Appendices*, HMSO, 1975.
5. For an account of this dispute, see R. Moore, *Racism and Black Resistance in Britain*, Pluto 1975.
6. Select Committee on Race Relations and Immigration, *op. cit.*, pp. 457–469.
7. *Op. cit.*, p. 459.
8. *Op. cit.*
9. Select Committee on Race Relations and Immigration, *Employment, Vol. 1, Report* HMSO, 1974, p. xxii.
10. TUC, *Report of 106th Congress, ibid.*, p. 536.
11. *Ibid.*, p. 536.
12. TUC, *Report of 107th Congress*, 1975, pp. 73–5.
13. See *Financial Times*, 25.9.75.

14. The motion in full was: 'Congress notes with alarm the growth of racialist and fascist activity in the U.K. and the support obtained by racialist groups in recent political local elections. Congress also condemns the provocative marches and demonstrations organized by the National Front and the National Party, which are designed to inflame racial hatred and intolerance of ethnic minority groups in this country and calls upon H.M. Government to take positive action within the law to ban them. Congress is mindful that the twin evils of unemployment and bad social conditions are the product of the system under which we live and are the enemies of all workers who should unite together in opposing them. In order to combat racialism in Britain, Congress calls on: (a) all affiliated unions to make every effort to warn members of the evils of racialism and of the dangers of a divided working class and to expose those organizations which spread race hatred and incite racial violence and to ensure equal employment opportunities between black and white workers; and (b) the General Council to initiate and organize a nationwide campaign through meetings, demonstrations and publicity material designed to combat the activities of the racialists to set worker against worker.'

15. See *The Times*, 8.9.76; *Financial Times*,8.9.76; *Guardian*, 8.9.76.

16. We have discussed the general meaning and implications of these disputes elsewhere. See R. Miles and A. Phizacklea, 'Class, Race, Ethnicity and Political Action', *Political Studies* 1977. For a critical evaluation of the meaning of these disputes, see S. Bentley, 'Industrial Conflict, Strikes and Black Workers: Problems of Research Methodology', *New Community*, 1976, Vol. 5 (1/2), pp. 127–38. (This volume 3.1.)

17. For accounts and evaluations of these two disputes, see Commission on Industrial Relations, *Mansfield Hosiery Mills Ltd.*, HMSO, 1974, and R. Moore, *op. cit.*

18. R. Miles and A. Phizacklea, 'The TUC, Black Workers and Immigration 1954–1973', *ibid.*

19. Commission on Industrial Relations, *op. cit.*

20. *Op. cit.*, p. 38.

21. *Race Today*, August 1973, p. 237.

22. R. Moore, *op. cit.*, pp. 77–83; Workers' Education Association/Runnymede Trust, *Trade Unions and Immigrant Workers*, Runnymede Trust 1974.

23. S. Bentley, *ibid.*, p. 131.

24. TUC, Report of 106th Congress, *ibid.*, p. 536.

25. At this time the TUC's International Committee had responsibility for 'race relations' matters.

26. TUC, *Report of 99th Congress*, 1967, p. 504.

27. This, along with other challenges to the General Council policy, is discussed in greater detail in R. Miles and A. Phizacklea, *ibid.*

28. Select Committee on Race Relations and Immigration, *Employment Vol. II*, *op. cit.*, p. 469–71.

29. Workers' Education Association/Runnymede Trust, *op. cit.*, pp. 21–2; *National Union of Public Employees Journal*, April 1974.

30. Workers' Education Association/Runnymede Trust, *op. cit.*, p. 22.

31. *Morning Star*, 10.1.75; *The Record*, March 1975.
32. C. T. Husbands, 'The National Front: a Response to Crisis?', *New Society*, 15.5.75; M. J. Le Lohé, 'The National Front and the General Elections of 1974', *New Community*, 1976, Vol. 5 (3), pp. 292–301.
33. M. J. Le Lohé, *ibid.* p. 301.
34. The *Financial Times*, 25.9.75, reported that the General Council was then considering establishing the Equal Rights Committee.
35. This point is emphasized by C. T. Husbands, *ibid.*, p. 404.
36. On the extent of disadvantage, see D. Smith, *op. cit.*, and Department of Employment, *The Role of Immigrants in the Labour Market*, DEP, 1977.

# CHAPTER 3.3

# THE STRIKE AT GRUNWICK*
## A. Phizacklea and R. Miles

## How it began

Grunwick Film Processing Laboratories Ltd develops and prints colour films, mainly from abroad. There are two factories in North-West London and in August 1976 they together employed 440 people, 50 of whom were clerical staff while the remainder were manual workers. On 20 August, some students, employed for the busy summer period (an exceptionally hot and dry one) were reprimanded for 'fooling around'; one (Devshi Bhudia, who had already secured a job elsewhere) was later summarily dismissed, and three or four others walked out in sympathy with him.[1] Near the end of the shift, Mrs Jayaben Desai was also reprimanded by a supervisor (who was reportedly disliked by some workers) for packing up early. She answered him back, asked for her cards, made a pointed speech to her fellow workers and marched out of the factory with her son Sunil. There they joined the others, who were still in the street outside. On Monday 23 August they were outside the factory gates with placards and at 3 pm there was a walk-out of about 50 at Chapel Road and a march round to the Cobbold Road Factory where some others joined the strikers and a scene ensued to which the police were called. During the next few days the numbers on strike increased to 137 (91 permanent staff and 46 students who would be returning to their studies in a week or so in any case).

Over the first weekend, Mrs Desai and the original nucleus had decided to build support for their plan to join a union. Sunil Desai went on Monday to the Citizens' Advice Bureau, where he was given the telephone number of Brent Trades Council (whose secretary, Jack Dromey, was to

* An edited version of an article from *New Community*, vol. VI, No. 3, Summer 1978, pp. 268–278.

become one of the strikers' chief advisers), and the TUC, where he was advised that a suitable union was an umbrella, white-collar union, the Association of Professional, Executive and Computer Staff (APEX). APEX accepted their applications almost at once and by the end of that week the 91 permanent staff on strike were members.

What followed fits a common pattern in such industrial situations. These APEX strikers began picketing the factory and formulated their demands, the most important of them being the right to belong to a union which received management recognition. The strikers believed that, having unionized themselves, they would be able to deal with their other grievances: these included low pay (some process workers received £28 gross for a 40-hour week), and the denial of dark-room and shift allowances, as well as welfare benefits (all paid by Grunwick's biggest commercial rival, Tudor Processing, which had a factory nearby). The strikers also objected to compulsory overtime, for which there was no prior warning, in the summer months, and to the management's refusal to provide transport home for the women late at night, even though buses were infrequent and harassment at bus stops common. All these latter issues, along with others, such as the recently-imposed practice of being timed whilst in the toilets, were, for the women, far more important issues than the question of wages.

Given that the majority of those who walked out on 23 August were women (and Asian immigrants, mostly from East Africa), it is important to understand the feelings of resentment that had been building up for a long time prior to the walk-out. One striker said:

> Management saw us as quiet Asian ladies who wouldn't answer back. Yes, we were quiet, we were quiet because we were respecting you, you who are our managers, that's why. But when you are treating us like this, we are going to show you what we can do. We knew our rights. We kept quiet because we didn't want to make trouble, but as things got worse, we said we can't keep quiet any longer, it's better to face them.[2]

Women and young men of immigrant status with little or no previous experience of factory work or trade unionism are a vulnerable section of the workforce. Film processing firms like Grunwick operate on low profit margins in a highly competitive market and, if costs are to be kept to the minimum, wages must be lower than most unions would like. It can therefore be argued that hostility towards union organization of the workforce and the locating of people willing to work for low wages are two means by which management could maintain profitability in such circumstances. George Ward, the Managing Director of Grunwick, denies using the former means, even though three van drivers and 24 process workers were sacked in 1973, subsequent to their joining a union. One of the sacked workers said the reason provided by the company for dismissal was lack of work, 'but one of the directors told me that they did not want a union in the factory'.[3]

The latter strategy would also be denied by the company, if it was interpreted to mean the conscious recruitment of Asian immigrants. However, this is not the view of those on strike: one striker reported to us that employment application forms asked for passport numbers and date of arrival in the UK. Whether there was a 'conscious' policy of recruiting Asians or not, the practice of recruiting relatives and friends through existing workers (so frequent in firms employing a largely Asian work-force), resulted in the company having, when the strike began, a workforce which was 80 per cent Asian, mainly from East Africa. Such a situation was to have less positive consequences for the company. A large proportion of workers at Grunwick in 1976 had a common language, religion, tradition and history. This meant that personal loyalties and a sense of community were strong among the minority who walked out of the factory, and this played an important part in both their ability to mobilize and in strengthening their solidarity and determination. [. . .]

## The issues raised by Grunwick

[The Grunwick dispute brought into question a number of issues, particularly the interpretation of the Trade Union and Labour Relations Act (1974) and the Employment Protection Act (1975), while other] [. . .] related issues, such as the law on picketing, gained undue prominence as a result of media attention. For instance, the amount of attention given by the national press to the initial walk-out was minuscule in comparison to the coverage given to the industrial action of the UPW or the violence on the picket line. [But this paper is concerned with another] but less well-publicized issue, ie the extent to which the Grunwick dispute is a test of the trade unions' changing attitude to coloured workers. Some early press reports drew attention to the fact that the majority of strikers were Asian immigrants and, as we will show shortly, certain parties to the dispute have made reference to this fact for varying reasons. Moreover, the beginning of the dispute coincided with the 1976 TUC Annual

Conference, which passed a major resolution on racialism and initiated a campaign against racialism in conjunction with the Labour Party.

## Coloured workers and the trade unions

To suggest that the Grunwick dispute may illustrate a changing trade union attitude to coloured workers implies an identifiable earlier position. We have argued elsewhere that up until 1974 the TUC held an extremely ambivalent attitude on the question of 'race relations' and racism.

Certainly, the TUC maintained a principled opposition to racial discrimination although those unions which represented the vast majority of coloured workers failed to speak in favour of the relevant motions, but the General Council also viewed these workers as a 'problem', in that it believed that they had not done enough to integrate themselves into the British workforce.[4] Moreover, during the early 1970s, there were a number of industrial disputes involving coloured workers in which allegations of racial discrimination were made against white workers and trade union officials. In one of these disputes, at Mansfield Hosiery Mills Ltd in 1972, not only the employer, but also the union, the National Union of Hosiery and Knitwear Workers, was found guilty of unlawfully discriminating against Asian employees.[5] The dispute at Imperial Typewriters Ltd in 1974 also received prominent attention, not least because allegations of racial discrimination were made against one of the biggest unions in the country, the Transport and General Workers' Union (TGWU). We have argued elsewhere that these disputes, along with two other factors, brought about a more positive attitude and policy to non-white workers on the part of the TUC, as demonstrated at the 1976 Congress.[6]

In considering whether this changed attitude and policy were instrumental, in bringing about the TUC and other trade union support for the Grunwick strikers, it is useful to compare the Grunwick dispute with one of the earlier disputes which featured allegations of racial discrimination, that at Imperial Typewriters Ltd. The latter dispute involved 1,100 East African Asian workers and arose out of very different grievances from those at Grunwick. The latter fact is central to our argument that Grunwick is, in the final analysis, *not* a test of the trade unions' changed attitude to coloured workers.

At Imperial Typewriters, the strikers were already members of a union, but claimed inadequate Asian representation on the shop stewards' committee. One of their basic demands was, therefore, a direct challenge to their trade union to ensure adequate representation of coloured workers. The management found an unexpected ally in the union (at branch and district level), whose initial unsympathetic attitude to the Asian workers became positively hostile when the Asians were forced to take unofficial strike action.[7] Thus the dispute at Imperial was characterized by a split between Asian strikers and local union officials, with the latter maintaining that '. . . in a civilized society the majority view will prevail. Some people must learn how things are done . . .'[8] This view was directly opposed to the strikers' position: they believed that the existing unions must be made to stand up for the rights of black workers when they failed in their duty to do so.[9] In contrast, [. . .] the basic demand of the Grunwick strikers has been trade union recognition. In their case, an employer has been refusing even to recognize a trade union and in these circumstances it is the Labour movement itself that is being challenged. The TUC and the trade union can therefore hardly be expected to do anything other than support the Grunwick strikers; and the fact that they are Asian immigrants is simply irrelevant in this context. The only sense in which the Grunwick strikers' immigrant status may be relevant is that the trade unions have traditionally been very concerned to recruit all immigrant workers into their membership. For example, the trade unions made their acceptance of the recruitment of East European Voluntary Workers in the late 1940s dependent upon their joining the appropriate trade union.[10] The issues raised by the two disputes are different and we would therefore maintain that the fact that Asian workers have been involved in both should not be interpreted to mean that both are, as a consequence, 'race relations' situations as well as industrial relations situations.

## The use of 'race' in the dispute

This is not to say that 'race' has not been viewed by some interested parties as a relevant dimension of the dispute. As the evidence stands, it cannot be shown that the management at Grunwick practised racial discrimination and the strikers themselves have been adamant in maintaining that their being Asians is irrelevant. They see the dispute as a conflict between workers and employers and, when we asked their feelings about one particular newspaper headline which read 'Asian Workers Strike for Union', we were told:

> It upsets us because we never talk about our own group. . . . We fight good for everyone who has to work in there. They are not all Asians. Once we have

the union in there, it will benefit everybody, not only Asians, so why call Asians by name.

Yet a number of interested parties have used to a varying degree, the 'race' dimension, and all of these have been on the *left* of the political spectrum. On the far left, the Socialist Workers Party (SWP) and the Communist Party (CPGB) have both, irrespective of their tactical differences, regarded support for the Grunwick strikers as a demonstration of solidarity with coloured workers. For example, the Brent Communist Party distributed a leaflet after a march in Willesden on 1 October 1976 which specifically referred to the strikers as 'Asian immigrants' and which urged workers not only to 'step up solidarity action with Grunwick workers', but also to 'reject racialism . . . one race, the human race.'

For present purposes the labour movement can be seen to consist of the trade union leadership, the trade union members, the local Trades Council and the different levels of the·Labour Party. The trade union leadership, in the form of the TUC General Council defined the dispute as between worker and employer over trade union recognition and their interest in it has concerned the viability of the Labour Government's industrial relations legislation. For example, the General Secretary of the TUC, Len Murray, declared at a meeting of the strike committee:

> Thatcher and Prior should tell the company to act like any decent employer and recognise the right of your employees to join a trade union . . . the fact that these are coloured men and women is not the essential issue. These are ordinary working people who deserve the help of every decent citizen.[11]

The response of APEX has been different. We have noted above that Roy Grantham made reference to the exploitation of Asian and West Indian workers in the context of a speech on Grunwick at the 1976 Annual Conference on the TUC. Early in 1977, he said: 'This is the first major dispute involving immigrant workers to which the unions have given full support.'[12] In this connection, it is interesting to note that APEX is one of the white-collar unions which has argued for a more positive policy on the part of the TUC toward coloured workers. At the 1974 TUC Conference, the union urged the TUC to create a sub-committee to deal with racism, to push trades councils into action against racial discrimination in employment, to counter the activities of the National Front and to campaign for the repeal of the 1971 Immigration Act. It could therefore be argued that, somewhat fortuitously, APEX, in being approached by the Grunwick strikers for assistance, was being given an opportunity in which it could show that its words did mean something in action. It may also be no coincidence that Tom Jackson, also Chairman of the TUC's Equal Rights Committee and Race Relations Advisory Committee, said in an interview with one of the authors in early 1977 that the unqualified (and unprecedented) support of the UPW was given because firstly Grunwick could be forced into negotiations, if starved of their mail and, secondly, it was an employer better suited to the nineteenth century, but also because it was a dispute involving coloured workers.

The Labour Government, apart from anxiously attempting reconciliation between the two sides, has made no reference to the strikers being Asian or immigrants, but a number of left-wing back-benchers have made references to the 'exploitation of coloured workers'[13] during parliamentary debates as a counter to the concerns of Conservative back-benchers about law and order.

As far as the trade union rank-and-file is concerned, we can only address ourselves to those we talked to in the Willesden area and in the course of our research. A significant feature of their response was the absence of hostility, often articulated in other contexts (notably in relation to housing), towards the East African Asian strikers. In this context, we found a willingness to put aside such prejudices and, instead, to indicate support for the strikers' demands. Also at the local level, it can be argued that it was not altogether coincidental that the substantial support of the Trades Council and Labour Party came only a month after they had launched a joint campaign against racialism in Brent. Undoubtedly, the dispute has been of some indirect benefit to both parties in that their support for the strikers could be used to show that this was a campaign of action and not of low-key propaganda. (For example, members of the local Labour Party, including the Chairman of the local Campaign Against Racialism, were arrested on the picket line.) An additional pay-off for the local Trades Council has been the number of enquiries made about trade union membership by previously unorganized coloured workers. Having said this we would argue that during the recent past the local Trades Council has tackled various industrial relations issues with the same degree of concern as it has shown towards the Grunwick dispute.

Thus on the left of the political spectrum, some interested parties, particularly those concerned about the extent of racism and racialist practice in Britain in general, have utilized the Grunwick dispute for their own ends and have therefore made 'race' a relevant issue. As one moves to the right of the political spectrum, however, one finds a complete absence of any reference to the ethnic origins of the Grunwick strikers. Among all shades of opinion within the Conservative party, and by George Ward himself and the NAFF, the issue that has been raised, with varying emphasis, by the Grunwick dispute, has been that of law and order. This may be a reflection of the view that there is more political mileage to be obtained from this emphasis rather than any other.

## Conclusion

The Grunwick dispute has already had a significant impact on industrial relations in this country. George Ward [. . .] effectively challenged, for nearly two years, what on paper appeared to be an extension of trade union influence granted by the Government's trade union and employment protection legislation. During the first year, rank-and-file trade unionists responded in their various ways, to the calls for support from the Grunwick strikers. But the response has seemingly proved increasingly embarrassing to the trade union leadership, particularly the use of direct action, which is viewed by some as a form of illegitimate coercion and which has undoubtedly aroused further hostility towards trade unions amongst some sections of the public at large.

For those with an interest in the relationship between the trade unions and coloured workers, the dispute may not provide evidence for a substantial change in the union leadership policy towards these workers. There are, however, features of the dispute which can be seen as encouraging. Firstly, the media have, in the main, portrayed the strikers simply as workers, rather than coloured workers. Although most national newspapers have referred at some point to the fact that the strikers were predominantly Asians from East Africa, this has been entirely subordinate to the publicity given to the UPW's action and the mass picketing. Secondly, in contrast to the disputes at Mansfield Hosiery Mills Ltd and Imperial Typewriters Ltd there has been little evidence of racial exclusion. Rather, both in the local area and nationally, solidarity action was forthcoming on a considerable scale.

## Notes and references

1. A more detailed chronology of events and viewpoints is to be found in Joe Rogaly's *Grunwick*, Penguin Special, September 1977; also in the Scarman Report on the Grunwick Dispute (cmnd. 6922).

2. Interview conducted with one of the strikers by one of the authors. Both authors were at the time carrying out research in the Willesden area on political conceptualization and action among the West Indian and English working class.

3. *Guardian*, 23 June 1977.

4. R. Miles and A. Phizacklea, 'The TUC, Black Workers and Immigration, 1954–1973', *RUER Working Paper* 1977.

5. Commission on Industrial Relations, *Mansfield Hosiery Mills Ltd.* (Report No. 76), HMSO 1974.

6. R. Miles and A. Phizacklea, 1978, *op. cit.*

7. Workers Educational Association/Runnymede Trust, *Immigrant Workers and Trade Unions*, Runnymede Trust, 1974.

8. *Race Today*, Vol. 6. No. 7, July 1974, p. 204.

9. This was expressed in a statement by the strike committee after the strikers had returned to work and cited in Counter Information Services, *Racism: Who Profits?*, CIS, 1976.

10. J. A. Tannahill, *European Volunteer Workers in Britain*, Manchester University Press, 1958.

11. *The Times*, 13 December 1976.

12. *Observer*, 20 March 1977.

13. *The Times*, 3 November 1976.

# CHAPTER 3.4

# RACE RELATIONS AT WORK
*Trades Union Congress*

In 1977 Congress carried a resolution calling upon the General Council to conduct a campaign against the activities of racialists in unions and to promote developments of equal opportunities. With regard to the campaign against racialism the General Council have issued a number of publications concerning race relations and have held two public demonstrations under the banner United Against Racialism. This general campaign goes on but the General Council are now focussing the emphasis on promoting good race relations at work and providing equal opportunities for all workers. As part of the development of effective equal opportunity policies, the General Council have been promoting the use of the TUC model clause on equal opportunities and it was following a review of progress on the use of that clause, that the General Council decided to organize this one day conference. [. . .]

Britain has for centuries been a multi-racial and multi-national society. Over the centuries many nationalities have made Britain their home. They have come to escape persecution, to find work, to find peace, and to enjoy prosperity. The most recent newcomers have been black and brown citizens of the Commonwealth who saw Britain as their mother country and who came to find, above all else, work.

Over the centuries newcomers to Britain have enriched British life. They have faced discrimination, hardship and opposition but they have made considerable and rapid progress. However, problems of discrimination, hardship and disadvantage remain. Racial discrimination, and indeed violence, are serious problems in British society today. The solution to these problems is not easy and requires action on many fronts. The trade unions

* An extract from the General Council's Discussion Document prepared for a Special Conference on Race Relations, July 17th, 1979.

have a special role to play in finding solutions to those problems concerning employment. [. . .] The TUC has pointed out that racial equality is in the interest of all trade union members. The basic principle of trade unionism is that unity is strength. The more union members there are in a workplace who are acting together, combining their knowledge and information and linking their support, the greater the influence of the union. Effective unity cannot exist if a union is treating any group of members with less consideration than other groups. While particular groups appear to be receiving less than an equal opportunity to secure jobs and indeed the jobs offering good pay and conditions, this weakens the Movement and damages its standing.

It has been argued that in the past the trade union Movement has not generally taken steps to ensure that they receive information about cases of discrimination within the union, nor have they always taken decisive action to combat discrimination when it has arisen. It has also been argued that little has been done to induct the new minority membership into the history, purposes and practices of the Movement.

The criticism of past activities of the trade union Movement even if not true for all sections of the Movement or for all times does point to a weakness which has existed and which cannot be ignored. For this reason, the TUC established an Equal Rights Committee and a Race Relations Advisory Committee in 1976. These Committees monitor and develop TUC policy on race relations in all its aspects, with special emphasis on trade unions' internal affairs and at the workplace.

There are relatively limited detailed statistics available about the extent of trade union membership of ethnic minorities. But evidence from the PEP Survey suggested that 'trade union membership is, if anything, higher among the minority groups than among the white population'. PEP found from its survey that among men from the minority groups who were in employment, 61 per cent are members of a trade union, compared with 47 per cent of white men. Trade union membership was rather lower among African Asians than among other Asians or West Indians, probably because comparatively few African Asians were manual workers. Thus Asians and West Indians half of whom arrived in Britain within the past ten years from countries having a different framework of industrial relations have been generally ready to put their trust in the trade union Movement.

From general observation it seems to be the case that ethnic minorities are underrepresented at every level of the trade union Movement. This is the case whether it be at full-time official level, at branch officer or shop steward level, or at attendance as delegates to policy making bodies or at branch.

Of course, one cause for the lack of representation lies in the fact that with many posts being filled by election it will take many years for ethnic minorities to work their way through the trade union Movement and gain the necessary experience to become office holders. It is also true to say that the disadvantages which hinder the progress of ethnic minorities at work will also prevent their progress in the trade union Movement.

Two issues arise. Firstly, what steps can trade unions take to develop the level of membership among ethnic minorities and second what efforts can they make to encourage participation by ethnic minority members in union affairs.

On both issues, it is obvious that any efforts with regard to ethnic minorities should be seen as part of a union's general efforts to develop its membership and to increase the participation of members in union activities. But unions need to examine whether they should take any special measures with regard to ethnic minorities.

Delegates' attention is drawn to the fact that the TUC has provided recruitment leaflets in five of the main ethnic minority languages for unions to use. An initiative is being taken in the East End of London by unions in association with the TUC's South East Regional Council. A joint committee has been formed to build up union organization in work-places in the East End which employ significant concentrations of ethnic minorities. [. . .]

## Collective bargaining and equal opportunities

The TUC suggested that unions, as a first step in the promotion of equal opportunities, should negotiate with employers the inclusion in their collective agreements an Equal Opportunities Clause; designed to secure the introduction of positive policies of equality of opportunity. The General Council have commended the following model clause:

> The parties to this agreement are committed to the development of positive policies to promote equal opportunity in employment regardless of workers' sex, marital status, creed, colour, race or ethnic origins. This principle will apply in respect of all conditions of work including pay, hours of work, holiday entitlement, overtime and shiftwork, work allocation, guaranteed earnings, sick pay, pensions, recruitment, training, promotion and redundancy (nothing in this clause is designed to undermine the protections for women workers in the Factories Act).

> The management undertake to draw opportunities for training and promotion to the attention of all eligible employees, and to inform all employees of this agreement on equal opportunity.
>
> The parties agree that they will review from time to time through their joint machinery, the operation of this equal opportunity policy.
>
> If any employee considers that he or she is suffering from unequal treatment on the grounds of sex, marital status, creed, colour, race or ethnic origins, he or she may make a complaint which will be dealt with through the agreed procedures for dealing with grievances.

In December 1977 the General Council decided to review how far unions had progressed with the inclusion of the clause into their collective agreements. Unions' views were also sought on whether the clause had helped to eliminate discrimination. Briefly, the report indicates that a number of unions in both the public and private sector have negotiated the inclusion of the clause in their collective agreements. However, the main conclusion of the General Council was that many unions had not appeared to have pursued the matter to any conclusion and that there was still a lot to be done by unions in considering the question of equal opportunities.

## Racialism

A final important aspect of race relations at work is the trade union Movement's role in the fight against racialist attitudes, which is essential if any of the policies and aims referred to earlier in this document are to be achieved.

Unlike the policies referred to in this document, which concern only the workplace, the campaign against racialist attitudes and values transcends dividing lines of organizations. All organizations, the media especially, have a moral obligation to counter racialism.

The TUC as part of the campaign has held two public demonstrations in London and Manchester under the banner 'United Against Racialism' and has issued leaflets to counter racialist propaganda.

The approach to the problem has been to promote the basic principle of trade unionism that unity is strength. A second strand of the TUC's campaign is to counter the fallacies about black people which are disseminated by racialists.

Finally, the TUC with the Labour Party has issued leaflets which condemn the fascist and racialist political parties and expose their dangers to our society.

Individual unions and Trades Councils have also been prominent in campaigns in their own industries or localities to increase awareness of the dangers of racialist propaganda.

A number of unions have also considered the problem of countering the activities of racialists within unions. The General Council has considered the matter and is particularly concerned about those trade union members who hold office within or on behalf of a union and may use their position to propagate their views and discriminate against a union's ethnic minority members. The General Council has therefore asked unions which have not yet adopted a policy on this matter, to seriously consider how best to deal with existing or possible future activities by racialists within their own organizations.

Trade unions will have to be vigilant in continuing to promote equal opportunities and opposing racialist views. Delegates may have suggestions as to what further programmes of action could be developed by the trade union Movement to counter racialism in the workplace.

# SECTION 4

# EQUAL OPPORTUNITY IN EMPLOYMENT

# INTRODUCTION

The need for positive action (see General Introduction) has been argued by the Commission for Racial Equality (Chapter 4.4). This contains an explanation of what is allowed under the Race Relations Act in terms of training and encouragement provided for specific ethnic minority groups. A wider discussion of the need for positive action is provided by Geoffrey Bindman (Chapter 4.5).

A survey conducted by David Smith (Chapter 4.1) revealed that in 1974 very few employers were interested in taking an active stance on equal opportunity. Many were prepared to accept equal opportunity in principle but did not feel it was necessary to take any action. The situation was little different in 1977.[1] Baroness Seear (Chapter 4.2) has argued that a positive stance by an employer (involving analysis of the facts, setting goals and timetables, monitoring, and training) is consistent with good management, and can be justified on grounds of self-interest. Both the TUC (Chapter 3.4) and the CBI (Chapter 4.3) have issued unequivocal statements supporting an active stance on equal opportunity. It may first be asked, how far should an employer go in the interests of achieving greater job equality between black and white workers? How far can employers, through separate and isolated action, break down the pattern of racially- based job inequality? By comparison with the United States, very few initiatives have been taken by British employers to promote equality of opportunity. Is state intervention therefore necessary, and, if it is, on what scale? These issues have been at the forefront of public debate in the United States where court-ordered hiring quotas, following successful complaints of discrimination against an employer, have been widely used for many years. A voluntary scheme by an employer giving preference to black employees in a craft training course was recently upheld as constitutional by the US Supreme Court on the grounds that such discrimination in favour of blacks 'mirrored' the purposes of the Civil Rights Act. The US Supreme Court also upheld the principle of giving preference to socially disadvantaged applicants to medical school in the

Bakke case. (The Court ruled, however, that the particular way in which the University of California operated the scheme was too rigid and thus declared it unlawful.)

It is often argued that any racially-based preference, whether in favour of whites or blacks, is unacceptable even if the purpose of the discrimination is benign (eg to compensate for discrimination in the past, or to reduce inequality or job segregation). An argument defending reverse discrimination has been put forward by Ronald Dworkin (Chapter 4.6). By contrast, Nathan Glazer (Chapter 4.7) argues that affirmative action (which in the United States frequently involves quota arrangements or goals and targets which are often de facto quotas) can yield short-term gains but has longer term disadvantages. It may well be that intervention of the kind advocated by Dworkin will be successful only where an expanding economy generates sufficient jobs to facilitate a reduction in an unequal pattern of employment or job opportunity. Given present economic conditions it may be doubted whether there would be sufficient political will to implement any large-scale intervention by central government specifically to improve the job prospects of black workers. And even if such action was taken, it may be wondered whether it would have much effect, in so far as many of the industries in which black workers are concentrated have been particularly hard hit by the decline in manufacturing output.

Thus future developments in equal opportunity policy will be discussed and formulated in the context of the persistent high levels of unemployment, the impact of micro-technology and the changing patterns of working life. The pattern of inequality and job segregation among women is similar to that among black people and the analysis and remedies are likely to have much in common. Despite high levels of unemployment, the vast majority of the labour force are in employment and are successfully seeking work. Therefore it is essential for employees to take equal opportunity seriously despite the recession. Thus an extract by David Wainwright (Chapter 4.8) is included in which he outlines an approach by which employees can achieve a wholehearted commitment to equal opportunity. Finally, an advertisement published by General Motors would have illustrated some of the results claimed by one major US employer but permission to reproduce this was refused.

## Reference

Carby, K. and Thakur, M. (1977) *No Problems Here?*, London, *Institute of Personnel Management*.

# CHAPTER 4.1

# RACIAL DISCRIMINATION – POLICY AND PRACTICE *
*David J. Smith*

A separate PEP project has shown, on the basis of tests in a variety of situations, that there is still substantial discrimination in recruitment for both skilled and unskilled jobs, though there is some indication that the incidence has decreased since the earlier PEP study carried out in 1966–67. The present study gives some insight into the employment practices that lie behind this situation, and it extends our understanding beyond recruitment to promotion and redundancy policies. It also allows us to assess the extent and effectiveness of policies to combat discrimination, and the studies at plant and head office level can be combined to yield an analysis of the reciprocating roles played by the centre and periphery in either combating discriminatory practices or allowing them to continue.

## Examples of discriminatory practices

The fourteen plants covered in the case studies form a good cross section by region and type of industry, but are not a representative sample in the statistical sense. The findings of this part of the study are not therefore intended to provide an exact measure of the incidence of discriminatory practices, but they do reveal some of the conditions in which these take root.

Out of the fourteen plants there were eight which clearly practised some form of discrimination, and in a further two cases discrimination seemed likely, though the facts were less clear cut.

At first sight it seems surprising that the managers of these plants – for

* Chapter II from *Racial Disadvantage in Employment*, Report no. 544, published by Political and Economic Planning (now Policy Studies Institute) June, 1974.

the most part decent and friendly people with a healthy respect for the law – should be doing things that are unlawful; all the more surprising, perhaps, when we find that they are not grossly prejudiced against the groups which they are treating unfairly. This paradox is explained by a number of factors; perhaps the most important of these is lack of awareness. Naturally managers know that racial discrimination is unlawful, but they are not usually familiar with the detailed provisions of the law, nor have they worked through its implications for their own practice. The result is that they have avoided facing up to the implications of what they are doing, and the law has not yet succeeded in applying enough pressure to make them face up to it.

This lack of awareness was vividly illustrated by a bakery in London which made a practice of employing considerable numbers of production workers on a so-called 'casual' basis. In fact these men were continuously employed, sometimes over a period of years, and were doing exactly the same jobs as the 'permanent' workers, yet their terms and conditions of employment were entirely different. The managing director explained the advantages of the system in these terms: 'They are on an hour's notice and there is no chance of redundancies and industrial trouble. I'm talking mainly about Indian staff. A few white men have jobs which involve a month's probationary period but there are no white casuals.'

This practice was contrary to the Contracts of Employment Act, because the men described as casuals would be regarded in law as permanent workers by virtue of their continuous employment over long periods. It would not therefore be legal to keep them on one hour's notice or to consider them ineligible for redundancy payments. There was also a serious element of racial discrimination. Among the workforce as a whole there was a preponderance of Indians, with a substantial minority of white workers, but virtually all the casuals were Indians. The managing director made it clear by the spontaneous remark already quoted that race was the main factor in deciding whether a man would be offered 'permanent' or 'casual' work. The same system was also being used in lieu of a proper selection procedure, for Indian employees only. 'I think you can really say that if you are an Indian here you would not get a permanent job anyway. You will be offered casual employment until we find out where we are'.

An advantage of the system, from the management's point of view, was that the 'casuals' could easily be laid off at the minimum expense. Redundancies were expected, because the bakery was about to modernize some of its plant, leading to a reduction in the workforce. Three months later we carried out further interviews with trade union representatives at the bakery. By that time some of the expected modernization had taken place; half of the 'casual' workers – all of them Indians – had already been dismissed.

It was remarkable that the managing director admitted so readily to practices that were unlawful on more than one count; this is a striking illustration of a lack of awareness of the implication of the law, which was also evident from other cases. For, if it had not been for his lack of awareness, this manager would never have made such admissions to a researcher whom he might be expected to treat with caution and suspicion.

It is easy for managers to put on blinkers to shut out the Race Relations Act from their field of vision, because the concept of discrimination is far less clear cut than the concept of an illegal act like stealing. The manager of the bakery does not approach his job in a reflective or analytical frame of mind, and it would not come naturally to him to measure his practices against what might seem like an obscure and irrelevant criterion. Indeed, such a manager will probably tend to ignore all constraints unless he is forced to take notice of them.

Besides a lack of awareness of the law, or a refusal to notice it, this case also illustrates another point. Racial discrimination does not usually spring up in isolation; it is typically just one knot in a tangle of bad employment practices. The system of employing production workers on a 'casual' basis was an unlawful method of exploitation which was adopted not as a means of discriminating on a racial basis, but to smooth the path for later redundancies, to prevent the possibility of organized resistance from the workforce and to avoid the necessity of having a proper selection procedure. The situation would probably not have been accepted by a white workforce, but this was not a factor that had been consciously weighed up by the management. The essential point was that they were prepared to adopt bad practices if they could get away with them, and it happened, almost incidentally, that these practices provided an opportunity for expression of a racial prejudice, and that all the 'casuals' were therefore Indians.

The case studies provide several illustrations of active and definite policies to regulate the numbers employed from various racial groups. Whether or not these policies are unlawful (this point is discussed below), they disprove an argument often put forward in favour of a *laissez-faire* approach towards race relations: that any specific policy in this field draws people's attention to the differences between races when they might otherwise tend to forget them. The fact that specific policies do already exist – but these are nearly always directed at limiting the numbers of Asians and West Indians employed.

The first such case was a large toy plant in London. Overall the proportion of employees from minority groups was about 25 per cent and this included about equal numbers of Asians and West Indians, with smaller numbers from various other groups. At one time management had tried to impose a quota of 10 per cent, and although this had been exceeded, they still tried to keep a balance between groups both overall and within each department. This led to some difficulties with employment agencies: 'You give them a job specification and the sort of person you want and they send you three or four applicants, all non-white, and because I've already got what I consider to be a balance in that department I have to turn these people down purely on the fact of their colour. One appreciates that ethically this might not be correct but on the other hand my concern is my company.'

By contrast the informant had never regretfully rejected white applicants because he had what he considered to be a balance in some particular department. At first sight it might seem that this policy would not be unlawful because of the 'racial balance' clause of the Act. In fact this company could not have satisfied the conditions of that clause. To do so they would have to show that their policy was designed to encourage mutual adjustment between people whose cultural backgrounds were different. In practice, however, they made no distinction between different minority groups, or between immigrants (whose culture might be alien) and Asians or West Indians who had been educated in this country. Their only concern was to limit the total number from the minority groups within each department. It is interesting, too, that the 'racial balance' clause had no influence in this case, because the management did not seem to know about it. They certainly did not invoke it to justify their policy, which they admitted was not ethically (or presumable legally) correct.

Two further cases show that the practice of controlling the levels of various racial groups in the workforce can work in opposite and paradoxical ways. In these cases the policies had nothing to do with racial balance, but were aimed at excluding a particular group. These plants were foundries a few miles distant from each other in the West Midlands, one three times as large as the other. At the larger foundry there were about 200 minority employees, almost all of them Indians. At the other there were 50 minority employees, almost all of them West Indians. At the larger foundry, employing Asians, the personnel manager said that West Indians were not particularly welcome, 'not for any reason of colour or race, but there is a strong feeling that they are very slow'.

This was in spite of the fact that, according to the same personnel director, 75 per cent of the Asians employed could not speak English, and there were severe problems of communication. The smaller foundry, which employed West Indians, had made the decision in the 1950s not to employ Asians, because of language problems. Since then recruitment had been by recommendation from existing workers, or in other words through the grapevine, and this had tended to exclude racial groups other than the whites and West Indians already at the foundry. Even so management must have had to discriminate to keep Asians out of the plant altogether. Thus, we have a case of two plants within a few miles of each other, each of them foundries with the same range of jobs, one excluding Asians, the other excluding West Indians, and each thinking it has excellent reasons for excluding the group that the other employs.

The personnel director of the larger foundry also illustrated another paradox. In spite of his prejudice against West Indian workers he was enthusiastic about making social contacts with Indians. He was often asked by Indian workers to social occasions such as weddings and always tried to attend. He was very much aware of the problems and anxieties of his Indian staff and had clearly thought about the ways in which they could be alleviated, for example by greatly improved induction processes. But the fact was that, mainly because of language, there existed in his plant the most complete barrier between the races that we encountered anywhere; and nothing had been done to avoid the industrial problems which could and did result from such a situation.

The cases of the two foundries, together with the toy factory in London, show that discriminatory policies may be aimed at restricting the minority workforce to Asians, or at restricting it to West Indians, or at keeping the ratio from the minority groups to an 'acceptable' level. When they are juxtaposed in this way these policies lose the appearance of having any objective basis.

The case of the smaller foundry also shows how a discriminatory policy of redundancies can be pursued without the men becoming aware of it, provided that management can avoid defining the criteria that are being used. One of the departments at the plant had been automated eighteen months before our visit. Before automation 80 men were employed in this department, of whom about 40 were West Indians. At the time of our visit the department employed 35, of whom 6 were West Indians. Thus about ten out of 40 whites were made redundant, compared with about 34 out of 40 West Indians. The works manager explained: 'We would have been silly if we didn't pick out people. It was largely left to the mill manager to pick the people out for the new mill and the rest were made redundant. So it was likely that they would adapt because we picked people with the right attitude. The coloured people – we needed fewer of them, so we had a wider choice.'

Management were able to do this because they succeeded in keeping the men in ignorance of the criteria that were being used to decide who was to be laid off:

*White foreman:* They could put their name down for redundancy.
*White crane driver:* No, it was on length of service.
*White assistant roller:* No, I had a mate who had worked here for years and he wasn't offered another job.
*West Indian pulpit operator:* They did it on whether you were a good worker.
*White assistant roller:* Older men were not offered jobs.

Like the case of the bakery, this case illustrates the way that discrimination can arise as one of a number of aspects of a bad employment practice. Whatever the racial constitution of the workforce, the criteria to be used in deciding redundancies could have been jointly agreed between management and men and, once having been agreed, they could have been clearly communicated to everyone in the department. Because this did not happen management was allowed to be arbitrary; it was allowed the scope to carry through policies that were racially discriminatory. The situation would not have been allowed to develop if the trade union had been stronger, and this point will be taken up later in the chapter on the role of the trade unions.

The case of the toy factory (discussed earlier) also illustrates a way in which the promotion of workers from minority groups can be avoided without apparent discrimination against existing staff. There were no minority charge-hands or supervisors, but on the other hand white workers were not promoted to these positions either. Instead the supervisory staff were recruited from outside. In this way management gave all groups of workers cause for grievance, in order to avoid having Asian or West Indian supervisors. There were signs that the union was about to take the matter up, so that a general labour relations problem would be created because of this roundabout discriminatory practice.

Discrimination in recruitment is perhaps most likely to occur – and certainly most difficult to prevent – in cases where the organization is fragmented, so that recruitment decisions are taken by the managers of a large number of small units. This was illustrated by the case of a group of food shops which we visited, in a part of London where the concentration of West Indians is exceptionally high. The group is medium sized, with shops in many parts of the country, but our case was confined to the four stores in one particular part of London. In total there are 65 employees in these shops, of whom 50 are women and fifteen men. The area personnel manager said that he did not know exactly how many West Indians were employed, but that he expected to see a few black faces when he went round the stores. In fact all of the employees of the stores in the area are white. This could only have happened as the result of discriminatory policies on the part of the four store managers, since there is a very high concentration of West Indians in the area (a high proportion of the customers are West Indians) and it is notoriously difficult to find counter staff for shops, so that there tends to be a very high labour turnover.

The local personnel manager changed twice during the course of our study, because the management of the whole group was in a state of flux at the time. This led to a general disorganization, which made it unlikely that the discriminatory policy was originating from a higher level. Our interpretation was that the individual store managers, being subject to little control from above, were allowed to pursue their discriminatory policies without interference.

Where recruitment decisions are fragmented, control will always be difficult, and this does not apply only to large shops. Another interesting case of the same kind was that of a scaffolding contractor which has countrywide operations, with a head office in the South East. At the head office, which employed several hundred, an estimated five to ten per cent of the staff were from minority groups. The manual workers, on the other hand, worked on their own in closely knit teams, and they had very little contact with their local depot and none with the head office. Recruitment was carried out by the depot managers in consultation with the charge-hands, and was not subject to any control from head office. Although there was no direct evidence of discrimination, it was readily admitted that a depot manager would never allocate an Asian or West Indian to a particular team if the charge-hand was against it. This meant, in effect, that the company could easily avoid having any workers from minority groups if they thought that their charge-hands would be prejudiced against them. It would be possible, of course, for the company to employ a proportion of minority workers by allocating them to charge-hands who did not object, but the whole recruitment process was so fragmented that general policies of this kind had never been contemplated. This may be an indication of more widespread problems that exist in the building industry.

These cases show that there is a strong danger of discrimination within highly fragmented organizations, but we are not suggesting that this is because junior staff are more likely to discriminate than senior staff. A number of factors are involved. Where the units are small and loosely controlled, personnel procedures tend to be informal and therefore less checkable; for this reason, when discrimination does occur, it is unlikely to be noticed by anyone outside the local unit. In general terms, control by higher levels over personnel matters tends to be limited. A completely separate point, which is well illustrated by the case of the scaffolding contractor, is that where the units are small and tightly knit, the higher levels will in any case be reluctant to force workers from minority groups into them against their will.

We have suggested that where industrial relations are not formalized, and where bad employment practices exist and are not resisted by the trade union, the opportunity for racial discrimination tends to arise in the midst of other industrial problems. Unfortunately, however, more formalized procedures, generally good employment practice and strong trade union representation do not automatically exclude the possibility of discrimination. In fact, where the trade union is strong it can help to bring about discrimination in recruitment, as well as influencing the practices adopted inside the plant. This was illustrated by the case of a plant in the South East, which is part of one of the largest British companies with a long record of forward looking personnel policies. Here, in a plant employing about 900 manual workers in essentially simple processes involving heavy repetitive work, there was a strong personnel function and virtually 100 per cent union representation, with fairly active participation in union affairs. Before the Race Relations Act the plant had excluded the racial minorities altogether, but since the Act it had begun to take on Asians in fairly small numbers. The personnel manager explained the policy by saying they 'did not want to be leaders in the field', so that when they did start recruiting the minorities they could benefit from the experience of other firms in the area.

Before deciding to recruit Asians and West Indians they had discussed the matter with the shop stewards, who had made 'hostile noises'; but they had decided to go ahead nevertheless. However, they had kept the proportion of workers from minority groups to five per cent and had ensured that they were thinly spread over the various departments. It was certain that this policy involved discrimination, because the proportion of the pool of manual labour in the area that belonged to minority groups was much higher than five per cent and the plant found it extremely difficult to get staff – the personnel manager estimated that there were five vacancies for every one unemployed person. In addition it was admitted that the majority of applicants were Asians and West Indians.

There was the possibility, in this case, that discrimination arose partly because of prejudice on the part of the personnel director. However, he did not express prejudiced views very readily, and it seemed that any prejudices that he might have were slight. The more important reason seemed to be genuine fear of opposition from white workers. A later interview with two shop stewards showed that these fears were far from groundless; one of the shop stewards happened to be prejudiced in an extreme and obsessive way. The generally good labour relations paradoxically encouraged management to discriminate, because they took serious account of workers' views, as they saw them. On the other hand, there was evidence from this and other cases that the opposition from white workers, though real, could be successfully opposed without producing serious disturbances. This question of the nature of white resistance and how it can be overcome is one that merits separate treatment.

# CHAPTER 4.2

# THE MANAGEMENT OF EQUAL OPPORTUNITY*
*The Rt Hon Baroness Seear*

Twenty years ago equal opportunity was not an issue, except among a small group of politically conscious people, mainly middle-class women. If discussed at all, it was seen as an aspect of class conflict. Today some form of legislation to promote equal opportunity is in existence or under consideration in most, if not all, of the major industrial countries. The reasons for this remarkable change lie outside the scope of this paper. It is, however, relevant that when most of today's managers and trade union officials were being trained, equal opportunity for women and for ethnic minorities was not on the syllabus, nor was it a subject which kept them awake at night.

This is one reason, though by no means the sole reason, why many managers have asked themselves why they should bother with these matters when it is a full-time job merely to keep the enterprise afloat.

The simplest and most obvious answer is, of course, that the Sex Discrimination Act 1975 and the Race Relations Act 1976 make it illegal to discriminate in nearly all the main aspects of employment on grounds of sex or marriage, or of colour, race, nationality, or ethnic or national origin.

At one level this is the end of the matter. We still believe we are a law-abiding people. Not many managers deliberately set out to defy the law. But obedience to legal requirements, though necessary, is not sufficient for the creation of equal opportunity. The law provides the essential foundation; only positive management action designed to suit the needs of each particular enterprise, can put flesh and blood on the legal bones.

* The 1979 Sir Alfred Herbert Paper presented to the Institution of Production Engineers. This is an edited version of 5000 words. Now also a Briefing Paper of the Runnymede Industrial Unit.

Legal considerations apart, there is clearly a strong case for equal opportunity in terms of elementary human rights. If there is a right to work, it is a right to be enjoyed by all, regardless of sex or colour. But many people who accept this principle point out that it has never meant that any particular individual has a right to a particular job in a particular place of work. Neither in this country, nor in the United States, where anti-discrimination law is much more powerful than in the United Kingdom, is it argued that employers are required to meet their equal opportunity obligations by reducing the efficiency of their enterprises.

On the contrary, since the manager's primary obligation to society is the creation of wealth and the provision of goods and services, the real question is how management can combine the application of an equal opportunity policy with the effective running of the business. If further it can be shown that such policies can in fact increase effectiveness, the elimination of discrimination appears in a different light. It then becomes not only a legal obligation, but also a positive element in good management.

Equal opportunity in employment means, in plain English, that no one is denied training or a job for reasons that have nothing to do with their competence and capacity. But if people who on merit would get a particular job are not appointed for some irrelevant reason, the job being filled by a less suitable person, the enterprise concerned is that much the poorer. Since it is management's contribution to make the most effective use of all available resources, financial, material and human it is clearly part of their job to see that such a waste of abilities is avoided.

If this argument is right, why is not equal opportunity a reality? Why does discrimination persist?

Some will no doubt say that I am making a mountain out of a molehill; that there is no discrimination; that given the known shortage of good people anyone with anything about him or her, can get on. There is no problem. 'No problems here' is in fact the title of a book written on this subject.[1] But the author did not find the claim could be substantiated. The assertion that there are no problems usually means there has been no overt trouble – no Industrial Tribunal cases, no awkward brushes with the Commission for Racial Equality or the Equal Opportunities Commission – or, and perhaps especially, no threatening noises from the unions, and no strikes.

But this relatively happy position does not in itself add up to equal opportunity. Whatever may be the circumstances in any one enterprise, the picture for the country as a whole makes it difficult, indeed impossible, to deny the existence of widespread discrimination.

In a study carried out by Political and Economic Planning in 1973–74[2] in London and the South East, in East and West Midlands, in Yorkshire and the North West, it was found that in 30 per cent of cases there was discrimination in selection against Asians or West Indians. A second PEP study,[3] looking into the level of work performed by members of ethnic minorities, reported: 'The findings show that there is a strong concentration of minorities in non-skilled manual jobs and a low concentration in non-manual jobs. Thus 10.1 per cent of the non-skilled manual workers are from minority groups compared with only 3.2 per cent of the non-manual workers. Male workers from minority groups are still more strongly concentrated in non-skilled manual jobs. The consequence of this is that the composition of the minority workforce by type of job is markedly different from that of the total workforce.'

The position with regard to women is not dissimilar, though the reasons for it are no doubt different. According to the 1976 New Earnings Survey[4] women comprised 39 per cent of the total labour force. They were, however, only 10.4 per cent of those employed in general management, 13.8 per cent of those in professional and related supporting management and administration, and 7.4 per cent in the category of professional and related supporting management in science, engineering, technical and similar fields.

Of course you may be right in believing that whatever happens elsewhere *you* are genuinely, to use a common American phrase, an 'equal opportunity employer.' But belief is not evidence. In the climate of today, with today's legal obligations, and today's apparent shortage of trained and trainable talent, it is necessary not only to believe, but to know. So far as possible you need to be able to prove it. How can you be sure you are not sitting on a gold mine of unused resources?

As with any issue facing management, the first task must be to establish the facts. How many women and members of ethnic minorities are employed and in what jobs? The answers to these questions call for an analysis of the employment position in terms of pay, and of levels of skill and authority. So far as women are concerned, this should not prove too difficult or time consuming, assuming the enterprise has reasonably good personnel records.

The case may be far less simple, however, in relation to ethnic minorities. In the early days of race relations legislation, many people believed that to compile records on the ethnic origin of employees was in itself an act of discrimination. The Race Relations Board and the Commission for Racial Equality have disagreed with this view. Unless records are kept which give information on ethnic origin, it is not possible for the analysis of facts to take place. Without such an analysis no management can answer the question 'Have we a problem?' nor can it take steps to solve the problem, or to see whether the attempted solutions are in fact working.

In some places trade unions do not accept the need to keep such records and oppose management attempts to set them up. This raises a real obstacle in the path of the establishment of equal opportunity within the enterprise. Differences of opinion between managements and unions are a familiar part of the daily round of industrial life, and at this point industrial relations can affect the establishment of equal opportunities. How then can management approach this aspect of the problem?

The leadership of the trade union movement has given the strongest possible support to equal opportunity for both women and ethnic minorities. As in so many other spheres this does not, of course, mean that all trade union members are equally keen. But support from the top, be it in management or in the unions, is always – or almost always – worth having. At local level it is up to management to learn where support for the official policy is enthusiastic and where it is at best lukewarm. Initial informal consultation on the development of policy is a well-tried and often most successful approach.

The problem of records is only one of a number of industrial relations issues that may need to be handled in this way. In most enterprises today it must be obvious that no equal opportunity policy has much chance of success without trade union support. It is perhaps less obvious that this is an issue which, personal prejudices apart, need not present great difficulties. The tough industrial relations problems are those that involve genuine conflict of interest between management and one or more unions, where there is, or appears to be, little common ground. Compromise is then the only solution.

Equal opportunity is not, in fact, such an issue. In an increasing number of cases both women and members of ethnic minorities are trade union members. The union has nothing to lose, and can have a good deal to gain, by underwriting a fair deal for them. At bottom the conflict, if there is one, is not between the management and union, but between the prejudiced and unprejudiced on both sides of the bargaining table. There could even be some unfamiliar alliances.

Once records have been established and the analysis undertaken, the basic facts are available for the development and application of policies.

Given the national figures, and the evidence of a number of enterprises in which such analysis has been undertaken, it is highly probable that a characteristic pattern will emerge for both women and ethnic minorities. In both cases it is likely to be found that they are heavily concentrated in a limited range of jobs and these jobs are predominantly the least well paid, the least skilled and the least likely to lead up the ladder to positions of authority. There will, of course, be variations and exceptions, but I would lay pretty heavy odds that this is the picture that would emerge in nine cases out of ten. This can in no way be regarded as a normal distribution, and for this reason, if for no other, it calls for further examination.

It seems likely that women and ethnic minorities fail to make the grade for one or both of two main reasons – either they suffer from some disadvantage which means that they cannot in fact hold their own in open competition; or they are discriminated against and so fail when in genuinely free competition they would win.

There can be no doubt that for both groups there are real disadvantages, and by no means all of them can be tackled by management, though it would certainly help if managements drew attention to them and threw their weight on the side of change. One of the most obvious of these disadvantages is the language barrier, which holds back some members of ethnic minorities. Some managements are doing a great deal to remove this disadvantage and to improve efficiency by introducing language teaching where it is most relevant, ie inside the place of work, using such bodies as the National Centre of Industrial Language Training. But there are still those whose command of English must reduce their effectiveness, and must also, incidentally, increase the risk that they may suffer an industrial accident.

Inadequate English is only one of many educational limitations affecting women and ethnic minorities when seeking employment or promotion. Despite some advance, girls still leave school ill-prepared to take craft or technical training or higher or further education in technological, economic or financial fields. Yet frequently it is just such a basic preparation which is required to get a foot on the rung of the ladder which leads to jobs of real scope and responsibility. Managements do not, and should not, control the education system. It is, however, increasingly accepted that bridges need to be built between schools and colleges, on one hand, and industry on the other, and the nature and extent of the disadvantage created by inadequate and inappropriate education is surely a priority subject for discussion.

Both women and ethnic minorities may continue to be at a disadvantage inside the place of work. Promotion to higher level jobs is frequently denied to candidates on the grounds that they have not had the right experience. It is, for example, frequently said of girls and women that they are not eligible for a particular job because they have not served a craft apprenticeship or have had no experience of line management, competent though they may have been in some specialist role. They are plainly at a disadvantage in comparison with a male candidate who has had the required experience.

Where this type of training and experience is in fact a valid qualification for the post sought, then clearly management is right to give the job to the appropriately qualified candidate. But the reasons the unsuccessful candidate lacks the right experience need be explored. Career ladders are all-important and the real question is why so few women and members of ethnic minorities get onto the ladders which can lead to high level jobs. The disadvantage of an inadequate general education and training is reinforced by the further disadvantages of inadequate job experience.

Women and members of ethnic minorities fail to make progress not only because they suffer from disadvantages which management may or may not be able to correct, but also because there is actual discrimination against them inside the enterprise, particularly in relation to initial selection, to training for promotion, and to promotion itself.

Sometimes this discrimination is deliberate and conscious.[5] The PEP study when testing the selection process obtained copies of letters sent by firms to black and white candidates, matched for qualifications. Two such letters read:

(To the white applicant)
    Date: 17 September 1973

Dear Mr X,
    We thank you for your interest in employment with this Company and would now ask you to complete and return the enclosed application form.
    We will make further contact with yourself when we have assessed all the applications for this position.

Yours faithfully,

(To the Pakistani applicant)

Date: 17 September 1973

Dear Mr X,
    We have received your letter with interest but regret to inform you that we have no suitable vacancy at the present moment.
    However, should a suitable vacancy arise in the near future we will make further contact.

Yours sincerely,


Training is often the key to promotion. Yet the figures for daytime release show that less than a quarter of all young people released by their employers for part-time study are women.[6] I have myself for many years taught on middle management courses attended by managers from a large number of enterprises. I can safely say that not two per cent of those attending the course have been women.

That direct discrimination of this type exists, no one would deny. In an investigation into equal opportunity for women for which I was responsible, some managers openly admitted not only that they did discriminate, but that they intended to continue to do so. Deeply entrenched ways of working, based on long-established custom and practice, are not easily altered, and it is not perhaps surprising that many people feel there can be little harm in continuing practices which, until recently, were very widely accepted by both men and women alike.

Discrimination against racial minorities is not in the same way based on long-established tradition, and is unlikely to be so openly, almost light-heartedly defended. There is also the important point that it remains good practice to be discriminating, provided the basis of the discrimination is neither irrational nor illegal. All selection methods are, after all, aimed at discriminating between those who are suitable for a certain job and those who are not. The purpose of equal opportunity policies is not to end the use of discrimination, but to ensure that the grounds for discrimination are both relevant and legal.

More subtle, more pervasive, and in many ways more important than open direct discrimination is the practice of indirect discrimination, also clearly banned in both the Race Relations Act and the Sex Discrimination Act. On the surface, indirect discrimination does not appear to be discrimination at all. A job or a promotion is, it is made clear, equally open to all comers. But the requirements and conditions of the job are such that in reality a substantial number of one sex or one ethnic group has no chance of being appointed. This does not, of course, mean automatically that the requirements have to be changed.

Neither here, nor for that matter in the United States, are organizations being forced to run with reduced efficiency. What can be challenged is the justification for the requirement or condition. Only if the employer, on being challenged, is unable to show justification will he be held to be discriminating. On the face of it, the removal of conditions which in fact cannot be justified should make for better, not worse selection. It also means that any managements who intend seriously to introduce an equal opportunity policy need to check through job by job to ensure that the alleged requirements do in fact make sense.

Answers to the questions which need to be asked may well set barking a number of sleeping dogs. Are age limits and seniority rules justifiable? In the now famous case of Linda Price against the Civil Service Department, an upper age limit was held to be unjustifiable. Is it really justifiable to require that only a person who has served an apprenticeship can be considered for a given post? Is it really the case that for certain prescribed driving jobs a Heavy Goods Vehicle Licence is required? Can mobility clauses in contracts be justified in all cases? And how about the need for the applicant to have a given number of O-levels?

Sometimes the answer will be yes. But these examples show how far-reaching can be the impact of equal opportunity legislation. They also show the link between the implementation of an equal opportunity policy and the validation of the firm's personnel management standards. Selection or promotion requirements which cannot be justified, cannot by definition be appropriate requirements and therefore should not exist.

Once the nature of discrimination both direct and indirect is clearly understood, existing policies and practices need to be explored to discover where change is necessary. Recruitment and selection, training, and promotion are the key areas.

Recruitment and selection are the areas that to date have attracted most attention in relation to equal opportunity. They appear to be the aspects most widely understood and have been the grounds of most of the cases which have been taken to Tribunals. It could be said that one of the major successes of the legislation has been the virtual elimination of the discriminatory advertisement. This can, however, prove a hollow victory, since a non-discriminatory advertisement can be followed all too easily by a discriminatory selection procedure. If the full implications of indirect discrimination have been grasped, it is clear that job analyses and job specifications need to be carefully checked.

If selection standards are closely linked with relevant job requirements, then the major cause of discriminatory selection processes will have been removed. It is not, however, a once and for all operation. Many selection procedures today are irrelevant and discriminatory because they have not been kept up to date – regular checking is part of the process of establishing equal opportunity. It is also essential if the selection methods are to remain valid. In relation to ethnic minorities, selection procedures may also raise the problem of cultural factors influencing test results. The Institute of Personnel Management report, 'Towards fairer selection – a code for non-discrimination'[8] pointed out that there are no truly 'culture fair' tests and that the test scores of members of minority groups cannot and should not be directly compared with those of the indigenous population unless research has shown this to be justified (which, in general, it has not).

The report then suggests ways by which some of these disadvantages can be reduced. Dr Pearn of the Runnymede Trust claims: 'With due regard to the reduction of bias in their use, validly used job-related tests can contribute to the removal of arbitrary barriers to the employment of black workers.'[9]

One further pitfall in selection arises from a tendency to generalize with insufficient regard for individual differences. Women, it is said, are more dextrous than men. But selection is always concerned with a particular individual, not with a whole category. Even if it could be shown that women in general tend to be more dextrous than men, it remains true that some men are more dextrous than some women. What the selection process needs to discover is the level of dexterity of the particular man or woman applying for a particular job. In one organization a job previously staffed 100 per cent by women became a job in which 25 per cent of the employees were men after the introduction of selection tests.

Selection for admission to a training course needs to be examined in much the same way as selection for an initial job. It is, however, important to remember that in the field of training, and in this field only, the legislation permits positive discrimination. Where in any job any particular ethnic group or either sex is under-represented, it is permissible to provide training on a preferential basis for that group or sex in order to help to redress the balance. The importance of this provision, which so far has scarcely been used at all, must be seen in relation to promotion policy.

With so few women trained for management or technical work, an equal opportunity policy in relation to promotion will operate very slowly indeed unless use is made of positive discrimination in training. And access to promotion is the crux of equal opportunity.

Training provides access to promotion – it does not ensure it. Any management that takes equal opportunity seriously needs to scrutinise its promotion policies and procedures in detail. If an organization is unable to explain clearly how it promotes from the existing white male population from which it draws the vast majority of its middle and senior managers, existing methods are not likely to contribute to equal opportunity. How are people identified for promotion? How are appraisals carried out? What use is made of appraisals in the promotion procedure? To these apparently obvious questions, by no means all organizations are able to give convincing answers.

It is not enough to review formal procedures. As every manager knows, what is supposed to happen according to the book and what in fact happens are often different. Differences that appear slight may none the less be of considerable importance. A management concerned to introduce a genuine equal opportunity policy must not only check its formal procedures, but must discover by a process of questioning what is really going on, and what are the real reasons for the perpetuation of discrimination.

Questioning serves two very important purposes. Obviously it is a means of establishing facts. But it is also the first stage in the essential process of raising awareness of equal opportunity issues and their implementation among managers and supervisors at all levels. The establishment of genuine equal opportunity calls for changes in attitude in most people.

Some of these attitudes are fairly superficial, resulting from an unquestioning acceptance of current practice. But some do have very deep roots and may indeed persist long after behaviour has altered to conform with new standards. Equal opportunity policies forced on managers and supervisors in the teeth of hostile attitudes may well create as many problems as they cure.

So the greatest attention needs to be paid to ways of influencing the attitudes as well as the behaviour of those who have to carry out the new policies. The more line managers and supervisors can be encouraged to question traditional practices and to suggest ways in which changes can be made, the more likely is the policy to be accepted and supported. Without such genuine acceptance, such policies may result in little more than reluctant window-dressing.

The fact-finding process is an important part of the policy of involving line management, as they begin to work through the problems raised by an equal opportunity policy. It must, however, be reinforced by formal and informal training programmes, probably involving role-playing and the use of case studies. The best training programmes will be those which are developed in response to queries and problems raised by the line managers and supervisors themselves.

Equal opportunity will not come about by itself. It requires management initiative and trade union cooperation if it is to become more than an empty phrase. Essentially it needs to be managed. This means, as with any other management activity, that there must be goals and timetables. Any organization can with the greatest of ease declare itself an 'equal opportunity employer'. There is a hard slog before the words are matched by deeds. Experience in the United States and in this country is showing that to make equal opportunity a reality, an organization must set out to achieve a realistic objective by a given date.

It may, for example, decide that at the end of three years it will have raised the percentage of women in line management positions from three per cent to nine per cent and the percentage of members of ethnic minorities in skilled trades from four per cent to eight per cent. Such goals must be clearly understood and accepted by everyone who will be involved in the process. The achievement of this goal will be regarded as a management task like any other management task, affecting the individual manager's assessments and promotion prospects. It is not suggested that these goals should be reached at the cost of the efficiency of the organization by taking on people who are not up to the job.

What is intended is something much more difficult – the discovery or development of people in the required categories who can in fact be selected or promoted on merit. What is required is what the Americans call an 'out-reach' programme to be carried out both within and outside the organization, involving a deliberate search for talent and the provision of appropriate training to bring potential candidates up to standard.

Initially there may well be difficulty in finding suitable candidates. There is a vicious circle to be broken. Because there have appeared to be no openings for women in posts requiring technical qualifications, no sensible girl in the past has invested her time in obtaining such qualifications. Once the word gets around that the demand exists, a supply will begin to come on stream. In one American bank, for example, a search for women with appropriate qualifications in finance was at first only moderately successful, but in a short space of time well qualified young women were knocking at the door. Equal opportunity, like anything else, needs to be marketed.

As in any other management enterprise, an equal opportunity policy cannot be installed and left to run itself. It is essential to monitor progress if timetables are to be kept and goals attained. Monitoring is a means both of checking progress and of identifying issues which require further investigation. The Civil Service Department, for example, which drew up an equal opportunity policy in 1973[10] engaged the Tavistock Institute of Human Rights to carry out work in 1976–77 to explore the possibility of developing a system of monitoring equal opportunity in the Civil Service.

The subsequent report[11] has aroused some controversy. It certainly showed a marked difference in the acceptance rate of majority and minority applicants.

This is not in itself evidence of discrimination, but it is evidence of the need for further investigation.[12] It also draws attention to 'hazards to fairness' which need to be corrected. A frequent finding of the studies was that reasons for rejecting applicants were often not recorded and sometimes not even clearly defined and agreed. Once pointed out, the danger is obvious, but it is a trap into which many organizations may well fall. Only careful monitoring can put those responsible fully on their guard.

Last but not least, the management of equal opportunity must be the responsibility of a senior manager with real influence and sufficient time. Without such leadership, words – however worthy the sentiments they express – will not be translated into deeds.

It all sounds very familiar. Get the facts; analyze the problem; set goals and timetables; train; communicate; cultivate and monitor. It makes the implementation of an equal opportunity policy sound what at the bottom it is – another job for competent managers running an efficient and responsible enterprise.

## References

1. *No problems here?* Keith Carby and Manab Thakur, Institute of Personnel Management, 1977.
2. *The Extent of Racial Discrimination*, Neil McIntosh and David J. Smith, PEP, The Social Science Institute, September, 1974.

3. *Racial Disadvantage in Employment,* David J. Smith, PEP, The Social Science Institute, June 1974.
4. New earnings survey reported in Second Annual Report of The Equal Opportunities Commission, 1977, published by HMSO.
5. *The Extent of Racial Discrimination, ibid.*
6. Equal Opportunities Commission, *ibid.*
7. Price v. Civil Service Commission, Industrial Relations Law Reports, 291 (1977).
8. *Towards Fairer Selection – A Code for Non-discrimination,* Institute of Personnel Management, 1978.
9. *Employment Testing and the Goal of Equal Opportunity: the American Experience,* Dr M. A. Pearn, Runnymede Trust, 1978.
10. 'Race Relations Policy: Equal Opportunity', General Circular GC/34, Civil Service Department (PMS), 19 November 1973.
11. 'Application of Race Relations Policy in the Civil Service', London: HMSO. November 1978.
12. 'Monitoring Equal Opportunity in the Civil Service', Dr M. A. Pearn, Runnymede Trust Briefing Paper, March 1979.

# CHAPTER 4.3

# 'STATEMENT' AND 'GUIDE ON GENERAL PRINCIPLES AND PRACTICE'*

## The Statement

The Confederation of British Industry wholeheartedly supports the principle of equal opportunities in employment and opposes all forms of discrimination on the grounds of sex, marital status, creed, colour, race, nationality, and ethnic or national origin. It regards the elimination of discrimination and the provision of equal opportunities as an essential step forward in the social and economic progress of the United Kingdom.

In addition the CBI favours the application by companies of constructive equal opportunities policies, and views such policies as a valuable contribution towards ensuring equal opportunities in employment based solely on merit and suitability of the job.

## Guide on general principles and practice

The CBI has prepared this Guide on company equal opportunities policies as an indication of general principles and practice so that member companies may assess their own policy on equal opportunities and take any appropriate action.

### The statutory duties of employers

As employers will know the Sex Discrimination Act 1975 and the Race Relations Act 1976 provide that it is unlawful for an employer to discriminate on the grounds of sex or race in offering employment or in the terms of employment. The only exception is where there is a genuine

---

* Confederation of British Industry.

occupational reason for the employment of a person of a particular sex or racial origin. Persons who believe that they have been discriminated against may complain to an Industrial Tribunal.

The Commission for Racial Equality and the Equal Opportunities Commission are both empowered to issue Codes of Practice relating to equal opportunities in employment. It is understood that they propose to exercise that right. The Codes will contain recommendations which though not legally binding will have persuasive force and will be of evidential value in any legal proceedings.

Discrimination may be direct or indirect. Direct discrimination consists of treating a person, on the grounds of race or sex, less favourably than others are or would be in the same circumstances. Indirect discrimination consists of unjustifiably applying a requirement or condition which, whether applied intentionally or not, adversely affects a considerably larger proportion of one sex or racial group than another.

In accordance with the relevant provisions of the legislation, legal penalties on an employer will follow if he is found by an Industrial Tribunal to have discriminated against an employee or potential employee. In addition the employer is liable for acts of discrimination on the part of his employees or his agents. He will, however, have a defence if he can prove that he took such steps as were reasonably practicable to prevent discrimination from occurring. For example, he might be able to show that he had taken adequate measures to instruct his employees on the company's equal opportunities policy.

It should be noted there is no provision in either of the statutes comparable to the requirement in the Health and Safety at Work etc. Act 1974 that employers should prepare and bring to the attention of employees a written statement of policy on health and safety at work. But although there is no legal obligation to have an equal opportunities policy or to evidence it in writing by means of a formal policy statement, the CBI believes that it is in accordance with the spirit of no one the legislation to have such a policy, and it is advantageous to commit it to writing so that it can be made known to all the employees affected by it. Employers may feel this would be part of good employment practice. In addition, many companies who operate a formal policy of equal opportunities in employment believe that it makes sound business sense in terms of developing the full potential of employees.

However, the CBI does not intend to issue a model company equal opportunities statement. Each company should decide for itself in the light of its own workforce composition and operational requirements the sort of policy that will be practicable for its organization. They will wish to decide in the light of their own experience what the content of any policy statement should be and to whom it should be published. In smaller companies, for example, a lesser degree of formality in the formulation and implementation of the policy will obviously be needed than would be the case in larger ones. Provided the policy is known to those it affects it may not be necessary to put it in writing.

## The contents of an equal opportunities policy

Aspects of employment which could be covered in an equal opportunities policy may include:

- ☐ the need to avoid racial and sex discrimination in recruitment, including advertising, placement, training, promotion or transfer, allocation of shift-work or overtime, discipline, redundancy and dismissal;
- ☐ the need for managers and supervisors to understand their personal responsibility for ensuring the effective operation of anti-discrimination policy and to act accordingly, particularly by avoiding direct or indirect discrimination in recruitment, promotion, training and dismissal of employees, and the arrangements for training them in that responsibility;
- ☐ arrangements for reviewing the policy and evaluating its operation;
- ☐ the role of employees, their representatives or any trade unions with regard to the policy;
- ☐ the availability of special facilities for certain categories of employees, eg language training;
- ☐ the use of grievance procedure where appropriate to resolve complaints of discrimination by employees and details of the outside agencies to whom employees may complain if they are unable to resolve the matter through the internal procedure.

Companies may also decide to include in any written policy statement a formal declaration of the company's commitment to the principle of equal opportunities.

## The operation of the policy

It is important that the policy should be seen to have the support of senior management, and is made known to all who will have to implement it, particularly personnel staff, line managers, and staff having direct contact with applicants eg gatemen and telephonists. It may therefore be sensible to issue a statement of the policy in the staff handbook, in management instructions or in a similar document. It may also be useful to include a reference to the company's policy in management and supervisory training.

Any equal opportunities policy will involve four stages; formulation, implementation, review and evaluation. Although careful formulation is essential, the success of the policy will depend primarily on the action taken to implement it. It will also obviously be necessary from time to time to review the policy and evaluate its operation to ensure that it is actually working.

The formality of any evaluation procedure will vary from company to company, but companies employing significant numbers of women or ethnic minorities may well find it useful to keep statistics. These can be examined to discover, for example, the extent to which such employees have been promoted in a given period as an indication of whether the promotion procedure is operating in a non-discriminatory way. Smaller companies may have difficulty in keeping records of this sort, but one of the ways in which they can evaluate the policy is to make regular enquiries to ensure that key employees remain aware of the company's policy and are carrying it out.

Companies may wish to consider the recommendations of the Commission for Racial Equality on monitoring the ethnic origin of employees in their booklet *Monitoring an Equal Opportunity Policy*. If employees are to be asked to specify their ethnic origins, or if visual identification is to be made by an official of the company, it will be essential that employees are aware of the reason for recording this information, and they should be reassured that the intention is to use it to avoid discrimination, not the reverse.

The active co-operation of all employees, particularly managers and supervisors, is essential to the success of the equal opportunities policy. They should be made aware of the policy and the need to carry it out effectively. Employers may wish formally to involve any employee representatives in the formulation and implementation of the policy through the existing consultative procedure, though as with other employment policy the ultimate responsibility lies with management. It is suggested that the monitoring of the policy is a matter for management alone, as the actions which result from it will have to be taken by them.

Where a trade union is recognized, the union may ask the employer to agree to an equal opportunities clause in a collective agreement. The decision as to whether to agree such a clause will have to take account of the circumstances of the company concerned, but no matter what its specific terms, management will wish to ensure that the agreement does not derogate from their rights and obligations as employers.

As in the case of statements, the CBI does not intend to issue a specimen clause or endorse any existing clause, because it does not think that such a clause drafted by any central organization would be likely to be suitable for adoption in its entirety into an individual agreement.

## Conclusion

In this guidance note it has been the CBI's intention simply to outline some of the standard characteristics of equal opportunities policies as an indication to employers of what might be included in their own policy. CBI staff would be glad to advise individual member companies on matters connected with equal opportunities policies, but are not able to draw up the policies for them.

# CHAPTER 4.4

## WHAT IS POSITIVE ACTION
## AND WHY IS IT NECESSARY?*
*Commission for Racial Equality*

1. Even if discrimination were stopped overnight this would not be sufficient to enable ethnic minorities to compete for jobs from a basis of genuine equality, for they would still suffer from the effects of past discrimination and disadvantage. They are still, for example, heavily under-represented in many areas of employment, particularly in supervisory and managerial positions and comparisons of employees with similar qualifications show that white men are significantly better represented in professional and managerial posts than men from ethnic minority groups.

2. The aim of positive action is to counteract these effects by enabling members of ethnic minority groups to develop their potential and 'catch up' with the experience of white applicants and employees. This does not involve the imposition of quotas or permit discrimination in selection.

3. The White Paper which preceded the 1976 Race Relations Act defined the need for such action. It argued that a principle of non-discrimination, interpreted 'too literally and inflexibly', might 'actually impede the elimination of invidious discrimination and the encouragement of equality of opportunity' because it would exclude such measures as special training courses for ethnic minority workers designed to help fit them for jobs from which they had previously been excluded, and special encouragement to them to apply for employment which, for various reasons, they had not previously sought. It therefore concluded that 'it would be wrong to adhere so blindly to the principle of formal legal

* Commission for Racial Equality, *Equal Opportunity in Employment: Why Positive Action?* A Guidance Paper, 1980.

equality as to ignore the handicaps preventing many black and brown workers from obtaining equal employment opportunities,' and promised:

> provisions allowing (but not requiring) employers and training organizations to provide special training facilities to members of such groups and to encourage them to take advantage of opportunities for doing particular work. There will be similar exemptions allowing the provision of special training facilities and encouragement by trade unions, employers' associations, and professional and trade organizations . . . the provision of facilities and services to meet the special needs of particular ethnic or national groups (for example in relation to education, instruction, training and health and social services) . . . and . . . discrimination in the employment, where necessary for these purposes, of persons of a particular ethnic or national group.

4. These provisions are now contained in Sections 5(2)d, 35, 37 and 38 of the Race Relations Act 1976, which are described later.

5. Ideally the need for these special provisions should not be a permanent one. Positive action is, in Lord Scarman's words, 'only a means to an end' – 'the law should declare the general principle of equal justice for all under the law, while recognizing the temporary and limited exception in favour of members of disadvantaged groups.'[1] A leading American legal authority has pointed out that Britain has the advantage of still having time to benefit from preventative action, since the situation here has not deteriorated to the worst kind of American experience of race relations.[2] Positive action is a stop-gap, and the sooner resources throughout the country are used to counteract the effects of discrimination and disadvantage, the sooner the gap will be closed.

6. There need not always be a clear practical distinction between positive action and action to prevent discrimination, particularly indirect discrimination, and some of the steps that we shall be recommending fall into both categories. Moreover, the scope for positive action goes very much wider than the special provisions of the Act. There are some types of action which may benefit the entire workforce, and meet the needs of disadvantaged employees or job applicants from any group.

## Does the employer gain any benefit?

1. It is to the advantage of any organization to have the widest and best choice for selecting its personnel. If staff or potential staff do not have

the chance of demonstrating their ability, employers are denied the opportunity of using it. Ensuring that a workforce is using its full potential benefits both employer and employee.

2. Specialized language and other training can improve communication, general efficiency, and therefore production.

3. Without the provision of specialized training, a situation can develop in which ethnic minority workers are concentrated in lower grades and white workers in higher grades, or in different shifts or sections. Dissatisfaction with race relations becomes dissatisfaction with industrial relations, and there can then be a decline in general operational efficiency. Positive action can improve industrial relations to the general benefit of any organization.

4. In many companies white workers are concentrated in senior posts because of length of service. When they reach retirement age, it is preferable to have replacements with experience of the company and its work. If ethnic minority workers are concentrated in the lower grades from which replacements are likely to be recruited, it makes sense to provide in-service training for them in readiness. This can be done by ensuring on-going training for current staff to maintain progress through all grades, or by forward manpower-planning in developing young trainees for a future senior role.

## Section 38(1) & (2). Training and encouragement by employers

Under Section 38(1) & (2) employers may afford only their employees from a particular racial group facilities for training to fit them for work in which that group has been under-represented in the previous twelve months or may encourage them to take advantage of opportunities of doing that work. For the purposes of these sub-sections, a racial group is under-represented in particular work if its proportion of the persons doing that work is small in comparison with its proportion of the workforce at that establishment or of the population of the relevant labour-market. No discrimination is allowed, however, at the point of selection for appointment or promotion.

The Metropolitan Police, for example, ran a recruitment campaign headed 'Is Racial Prejudice keeping *you* out of the Metropolitan Police?' and stating: 'if you happen to be coloured, you'll be especially welcomed because there aren't anything like as many officers from coloured communities as we would like to have.' But while members from ethnic minorities were encouraged to apply, there was no discrimination at the point of selection.

One company had a number of Asian supervisors with the experience to equip them for promotion to posts in which Asians were under-represented, but without command of the specialized technical language required for the appropriate training course. In co-operation with the local industrial language training centre, the company organized in-service training courses to help fit them for such posts.

Another company has set up a Youth Development Scheme to encourage more applications for its craft apprenticeships from black youths who are potential trainees but lacked the necessary educational qualifications. This is a one-year 'pre-apprenticeship course' comprising block release to a local technical college for off-the job instruction, with criteria such as manual dexterity and willingness to learn used as entry qualifications. If on completion trainees can demonstrate improvement to a standard comparable with the normal apprenticeship intake they can be admitted to the standard apprenticeship scheme. Otherwise they can continue on what is in effect an alternative apprenticeship course, which does not reduce standards but provides an alternative approach to similar qualifications. The company does all that it can to ensure permanent jobs for trainees who successfully complete the course.

## What, in addition, does the Race Relations Act allow?

*Section 5(2)(d). Where being of a particular racial group is a genuine occupational qualification for a job*

Where a particular post is concerned with the provision of services promoting the welfare of persons of a particular racial group, and where these services can most appropriately be provided by a member of that group, membership of the racial group concerned may be a genuine occupational qualification for appointment to the post. (A 'racial group' is a group of persons defined by reference to colour, race, nationality or ethnic or national origins.)

For example, several local authorities have appointed ethnic minority social workers to work particularly with local ethnic minority communities with whom they share cultural backgrounds. One local authority has appointed four Asians to work with the Asian community in Housing Action areas under its Urban Renewal Programme.

## Section 35. Measures to meet the special needs of particular racial groups

Section 35 allows action to be taken to afford members of a particular racial group access to facilities or services to meet the special needs[3] of persons of that group in regard to their education, training, welfare and ancillary benefits. Industrial language training is an obvious example.

## Section 37. Training and encouragement by training bodies[4]

Under Section 37 training bodies may afford only persons of a particular racial group access to facilities for training for particular work, or encourage them to take advantage of opportunities for doing that work, when they have been under-represented in that work either in Great Britain as a whole or any part of Great Britain.

For the purpose of this sub-section a racial group is under-represented in particular work where it appears to the training body that at any time within the preceding twelve months there were no persons of that group among those doing that work in Great Britain; or the proportion of the group among those doing that work in Great Britain was small in comparison with its proportion of the population of Great Britain. Where the conditions are met for only a particular area, training or encouragement can only be provided for persons who appear likely to take up that work in that area.

One ITB, which has assisted with industrial language training for several years, has extended their field of interest to cover courses for 'immigrant spokesmen' – to give training in the industrial relations systems within a company and the procedures which follow from these. The aim of the courses is to help ethnic minority shop floor representatives to understand industrial relations procedures and use the system constitutionally. It is hoped that the representatives will then go on to train their members along the same lines.

One local community project applied for designation in order, with Urban Aid support, to operate a scheme to train young people from ethnic minorities in the caring professions, with the intention of fitting them for employment as local authority community workers or with local voluntary organizations.

## Section 38(3), (4) & (5). Training and encouragement by trade unions, employers' associations and similar organizations

Under Section 38(3), (4) & (5) trade unions, employers' associations and similar organizations[5] may afford only those members who belong to a particular racial group access to facilities for training to fit them for posts in which that group has been under-represented in the previous twelve months or may encourage then to take advantage of opportunities for holding such posts. For the purposes of these sub-sections a racial group is under-represented in a particular post if its proportion of the persons holding such posts is small in comparison with its proportion of the membership as a whole. Trade unions, employers' associations and similar organizations may also encourage members of a particular racial group to become members where, during the previous twelve months, that group's proportion in membership was small in comparison with its proportion among those eligible for membership.

The TUC and individual trade unions have translated courses and information on trade unionism into Asian languages in order to encourage participation by Asian workers, both as members and shop stewards, on a scale more closely related to their numbers in the work-force.

## Section 29(2). Advertising

Under Section 29(2) it is not unlawful to publish an advertisement which indicates an intention to take any action which is allowed by Sections 5(2)(d), 35, 37 and 38.

## Notes and references

1. Minority Rights in a Plural Society, the Sixth Minority Rights Group Annual Lecture, by the Rt. Hon. Lord Scarman PC OBE.
2. Professor Archibald Cox lecturing on the Bakke case at the American Embassy on 3 July 1978.
3. A variety of provisions could be eligible under Section 35, but each would have to be judged on the individual factors involved. Under-representation in a particular sphere, for example, is not of itself sufficient grounds to justify 'special needs'. Such 'special needs' could be interpreted as not being required to be exclusive to a particular racial group, but must be special to the relevant category of persons of the particular racial group, viewed as a racial group. To illustrate from the example of language training given above, the fact that a white indigenous person has a special need for remedial tuition in literacy does not in any way prevent members of a particular ethnic minority group from having special needs for language training as a result of their racial background. The criterion for the special nature of the needs would be that persons of the racial group suffer disproportionately in comparison with persons of other racial groups from the need for the particular facility or service which is to be provided for their education, training or welfare.

4. For the purposes of this Section, training bodies include Industrial Training Boards established under Section 1 of the Industrial Training Act 1964; the Manpower Services Commission, including the Employment Services Division and the Training Services Division; and any other person designated for the purposes of this Section by the Secretary of State. Groups seeking designation can apply to the Manpower General Division, Department of Employment, Caxton House, Tothill Street, London SW1H 9NA.

5. This section applies to organizations of workers or employers or any other organization whose members carry on a particular profession or trade for the purposes of which the organization exists.

# CHAPTER 4.5

# POSITIVE ACTION*
## Geoffrey Bindman

## 'Equal opportunity' and 'affirmative action' policies

It has been pointed out that the striking superiority in the effort being made in the United States is the widespread implementation of equal opportunity and affirmative action policies. What sort of policies are these? How are such policies stimulated and what stands in their way in Britain?

The expression 'equal opportunity policy' is in common use in Britain, but its meaning has not been defined with precision. In its most limited sense it is used to refer to a policy whose object is solely to prevent unlawful discrimination by the firm or institution which adopts it. In a broader sense it includes giving greater encouragement to members of ethnic minorities to take advantage of opportunities than to others. An equal opportunity policy in this sense goes beyond the negative requirement of the law to abstain from discrimination. It encourages the acquisition of a fairer or more nearly equal share of the benefits of society for members of ethnic groups who are disproportionately denied them. 'Affirmative action' is the term most commonly used in the United States to describe such policies, but invariably it has the second broader sense with often additionally the implication that preferential treatment may be given in certain circumstances to minorities with a view to redressing the balance between them and more favoured groups. The Race Relations Act does not require the adoption of an equal opportunity policy even in the narrowest sense, though ordinary prudence or routine practice might cause many institutions to take some precautions to avoid breaches of the law.

* An extract from the article which appeared in *New Community*, Winter 1980, vol. VIII, No. 3.

The duty imposed by the Act is negative: not to discriminate by or against any person by reference to their supposed membership of a racial group whatever it may be. From this it follows that preferential treatment or reverse discrimination in favour of a racial group is in principle unlawful. It becomes lawful only where there is a specific exemption allowing it.

The Act does, however, give some recognition to the obvious fact that the rigid application of the negative principle of non-discrimination will, even if it is fully successful, result in no more than the perpetuation of existing inequalities. As the White paper previewing the 1976 Race Relations Act says: 'The Government considers that it would be wrong to adhere so blindly to the principle of formal legal equality as to ignore the handicaps preventing many black and brown workers from obtaining equal employment opportunities.'[1] The Act therefore does contain some exemptions for voluntary 'positive action' which might otherwise be construed as unlawful discrimination notwithstanding its benevolent intent.

## Preference in the pre-selection stages

The interpretation of sections 37 and 38 also has limitations and uncertainties. Both have been narrowly defined with the apparent intention of retaining the prohibition of giving preference at the stage of selection for employment or promotion. There is exemption only for the stages leading up to selection, ie the process of seeking candidates and training to achieve the necessary qualifications. As the training or encouragement of those who do not belong to the relevant minorities is not obligatory, however, an employer who wished to carry his preference to the selection stage could often in practice do so. The firm statement in the Home Office Guide to the Act: 'This exception does not, however, make it lawful for the employer to discriminate at the point of selection for such work'[2] is literally correct, but it may lead the employer who wishes to increase minority representation to underestimate the possibilities.

Using the parallel provisions in the Sex Discrimination Act, the Engineering Industry Training Board has proposed a scheme for making grants to employers to encourage them to recruit female trainee technicians where few or none are already employed. The scheme is supported by the Manpower Services Commission and funds have been secured from the European Social Fund.[3] The practical effect of recruiting additional female trainees is obviously to give them preference in recruitment, assuming only that there are enough vacancies after they have completed their training to absorb all who have been trained. Such schemes are as appropriate for under-represented ethnic minorities as for women and are equally to be encouraged.

The special programmes administered by the Manpower Services Commission for the unemployed are not, of course, designed specifically to help ethnic minorities although, to the extent that their members are represented among the unemployed, they benefit from these schemes. A joint working party of the CRE and the MSC has considered the implications of such schemes for ethnic minorities and the extent to which special measures for ethnic minorities are justified.[4] A number of local initiatives taken by community relations councils and others to encourage self-help groups and training schemes are commended. The CRE has provided funding for several of these and so has the MSC. In a few cases relationships have been established with employers who participate in training and who in some cases place trainees in employment.

The CRE has, however, recently expressed disappointment that the recommendations of this working party and of another joint CRE and MSC group, the Ethnic Minorities Task Group, have not been accepted.[5] These included the monitoring of ethnic minority participation in special programmes and a greater contribution by employers to such schemes. Apart from the few schemes which directly involve employers,[6] the weakness of the special programmes supported by MSC lies precisely in the absence of incentive for employers to make special provision for ethnic minorities. It is significant that only one training scheme based on minority under-representation had led to designation of a training body under section 37 (at the time of writing). This was the North Lewisham Project in South London, which sought to provide basic training in community work for West Indians without appropriate academic qualifications for established courses.

## Promoting equal opportunity policies

The opportunities for positive action allowed by the Race Relations Act are by no means insignificant, though some of the restrictions seem arbitrary. The CRE encourages positive action and has issued detailed guidance about it, yet there is no evidence of any widespread adoption of equal opportunity policies incorporating positive action. Only a handful have been introduced by private employers. A few local authorities have adopted them, notably Camden, Lambeth and Hackney. The education authorities referred to earlier have done so, but there is little other evidence of schemes initiated by or encouraged by Government. Even those policies which seek to do no more than to ensure the absence of unlawful discrimination are not believed to be numerous, though it is impossible to establish how many exist. This is so notwithstanding the specific defence to legal proceedings brought under the Race Relations Act against an employer (who would otherwise be liable for acts of his employee done in the course of his employment) 'that he took such steps as were reasonably practicable to prevent the employee from doing that act, or from doing in the course of his employment acts of that description'.[7] This might be expected to stimulate reasonable efforts but appears rarely to have done so.

Considerable attempts have also been made by the CRE to promote equal opportunity policies generally, and to demonstrate that such policies are in the interest of employers as well as in the public interest. In 'Equal Opportunity in Employment – A Guide for Employers',[8] the Commission asserts the vital importance of equality of opportunity regardless of race, 'not only for employees to have a fair and equal chance of developing their abilities and realizing their expectations, but also for employers to make full and effective use of their manpower and to improve their industrial relations.' Such policies must be more than a mere pious statement of intent.

Employers are advised in drawing up a programme to:

(a) allocate overall responsibility for the policy to a member of senior management;

(b) hold discussions and, where possible, reach agreement with trade unions or employee representatives on the policy's contents and implementation;

(c) issue a statement to all employees setting out the policy and to make the policy known to potential job applicants;

(d) provide training and guidance for persons in key decision-making areas in order to ensure that they understand their responsibilities under the law and the company's policy;

(e) examine existing procedures and criteria and, where it is found that they are operating or could operate against equal opportunity, to change them, where appropriate, after consultation with trade unions or employee representatives;

(f) carry out an initial analysis of the ethnic composition of the workforce in order to identify possible areas for action;

(g) monitor the ethnic composition of the workforce and of job applicants on a regular basis in order to evaluate the progress of the policy.

Other bodies and personnel specialists have published similar recommendations and detailed guidance.[9]

## Monitoring and setting an example

An essential element in an effective equal opportunity policy (even one designed to do no more than ensure compliance with the law) is knowledge of the facts about minority employment and recruitment within the organization. This entails record-keeping and monitoring in all but those small firms and institutions where the facts are obvious or already well-known. Yet only a handful of large private firms are known to have fully developed policies which include ethnic records and monitoring. Much opposition to monitoring is based on misunderstanding or is a way of expressing general opposition to equal opportunity policies. The collection of ethnic statistics is not itself discriminatory, for statistics are neutral and it is the use to which they are put which alone need cause concern. The fear that racial statistics would help an employer to discriminate is an understandable one, and it was a similar fear which led some coloured people and groups to oppose the inclusion of a question about racial origin in the 1981 census. But an effective equal opportunity policy without knowledge of the facts is virtually impossible, and the risk of any discrimination occurring which would not have occurred without record-keeping must be an extremely small one. Those firms which do keep records and monitor have reported no difficulties. Nor is there any reason to suppose that the cost is a significant factor, balanced against the advantages of an effective policy.

There is a conspicuous absence of leadership from the Government in bringing about equal opportunity policies either in its own employment or in private employment where its influence could be decisive. The Tavistock Institute of Human Relations was commissioned by the Civil Service Department to conduct a study of the effectiveness of the policy on race relations in the Civil Service and its report was published in November 1978.[10] The report showed that in several departments there were substantially fewer ethnic minority employees than would have been anticipated in the absence of discrimination. A joint working party of management and trade unions was established after the publication of the report to consider what action should be taken. One of the main non-industrial Civil Service unions, the Civil and Public Services

Association, has acknowledged that a policy of no racial discrimination cannot be demonstrated without a detailed monitoring system and has called on the Government to make the necessary resources available to ensure that records of ethnic background can be collected, analysed, regularly updated and follow-up action taken where necessary. Yet the joint working party has still not reported and the Government has shown no sign of readiness to introduce effective policies.[11]

As well as setting an example to private employers in its policies for employment in the Civil Service, the Government could use its commercial power by insisting on satisfactory policies as a condition of eligibility for Government business. It has made gestures in this direction but with no known practical effect. From 1969 all Government contracts have contained a standard clause requiring compliance with the provisions of the Race Relations Act 1968 relating to discrimination in employment and to take all reasonable steps to ensure that their employees and subcontractors did the same. Of course the inclusion of such a clause without any arrangements for checking whether it is being obeyed is of little value. The Street Committee in 1967 had recommended that the Race Relations Board should be given the task of policing the non-discrimination clause[12] but this was not implemented. The 1975 White Paper reverted to the topic:

> The Government has considered whether its duty to take an active role to eliminate discrimination requires something additional. It would be an unacceptable burden to require all contractors to supply as a matter of form full particulars of their employment policies; but the Government cannot passively assume that a formal condition in a contract is all that is required. It is therefore intended that it should be a standard condition of Government contracts that the contractor will provide on request to the Department of Employment such information about its employment policies and practices as the department may reasonably require.[13]

It was not expected that any provision would appear in the Race Relations Bill to give effect to this commitment in the White Paper, since it is a matter for executive action by the Government. It is surprising, however, that even the very limited extension proposed has still not been brought into effect. No doubt the precise mechanism needed consideration and at the time of the change of Government in May 1979 consultations were still in progress. Before the General Election the CRE had submitted detailed arguments and suggestions on the effective monitoring of the equal opportunity clause but even at the time of writing (August 1980) no response had been received. The clause remains as ineffective as before.[14]

Another source of persuasion to employers to adopt effective equal opportunity policies is the Code of Practice which the Race Relations Act permits the CRE to issue, containing practical guidance for 'the elimination of discrimination in the field of employment' and 'the promotion of equality of opportunity in that field between persons of different racial groups'.[15] The CRE has prepared a draft Code and has issued it for public consultation.[16] The Code can only be formally issued after it has been approved by the Secretary of State for Employment and laid before Parliament. As well as the persuasive authority of a code approved by Parliament, a Code of Practice which has been formally issued has some albeit very limited legal consequences: an industrial tribunal in deciding any question in proceedings under the Race Relations Act must take any provision of the Code into account which appears to it to be relevant.[17]

The CRE's draft code recommends that employers should 'adopt, implement and monitor' a formal equal opportunity policy to ensure that there is no unlawful discrimination and that equal opportunity is genuinely available. It sets out the ingredients of an effective policy as they appear in its earlier guidance document. It recommends a method of monitoring which includes the keeping of records and regular analysis of them, though conceding that alternative methods of monitoring are acceptable if they can be shown to be effective. It is not yet known, of course, whether the code will be issued in its present form or will be amended before obtaining Government and Parliamentary approval (or indeed whether it will be issued at all). If it is issued in its present form it may prove to be a stimulus for effective equal opportunity policies, though without coercive force.

## Comparisons with the US

Comparing this picture with the United States, it is useful to bear in mind the three ways in which equal opportunity policies can be stimulated: by a vigorously enforced law against discrimination which creates a strong motivation to take steps to avoid the risk of legal action; by making the adoption of suitable policies itself a legal requirement; and by the Government using its commercial and other executive powers to stimulate equal opportunity policies.

The basic principles underlying the law are not significantly different between the two jurisdictions. In the United States discrimination in a wide range of activities is made unlawful where it occurs because of a person's race or national origins.[18] As under the Race Relations Act the prohibition of discrimination is in negative terms: to comply with the law it is sufficient to refrain from discriminating. There is no general legal obligation to undertake affirmative action policies save that, by contrast with the Race Relations Act, a court may order affirmative action by way of remedy for discrimination already proved to have taken place.

Two factors, however, make the persuasive effect of the law much greater in the United States: the prospect of successful litigation against those who discriminate is much greater and the economic consequences for those successfully sued are vastly greater. The prospect of success is greater because judicial attitudes in the United States differ from those which have so far manifested themselves among the judiciary in the United Kingdom. To some degree this stems from fundamental differences in judicial philosophy. In the United States the judges (led by the Supreme Court) have understood and accepted the major importance of measures to end racial discrimination and have been prepared to interpret the law broadly to give it maximum effect. The concept of indirect discrimination, as has been said, was created in the United States without legislative intervention. Such an imaginative and innovative approach may go beyond the capacity of British judges not merely for reasons of temperament but because the canons of statutory interpretation which prevail in our courts do not permit it. Nevertheless, there is no doubt that US judges on the whole have an understanding of discrimination which enables them to identify it much more readily than nearly all British judges and Industrial Tribunals, who are much less willing to accept that discrimination has been proved.

In the US, moreover, the economic consequences of a finding of discrimination are potentially much greater because heavy damages may be awarded both for direct and indirect discrimination. Under the Race Relations Act no award of damages at all can be made in an indirect discrimination case if the discriminator proves that the indirectly discriminatory requirement or condition was applied without the intention of treating the victim unfavourably on racial grounds.[19] This will usually be the case, since the whole point of indirect discrimination is that it arises out of practices which unintentionally (though unjustifiably) operate to the disadvantage of minorities.[20] Even where compensation can be awarded in Britain, the amounts have often been derisory.[21] Furthermore, the procedural device of the 'class action', available in the US but not in Britain, enables claims to be pursued in the US courts simultaneously on behalf of a large number of claimants, each of whom may be entitled to compensation. The deterrent effect of damages claims is also diminished in Britain by the greater difficulty which faces those who wish to pursue them. Legal aid is not available in the Industrial Tribunals and the CRE is the only major source of advice and assistance. In the US the contingent fee system, which allows lawyers to take an agreed percentage of whatever damages are awarded as their fee, means that lawyers are always available where there is a prospect of large awards, and, even when there is no prospect of gain, there are large and efficient civil rights organizations which specialize in litigating discrimination cases with widespread significance and impact.

The Equal Employment Opportunities Commission, a statutory agency, also brings cases to court where patterns and practices of discrimination are alleged. Although the law against discrimination requires only the absence of discrimination, it has long been established that US courts which find unlawful discrimination may make detailed and wide-ranging remedial orders designed to prevent the recurrence of discriminatory practices and rectify the effects of past discrimination. These orders customarily require numerical hiring and promotion goals. Thus an employer who does not voluntarily adopt an affirmative action programme may find he is compelled by a court to do so. Even if he believes he can successfully defend a lawsuit, he may find it prudent and less costly than fighting it to reach a compromise in which he would submit to a court-ordered affirmative action programme, perhaps in return for the waiver of the claim for damages.

The influence and leadership of Government is extremely powerful in the United States. By contrast with the failure of the British Government to implement even the very modest commitment of the White Paper concerning Government contracts, the US Federal Government has for a number of years compelled those who enter into contractual relationships with it to undertake strict monitoring to ensure non-discrimination.[22] Every contractor having 50 or more employees and a contract amounting to $50,000 or more annually must file an annual report, or, in the case of a new contractor, within 30 days of the award of the contract. The report contains a detailed analysis of the ethnic origin of the work-force at every level. The sanctions for breach of any of these requirements include cancellation or suspension of the contract and disqualification from receiving further contracts. A separate agency, the Office of Federal Contract Compliance, is responsible for enforcing these requirements, because it is regarded as self-evident that contracting departments cannot be their own policemen.

Furthermore, Title VI of the Civil Rights Act 1964 prohibits discrimination in 'any program or activity receiving federal financial assistance'. Every federal department and agency with power to give financial assistance through grants, loans or other means is under a duty to ensure that this rule is observed. This normally entails proof that effective policies are in operation on terms similar to those applied to Government contractors.

Detailed guidelines for affirmative action are published by the Equal Employment Opportunities Commission,[23] and by other Government departments and agencies. The avowed aim of such guidance is to encourage policies which will not merely avoid discrimination but will increase representation of minorities in all fields and levels of employment. The foreword to the EEOC guidelines of 1974 stresses the need for positive affirmative action beyond the establishment of neutral 'non-discriminatory' and 'merit-hiring' policies. It goes on:

> Experience in administering equal opportunity laws over the past 30 years has shown that many discriminatory practices of the past remain so deeply embedded in basic institutions of society that these practices continue to have extremely unequal effect on certain groups in our population, even when the employer has no conscious intent to discriminate. The legal necessity for positive affirmative action to remove these discriminatory practices which still pervade every phase of employment has been firmly established by the courts. Many people who suffer effects of past and present discrimination are already qualified for better jobs, but continuing barriers throughout employment systems deny them equal opportunity. The major part of an Affirmative Action Program must be recognition and removal of these barriers . . . There are other people who, because of a lifetime of unequal opportunity in many institutions of society, may need additional aid to become qualified for jobs on an equal basis. This, too, is part of affirmative action.

Thus in 1974 the main emphasis of an affirmative action programme was to be the elimination of direct and indirect discrimination, both of which the law prohibited, with in addition positive action to train members of disadvantaged ethnic minorities to reach the level at which they could compete on equal terms. The preference desirable at the training stage was, as has been seen in relation to sections 37 and 38 of the Race Relations Act, not seen as extending to the stage of recruitment. But the EEOC guidelines also went on to recommend strongly that affirmative action programmes should set 'specific, measurable, attainable hiring and promotion goals, with target dates, in each area of underutilization'.[24] Such goals should be fixed after analysing the existing work force to identify jobs, departments and units where minorities (and females – for sex discrimination is also within the EEOC's mandate) were underutilized.

The willingness of the courts to infer discrimination from statistical disparities led the EEOC to state:

> If a statistical survey shows that minorities and females are not participating in your workforce at all levels in reasonable relation to their presence in the population and the labour force, the burden of proof is on you to show that this is not the result of discrimination, however inadvertent.[25]

## The Bakke case and after

These pressures towards policies which include a measure of positive action led to attempts in the later 1970s to define the limits of positive action in American law. The Bakke case[26] is the most famous example. Allan Bakke, an applicant for a medical school place challenged the validity of a scheme voluntarily introduced by the school which in effect gave preference to a limited number of ethnic minority candidates, to the detriment of Allan Bakke, who would otherwise have gained admission. The Supreme Court upheld Bakke's claim in the sense that they struck down the particular scheme, but they also declared that a programme that took race into account as one factor in determining eligibility would be lawful.

In the employment field the Supreme Court has also, since Bakke, held that an affirmative action programme incorporated in a collective bargaining agreement between the United Steelworkers of America and the Kaiser Aluminum and Chemical Corporation is lawful. Under this programme, designed to eliminate 'conspicuous racial imbalances in Kaiser's then almost exclusively white craft work forces', 50 per cent of the places in certain in-plant training programmes were reserved for black employees.[27] The court took the view that to prevent such schemes would be to allow the effects of past discrimination to persist forever. Without expressing the precise limits of positive action they indicated factors which made the Kaiser plan acceptable: it did not unnecessarily disturb the interests of white workers by requiring their discharge and their replacement by black workers; it did not create an absolute bar to the advancement of white workers, since half of those trained in the programme would be white; and the plan was a temporary measure intended to eliminate a manifest racial imbalance, so that preferential selection would end as soon as the percentage of black skilled craft workers reached approximately the percentage of blacks in the local labour force.

Approval of the courts for affirmative action has been endorsed and welcomed by the US Government. President Carter said in a memorandum to heads of executive departments and agencies on 20th July 1978, following the Bakke result:

> That historic decision indicates that properly tailored affirmative action plans, which provide minorities with increased access to federal programs and jobs and which are fair to all Americans, are consistent with the Civil Rights Act 1964 and the Constitution. I want to make certain that, in the aftermath of Bakke, you continue to develop, implement, and enforce vigorously affirmative action programs. I also want to make certain that the Administration's strong commitment to equal opportunity and affirmative action is recognized and understood by all Americans.[28]

The opportunities which the law in the US allows for positive action are greater and more flexible than those allowed by the Race Relations Act and their scope has raised complex moral and political issues. The Bakke case, which has already produced several books[29] and innumerable articles, has evidently stirred up very deep-seated anxieties and differences about the distribution of wealth and status in American society. To prefer one person to another by reason of his involuntary membership of a group, whether identified by race or any other criterion, can always be seen as unfair to an individual whose claims are no less, but who is not a member of the group. Yet group preferences are accepted in many spheres in aid of a broad social justice which could not be achieved individually on purely practical grounds.[30]

In Britain, just as the concentration of the Race Relations Acts 1965 and 1968 on cases of direct discrimination against individuals could not hope to make any serious inroad on the patterns of inequality attributed to indirect discrimination, so it is now clear that the remedies provided by the law against indirect discrimination fall far short of the measures needed to bring about a distribution of the social and economic benefits of society among the ethnic groups in the population in proportion to their numbers.

Even the much shorter path to the abolition of new inequalities has yet to be travelled. Department of Employment statistics show that unemployment among ethnic minorities rose four times as fast between February 1979 and February 1980 as overall unemployment.[31] The remote risk of injustice from affirmative action schemes to members of the advantaged majority seems of little more than academic interest in the face of such a trend.

The limitations imposed by the US courts on affirmative action provide more than adequate safeguards, and the provisions of the British Race Relations Act will need to be amended to give them at least comparable strength and comparable flexibility. The most pressing need, however, is not for changes in the law but for a substantial strengthening of the legal and economic powers and inducements to apply effective equal opportunity policies. This will come about only if there is greater readiness by the courts and tribunals to enforce the law, if more resources are provided for law enforcement and if the Government demonstrates its commitment to racial equality by using its executive powers.

## Notes and references

1. *Racial Discrimination* (Cmnd. 6234), (HMSO September 1975) para. 57.
2. *Racial Discrimination – A Guide to the Race Relations Act 1976*, (HMSO 1977) para. 7.11.
3. Information supplied by the Equal Opportunities Commission.
4. *Special Programmes Special Needs*, (CRE October 1979).
5. *Ethnic Minority Youth Unemployment – A Paper Presented to Government* (CRE July 1980).
6. For example, those of Fullemploy and Camden Community Relations Committee's Operation Springboard. For the former see *Special Programmes Special Needs* Supra, n. 14. For a description of the latter, see the CRE's Employment Report for June 1980, at p. 6.
7. Section 32(3).
8. CRE July 1978.
9. For example, the Institute of Personnel Management in *Towards Fairer Selection – A Code for Non-Discrimination* (August 1978) and David Wainwright in *Discrimination in Employment* (Associated Business Press 1979).
10. *The Application of Race Relations Policy in the Civil Service* (HMSO 1978).
11. CRE 1979 Annual Report at p. 5. At the time of writing the position had not changed.
12. *Anti-Discrimination Legislation: the Street Report*, Street, Howe & Bindman (PEP 1967) at p. 131.

13. Supra para. 20.
14. CRE 1979 Annual Report at p. 5.
15. RRA 1976 S.47(1).
16. February 1980.
17. RRA 1976 S. 47(10).
18. In relation to employment, for example, see Title VII of the Civil Rights Act 1964, as amended, sec. 703.
19. RRA 1976 S. 56(1)(b) and 57(3).
20. In 1979 £75 was a typical award for injury to feelings. The highest total award record by the CRE was £515.80. In 1978 there was an award of £1,925.63 including £150 for injury to feelings. See CRE Annual Reports of 1978 and 1979. In the United States, nearly $15 million in back pay was received by employees of the American Telephone and Telegraph Company as long ago as 1974, and there have been even bigger awards since.
21. Bindman, Indirect Discrimination and the Race Relations Act, *New Law Journal*, April 26, 1979, p. 408.
22. Executive Order 11246 issued on 24th September 1965 (Schlei & Grossman, op. cit. ch. 25).
23. *Affirmative Action and Equal Employment* (January 1974) volume 1, p. 1. The guidelines were amended on 20th February 1979: see *Towards an Understanding of Bakke*, (US Commission on Civil Rights May 1979).
24. *Affirmative Action and Equal Employment* Vol. 1, p. 3.
25. Ibid. p. 7.
26. 438 U.S. 265 (1978).
27. Weber v. Kaiser Aluminum Chemical Corp. and United Steelworkers of America, AFL-C10. 99 S.Ct 2721 (1979).
28. In Bakke the Supreme Court held that an explicit racial quota was unlawful in university admissions, but in Weber what was tantamount to a quota of trainees for employment was permitted.
29. Quoted in *Toward an Understanding of Bakke* supra, note 34 at p. 175.
30. Opposing points of view are illustrated in J. Dreyfuss and C. Lawrence, *The Bakke Case – The Politics of Inequality*, (Harcourt Brace Jovanovitch 1979), supporting positive discrimination, and T. Eastland and W. J. Bennet, *Counting by Race* (Basic Books 1979) opposing it. A passionate attack on positive discrimination and affirmative action generally has been made by Nathan Glazer. (See Ch. 4.7 this volume.)
31. Moral arguments for positive discrimination are analyzed (and approved) by Alan H. Goldman, *Justice and Reverse Discrimination* (Princeton University Press 1979) and Ronald Dworkin in three articles in the *New York Review of Books:* 'Why Bakke Has No Case' (10 November 1977). 'The Bakke Decision: Did it Decide Anything?' (17 August 1978), and 'How to Read the Civil Rights Act' (20 December 1979). In fields where race is not an explicit criterion the morality of positive discrimination is accepted with little debate eg urban aid programmes and the rate support grant. Quoted in *Ethnic Minority Youth Employment*, note 14 Supra.

# CHAPTER 4.6


# REVERSE DISCRIMINATION*
### Ronald Dworkin


In 1945 a black man named Sweatt applied to the University of Texas Law School, but was refused admission because state law provided that only whites could attend. The Supreme Court declared that this law violated Sweatt's rights under the Fourteenth Amendment to the United States Constitution, which provides that no state shall deny any man the equal protection of its laws.[1] In 1971 a Jew named DeFunis applied to the University of Washington Law School; he was rejected although his test scores and college grades were such that he would have been admitted if he had been a black or a Filipino or a Chicano or an American Indian. DeFunis asked the Supreme Court to declare that the Washington practice, which required less exacting standards of minority groups, violated his rights under the Fourteenth Amendment.[2]

The Washington Law School's admissions procedures were complex. Applications were divided into two groups. The majority – those not from the designated minority groups – were first screened so as to eliminate all applicants whose predicted average, which is a function of college grades and aptitude test scores, fell below a certain level. Majority applicants who survived this initial cut were then placed in categories that received progressively more careful consideration. Minority-group applications, on the other hand, were not screened; each received the most careful consideration by a special committee consisting of a black professor of law and a white professor who had taught in programmes to aid black law students. Most of the minority applicants who were accepted in the year in which DeFunis was rejected had predicted averages below the cutoff level, and the law school conceded that any minority applicant with his average would certainly have been accepted.

* *Taking Rights Seriously,* Duckworth & Co Ltd, 1977.

The *DeFunis* case split those political action groups that have tradititio-nally supported liberal causes. The B'nai Brith Anti-Defamation League and the AFL-CIO, for example, filed briefs as *amici curiae* in support of DeFunis' claim, while the American Hebrew Woman's Council, the UAW, and the UMWA filed briefs against it.

These splits among old allies demonstrate both the practical and the philosophical importance of the case. In the past liberals held, within one set of attitudes, three propositions: that racial classification is an evil in itself; that every person has a right to an educational opportunity commensurate with his abilities; and that affirmative state action is proper to remedy the serious inequalities of American society. In the last decade, however, the opinion has grown that these three liberal propositions are in fact not compatible, because the most effective programmes of state action are those that give a competitive advantage to minority racial groups.

That opinion has, of course, been challenged. Some educators argue that benign quotas are ineffective, even self-defeating, because preferen-tial treatment will reinforce the sense of inferiority that many blacks already have. Others make a more general objection. They argue that any racial discrimination, even for the purpose of benefiting minorities, will in fact harm those minorities, because prejudice is fostered whenever racial distinctions are tolerated for any purpose whatever. But these are complex and controversial empirical judgements, and it is far too early, as wise critics concede, to decide whether preferential treatment does more harm or good. Nor is it the business of judges, particularly in constitutional cases, to overthrow decisions of other officials because the judges disagree about the efficiency of social policies. This empirical criticism is therefore reinforced by the moral argument that even if reverse discrimination does benefit minorities and does reduce prejudice in the long run, it is nevertheless wrong because distinctions of race are inherently unjust. They are unjust because they violate the rights of individual members of groups not so favoured, who may thereby lose a place as DeFunis did.

DeFunis presented this moral argument, in the form of a constitutional claim, to the courts. The Supreme Court did not, in the end, decide whether the argument was good or bad. DeFunis had been admitted to the law school after one lower court had decided in his favour, and the law school said that he would be allowed to graduate however the case was finally decided. The Court therefore held that the case was moot and dismissed the appeal on that ground. But Mr Justice Douglas disagreed with this neutral disposition of the case; he wrote a dissenting opinion in which he argued that the Court should have upheld DeFunis's claim on the merits. Many universities and colleges have taken Justice Douglas's opinion as handwriting on the wall, and have changed their practices in anticipation of a later Court decision in which his opinion prevails. In fact, his opinion pointed out that law schools might achieve much the same result by a more sophisticated policy than Washington used. A school might stipulate, for example, that applicants from all races and groups would be considered together, but that the aptitude tests of certain minority applicants would be graded differently, or given less weight in overall predicted average, because experience had shown that standard examinations were for different reasons a poorer test of the actual ability of these applicants. But if this technique is used deliberately to achieve the same result, it is devious, and it remains to ask why the candid programme used by the University of Washington was either unjust or unconstitutional.

DeFunis plainly has no Constitutional right that the state provide him a legal education of a certain quality. His rights would not be violated if his state did not have a law school at all, or if it had a law school with so few places that he could not win one on intellectual merit. Nor does he have a right to insist that intelligence be the exclusive test of admission. Law schools do rely heavily on intellectual tests for admission. That seems proper, however, not because applicants have a right to be judged in that way, but because it is reasonable to think that the community as a whole is better off if its lawyers are intelligent. That is, intellectual standards are justified, not because they reward the clever, but because they seem to serve a useful social policy.

Law schools sometimes serve that policy better, moreover, by supplementing intelligence tests with other sorts of standards: they sometimes prefer industrious applicants, for example, to those who are brighter but lazier. They also serve special policies for which intelligence is not relevant. The Washington Law School, for example, gave special preference not only to the minority applicants but also to veterans who had been at the school before entering the military, and neither DeFunis nor any of the briefs submitted on his behalf complained of that preference.

DeFunis does not have an absolute right to a law school place, nor does he have a right that only intelligence be used as a standard for admission. He says he nevertheless has a right that race *not* be used as a standard, no matter how well a racial classification might work to promote the general welfare or to reduce social and economic inequality. He does not claim, however, that he has this right as a distinct and independent political right that is specifically protected by the Constitution, as is his right to freedom of speech and religion. The Constitution does not condemn racial classification directly, as it does condemn censorship or the establishment of a state religion. DeFunis claims that his right that race not be used as a criterion of admission follows from the more abstract right of equality that is protected by the Fourteenth Amendment, which provides that no state shall deny to any person the equal protection of the law.

But the legal arguments made on both sides show that neither the text of the Constitution nor the prior decisions of the Supreme Court decisively settle the question whether, as a matter of law, the Equal Protection Clause makes all racial classifications unconstitutional. The Clause makes the concept of equality a test of legislation, but it does not stipulate any particular conception of that concept. Those who wrote the Clause intended to attack certain consequences of slavery and racial prejudice, but it is unlikely that they intended to outlaw all racial classifications, or that they expected such a prohibition to be the result of what they wrote. They outlawed whatever policies would violate equality, but left it to others to decide, from time to time, what that means. There cannot be a good legal argument in favour of DeFunis, therefore, unless there is a good moral argument that all racial classifications, even those that make society as a whole more equal, are inherently offensive to an individual's right to equal protection for himself.

There is nothing paradoxical, of course, in the idea that an individual's right to equal protection may sometimes conflict with an otherwise desirable social policy, including the policy of making the community more equal overall. Suppose a law school were to charge a few middle-class students, selected by lot, double tuition in order to increase the scholarship fund for poor students. It would be serving a desirable policy – equality of opportunity – by means that violated the right of the students selected by lot to be treated equally with other students who could also afford the increased fees. It is, in fact, part of the importance of DeFunis's case that it forces us to acknowledge the distinction between equality as a policy and equality as a right, a distinction that political theory has virtually ignored. He argues that the Washington Law School violated his individual right to equality for the sake of a policy of greater equality overall, in the same way that double tuition for arbitrarily chosen students would violate their rights for the same purpose.

We must therefore concentrate our attention on that claim. We must try to define the central concept on which it turns, which is the concept of an individual right to equality made a constitutional right by the Equal Protection Clause. What rights to equality do citizens have as individuals which might defeat programmes aimed at important economic and social policies, including the social policy of improving equality overall?

There are two different sorts of rights they may be said to have. The first is the right to *equal treatment*, which is the right to an equal distribution of some opportunity or resource or burden. Every citizen, for example, has a right to an equal vote in a democracy; that is the nerve of the Supreme Court's decision that one person must have one vote even if a different and more complex arrangement would better secure the collective welfare. The second is the right to *treatment as an equal*, which is the right, not to receive the same distribution of some burden or benefit, but to be treated with the same respect and concern as anyone else. If I have two children, and one is dying from a disease that is making the other uncomfortable, I do not show equal concern if I flip a coin to decide which should have the remaining dose of a drug. This example shows that the right to treatment as an equal is fundamental, and the right to equal treatment, derivative. In some circumstances the right to treatment as an equal will entail a right to equal treatment, but not, by any means, in all circumstances.

DeFunis does not have a right to equal treatment in the assignment of law school places; he does not have a right to a place just because others are given places. Individuals may have a right to equal treatment in elementary education, because someone who is denied elementary education is unlikely to lead a useful life. But legal education is not so vital that everyone has an equal right to it.

DeFunis does have the second sort of right – a right to treatment as an equal in the decision as to which admissions standard should be used. That is, he has a right that his interests be treated as fully and sympathetically as the interests of any others when the law school decides whether to count race as a pertinent criterion for admission. But we must be careful not to overstate what that means.

Suppose an applicant complains that his right to be treated as an equal is violated by tests that place the less intelligent candidates at a disadvantage against the more intelligent. A law school might properly reply in the following way. Any standard will place certain candidates at a disadvantage as against others, but an admission policy may nevertheless be justified if it seems reasonable to expect that the overall gain to the community exceeds the overall loss, and if no other policy that does not provide a comparable disadvantage would produce even roughly the same gain. An individual's right to be treated as an equal means that his potential loss must be treated as a matter of concern, but that loss may nevertheless be outweighed by the gain to the community as a whole. If it is, then the less intelligent applicant cannot claim that he is cheated of his right to be treated as an equal just because he suffers a disadvantage others do not.

Washington may make the same reply to DeFunis. Any admissions policy must put some applicants at a disadvantage, and a policy of preference for minority applicants can reasonably be supposed to benefit the community as a whole, even when the loss to candidates such as DeFunis is taken into account. If there are more black lawyers, they will help to provide better legal services to the black community, and so reduce social tensions. It might well improve the quality of legal education for all students, moreover, to have a greater number of blacks as classroom discussants of social problems. Further, if blacks are seen as successful law students, then other blacks who do meet the usual intellectual standards might be encouraged to apply, and that, in turn, would raise the intellectual quality of the bar. In any case, preferential admissions of blacks should decrease the difference in wealth and power that now exists between different racial groups, and so make the community more equal overall. It is, as I said, controversial whether a preferential admissions programme will in fact promote these various policies, but it cannot be said to be implausible that it will. The disadvantage to applicants such as DeFunis is, on that hypothesis, a cost that must be paid for a greater gain; it is in that way like the disadvantage to less intelligent students that is the cost of ordinary admissions policies.[3]

We now see the difference between DeFunis's case and the case we imagined, in which a law school charged students selected at random higher fees. The special disadvantage to these students was not necessary to achieve the gain in scholarship funds, because the same gain would have been achieved by a more equal distribution of the cost amongst all the students who could afford it. That is not true of DeFunis. He did suffer from the Washington policy more than those majority applicants who were accepted. But that discrimination was not arbitrary; it was a consequence of the meritocratic standards he approves. DeFunis's argument therefore fails. The Equal Protection Clause gives constitutional standing to the right to be treated as an equal, but he cannot find, in that right, any support for his claim that the clause makes all racial classifications illegal.

We therefore have the distinctions in hand necessary to distinguish *DeFunis* from *Sweatt*. The arguments for an admissions programme that discriminates against blacks are all utilitarian arguments, and they are all utilitarian arguments that rely upon external preferences in such a way as to offend the constitutional right of blacks to be treated as equals. The arguments for an admissions programme that discriminates in favour of blacks are both utilitarian and ideal. Some of the utilitarian arguments do rely, at least indirectly, on external preferences, such as the preference of certain blacks for lawyers of their own race; but the utilitarian arguments that do not rely on such preferences are strong and may be sufficient. The ideal arguments do not rely upon preferences at all, but on the independent argument that a more equal society is a better society even if its citizens prefer inequality. That argument does not deny anyone's right to be treated as an equal himself.

We are therefore left, in *DeFunis*, with the simple and straightforward argument with which we began. Racial criteria are not necessarily the right standards for deciding which applicants should be accepted by law schools. But neither are intellectual criteria, nor indeed, any other set of criteria. The fairness – and constitutionality – of any admissions programme must be tested in the same way. It is justified if it serves a proper policy that respects the right of all members of the community to be treated as equals, but not otherwise. The criteria used by schools that refused to consider blacks failed that test, but the criteria used by the Washington University Law School do not.

We are all rightly suspicious of racial classifications. They have been used to deny, rather than to respect, the right of equality, and we are all conscious of the consequent injustice. But if we misunderstand the nature of that injustice because we do not make the simple distinctions that are necessary to understand it, then we are in danger of more injustice still. It may be that preferential admissions programmes will not, in fact, make a more equal society, because they may not have the effects their advocates believe they will. That strategic question should be at the centre of debate about these programmes. But we must not corrupt the debate by supposing that these programmes are unfair even if they do work. We must take care not to use the Equal Protection Clause to cheat ourselves of equality.

## Notes and references

1. *Sweatt v. Painter*, 339 U.S. 629, 70 S. Ct. 848.
2. *DeFunis v. Odegaard*, 94 S. Ct. 1704 (1974).

3. There are circumstances in which a policy violates someone's right to be treated as an equal in spite of the fact that the social gains from that policy may be said to outweigh the losses. These circumstances arise when the gains that outweigh the losses include the satisfaction of prejudices and other sorts of preferences that it is improper for officials or institutions to take into account at all. But the hypothetical social gains described in this paragraph do not include gains of that character. Of course, if DeFunis had some other right, beyond the right to be treated as an equal, which the Washington policy violated, then the fact that the policy might achieve an overall social gain would not justify the violation. If the Washington admissions procedure included a religious test that violated his right to religious freedom, for example, it would offer no excuse that using such a test might make the community more cohesive. But DeFunis does not rely on any distinct right beyond his right to equality protected by the Equal Protection Clause.

# CHAPTER 4.7

# FROM EQUAL OPPORTUNITY TO STATISTICAL PARITY*
*Nathan Glazer*

It may be granted that the Federal civil rights enforcement agencies, with their scheme of 'affirmative action,' based on an estimate of 'underutilization.' and the courts, with their strange definitions of 'discrimination,' are engaged in a process of requiring all the major employing institutions in the country to employ minorities in rough proportion to their presence in the population. While this may be of concern to the legal specialist or the moralist, how can it be anything but a matter to applaud for the social analyst concerned for the good of the country, for the welfare of the groups within it, and for the future of the relations of the groups that make it up? We are acquainted with the despair of the ghetto, a despair that broke out in riots in the 1960s, in extremist political demands accompanied by terrorism at the turn of the 1970s, and in an enormous increase in crime which has made life in the cities miserable and dangerous. Whatever the means, can it be denied that a process of requiring equal representation of employment is good not only for the minority groups but for the country?

Let me first clear away one issue that is generally raised in the discussion of affirmative action: I oppose discrimination; I fully support the law; I think there is nothing which so degrades a nation as the exclusion of one group from its opportunities – including employment and education and political participation and access to the multifarious benefits of government – because of race, colour, national origin, religion, and, I will add, as the law does, sex, although that is not at issue here. But what I have been describing and criticizing is not an attack on discrimination. Where the EEOC takes up

* Extracts from Chapter 2 of *Affirmative Discrimination: Ethnic Inequality and Public Policy*, New York, Basic Books Inc. Copyright © 1975 by Nathan Glazer. Reprinted by permission.

a case of discrimination and gets a job and compensation for the victim, I applaud it. The fact is that much of the work of the government agencies has nothing to do with discrimination. One may review these enormous governmental reports and legal cases at length and find scarcely a single reference to any act of discrimination against an individual.

The downgrading of acts of *discrimination* in the legal and administrative efforts to achieve equality for blacks and other minority groups in favour of statistical pattern-seeking has some important consequences. It is one thing to read that an upstanding, hard-working, and ambitious young man has been turned down for a job, or a school admission, or a house because he is black. It is quite another to read that the percentage getting such and such a job, or buying houses in this place, or being admitted to this programme is thus and so. In the latter case, one does not know why the percentage is the way it is – nor is there any necessary reason given why it should be higher or lower. The sense of concrete evil done which can, and does, arouse people disappears. If any concrete connection with the Negro condition is made, it cannot be that this and that qualified black has been denied a job or admission – for the evidence is now all too clear that the qualified (and a good number of the unqualified, too) get jobs and admissions. The concrete connection with an individual's personal fate that is likely to be made tends to be in this form: if more blacks were given these jobs, perhaps less would be on the street, or drug addicts, or killing unoffending shopkeepers. It is one thing to be asked to fight discrimination against the competent, hard-working, and law-abiding; it is quite another to be asked to fight discrimination against the less competent or incompetent and criminally inclined. The statistical emphasis leads to the latter. Undoubtedly even those of lesser competence and criminal inclination must be incorporated into society, but one wonders whether this burden should be placed on laws against discrimination on account of race, colour, religion, or national origin.

The emphasis on statistics, rather than personal discrimination, raises another problem. The argument from statistics *without cases* is made not only because it is an easier argument to make, and will lead to more sweeping remedies, but also for two other reasons.

First, those who make it believe that there is such a deeply ingrained prejudice in whites, leading to discrimination against black and other minorities, that it can be assumed prejudice is the operative cause in any case of differential treatment, rather than concern about qualifications. To this assumption there can be no answer. One can only, as an individual, search one's own motives and actions; and those of the institutions and bodies with which one is involved. The ordinary public opinion surveys do show a substantial decline in prejudice, but certainly no one who believes in the persistence of an ingrained and deeply based prejudice which will make itself felt in every situation will accept such admittedly crude and broad-brush evidence. There is no answer to the argument that every case of differential treatment must be based on prejudice since we are all prejudiced. We will each make our own response to this, depending on our experience and on our sense of the motives of ourselves and our fellowmen. Clearly, the decisions of the anti-discrimination agencies are the least charitable possible. But they have support in liberal opinion, which continually insists on the guilt for racist actions of each and every one of us.

However, there is another justification for the statistical approach which may be easier to deal with in open discussion: This is the justification from 'institutional' causes. A reference to 'institutional forms of exclusion and discrimination' occurs in an official document of the Office for Civil Rights of HEW.[1] We also know the term as 'institutional racism.' This term has not been subjected to the analysis it deserves. It is obviously something devised in the absence of clear evidence of discrimination and prejudice. It suggests that, without intent, a group may be victimized. Racism, in common understanding, means an attitude of superiority, disdain, or prejudice toward another person because he is of another race, and a philosophy or ideology that justifies such attitudes on the basis of the inferiority – genetic, cultural, moral, or intellectual – of a race. The rise of the popularity of the term 'institutional racism' points to one happy development, namely, that racism pure and simple is less often found or expressed. But the rise of this term has less happy consequences in that it tends to assume that all cases of differential representation in an institution demonstrate 'institutional racism'. But each institutional form of exclusion must be judged in its own terms. Thus whether the requirement of a high school diploma, or a grade in a test, or employment on the basis of some skills or talents is 'institutional racism' and to be corrected must depend on the judgement of whether it is justified in terms of the end of the institution; whether, even if not fully justified, it is convenient (in which case, a sound public policy might call for its change, but without the implication that it had any racist intent); or whether it is actually designed to exclude some minority group, in which case it is clearly unjust and illegal. The term 'institutional racism,' however, tends to push the decision as to what we deal with increasingly towards the interpretation that *any* institutional effort to make distinctions is unjust or illegal.

Against the argument that, whatever the moral or legal faults of these procedures, they are socially good, I would make three points.

First, they became institutionalized and strengthened at a time when very substantial progress had been made, and was being made, in the upgrading of black employment and income, a progress that had, oddly enough, taken place without benefit of such extreme measures. Second, it is questionable whether they reach in any significant way the remaining and indeed most severe problems involved in the black condition. And third, unnecessarily and without sufficient justification, they threaten a desirable, emergent pattern of dealing with ethnic differences, one which does not give them formal, legal acknowledgement, neither encourages nor discourages group allegiance and identification, and treats every individual as an individual and not as a member of a group. This is now threatened by public policies which emphasize rigid lines of division between ethnic groups and make the ethnic characteristics of individuals, because of public determinations, primary for their personal fate.

I have already given some evidence on the marked progress in the economic position of blacks which was evident before the most extreme and still current form of affirmative action was established in 1971. A substantial measure of income equality has been reached in North and West for younger, complete families, and we are close to it in the South.

In addition to this change in the income position of blacks, there were remarkable changes in occupational distribution. The causes of these changes were numerous: the improved economic situation, the improved education of blacks giving them access to more jobs,[2] the population movement from South to North and from rural and small town to large city, the pressure of the black revolution and the changing attitudes of whites, and the actions of businesses and colleges and universities in increasing opportunities for minorities. The legal measures of proportional representation we have described could not very well have had much effect before 1971. They seemed to have been instituted just at the point when black progress, economically and educationally, seemed solidly institutionalized, and was maintaining itself despite the decline of riots.[3]

My second argument against proportional representation is that I do not see how it is effective in reaching the really severe problems of the black population. Among the most serious economic problems of the black population in the past decade have been high rates of unemployment

–even higher rates among the youth – and a substantial decline in participation in the labour force. Now these developments occurred during a decade of economic expansion when, in most metropolitan areas, substantial numbers of unskilled jobs were available. Consider one analysis of developments in New York City, where there has been a substantial decline in the number of blacks in the labour force:

> . . . [N]either rates of unemployment by sex nor by race show the New York labor market to have been weak in early 1970, either in the New York region or in New York City . . . [W]ages of unskilled workers are relatively high and have been rising sharply in the New York region, suggesting that there is a strong demand for workers at the unskilled level. [Yet] the Bureau of Labor Statistics reported a dramatic decline in the labour-force participation in New York among 'Negroes and other races' twenty years and older from 61 per cent of the population in 1970 to less than 55 per cent in 1972. . . .
>
> Any attempt to expand New York employment will have to deal with the supply as well as the demand for labour. And any attempt to deal with the supply of labour should take into consideration the possibility that at least a portion of the decline in labour-force participation is due to the existence of attractive alternatives to working.[4]

Many of the features of this analysis could be duplicated in other metropolitan centres. Since 1948 there has been a long-range decline in the labour-force participation of non-white males from 97 per cent to 92 per cent among 35- to 44-year-olds, from 95 per cent to 87 per cent among 45-to 54-year-olds.[5]

Poverty among blacks is increasingly concentrated among female-headed families. Of Negro families in poverty, those families with male heads dropped from 1,300,000 to 550,000 from 1959 to 1973; with female heads, they increased in this period from 550,000 to 970,000. As a result, in 1973, of black families in poverty, female-headed families formed almost two-thirds. It is not easy to see how this group could effectively be reached with anti-discrimination programmes, in view of the levels of education among them, the nature of the jobs for which they are best qualified, and the alternative attractions of welfare.[6]

During the 1960s, when discrimination was declining, the income of blacks as a proportion of white income was rising and the percentage of blacks in white-collar and stable blue-collar work was also rising, there was simultaneously a great increase in female-headed families among blacks, of youth unemployment, and of crime among blacks. No one has given a very convincing explanation of this tangle of pathology in the ghetto, but it is hard to believe it is anything as simple as lack of jobs or discrimination in available jobs.

At the moment of writing, we are in a deep recession, and black unemployment, as white, has gone very high. But clearly it was not the absence of jobs in the late 1960s that explained the situation of a decline in labour force participation and the existence of many jobs for which there were no takers. For example, an analysis by two authorities[7] of the problems of black youth points out:

> Because illicit activities can be an attractive alternative to work and because few youths have family responsibilities, many are not interested in taking jobs that pay low wages and have little status. When unemployment rates were at a low in 1969 and jobs were relatively plentiful if proved to be difficult in many cities to recruit eighteen and nineteen-year-old youths for public employment at minimum wages, even though unemployment for males of this age continued to be high. . . .
> The limited evidence does not disprove the notion held by many employers that youths are reluctant to work at the going wage. . . .

The authors do go on to say: 'Nevertheless, the evidence suggests that a majority of teenage males have realistic wage expectations.' These, of course, may be the ones who are working.

It seems clear that the main impact of preferential hiring is on the better qualified – the professional and technical, who are already the beneficiaries of an income bonus on the basis of their relative scarcity; the skilled worker already employed, upgraded through governmental pressures; the unskilled worker already regularly employed, also given opportunities of upgrading. Undoubtedly some of the benefit reaches down, but the lion's share must inevitably go to the better qualified portion of the black population.

Nothing I have said, I repeat, should be taken as justifying discrimination; the real question is what part of the severe problems of the black population can be reached by programmes of preferential hiring or is the result of present discrimination in employment. (Perhaps all of it can be attributed to *past* discrimination in employment, but that does not mean these problems can be *presently* reached by programmes of preferential employment.)

If the conditions of the black population can be improved by these programmes, then undoubtedly that would be the best reason for them. For me, no consideration of principle – such as that merit should be rewarded, or that governmental programmes should not discriminate on grounds of race or ethnic group – would stand in the way of a programme of preferential hiring if it made some substantial progress in reducing the severe problems of the low-income black population and of the inner cities. Because I have doubts as to what this contribution will be, I take more seriously the third objection I have raised to preferential hiring: the creation of fixed ethnic-racial categories, the danger of freezing them, and the danger of their spreading.

The Department of Labour, apparently, was the organization which decided that the 'affected' or 'protected' classes should consist of Negroes, Spanish-surnamed Americans, Native Americans, and Orientals.[8] It is a strange mix. Why just these and no others? We understand why Negroes and American Indians – they have been the subjects of state discrimination, and the latter group has been, in a sense, a ward of the state. Puerto Ricans, perhaps, are included because we conquered them and are responsible for them. We did not conquer most of the Mexican Americans. They came as immigrants, and why they should be 'protected' more than other minorities is an interesting question. Other Spanish-surnamed Americans raise even more difficult questions. Why Cubans? They have already received substantial assistance in immigration and have made as much progress as any immigrant might expect. Why immigrants from Latin America, aside from Puerto Ricans, who must also be included among the 'protected,' 'assisted' – and, of course, therefore counted – classes? Why Oriental Americans? They have indeed been subject in the past to savage official discrimination, but that is in the past. Having done passably well under discrimination, and much better since discrimination was radically reduced, it is not clear why the government came rushing in to include them in 'affirmative action' – unless it was under the vague notion that any race aside from the white *must* be the victim of discrimination in the United States.

We could go on. Why Spanish immigrants? In what sense have they been treated worse than immigrants from Italy or Greece? And why (if they are included among the Spanish-surnamed) Sephardic Jews? Why not the Portuguese in New England, and the French Canadians? And why not dark-skinned immigrants from India, who are now a very substantial part of the new immigration?

It is perhaps easier to understand who is included – even though there are anomalies – than to understand who is excluded. Another set of guidelines ominously states:

> Members of various religious and ethnic groups, primarily but not exclusively of Eastern, Middle, and Southern European ancestry, such as Jews, Catholics, Italians, Greeks, and Slavic groups, continue to be excluded from executive, middle-management and other job levels because of discrimination based upon their religion and/or national origin. These guidelines are intended to remedy such unfair treatment.[9]

Clearly, these guidelines have been issued less because of a powerful need or demand of these groups for redress (though what is asserted is undoubtedly true) than because either these groups must have decided they need protection for themselves owing to the preferred position that other groups are attaining or because equity seemed to demand of the guideline-setters that they be included, too. Thus groups that were once content to press their advance through education, business, informal pressures, and specific complaints because of discrimination to state and Federal agencies may find, in self-defence or the desire not to lose an advantage, that they, too, must enter the arena of conflict that the government has defined by creating what we must now call, I assume, 'more protected' or 'more affected' classes – ethnic groups number 1, as against 2, in terms of their claim to governmental consideration.

Thus the nation is by government action increasingly divided formally into racial and ethnic categories with differential rights. The Orwellian nightmare '. . . all animals are equal, but some animals are more equal than others, . . .' comes closer. Individuals find subtle pressures to make use of their group affiliation not necessarily because of any desire to be associated with a group but because groups become the basis for rights, and those who want to claim certain rights must do so as a member of an affected or protected class. New lines of conflict are created, by government action. New resentments are created; new turfs are to be protected; new angers arise; and one sees them on both sides of the line that divides protected and affected from nonprotected and nonaffected. We should not underestimate the effects of government benefits. If people begin by feeling they do not deserve them, they will soon change their minds to decide they do after all (otherwise, why would the government give it to them?) and angrily rise up to protect them.

Conceivably, there have been benefits as we have moved from nondiscrimination to soft affirmative action to harder goals and deadlines. But there have been losses, too.

## Notes and references

1. Speech by Senator James Buckley, May 22, 1973, Congressional Record.
2. The following table indicates the rate of change, the degree to which equality in proportion of high school graduates has been reached, and the remaining disparities:

| Level of Schooling Completed by Persons 20 to 24 Years Old | | | | |
|---|---|---|---|---|
| | Male | | Female | |
| | Black | White | Black | White |
| **Percent completed 4 years of high school or more:** | | | | |
| 1965 | 50 | 76 | 48 | 77 |
| 1973 | 70 | 85 | 72 | 85 |
| **Percent completed 1 year of college or more:** | | | | |
| 1965 | 14 | 36 | 15 | 26 |
| 1973 | 27 | 46 | 25 | 37 |

| Percent of Population 25 to 34 Years Old Who Completed 4 Years of College or More | | | | | |
|---|---|---|---|---|---|
| | Black | | | White | | |
| | Total | Male | Female | Total | Male | Female |
| 1966 | 5.7 | 5.2 | 6.1 | 14.6 | 18.9 | 10.4 |
| 1973 | 8.3 | 8.0 | 8.5 | 19.0 | 22.6 | 15.5 |

Source: *The Social and Economic Status of the Black Population in the United States, 1973*, p.69.

3. I have concentrated on the black population in this discussion because they are by far the largest minority – over eleven per cent of the population. The next largest minority, as the Federal government lists minorities, the Mexican Americans, do not number even three per cent of the population, the Puerto Rican not even one per cent. I do not consider other 'Spanish-surnamed' minorities necessarily deprived economically – the largest among them, the Cubans, have made good economic progress. 'Orientals' are economically and educationally no worse off than the white population. From my own point of view, each group is so distinct that to deal with their problems in general would not make much sense. For this reason, I have concentrated on what is by far the largest group, blacks.
4. 'Why Are New York's Workers Dropping Out?' in *Monthly Economic Letter*, August 1973, New York: First National City Bank, pp. 12–13.

5. Martin Feldstein, 'The Economics of the New Unemployment,' *The Public Interest,* Fall 1973, pp. 3–42.
6. Bureau of the Census, *op. cit.,* Table 19.
7. Sar A. Levitan and Robert Taggart III, in *The Job Crisis for Black Youth,* Report of the Twentieth Century Fund Task Force on Employment Problems of Black Youth, New York: Praeger, 1971, p 63.
8. Buckley, *op. cit.*
9. *Federal Register,* 'Guidelines on Discrimination because of Religion or National Origin,' January 19, 1973, Part (b) of 60–50.1.

# CHAPTER 4.8

# A PROGRAMME FOR CHANGE*
*David Wainwright*

An audit of the employment situation in an organization may reveal obvious areas of discrimination which can be rapidly changed. In addition it will probably uncover a range of difficult attitude-based problems related to the access of women and ethnic minorities to certain jobs. These problems are more difficult to solve because they will require work over a period of time to change behaviour and the process of making the change will be peculiar to that particular organization. Collecting the information for the audit of personnel policies may be a new procedure which may produce information hitherto not available to the organization, but what is collected will not change from one organization to another – it is how the information is used to change behaviour which will vary. For example, two different organizations might have the same problem, that women and ethnic minorities are under-represented at the first level of supervision because of criteria for promotion which indirectly discriminate against them. The process of changing the criteria will depend on a whole range of factors, but usually the process of change to prevent discrimination will have to be in harmony with the customary ways of making change in the organization. If change normally comes about by a consultative process, then it is advisable to use that process to change the criteria for selection.

## The elements in a programme

There are elements of an organization that have important implications for the way in which changes to behaviour are attempted. Later discussion of different ways of changing behaviour will be easier if these elements are identified now. The first part of the organization that needs to be

* Extracts from Chapter 10 of *Discrimination in Employment*, Associated Business Press, 1979.

considered is its formal systems, that is the policies and procedures that state how certain functions should be performed. The *formal systems* of an organization are the visible systems consisting of organization charts, policy manuals and memos on procedure, etc. The second part of an organization that needs to be considered is the *informal systems* – the cultural norms of behaviour and the values which can influence the behaviour of employees just as much as the formal system of rules and procedures. For example, the formal system for promotion might state that this is on merit and that performance appraisal is the evidence of merit. But the informal system may be that 'around here if you want promotion you need more service than anyone else in the department'. In such a situation to follow the formal system and appoint a short service employee would break the informal system or the norms on promotion. Change on promotion policy in this example must be easier if it is in line with the informal norms, because the informal system is the system in reality. Change can alter the informal system but it is obviously more difficult than re-writing a policy and issuing a new procedure.

An organization also has *objectives* – the basic objective probably being survival. Different departments within an organization may have different objectives and sometimes these may conflict. Any attempt at changing behaviour must be made in full awareness of the objectives of the organization and the departments, because it can only succeed if it is consistent with group and individual objectives.

The formal and informal systems of an organization, with its objectives, do not exist in a vacuum. The external environment interacts with the organization and is a pressure that encourages or resists change. For example, one reason for the development by United States corporations of elaborate formal systems to comply with their laws on equal opportunity, is that the external environment in the US creates more pressure for change.

The audit of personnel procedures identifies procedures where planned change is necessary; after a review of the objectives, and the formal and informal systems of an organization, the strategy for the change process should become clearer. Change may be aimed at a formal system or an informal 'norm' or a change to the objectives of the organization. Very often the change strategy will be intended to change both a formal system and employee attitudes, but the person responsible for change will have to be clear as to the focus of the change strategy and how changing one will affect the other.

Before it is possible to plan any kind of change, it is necessary that there should be acceptance among the people who will be affected that a problem does exist. The audit may generate the first awareness of a problem but one reaction to information is to deny that it is the responsibility of the organization to change. For example, if the audit shows a low participation of women and ethnic minorities in a particular job then it can be argued that the reason is:

a. women and ethnic minorities don't apply for the jobs; or
b. they don't have the right previous experience; or
c. they don't have the right qualifications by the right age, eg their educational career is different from the men we usually employ; or
d. their expectations and career prospects are different.

Each of these arguments must be dealt with in order to reach the first stage of the change process, which is a feeling that change is necessary in the organization. Once it is accepted as necessary then it can be directed at individuals, groups or the entire organization. If behaviour is the target for change, then groups who are influential in setting or enforcing the informal system will be a natural focus. If formal systems need to be changed, then the person responsible for the system will be the focus. Since the ultimate objective is to change the entire organization the effort will eventually be directed at most employees. Strategies can make their initial efforts at the top level of the organization and spread downwards, or at the bottom and spread upwards. To start at the top may be a high risk, but to start at the bottom may lead to the change being seen as unimportant and it can be difficult to move away from the area where the change starts.

## The traditional strategy on equal opportunity

Most of the change strategies aimed to introduce equal opportunity have emphasized changes to formal systems. Previously this author has suggested[1] an 'affirmative action plan' for organizations which concentrated almost entirely on formal systems. The Commission for Racial Equality and the Equal Opportunity Commission have both made suggestions which relate entirely to formal systems. At the same time everyone would agree that attitudes need to change if equal opportunity is to be a reality and not just a series of ringing declarations of good intentions. In hierarchical and bureaucratic organizations changes to formal systems may encourage real change to behaviour, but in most organizations it is possible for the policy manual to provide instructions that are ignored, in practice, by everyone. It is particularly easy for employees to ignore general statements that the company intends to act lawfully when it does not positively tell individual employees what they should do; only what is to be avoided.

An alternative way of trying to bring about a change in behaviour is to provide training for managers which helps them understand how direct and indirect discrimination works against women and ethnic minorities. Typically this training would consist of lectures and case studies and would produce a greater awareness of the issues. It need not necessarily lead to a change of behaviour and is highly unlikely to do so unless the work environment also encourages change and supports it when it happens. To change behaviour by providing training it would be necessary for:

a.  the informal systems to encourage and support a change of behaviour;
b.  the managers to feel a need to change;
c.  an alternative behaviour to be agreed between all involved;
d.  there to be an opportunity to practise the new behaviour and to have it checked as effective after the training course.

An equal opportunity programme in a company is unlikely to succeed if it only changes the policies or if it only makes managers aware of the law and how personnel policies can be unlawful. What is required is an organizational development (OD) programme which as defined by Kahn as 'changing the pattern of recurring behaviour'.[2]

It is assumed that by producing information for the audit a number of clear cases of direct or indirect discrimination against women and ethnic minorities will have been recognized. To obtain the commitment that an OD type programme in this area will require means that this information needs to be shared with top management. The aim must be to produce a feeling at the highest level in the organization that something will have to change. It should not be necessary, and would be impossible, to provide a detailed set of recommendations on what exactly must change. Part of the programme will be the discovery of the 'recurring behaviour' which has to change. Once the need to change is felt, it can be agreed that it is necessary to carry on producing information so that the position can be analyzed as the programme progresses. This regular flow of data will help identify any problems that a change produces and will help sustain interest and motivation to actually achieve the change in behaviour.

Collecting the data and producing a feeling that things need to change will not produce the change itself and the first step might be introduced through formal systems changes, training courses or consultation between employees and managers. Choosing the activity which is to be the means to introduce the change must depend on the people and the organizations. The pattern is set out in Fig. 1.

**Figure 1**    Organization development programme for equal opportunity

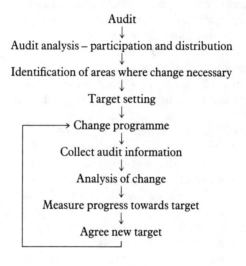

Audit
↓
Audit analysis – participation and distribution
↓
Identification of areas where change necessary
↓
Target setting
↓
Change programme
↓
Collect audit information
↓
Analysis of change
↓
Measure progress towards target
↓
Agree new target

The alternative components are presented in this chapter in terms of formal interventions to change policies and procedures, and informal interventions aimed at changing the attitudes and norms that make up the informal systems. An intervention in the informal system may be necessary to produce a 'felt need' for change in the organization. The overall objective is to find a way of combining formal and informal interventions in such a way that a method of monitoring equal opportunity policies becomes part of the organization in the same way as a financial control system or a sales forecast.

## hy the traditional strategy fails

The objective is not new. The Race Relations Board and the Institute of Personnel Management, among others, were both advising organizations to adopt equal opportunity policies in the late sixties. But, after ten years of exhortation and advice on what policies are required, few British organizations have developed the policies, and of those even fewer have attempted to see that behaviour is in line with the good intentions stated in them. Before another attempt is made to explain what is required, some explanation must be offered as to why the law and the exhortation seem to have made so little difference. Among the reasons are the following.

a.  The people with the power and influence to make equal opportunity policies effective do not feel any need for such policies. The majority of them are white and male and have no direct experience of the problems. Women and blacks in Britain are usually passive when organizations discriminate and do not express any resentment at their treatment. The minority who press for change can be ignored as unrepresentative of the feelings of the group.

b.  The suggested changes to formal policies in organizations are not in harmony with other systems in the company. For example, it would be unrealistic to suggest to an organization that does not have formal systems for monitoring sales or cash flow that they introduce a formal system to monitor equal opportunity policy. Where an organization manages its business without written policies and procedures in every other area, it is unlikely to manage the issue of equal opportunity by adopting policies and procedures. If the organization does act out of character and issue a formal policy, it is unlikely to work. Managers will conclude that the written policy is merely a public relations exercise, because from their experience they know that when the company really wants change it goes about it in a different way.

c.  Where organizations do bring about change by formal alterations to policies and procedures on most issues, it may not work when applied to equal opportunity. There is a possibility that the new policy will be understood intellectually but in fact only superficial changes will be made. This is because on an issue like equal opportunity it is impossible to spell out all the implications and there is genuine confusion about indirect discrimination and reverse discrimination. A policy manual will not change attitudes and assumptions about blacks and women that were acquired unconsciously as part of the process of growing up.

d. There may be very different expectations about the pace of change that will follow a change in policy. It can be argued that changes in policy will change behaviour very gradually and that visible signs cannot be expected. This argument is unlikely to reassure individuals who feel they are losing opportunities now.

Many of the changes that organizations are urged to introduce to promote equal opportunity are changes that were introduced in the United States, and that were successful in terms of their impact on the job opportunities of blacks and women in that country. There was a feeling that if a policy was introduced and more women and blacks were subsequently recruited then the events were linked as cause and effect. However, there were at least two major differences in the society that may explain why similar law in a similar industrial country had a different effect. In the USA the law followed the burning of the industrial city ghettos. This period of social conflict prepared people for the idea that change was necessary. Formal policies were needed in the USA when the Equal Employment Opportunities Commission began to ask for detailed statistical returns. The information required by the government in the USA made organizations feel they needed formal system changes to provide the data. Since the British enforcement agencies have not imposed any formal systems on organizations, they are often ignorant of the situation in an organization. For example, records of ethnic origin have been suggested by the Race Relations Board and the Commission for Racial Equality but most companies do not have records and therefore do not have any system that might prompt them to ask why certain departments or areas only employ white males.

## An alternative strategy

Once an organization accepts that it will be necessary to bring about change in attitudes and behaviour to ensure compliance with the laws in discrimination in employment, it needs to consider the steps in that change. Set out below are some suggestions as to how this might be done. The suggestions are general but follow the pattern of trying to produce a 'felt need for change' before the change is designed.

It is suggested that all the steps in the programme involve employees. The general suggestions on strategy are followed by:
a. specific formal policies that can be used as examples and adapted to particular organizations;

b. cases and training exercises to stimulate a discussion of attitudes;
c. a monitoring programme;
d. the reasons for a participative approach.

## General strategy steps

The general strategy consists of eight steps which need not always follow one on the other and may overlap. Since the initial steps are for the information and training of the employees responsible for the programme as well as for making changes, it is possible that it may be necessary to return to the first few stages in the light of later progress.

*Step 1:* The management group or the individual initiating the interest in an equal opportunity programme should consider who will be responsible for the development and for sustaining its momentum in the long term and who will be responsible for acquiring resources for the work, eg time for meetings. The executive authority, *what is done,* need not be the same individual as the authority for the process of change, *how it is done.*

At the beginning it will be necessary for management to agree on how employees are to be informed of the programme in a regular manner, preferably making use of an existing line of communication. The content of the communication need only tell employees that the company wishes to review information with employees – it should avoid any statement of objectives or philosophy and rely on a general statement about an intent to see that the company meets legal requirements.

*Step 2:* Once the employee group to be involved has been identified, information on the audit, the law and company policy to meet the legal requirements can be discussed. These three pieces of information should help the group to discuss the problems that are exposed by the audit information, what situation they would expect to see and whether they can connect the two. It should not be necessary to try to prove anything about past behaviour and an 'adversary' relationship should be avoided. The group should be asked why they think the present levels of participation and

distribution among women and ethnic minorities exist. Clarification may be sought, but if there is disagreement in some areas these can be left; the areas of agreement can be examined to begin with. At this stage an overall plan should be avoided. Specific issues like school leaver recruitment or promotion should be discussed and a joint plan made to change the situation, with targets and implementation agreed.

*Step 3:* From the small projects in Step 2 there will probably be recommendations to change certain formal systems to continue the process. After implementing these specific changes, it may then be possible to widen the study to include a review of all the formal systems in an area. For example, from a study of school leaver recruitment may come a recommendation to change the media used for recruitment. Once that has been implemented, it may be appropriate to ask how that change will affect other formal systems relating to the recruitment of staff other than school leavers. This would involve a review of all policies and procedures on recruitment, which would then lead back to the audit information to look at participation and distribution figures for women and ethnic minorities at each stage of the recruitment process.

*Step 4:* From the first study system and its implications it can be expected that certain attitudes and individual assumptions will be identified. It may be decided in some circumstances that a change in systems will be unproductive without a change in attitudes within the responsible group. It could at this stage be useful to study attitudes in more detail – either through the type of study of management attitudes completed by Audrey Hunt[3] or through a discussion among the employees of the group norms on the employment of women and ethnic minorities. The type of questions that could be used to build a picture of norms are shown in Fig. 2. They examine how things really are rather than attitudes. The objective of either a study of norms or a more conventional attitude survey is to produce a wider appreciation of a felt need to change attitudes towards the employment of women and ethnic minorities.

*Step 5:* The attitude survey or the questions on norms will provide information on the expectations and assumptions one group has about another. Training could be provided to tackle issues of cultural bias and stereotyping of certain groups of employees if these exist. The organization can make clear in the training that behaviour based on cultural bias or stereotyping is not acceptable. The training can be provided in an interesting way without attributing blame.

*Step 6:* Once one main area or formal system such as recruitment or training or promotion has been studied, objectives set and attitudes discussed, the process can be extended into other areas of formal systems. At this stage it may also be useful to begin to involve other people, so that if a group of ten employees have been working on Steps 1–5 then maybe two of them could be replaced by other employees with a particular interest in the subject or by those who will be particularly involved in the

**Figure 2**   Cultural norm indicator

| If a member of your group were to: | Most other members would | | | |
|---|---|---|---|---|
| | approve and encourage it to encourage it | approve but do nothing to encourage it | consider it unimportant | disapprove but do nothing to discourage it | disapprove and discourage it |
| 1  Take time to show a West Indian employee how to do a job | | | | |
| 2  Refuse to take orders from a female supervisor | | | | |
| 3  Ask for six weeks unpaid leave to visit relatives in Canada | | | | |
| 4  Encourage a cousin to come and work with the organization | | | | |
| 5  Suggest that the canteen put on food for Muslim employees | | | | |
| 6  Suggest that unemployed people born in Britain should be given preference for any vacancies | | | | |
| 7  Fail to treat a woman employee with respect | | | | |
| 8  Suggest English language training courses are held in work time | | | | |
| 9  Encourage his daughter to apply for skilled work | | | | |
| 10  Refuse to sit next to an Asian on the bus | | | | |
| 11  Say that his daughter must leave school no matter what | | | | |
| 12  Suggest a work meeting is held in the evening | | | | |
| 13  Expect women employees to make tea if required | | | | |
| 14  Swear at a woman | | | | |
| 15  Be proud of a daughter studying engineering at university | | | | |

© TMS (Europe) Ltd.

next major area of study. As new areas of formal systems are studied, it could be that it will be necessary to refer back to information and decisions taken in earlier meetings of the employee group. If changes are to be made to formal systems there should always be a discussion about whether a particular change is positive in that it is in accordance with the informal attitudes and norms, or negative in that it is in conflict with the attitudes and norms. If the employee group want to alter the formal system in a way that will conflict with attitudes and norms, then they must also consider what aspects of the informal system need to be worked on in order that the change will be supported.

*Step 7:* From Steps 1–6 should come information on attitudes and changes to systems that can be communicated to all employees. With the making of each change, information will have been given to those who are directly involved. Once a regular method of working and some achievements can be shown, the plan for the future can be more widely communicated. Past achievements and how they were planned can be used as examples. The general message of intent for the future is also the point at which it becomes clear that equal opportunity policies are to be part of the organization's future. At this stage the employee group might be given more permanent status, together with some formal procedures for representing employees.

*Step 8:* The final stage takes the form of positive steps to increase the participation and distribution of women and ethnic minorities, including special training arrangements to allow women or minorities to meet the criteria for promotion that have been established as necessary for the organization.

In the first seven steps the focus has been on removing direct and indirect discrimination and getting the commitment of employees to those changes. There may however be some barriers that the employer cannot change, such as qualifications or age requirements. In those circumstances, possibly the employees will suggest special training or experience to correct the effects of discrimination that they have iden-tified as having been endemic practice for a number of years. For example, in a situation where certain types of experience have been a prerequisite for promotion to a supervisor grade, it might be necessary to provide that experience before those who suffered discrimination can reach that grade. Once they reach the supervisor grade the organization must then decide whether to allow accelerated movement through the supervisors' ranks to compensate for the period when discrimination held them back. At British Airways women were barred from the higher grades of cabin staff until recently and it was necessary to be the most senior man in a grade in order to be offered a job in the grade above. When the bar was removed women were in the lower grades although some had longer service with BA than men in the grades above. With eighteen grades it would obviously take a long time for women to reach the top if they had to move through each one. In fact British Airways removed the bar and took all the women's service into account when promoting. This meant that when a top grade job came up, some long-service female staff who had not yet reached the grade immediately below that of the vacancy nevertheless jumped several grades because they had more service in total. Such accelerated promotion was fair to the women but obviously some men who had been 'waiting' at the head of the queue for the higher grade job were disappointed.

## Notes and references

1. Wainwright, David, *Race and Employment: Managing a Multi-Racial Labour Force*, 1971, IPM.
2. Kahn, R. L., 'Organizational Development. Some Problems and Proposals. *Journal of Applied Behavioural Science*. Vol. 10, No. 4, 974.
3. Hunt, Audrey, *Management Attitudes and Practices towards Women at Work* HMSO.

# SECTION 5

# THE IMPLICATIONS OF UNEMPLOYMENT

# CHAPTER 5.1

# BLACK WORKERS IN BRITAIN: FROM FULL EMPLOYMENT TO RECESSION*
## Ed Rhodes and Peter Braham

Earlier articles have drawn out the economic factors which underlay the mid-twentieth century migration of labour to the UK and other countries of North-Western Europe. This migration and the prolonged economic boom from the 1940s to the 1970s were interdependent in the sense that rapid economic expansion resulted in labour shortages which produced the demand for migrant labour. These boom conditions probably could not have been sustained without the availability of a new, adaptable, and mobile addition to the indigenous workforces. Together with the absorption of political refugees, a continued move from agriculture and increases in female employment, migrant workers contributed to employer containment of wage costs and facilitated the continuing expansion of output. The character of migration gradually changed, as Böhning suggests (pp. 36–39), towards a stage of maturity. In Britain this was apparent by the 1970s, when, according to the TUC: 'The stage of permanent settlement and full participation has now been reached by large numbers of the immigrant workforce and their children resulting in the emergence of emphasis on questions . . . of advancement rather than of initial adaptation.'[1]

But while immigrant workers and their dependants were becoming transformed into settled communities, the economic conditions which had produced a demand for their labour had given way to low and sometimes negative rates of growth. By 1981, registered unemployment in the 24 OECD countries had reached 26 million – more than the total UK workforce. In the UK registered unemployment had started to rise in the mid-1960s – earlier than in other industrialized countries. By the early

1980s it exceeded three million or more than twelve per cent of the workforce with evidence of considerable additional but unregistered unemployment. By the early 1980s there was general recognition that high levels of unemployment and reduced levels of economic activity were likely to persist into the 1990s and perhaps beyond. The emphasis of much economic and social policy has changed markedly in these circumstances. Many of the underlying assumptions which were elevated to unquestioned status in previous years became subject to reassessment. For example, much of the accumulated body of knowledge about the problems facing black and other migrant workers, as well as the development of policies designed to combat aspects of discrimination and disadvantage, has been assembled in the context of expanding resources and relatively low levels of unemployment. To what extent will the continuance of high unemployment change the problems which black workers face and affect their prospects for equal opportunity and for the advancement referred to by the TUC?

In considering this question it is important to be aware of the broader context of migration and settlement of black workers. To those unfamiliar with studies of international migration both the arrival of black workers and their subsequent problems may appear to be without parallel. However, Britain's experience of migration is not unusual but part of a long-standing and broadly based pattern of population movement. Moreover, while migration to Britain between the 1950s and 1970s did take place on a large scale, this was by no means the only mass movement of population into the country. As was the case with earlier phases of immigration, the arrival of black migrants has emphasized a variety of social issues and it is these that have tended to receive the bulk of attention and investigation. But the fundamental nature of issues such as disadvantage in the field of education, the housing market or in occupational placement, cannot be fully understood without reference to the underlying factors which shape the timing, direction and scale of migration and the subsequent experience of work and settlement.

Of course, migration does not always take place for economic reasons as the Jewish experience demonstrates (Chapter 2.9). Nor can economic factors always be separated from political pressures but while factors such as religious, political or tribal persecution may vary greatly in intensity, the economic pressures underlying latent or manifest 'push factors' in migration are likely to exert a continuous effect so long as wide disparities in the international division of wealth persist. Economic factors are particularly evident on the demand or pull side although governments have perceived additional numbers to be a buttress against the political expansionism of powerful neighbours. Inward migration, whether forced or voluntary, within or across State frontiers, has been central in the processes of economic development, whether in the establishment of plantation economies or in the construction of industrial economies. The result has been movement from and to most parts of the world and over long periods of time. In the USA for example:

> Covered wagon pioneers, it was said, opened up the West for the white man – and closed it for the Indian. But those who were to do the hardest, heaviest, least rewarding work came by ship or freight train over the sea from China and over the rails from the East. . . . The employers imported Chinese labourers. They worked them under contract and in gangs. Cheap labour, forced labour, not free to move or settle. When mobile US workers replaced the Chinese the employer had less responsibility. They arrived on their own, at each job, as needed. They left on their own when no longer needed. The employer paid them the least they'd work for, only so long as he needed them. They were free men – free to go wherever the job called, and free to starve if they couldn't find one.[2]

Many of those who came 'over the rails from the East' came from Europe. Between 1846 and 1932 some 52 million people left Europe for overseas destinations. By the end of this period one-eleventh of the population of the world were people of European origin living outside Europe.[3] It is often thought that large-scale migration came to an end soon after the First World War when increasing restrictions were imposed on the movement of population. This is quite incorrect. For example, a conservative estimate places the number of refugees forced to leave one country for another in the period 1945–55 at 45 million – equivalent to the entire overseas migration from Europe in the *century* before the First World War.[4] And between 1945 and 1975 approximately fifteen million workers and their dependants settled in the industrialized countries of North-West Europe, a rate of immigration which comfortably exceeded that of immigration to the USA between 1846 and 1932.

It is often forgotten that the UK has long played an important role in the international movement of labour not only as a sending and a receiving country but also in moving labour between other countries: 'Leaving aside her innovative and long involvement in the African slave trade, there were contract labour systems bringing Indians to Malaya, East and South Africa and the Caribbean.'[5] Moreover, many international migrants came from

Britain itself. Descloitres suggests that between 1800 and 1860 Britain accounted for two-thirds of all emigrants from Europe.[6] With the exception of the 1930s and the period 1958–63, emigration from Britain has exceeded immigration.[7] Nonetheless immigration, particularly from Ireland, played an important role in the industrialization of the UK. By 1851, Irish immigrants formed a similar proportion of the population of England and Wales – some 2.9 per cent – as does the present black population.[8] In turn, while black migration and settlement have commanded most attention in the recent past, this was preceded by the large scale settlement of Italians and displaced persons from Eastern Europe and accompanied by migration – generally short term – from other West European countries and from the white Commonwealth countries.

The post 1940s movement of labour into the UK, as we suggested earlier, was part of a wider international movement of labour which, at that time, particularly affected North-Western Europe.[9] The case of the German Federal Republic is probably the most striking. Migration was limited until the 1960s because, in contrast to the UK, there remained a large agricultural workforce to absorb into industrial employment, and prior to the construction of the Berlin Wall, some ten million people had arrived from Eastern Europe. In 1959 there were less than 200,000 non-German workers in the Republic but by 1966 this had risen to 1.3 million and by 1971 to two million.[10]

However, movement into West Germany, as elsewhere, has not been continuous. Amongst other things the rate and direction of movement was related to changes in levels of economic activity. In the case of West Indian migration to the UK, for example, Peach found there was 'a substantial and significant inverse correlation between unemployment and net West Indian immigration' between 1955 and 1974 – as unemployment rose so immigration fell.[11] To some extent levels of unemployment may provide a 'natural' regulator on rates of migration, helped by the flow of information from those who have migrated. Whether or not the flow of immigrants is regulated by the economic cycle, more reliance has been generally placed on other forms of control. This is particularly so as unemployment rises when there is likely to be an intensification of pressures for immigration legislation. Generally speaking, immigration controls in both Europe and North America were established (or, if already in existence, were tightened) as the depression of the 1930s grew in intensity. During the 1914–18 war, for example, the French Government recruited over one million workers from Southern Europe and its overseas colonies. After the war recruitment contracts were concluded with several labour-exporting countries. The number of foreigners working in France grew steadily until in 1930 it reached three million. With the onset of the depression, foreign workers had their work permits cancelled and they were quickly repatriated.[12] Britain likewise drew in civilian colonial workers to assist in the war effort between 1914–18 but subsequently repatriated them.

After the 1940s, however, governments in labour-importing countries generally avoided compulsory repatriation. Instead, they have sought to develop controls which are sufficiently flexible to ensure that in time of economic expansion the recruitment of less-skilled workers (but not their dependants) is facilitated, whereas in time of economic contraction the less-skilled are encouraged to return to their country of origin, while those with skills still in demand continue to be allowed to enter. In the 1970s the UK sought to emulate this general pattern by immigration legislation and other means. This has entailed an increased use of quotas related to skill, and of restrictive and short-term labour permits, described by Blackburn and Mann as, in effect, a system of bonded labourers (p. 80–81).

The migration of black workers thus fits within a pattern which can be identified throughout the processes of industrial development – and indeed of much pre-industrial development – and in which many of the issues and responses are recurrent. If and when there is a post 1980s upswing the issues of inward migration may well become significant again, unless, as Sivanandan suggests (pp. 61–63) there has been a permanent shift in the relationship between capital mobility and labour mobility. This emphasizes a further context within which migration needs to be viewed – the continuous processes of adaption and expansion of the labour force which have been central to industrialization and capital accumulation. Capitalism depends upon what Schumpeter[13] characterized as a process of creative destruction. Even during depression, products and markets are in continuous transition as are methods of production, requiring continuous adaptation and relocation from the workforce. During the upswing labour shortages are likely to develop and limit the duration of the boom, unless a reserve supply of labour can be tapped from among the unemployed and elsewhere in order to avoid the escalation of wage costs that would follow from labour shortages.

Agriculture has long been one of the most significant areas of labour reserve. It was, for example, of key importance in the post-war development both of Japan, where some seven million labourers left the land between 1950 and 1965, and of Italy.[14] Though in Britain the agricultural workforce was too small to serve the same function as in Italy or Japan, a reservoir of male labour was provided by the decline of, for example, the railways, of coal mining and of the steel industry. On the other hand, the supply of labour was diminished by changes in the school leaving age, the extension of higher education, by earlier retirement and, not least, by emigration.

The most significant *internal* source of additional labour available to the majority of industrialized countries lay in the expansion of the female labour force. In Japan, the number of working women rose from three million in 1950 to twelve million in 1970.[15] In the USA the percentage of women in the workforce rose from 29 per cent in 1951 to 39.6 per cent in 1971.[16] In Britain, the percentage of women in the workforce was high in comparison with the USA (twenty per cent in 1901), but stable throughout the first half of the century at about 34–35 per cent. Coincident with the migration of black workers, however, there was a major increase in the percentage of the economically active workforce who were women. This grew from 34.9 per cent in 1951 (6.3 million female employees) to 42.6 per cent (8.3 million female employees) in 1971. The increase is largely accounted for by the development of a bimodal pattern of employment as married women have more frequently returned to work when their children reach school age.

Women have thus formed a significant element in the reserve army of labour. Like black workers, but more so, they form a clearly disadvantaged group in terms of their occupational distribution. Together with other categories of workers they are more likely to be vulnerable to unemployment in recession, when the virtues of domesticity and the supposedly 'secondary' nature of women's earnings may be emphasized. After the 1939–45 War, for example, it was thought likely that there would soon be a recession as was the case after the war of 1914–18. Women were encouraged to return from the Homefront to the homefront, partly through the dismantling of nursery and other facilities which had been established to increase the female activity rate in order to counteract the shortage of male manpower. Likewise when labour shortages developed in the post-war period, attitudes to the employment of EVWs and black workers were shaped by the expectation that the boom would be shortlived.

The option of importing labour thus recommended itself precisely because it may have seemed the ideal solution to what appeared likely to be a temporary problem. Should economic expansion and full employment not persist, immigrant workers could return to their countries of origin. Alternative solutions, such as a substantial rise in wages to tempt indigenous workers back into unpopular occupations, might have had consequences which would be less easily reversed after the conditions which gave rise to their adoption had ended.

Moreover, the employment of immigrant labour offered a number of additional advantages to the receiving economy. For example, if immigrants arrive ready to work and unaccompanied by their families, and leave either at the end of their working life or when there is no work available, then the receiving economy will avoid responsibility for much of what is termed the 'social wage', ie the cost of food, clothing, housing, unemployment benefit, retirement etc, except at the actual point of production.

Above all, immigrant labour is likely to be cheap labour in so far as migrants are willing to perform less desirable jobs at wage levels at which insufficient local labour would be forthcoming. Immigrant workers can be seen as both more available, yet more disposable, and as having lower economic expectations than indigenous labour. In this context, we may recall Cohen and Jenner's hypothesis (Chapter 2.2) that the immigrant worker newly established in a country is near to the economist's ideal of economic man: he may be constrained by lack of skill, by language problems or by discrimination to work long and unsocial hours, in poor conditions, in order to earn as much as possible. (See also Blackburn and Mann, Chapter 2.4.)

Ideally the labour reserve should be mobile not only in the sense of readiness to move into areas of labour shortage, whatever the type and location of job, but also in terms of ability to move out of the workforce when unemployment rises to high levels. Women may fulfil this role if they can be persuaded to return to domestic tasks. In some circumstances migrant labour has the same potential. This can be clearly seen in the case of West Germany. In the minor recession of 1966–67 for example, some 30 per cent of the non-German immigrant workforce, 400,000 workers, were obliged to return home. But as the economy moved towards expansion again, the pace of inward migration again increased. The subsequent behaviour of *Gastarbeiter* (guestworkers) in the much more prolonged recession which followed the 1973 oil-crisis revealed, however, that their 'mobile labour potential' had become much lower than either the German Government or the employers' organizations might wish. Nevertheless, a sharp contrast is evident between the working of the early Gastarbeiter system in Germany, say up to the late 1960s, and the recruitment of black labour in Britain in the same period.

In Germany the mass recruitment of foreign workers, most of whom were employed on one-year contracts, facilitated the adjustment of the labour force to short-term changes in demand. The availability of an additional labour supply, which could be relied upon to depart when no longer needed, encouraged sustained investment and led to strong productivity gains in periods of economic downturn.[17] But even during depression there is likely to remain some considerable demand for migrant labour. Thus it is useful to distinguish between that part of the immigrant labour force which acts (in the words of a former chairman of the German equivalent of the CBI) as a 'mobile labour potential', which can be exported as demand for labour contracts; and that part which performs jobs which indigenous workers will be reluctant to fill even in time of recession.

The pattern followed by the UK was somewhat different. The chosen economic path was less capital-intensive than that of Germany (see Sivanandan, Chapter 1.3 for example). In addition, the immigration of black workers did not provide the same degree of 'mobile labour potential' because black immigrants – unlike Gastarbeiter – were full citizens and thus were not obliged to depart when their labour was no longer required. The 1962 Commonwealth Immigrants Act was passed at a time when the Government acknowledged that shortages of labour were restricting economic growth. Nevertheless, the Act both limited the supply of additional workers and transformed the composition of the black population. As full citizens, black immigrants had possessed the right to bring in dependants. Prior to 1962, therefore, there had developed a 'black reproductive sector' (spouses, children etc, not in employment) in addition to the black labour force. However, workers considerably outnumbered dependants. The prospect of controls transformed the existing pattern of migration. Previously, the flow of black immigrants largely consisted of workers coming in response to demand for their labour; after 1962 it largely consisted of dependants intent on permanent immigration. The effect of the Act was thus to limit the supply of labour at a time of excess demand and to expand the number of dependants who, partly because of the difficulty of re-entry, would be likely to remain even when the period of excess demand had ended.

Black workers originally occupied a 'helot' role in the economy. Few of them have since been able to move out of the type of undesirable employment for which they were first recruited. This can be explained to some degree by the level of discrimination which has faced black workers not only when they apply for jobs but also when they are in line for promotion. Comparison of the 1971 Census returns and the 1977–78 NDHS[18] appears to indicate some improvement during the 1970s at least. But it is unclear to what extent this is more than a consequence of successive changes in immigration control which have progressively confined access to the more highly skilled. The extent of discrimination caused Smith to conclude that 'there is little evidence that racial inequalities in the employment field will be quickly corrected by upward mobility of Asians and West Indians'. [19]

In seeking to understand the mechanisms whereby disadvantage arises in the employment of black and other workers, it is important to look at the processes through which employees are recruited, upgraded and promoted. In large organizations at least, associated with the advance of formal personnel management, processes of recruitment and promotion have increasingly been organized on lines which appear to equate with the Weberian model of selection based solely on technical competence. Criteria such as levels of qualification, skill, experience and achievement are used to provide 'objective' means of selecting one recruit rather than another. Were such objectivity a reality, it would seem to be only a matter of time before suitably qualified members of disadvantaged groups such as women and black workers, for example, achieved equal status with white male workers.

In practice, however, there are a number of reasons why the concept of objectivity in selection is difficult to achieve in practice even if it is desired by those in control of organizations. Small firms may not have the resources or the desire to develop complex procedures; while in large organizations the exercise of responsibility for selection, like much day to day operation, has in practice to be delegated. At a general level, as Bendix points out, those 'who command must control, but cannot superintend, the executions of their directives'.[20] Furthermore it is difficult to establish criteria that are 'objective' in any meaningful sense. Passage to skilled status, for example, is generally achieved not by exam, but by serving the fixed time period of apprenticeship and thus covers a wide range of technical competence. Examinations such as degrees or GCEs tend to be general rather than of direct relevance to specific occupations. Even so, how do you distinguish between candidates with equivalent educational achievements and how do you evaluate one pattern of experience against another that is similar? Finally, as Blackburn and Mann's study of Peterborough suggests, at the level of unskilled and semi-skilled work, there is little to distinguish between jobs in terms of prerequisite skills or experience. They concluded that, apart from those workers 'with mental or physical deficiencies, workers who are non literate (usually immigrants), workers nearing retirement and losing both strength and adaptability . . . we have estimated that in Peterborough about 85 per cent of the workers possess the necessary ability to undertake 95 per cent of the jobs' (ie those in the unqualified labour market which they were studying).[21] In other words, most workers can perform most jobs. In non-skilled jobs it is particularly easy for employers to establish seemingly objective entry or promotion requirements which are in practice not generally relevant to the jobs concerned but which, wittingly or otherwise, serve to exclude one category of workers or another. For example, women workers have been excluded by lifting requirements, which it was assumed no woman would be able to fulfil, or by requiring that all employees in a category accept the firm's right to transfer them between locations.[22] Likewise literacy tests may serve to exclude black applicants or restrict their advancement.

Given the difficulties in differentiating between one applicant and another in terms of ability to satisfy the requirements of a job, employers use what Offe[23] terms 'ascriptive qualifications' as a secondary –sometimes perhaps, the only – system of screening. Thus various general characteristics tend to be ascribed to workers by employers. A record of frequent job changes, for example, may be regarded as a sign of instability among manual workers, whereas for young executives this may be perceived as an indicator of drive and initiative. And mature single male workers are likely to find it more difficult to gain employment than their married contemporaries, because single status is believed to be associated with unreliability, with higher levels of alcoholism and mental instability.[24] Most pervasive are the assumptions that are often made about the supposed behavioural characteristics and physical or other limitations of women as workers.

These assumptions, which have effectively restricted them to a limited, usually low level range of occupations, may provide a valuable insight to the problems faced by black workers. Hunt[25] examined managerial attitudes to women workers and his findings could be applied equally to black workers:

that a majority of those responsible for the engagement of employees start off with the belief that a woman applicant is likely to be inferior to a man in respect of all the qualifications considered important. The higher the level of the job, the greater the proportion who considered men were more likely to have the required attributes. Assuming identical attributes of both a man and woman applicant, the majority would give preference to a man rather than to a woman for all types of work, with the exception of catering and domestic work, where women were preferred, and office work where the majority expressed no preferences.[26]

(However the pattern of employment in both cases is, of course, a consequence of actions and policies in many areas besides employment which may shape aspirations in relation to work or, as in the case of apprenticeships or medical training, deny access at the point of entry.)

Apart from a range of assumptions about their work behaviour, black workers also suffer from pernicious beliefs about aspects of personal behaviour which may be held to affect work performance. The 1967 PEP Survey found that:

> The occupational characteristics attributed to immigrants were a general ignorance of the British way of life and in particular poor spoken English or none at all, a low level of formal qualifications and a tendency to over-claim qualifications, and a habit of continually changing jobs, or high occupational mobility. To these can be added certain qualities such as idleness, slowness or unwillingness to learn, and unwillingness to take orders which manifested itself in surliness and aggressiveness. The personal characteristics also included dirtiness, smelliness, unattractive eating habits, sexual virility and appetite, and a 'chip on the shoulder' or a marked sensitivity to colour which made them attribute all failures and misfortunes to that.[27]

The 1974 PEP Survey[28] and much of the evidence submitted in the same year by employers, careers officers and others to the House of Commons Select Committee[29] suggests that such stereotyping is highly durable. Brooks[30] indicates that black workers may be accepted as employees, workmates and individuals without disturbing stereotypical categorizations.

A belief that the work performance of black workers is in some respects likely to be unsatisfactory need not reflect a general racial prejudice, but may be sufficient to influence the selection process.

Such beliefs are evident across a wide spectrum of work. As the extracts from Smith (Chapter 2.8) and Ballard and Holden (Chapter 2.7) demonstrate, black applicants may hold suitable qualifications for white-collar and graduate appointments, but they will be significantly less successful than equally qualified white applicants.

For many workers, then, decisions about their suitability for employment or promotion are likely to be influenced or determined by characteristics attributed to the various categories into which managers may place them. For those seeking to improve the prospects for advancement of black workers and others, or to limit their vulnerability to unemployment, this represents one of the most intractable problems. This is partly the case because the influence of ascriptive criteria is often hard to identify. For example, the PEP Studies showed that many individuals were unaware that they had been discriminated against.

Of equal importance are factors such as the pressures of operational efficiency, and the relationship between organizational performance and managerial careers. Translated into the area of selection, operational efficiency *requires* that managers recruit those workers whom they *believe* to be the best available in the prevailing circumstances – ie those from whom they will secure the highest return. Given the problems of sifting between the often marginal differences in applicants' backgrounds they are most likely to be influenced by assessments of 'stability', 'dependability' and 'acceptability'. All other things being equal, the most suitable candidate for many jobs is likely to be the one who is thought least likely to disturb the unity and level of work effort of the workgroups he or she will encounter. The characteristics which are ascribed to individuals, consciously or otherwise, through stereotyping may be crucial in deciding to prefer one candidate and reject others, or to decide which among existing employees should be dismissed.

This is not to suggest that ascribed characteristics are the only factor determining entry or movement in the internal labour market or that the characteristics ascribed to black workers are necessarily negative. Amongst other things, there is likely to be a structure of workplace rules, particularly in unionized workplaces, which may influence upward progression, or which regulate dismissal or redundancy. Seniority rules, or first in last out, will, at least, protect those black workers with fairly long service and should ensure equal treatment. Whatever misgivings managers may have had when black and other migrant workers were first recruited, these are likely to have been modified by experience: 'coloured workers were more honest than whites, Pakistanis were reliable but they "need feeding up before they can do heavy work", Italians were "hard workers but a little reckless"'.[31] However the effects of such positive experience may be limited. They do not necessarily disturb assumptions that black or other workers are most suited for certain types of work.

Indeed they may merely be regarded as proof that they are good at that sort of work. On the other hand, the significance of the attitudes of other groups of employees should not be forgotten. Attitudes to recruitment or promotion, particularly to supervisory positions may provide a strong deterrent to change.

It is useful to think of the flow of candidates through selection processes in terms of a queue system. An individual's position in the queue is likely to be related to the combination of the desirability or otherwise of a job, the categorization which is attached to the job – 'women's work' etc – and to the work characteristics believed by employers to be associated with factors such as age, sex or colour. Position in the queue is also a consequence of the level of employment. As unemployment rises, those with disadvantages are more likely to be pushed towards the back of the queue, particularly for the more desirable jobs. This is of course something of a caricature. Ascriptive qualifications may be less important to some employers than others; and individuals in categories that can be regarded as disadvantaged do succeed against more advantaged candidates. Additionally, the structure and composition of 'queues' is modified by the preferences of workers. For example, those who are unemployed may choose not to seek certain types of jobs. This was evident during full employment when indigenous workers deserted the undesirable jobs for which black workers were recruited. During periods of rising unemployment there may be little or no downward shaping of work attitudes and expectations; some individuals may decide to extend the job search process rather than accept jobs of a type which are not reasonably close to their preferences.

Whatever qualifications there might be about the concept of a queue, it does accord with much of the statistical evidence about the characteristics of the unemployed. Broadly, there are two sets of factors which may explain why particular individuals become unemployed and why they remain unemployed for different periods. At one level there are the characteristics of the individuals themselves; and at another there are the broad economic factors of frictional and structural change which may increase the level of risk experienced by any group. Where the first of these is concerned, the statistical evidence[32] shows quite clearly that particular groups are at risk. These groups face higher than average chances of becoming unemployed, and of remaining unemployed for long periods. Many members of the working population never experience unemployment, but as Smith and Nickell show, its incidence 'is heavily trated among particular groups'.[33] The incidence of unemployment is, for example, clearly related to age. Apart from the acute problems of school leavers, young workers generally have a higher propensity to quit which may reflect both lower levels of financial commitments and a search for improved longer term employment conditions. They are also most at risk of becoming unemployed involuntarily through the operation of 'last in, first out' redundancy clauses and through other factors. Although they may experience less difficulty than rather older workers in finding new employment, the consequence is that, as unemployment rises, the percentage of youth unemployment increases much faster. For each one per cent increase in the unemployment rate, youth unemployment rises by 1.7 per cent.[34] At the other end of the scale workers over the age of 55 are also more likely to become unemployed, but predominantly involuntarily so. Those most at risk also include the disabled, those suffering from ill-health, black workers and, possibly, women. The evidence is less clear in the latter case because of their much lower unemployment registration rates, probably between 44 and 55 per cent compared with 74 to 87 per cent for men.[35]

(The evidence gathered by Smith[36] and others suggests that registration rates for black workers are similar to those of the population as a whole)

Further categories of risk are related to specific occupations: risks increase for those employed by small firms, without qualifications, with short periods of service in their current or most recent job, with low earnings, and in low status occupations. The various categories of risk vary in their effects however. Youth is a temporary factor, and ill-health, lack of qualification or single status may be changed. But where sex, disablement and skin colour are concerned it is only wide social attitudes and policies which can change the level of risk. For black workers as for women, the handicapped and the disabled, the other factors represent additional hazards to which they may at various times also be prone.

The chief source of risk of being unemployed resides in category of occupation. The proneness of the non-skilled to unemployment was demonstrated by a study of the returns from the 1972 General Household Survey.[37] This indicated an unemployment rate of 14.2 per cent for unskilled male manual workers and 6.7 per cent for the semi-skilled, compared with an average male rate of 4.5 per cent, 4.0 per cent among skilled male manual workers and foremen and 1.2 per cent among senior and intermediate non-manual workers. This is not simply a matter of incidence of unemployment: unskilled male manual workers were also found to remain out of work for longer periods than average. During a depression, firms are more likely to lay-off the unskilled and semi-skilled and to halt their recruitment, hence Smith's[38] parallel finding that the unskilled male manual worker was six times more likely to be unemployed than a male non-manual worker.

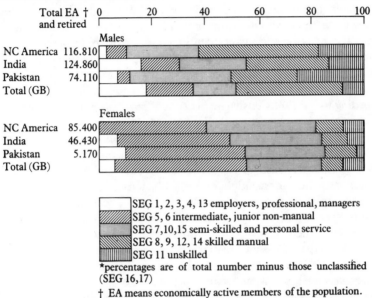

SEG 1, 2, 3, 4, 13 employers, professional, managers
SEG 5, 6 intermediate, junior non-manual
SEG 7, 10, 15 semi-skilled and personal service
SEG 8, 9, 12, 14 skilled manual
SEG 11 unskilled
*percentages are of total number minus those unclassified (SEG 16, 17)

† EA means economically active members of the population.

Source: G. Lomas: Employment and Economic Activity, 1972 Census Data in *New Community*, Vol. VII No. 2, Summer, 1979, p. 221

**Figure 1:** Distribution by socio-economic group, Great Britain, 1971.

To the extent that black or other groups of workers disproportionately occupy specific socio-economic categories, so they will be disproportionately at risk. The 1971 Census and the 1977–78 National Dwelling and Housing Survey both indicate that the socio-economic distribution varies considerably between male black workers. As can be seen in Figure 1, West Indian and Pakistani/Bangladeshi men were under-represented among employers, professionals and managers but over-represented among unskilled workers. For West Indian men as a whole this was more than counterbalanced by their high occupancy of skilled work, while Indian men are closer to the distribution of the population as a whole. The employment profile of black women is more uniformly closer to the general distribution. Generally, however, the pattern of distribution and its implications for unemployment needs to be considered in the context of the PEP finding[39] that black workers tend to be overqualified for the jobs they do compared with the population as a whole.

A further element of risk is attached to the particular industry in which an individual works. Workers in manufacturing have generally been more vulnerable than workers in service industries. Within this general pattern, however, there are variations in rates of decline and some sectors such as insurance, banking and finance continued to expand in terms of numbers of employees even as unemployment rose. An examination of the distribution of black workers in the labour market shows that they are disproportionately concentrated in manufacturing industry. Thus, according to the 1971 Census, 47 per cent of black males were employed in manufacturing compared with 33 per cent of white males. There are particular concentrations of black employees in a number of manufacturing industries, eg vehicle production, metal manufacture and textiles. Black workers are also disproportionately concentrated in a number of service industries, for example, transport, catering and the health service. But the implications of this concentration are unclear. Smith found that most industries gave rise to a degree of unemployment which was broadly in line with their share of total workforce. This applied whether the workforce was taken as a whole, or whether separate analysis was made of the white, West Indian and Asian workforces. The major exception to this pattern was the association between the decline of the textile industry and the rate of Asian unemployment. In 1971 22 per cent of unemployed Asian men had been previously employed in textiles, though the industry employed only 10.5 per cent of Asian men in work and 2.1 per cent of all men in work.[40]

The data for Smith's research were gathered in 1979 and it is possible that the subsequent more rapid fall in employment and industrial output has produced a closer association between high rates of black unemployment and the decline of certain industries. However, to seek to explain black disadvantage in unemployment (or in employment) principally in terms of a concentration of black workers in 'disadvantaged' – in the sense of declining – industries is to misunderstand the genesis of black migration. In the initial phase of their immigration, black workers were undoubtedly required to man declining industries and industries which offered seasonal unemployment or little job security. On the other hand, their labour was also required in expanding industries and advanced sectors of the economy. The call for migrant labour arose less because indigenous labour was abandoning declining industries than because it was abandoning disadvantaged *jobs*. Even in the textile industry the recruitment of Pakistani workers was associated with, and facilitated, new capital investment. (Cohen and Jenner, Chapter 2.2, p. 122.) As Böhning argues, 'it is not the economic sector as such but the incidence of socially undesirable jobs that matters and there is practically no sector where there are no badly paid and undesirable jobs'. (Chapter 1.1, p. 30.)

Finally, higher risk of unemployment is associated with geographical location in terms of the different regional rates of unemployment and of the differing ratios of vacancies to numbers of unemployed. For example in the West Midlands, an area where black workers are disproportionately concentrated, the unemployment rate for the West Midlands in mid-1980 was close to the average of 6.1 per cent but the ratio of unemployed to vacancies of 29:1 was higher than in the other regions. In general however, black workers have been concentrated in areas that, until the 1980s, at least, were lower risk – primarily London, the South East, and the West Midlands. (By 1981 however, the West Midlands unemployment rate was one of the highest, above that of Scotland.) But this does not necessarily limit the level of risk because of mixed experience within regions. A DES Survey based on 1977–78 NDHS data looked at the characteristics of the unemployed in ten English cities. All workers were classified by age, sex and socio- economic group as well as ethnic origin in an attempt to establish the extent to which ethnic origin was significant in explaining the incidence of unemployment. In seven of the cities, accounting for about ten per cent of the black population in England, it was found that unemployment rates were similar across all ethnic categories. In London, Birmingham and Leicester, which together accounted for 56 per cent of the black English population, the proportion of unemployed black workers was significantly higher even after the effects of different age and skill distributions were allowed for. In other words, being black was a significant factor determining unemployment and thus suggests that the level of black unemployment cannot be explained only by virtue of their disproportionate occupancy of lower level jobs.[41]

There is, then, a wide range of factors which may increase the prospects of becoming unemployed for any man or woman. How important is race in this process? Smith suggests that 'the extra risk of being unemployed that arises from being an Asian or a West Indian is small compared with the extra risk from being an unskilled manual worker rather than a senior manager or a university professor'.[42] The importance of race should not be exaggerated: unemployment magnifies racial inequalities, but it magnifies other inequalities as well. Unemployment has implications and consequences for all but the most privileged sections of the population; it is a general problem, and one unlikely to be resolved merely by paying special attention to the difficulties of particular sections of the workforce, be they black workers or other disadvantaged groups. Nevertheless, the seriousness of the problems that face black workers, and the extent to which these problems illuminate general societal inequalities and disadvantages, should not be underestimated. If we are to seek an explanation of why it is that black workers face a greater risk of unemployment than does the labour force as a whole, we must examine the circumstances of their initial recruitment into specific occupations and industries.

During the early 1960s, the prospect of controls on immigration led to a dramatic increase in immigration. The rate of arrival was such that the labour market became temporarily 'flooded'. Thus in February 1963 (more than six months after the imposition of control) black workers formed six per cent of the unemployed though they accounted for only one and half per cent of the workforce.

Between 1963 and 1966 there was a sharp fall in black unemployment expressed as a percentage of total unemployment. This trend was interrupted by a minor recession which occurred between 1966 and 1968, but it was resumed once again from 1968 to 1970, by which time the rate of unemployment among black workers – at about 2½ per cent – was roughly equivalent to their numbers in the total workforce.[43] Having achieved a normal distribution in terms of the incidence of unemployment, the relative position of black workers deteriorated progressively through the 1970s. As can be seen in Figure 2, when the absolute level of male unemployment rose so the proportion of the unemployed males who were black rose rapidly.

When there was some downward movement in the numbers of unemployed, the proportion of unemployed males who were black dropped with similar rapidity. This appears to be explained by the greater preparedness of unemployed black workers to move down the job hierarchy in an attempt to find work. But the long term unemployment trend during the 1970s was upwards, rapidly so at the end of the decade. The disproportionate effects can be seen in the figure. However it is not simply the numerical increase that is significant; equally important, the average duration of unemployment was increasing. Between 1976 and 1978, for example, the number of men among the unemployed who had been without work for more than six months increased from 34 per cent to 43 per cent.[44]. Smith[45] found that compared with white workers a higher proportion of black unemployed workers were longer term unemployed. Moreover a broader range of black workers was found to be at risk: whereas for native workers unemployment, as we have seen, tends to be concentrated among the non-skilled, black workers are more at risk across all categories of occupation. Finally there are the particular problems of groups within the black population, most notably young West Indians.

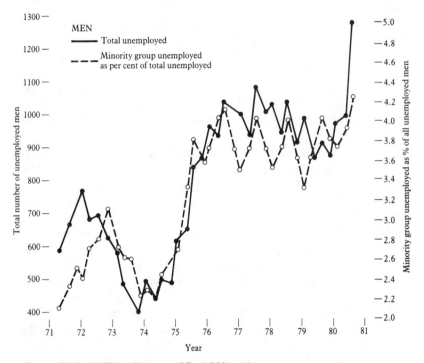

*Source:* D. Smith *Unemployment and Racial Minorities,*
Policy Studies Institute, 1981, p.4.

**Figure 2:** Minority unemployed as a percentage of all unemployed, men, 1971–81.
*(To understand the full impact of this figure it should be remembered that if the black proportion of the unemployed were to equate to their relative presence in the workforce, the dotted line should remain more or less level from the three per cent point on the right hand axis.)*

Black workers occupy a specially disadvantaged labour-market position in so far as eg they may be more likely than white workers to be dismissed in the event of a fall in economic activity, they may find greater difficulty in finding employment and they tend to occupy jobs at lower levels than similarly qualified white workers.[46] Such discrimination may keep black workers disproportionately concentrated in the type of less-skilled jobs, involving low pay and poor conditions, for which their labour was first required; that is, in the very jobs most threatened by rising unemployment.

We have sought to establish the scale of the problems faced by black workers. Two important questions remain. First, is it possible that the problems associated with the high level of unemployment reached in the early 1980s will become still more acute? Second, given that the problems posed by unemployment for black workers are but a part of a much wider set of economic and social problems, to what extent is there some prospect of action to alleviate the added risks which are faced by all categories of black worker?

It is, of course impossible to predict with any confidence the course of domestic or international economic trends and policies, nor of the political changes which may shape or be shaped by economic pressures. Nonetheless there are good reasons for believing that the level of unemployment will remain high throughout most, if not all, of this decade. Apart from the depth of the current recession, from which recovery must necessarily be slow, the shift to economic policies which emphasize the significance of the regulatory or controlling effects of unemployment, and shifts in state expenditure patterns towards areas such as armaments, technological and organizational change, seem likely to have marked effects on the levels, types and locations of employment for a considerable number of years. Where the domestic economy is concerned, there are long standing processes of structural change which will continue to shift the location of employment away from areas such as the metal and other heavy industries, towards a limited range of manufacturing activity and towards professional and other services. But beside such consistent and long standing changes it is frequently suggested that changes in micro-electronic technology, such as the development of micro-processors, will have more extensive and radical effects on employment and the content of work. Much has been written about the 'micro-processor revolution', and it would be inappropriate to re-cover the ground here. This is particularly so because much of the material is highly tentative and speculative, as well as being ephemeral, given that the pace of change is so very rapid. We can do no more than note some of the general consequences which appear likely to have particular effects for the employment of black workers.

Firstly, the logic of existing developments suggests that the progressive process of deskilling which has gradually affected most manual, and much non-manual, work will continue. This will intensify the competition which black workers face, and reduce the availability of skilled, more highly paid jobs which West Indians in particular, have tended to occupy. For example, small batch production in the engineering industry, accounting for more than 40 per cent of engineering output and largely the preserve of the skilled craftsman, has mostly been untouched by automation until now. Micro-processor technology will radically change production methods and reduce the need for skilled men. Secondly, we would point to the likelihood that the expectations of second generation black workers will remain similar to those of their white age-cohorts. However, the extent to which these expectations will be realized becomes more problematic when the impact of micro-processors and other instruments of office automation are taken into account. Furthermore, the relatively low cost, simplicity and adaptability in use of micro-processors is likely to extend aspects of shopfloor and office automation to small firms which until now have been largely immune. The net effect is likely to be a continuing squeeze on jobs and additional constraints on upward mobility.

The other aspect of technological change and related organizational change is that brought out by Sivanandan (Chapter 1.3, pp. 61–62). Amongst other things he emphasized the role of communications and other technology in making possible a change in the international relationship of capital and labour. The relative attractions of importing labour have diminished as it has become easier to relocate and control industrial enterprises of many types in the existing areas of low cost reserve labour.

Frobel *et al* have identified three main reasons for this:
1. There exists in the Third World an almost inexhaustible supply of cheap, disposable labour, which has been displaced into urban areas by a variety of social and economic developments. Given the extent of poverty and in the absence of trade union organization, this labour will be willing to work long hours in whatever system of shift-work suits the employer.
2. The fragmentation of the production process is now so advanced that more and more tasks can be carried out with minimal skills and training.

3. Improvements in transport and communications are such that complete or partial production processes may be sited almost anywhere in the world without being rendered uneconomic by organizational, technical or cost problems.[47]

Their main thesis is that a new international division of labour has replaced that in which Third World Countries were valued only as providers of labour and raw materials. In this new phase production processes can be subdivided and re-located according to where the optimum combination of capital and labour lies. In this developing world-wide economy companies will seek where possible to move production from high wage economies to economies (or economic enclaves offering special tax concessions) in which wage costs are low and where they will be kept low by the virtually inexhaustible supply of labour.

Frobel et al's detailed analysis of developments in the German textile and clothing industry may be of particular relevance for black workers in Britain. Their examination shows that the number of workers employed within Germany has declined steadily since the 1960s, while in the same period German-owned factories have been established in South East Asia and North Africa. In one case, parts of trousers were cut out on automatic machines in Germany, then flown to a German-owned factory in Tunisia to be sewn together, and finally flown back to Germany to be sold, an illustration of the extent to which the production process can be divided between high-wage, capital-intensive and low-wage, labour-intensive elements.

Frobel et al also studied the foreign operations of some 600 companies outside textiles. This revealed that by the mid-1970s German companies employed more than half-a-million workers outside Germany, by which point German overseas investment approached DM 50,000 million. According to another recent study of the German economy, the industries which are most affected by this relocation are those which employ the largest number of immigrant workers.[48]

In this article, and in the content of this Reader as a whole, we have sought to establish the extent of disadvantage faced by black workers and to identify specific explanations of that disadvantage through examination of wider historical and economic contexts. In conclusion there remains the question of whether there can be any substantial progress towards the alleviation or resolution of aspects of black disadvantage in employment at a time when unemployment seems likely to remain at high levels and when economic and social inequalities in general are increasing. The short answer is probably that little can be done until the economic situation improves. Black workers are only one of several groups for whom disadvantage has become more acute and for whom a special case can be advanced.

Action to ameliorate the problems of one or more such groups can either come about by a general redistribution of wealth and resources (which seems highly unlikely), or by extending or creating disadvantage elsewhere. Without wider action the employment prospects of black workers can only increase at the expense of decreased employment prospects for others, which would probably cause some increase in racial tension. Black workers face the same problem as others such as young workers, that 'if significant changes in youth unemployment are to be made, policies which affect the whole economy (either the local economy or the United Kingdom's economy as a whole) are essential'.[49]

However, for some considerable time to come, measures to increase the general level of economic activity are more likely to stabilize the level of unemployment or to effect modest reductions rather than sharply to reduce it. In any event, it is unlikely that unemployment will fall to the levels of the 1940s–1960s.

Yet this does not mean that there is nothing that can or should be done. It is simply to emphasize the extent of the constraints. There is no overriding reason why the extent of discrimination should not be progressively minimized, or why sources of disadvantage should not be modified or removed, in order to reduce the gap between black disadvantage and that of the population as a whole. Unemployment does not prevent pursuit of goals suggested by the CBI: 'to reduce the level of passive discrimination and in particular . . . to make arrangements which ensure that everyone concerned has opportunities to get into, first, the high paying areas within a factory, (sic) and second, the promotion that they deserve on merit.'[50] The obstacles in the way of such action may have increased, but so from many points of view has the need for them. What problems there are not solely a consequence of unemployment but of the attitudes and policies of those who are directly or indirectly involved in regulating the issues of work and employment.

The law clearly has a role to play in shaping attitudes and in providing a clear basis for the establishment and operation of non-discriminatory policies etc, but its effects are likely to remain limited. Change is more likely to come from the actions of trade unions and, more significantly, of employers. Moreover, legal intervention is limited in so far as it is primarily concerned with individual cases. It is, however, at a collective level that many employment issues are regulated and administered. Individual cases often do not get referral either because individuals may be unaware that they have been discriminated against or because they are reluctant to involve themselves in what appear to be cumbersome and uncertain procedures. Legal provision may produce some incremental and possibly marginal changes, but there is a large gap between implementing those formal measures which may be necessary to secure minimal compliance with legal requirements, and the policies and practices which may achieve something approaching the underlying intention of legislation. What evidence there is suggests that the effects of race relations legislation are more apparent than real. The difficulties can perhaps be more clearly seen in the parallel legislation against sex discrimination. Male social attitudes being apparently more open than attitudes on race, limitations on the law become more visible:

> . . . most organizations did very little as a result of the legislation. Discrimination continued and our findings on managers' intentions to discriminate indicated that instances of discrimination might increase when more vacancies occurred. This response to the legislation seems to have been due to two common attitudes: first, that the legislation was unnecessary and irrelevant because 'we already have equal opportunities'; and second, that where an organization was discriminating, this was acceptable and the legislation would not require any real changes. 'Legislation does not mean a company will act differently. We will not change our personnel decisions, just how we go about them. . . . Just as we keep a "good" mix on race by finding reasons to reject most Asians, so we will find reasons to reject women for some jobs' (a personnel manager).
> The first attitude was common among many managers who felt that women were free to apply for jobs, especially where all jobs were openly advertised. They believed women were in the jobs they could do best and which they wanted to do, as were men. Many of these managers were line managers who had not thought deeply or seriously about discrimination and they were often in organizations which had not issued detailed guidelines on the legislation. They were not fully aware of the Act and its implications. Given their lack of knowledge and interest and their belief that women already had equal opportunity, they were likely to continue to discriminate without being fully aware that they were doing so.[51]

We suggested earlier that the original profile of black employment was related largely to economic need, and that once a disadvantaged employment pattern becomes established it is in a sense self-perpetuating.

Assumptions develop about the capabilities of individuals on the basis of past work records. Certain categories of work become associated with certain categories of worker. To overcome these assumptions and the effects of discrimination requires both a level of awareness and a modification of priorities. As the CBI explained to a Select Committee hearing:

> Employers have a great deal to think about and they are questions of immediate survival and . . . (the removal of discrimination) . . . does not strike them as being in that kind of category. They will, therefore, tend to put it off for as long as they can, not because they do not wish to do the right thing and all that, but for purely practical reasons . . . The difficulty . . . (of a positive policy) . . . is a matter of timing because it will always be somewhere near the bottom of the pending tray.[52]

Thus the pressures of day-to-day operations may be of more significance than the influence of prejudiced attitudes. One can only speculate about the current position of such issues in the 'pending' tray, given the intensification of questions of immediate survival since 1974.

The CBI itself is hardly in a position to produce a change in priorities. Beside other limitations it has no power and, at best, limited influence over its members, particularly those smaller companies who are in membership – the majority are non-members. But where equal opportunity and other policies are established as even moderately important priorities in employing organizations there remain many difficulties. In large companies, it can be just as difficult to translate formal policies into actions that represent more than overt compliance as it may be to enforce legal provisions. This is partly because it is the actions of subordinate groups of managers, or of individual managers, who directly or indirectly shape practice in recruitment, promotion or work allocation.

There may also be constraints on the application of company policy, real or imagined, which are derived from employee attitudes and actions. The shift in TUC policy toward black workers which took place in the 1970s, described by Miles and Phizacklea in Chapter 3.2 may have done something to affect the attitudes of union members. The change in TUC policy has been accompanied by corresponding changes in the larger unions such as the T & GWU and NUPE. But the effect of these changes should not be overestimated. As with employers, it seems likely that other than where unavoidable issues arise, the translation of formal declaration of policy into shopfloor action will be limited. Full-time union officers tend to play a predominantly 'fire fighting' role, being overstretched and pre-occupied with active issues of pay and redundancy, rather than the shaping of more general union workplace policy. The extent to which issues of discrimination and equal opportunity are accepted as priorities, and are not totally overwhelmed by other issues, is limited. This is partly because unemployment together with legal changes since 1980 has weakened trade unions in relation to employers. In any event, the power of collective bargaining and the general pattern of workplace regulation are themselves more limited in extent and effect than is often held to be the case.

Many issues such as recruitment and wider aspects of organizational policy remain outside the managerially accepted area of union- management relationships in all but the most highly union organized workplaces. Management remain the initiators of policy. The making of workplace rules, like policy interpretation and application as a whole, remains as Armstrong *et al* observe, 'a management process and . . . becomes material for "industrial relations" only as an exception and by way of reaction to the general process of management rule making.'[53] It should also be remembered that there remain many non unionized workplaces in which a significant number of black workers must be employed. Thus the extent to which unions can modify black disadvantage is limited.

At a time of increased competition for jobs, divisions between groups of workers are likely to become more apparent. Attempts may be made to strengthen or extend the boundaries and defences of employment territories in order to reduce job competition. This is not to suggest that such an extension will be made in racial terms. As Bentley shows (Chapter 3.1 pp. 227–244), there is little evidence of divisions along these lines. What it does suggest is a possible conflict between the maintenance of such defences against unemployment, and attempts to reduce black disadvantage.

Again we should emphasize that we are not arguing that no progress towards the removal of black disadvantage is likely to be made. We seek rather to emphasize that where positive change takes place it is likely to be both slow and limited, at least in the medium term. The CBI's spokesman in 1974 regarded it as being 'crucial that in the next two or three years we tackle them (ie the issues of promotion etc, referred to above, p. 387) and end up on the right side'.

Yet recent studies, eg of the job prospects of young blacks in Nottingham and Lewisham in South London and Smith's study of unemployment,[54] demonstrate the persistence of black disadvantage. In the absence of wider action that would substantially reduce unemployment or tackle disadvantage, it seems likely that the most effective means of mitigating the effects of unemployment will come from the resources of the black community itself. The experience of Jewish immigrants as Kosmin (Chapter 2.9, p. 188) suggests, shows the importance of finding a niche in the economic structure where competition with the native labour force is limited. To some extent this may be found within the conventional employment structure but the development of independent sources of income and employment generates an element of independence from and insulation against employment discrimination and the pressures and vagaries of the wider economy. An extreme version of this is what Wilson and Porte term 'enclave economies'.[55] They suggest that this concept needs to be related to the dualist hypothesis (see Blackburn and Mann, Chapter 1.4) which has more relevance in the US context. Of particular significance for 'unmeltable' ethnics, for whom the barriers against entry to the more attractive jobs are most tenacious, jobs in the enclave economies may provide an attractive option to working in the mainstream economy. In the ideal model, these may develop within a distinct ethnic product market. This will contain reliable and culturally appropriate sources of supply, and it will gradually extend vertically in the production process, for example, through the extension back from retailers to wholesalers to processing or manufacturing and even back to initial sources of supply.

In this country it seems clear that ethnic-owned businesses provide an important source of employment and other economic support, but they tend to rely less exclusively on the ethnic communities than Wilson and Porte's model would suggest. The textile trade, for example as Werbner points out,[56] is one in which immigrants have tended to do well (see Kosmin Chapter 2.9 and Shah, Chapter 2.10). It is suitable for the small scale investment that reflects limited immigrant financial resources. While it is not a new industry, it is one to which the successive groups of migrant workers have brought revival, finding new demands. But success in this as other areas has substantially depended on custom from the wider community. Werbner's Asian wholesalers supplied English traders as well as fellow Pakistanis. A study of Asian retailers in Croydon[57] likewise found trade from the white population to be important – in this case highly so. Asian traders had come to own ten per cent of all independent retail outlets and 34 per cent of all independent groceries. Their success appears to have been related to the retention of the personal service not available in supermarkets and to their readiness to provide an additional service by remaining open for long hours.

More evidence is required before the general importance of ethnic businesses for the ethnic communities and for the economy as a whole is established. On the evidence that is available this may be an area in which government might usefully undertake a new initiative towards the alleviation of black disadvantage within the general context of present economic and social policies. We have already referred to doubts about government's ability significantly to lower unemployment for some time – the area from which a positive improvement is most likely to come. At the same time, it is difficult to identify areas where governments are both able and prepared to introduce measures that will substantially improve the prospects of black workers, which do not seek to tackle the problem of high levels of unemployment among all workers. Meanwhile resources might be more effectively directed towards enabling the black communities to take action themselves on the problems of unemployment and lack of opportunity faced by many of their members by facilitating the expansion of businesses and other work providing organizations. It would also provide a useful recognition and acceptance of cultural plurality, as well as the positive economic contributions of the black community. It would fit well with the declared intention of governments to assist small businesses and to encourage new areas of economic activity. But even at a level beyond that of a cosmetic policy, such action can only benefit a minority of a minority. It carries the danger of emphasizing a narrow and divisive focus, treating the issues of black employment or unemployment as a discrete issue. In contrast, we have tried to emphasize that the issue of discrimination and disadvantage, in employment or in unemployment, is part of much wider social issues and problems and can only be meaningfully approached in this way. However, to reiterate, this is to emphasize the difficulties and limitations facing action, not to suggest that no action can be taken. Simply bringing the level of black disadvantage to that of the population as a whole remains an important interim objective but there remains the separate problem of combatting racial discrimination and hostility. It would perhaps be timely for many of those involved in the regulation of employment to examine whether the passive support of equal opportunity, contrived compliance with legislative requirements or the occasional verbal rejection of racialist views or actions, remains adequate. The priorities of the pending tray, in the CBI's phraseology, might well be reviewed. In particular there is a case for looking again at the way that 'positive inaction' may amount to acquiescence in the maintenance or advance of discriminatory practices. 'Positive inaction' may provide cover for policies or practices which, at the point of implementation, may be regarded by the initiators or victims of racial prejudice as legitimating those feelings. Governments for example have effectively achieved this through immigration legislation which however carefully designed is clearly perceived as being discriminatory in effect, if not in intention. The argument that immigration controls are set in context by anti-discrimination legislation falters both because there is reluctance to use the legal machinery and because to go to law may involve coming into conflict with prevailing judicial attitudes.[58] A proper assessment of the problems of black workers must take account of factors such as these, as well as of the actions of employers, trade unionists and the state in the changing employment conditions faced by the black workers. Effective action to overcome the problems of black workers during the period of their entry into the labour force was difficult enought despite the prevailing excess demand for labour; in the circumstances of deepening recession and rising unemployment, such effective action will be all the harder.

## Notes

1. Evidence to the Select Committee on Race Relations and Immigration, Minutes of Evidence – volume II, 1974, session p. 451.
2. De Caux, L: *The Living Spirit of the Wobblies*, International Publishers, New York, 1978, p. 4.
3. Thomas, B.: 'Economic Aspects of Migration' in *International Encyclopedia of the Social Sciences*, 1968, p. 293, Macmillan and the Free Press, USA.
4. Thomas, op cit, p. 293.
5. Allen, S: 'White Migrants, Black Workers' in *New Community*, vol XX, 1978, p. 12.
6. Descloitres, R: 'The Foreign Worker,' OECD, Paris, p. 22 quoted in Castles, S. and Kosack, G: *Immigrant Workers and the Class Structure in Western Europe*, OUP, 1973, p. 15.
7. Allen, S, op cit.
8. Castles, S and Kosack, G, op cit, p. 17.
9. There were also, of course, consequences for the sending countries; see, for example, Paine, S: *Exporting Workers – the Turkish Case*, CUP, 1974.
10. Mandel, E: *Late Capitalism*, New Left Books, London, 1975, p. 170.
11. Peach, C: 'British Unemployment Cycles and West Indian Immigration, 1955–74' *New Community*, vol. vii, no. 1, Winter 1978/9.
12. Power, J: Western Europe's Migrant Workers, Minority Rights Group, Report No. 28, 1978.

13. Schumpeter, J. A: *Capitalism, Socialism and Democracy*, Allen and Unwin, 1943.
14. Mandel, op cit, p. 171.
15. Mandel, op cit.
16. Hakim, C: *Occupational Segregation*, Department of Employment Research Paper No. 9, 1979, p. 13.
17. Schmid, G: 'Foreign Workers and Labour Market Flexibility, *Journal of Common Market Studies*, vol. ix, no. 3.
18. Barber, A: Labour Force information from the National Dwelling and Housing Survey, Department of Employment Research Paper 17, May 1981.
19. Smith, D: *Racial Disadvantage In Britain*, Penguin, 1977, p. 190.
20. Bendix, R: *Work and Authority in Industry*, University of California press, 1974.
21. Blackburn, R and Mann, M: *The Working Class in the Labour Market*, MacMillan, 1979, p. 12.
22. For examples, see Snell, M W, Glucklich, P and Povall, M: *Equal Pay and Opportunities*, Research Paper 20, Department of Employment, April 1981.
23. Offe, C: *Industry and Inequality*, Edward Arnold, 1976.
24. Nickell, S J: 'A Picture of Male Unemployment in Britain', *The Economic Journal*, December 1980, p. 784.
25. Hunt, A: 'Management Attitudes and Practices Towards Women at Work', HMSO, 1975.
26. Summarized in Hakim, op cit.
27. Daniel, W W: *Racial Discrimination in England*, Penguin Books, 1968, pp. 85–6.
28. Smith, D: *Racial Disadvantage in Employment*, PEP, 1974.
29. Select Committee on Race Relations and Immigration, op cit.
30. Brooks, D: *Race and Labour in London Transport*, OUP for IRR, 1975.
31. Blackburn, R and Mann, M, op cit, p. 106.
32. There is a wide range of sources, but most useful are the Department of Employment Gazette, including its occasional special articles; several of the Department of Employment's Research Papers; Smith D: *Unemployment and Racial Minorities*, Policy Studies Institute, 1981; and Nickell, op cit. is a useful general review.
33. Nickell, S J, op cit, p. 784.
34. Makeham, P: *Youth Unemployment*, Department of Employment Research Paper No. 10, 1980.
35. Smith, D, 1981, op cit.
36. Barber, op cit, Table 5, p. 29.
37. Nickell, op cit.
38. Smith, D, 1981, op cit.
39. Smith, D, 1977, op cit, pp. 74–6.
40. Office of Population Census and Surveys, *Census 1971, Economic Activity, Part III*, HMSO, 1975; Lomas, G and Monck, E, The Coloured Population of Great Britain, Employment and Economic Activity, 1971, *Analysis of Special Census Tabulation*, Runnymede Trust, 1977; Smith, D, 1981, op cit, pp. 34 and 151.

41. Barber, op cit, pp. 12–17.
42. Smith, D, 1981, op cit.
43. Smith, D, 1977, op cit, p. 68.
44. Hawkins, K: *Unemployment*, Penguin, 1979.
45. Smith, D, 1981, op cit.
46. See, for example, CRE 'Looking for Work – Black and White School Leavers in Lewisham', Commission for Racial Equality, 1978.
47. Frobel, F, Heinrichs, J and Kreye, O *The New International Division of Labour:* structural unemployment in industrialized countries and industrialization in developing countries, Cambridge University Press, 1980, p. 13.
48. Heimanz, V and Schatz, K, *Trade in Place of Migration*, Geneva, International Labour Office, 1979.
49. Makeham, 1980, op cit.
50. Select Committee on Race Relations and Immigration, op cit, Minutes of evidence, S1434.
51. Snell *et al*, op cit, pp. 86–7.
52. Select Committee on Race Relations and Immigration, op cit. Minutes of Evidence, S1412 and 1413.
53. Armstrong, P J, Goodman J F R and Hyman, J D, *Ideology and Shop Floor Industrial Relations*, Croom Helm, 1981.
54. Hubbuk, J and Carter, S: *Half a Chance?*, CRE; 1981; CRE, 1978, op cit.; Smith, D., 1981, op. cit.
55. Wilson, K and Porte, A: 'Immigrant Enclaves: an Analysis of the Labour Market Experiences of Cubans in Miami', *American Journal of Sociology*, vol. 86 No. 2 September, 1980.
56. Werbner, P: 'From Rags to Riches: Manchester Pakistanis in the Textile Trade', *New Community*, vol viii nos. 1, 2, Spring 1980.
57. Mullins, D., 'Asian Retailing in Croydon', *New Community*, vol. vii no. 3, Winter 1979.
58. We have not looked at the role of the courts but clearly this is central in determining the effectiveness of legislation to limit discrimination or improve equality of opportunity. Griffith has pointed out that the judiciary have interpreted race relations registration as 'primarily an interference with the rights of individuals to discriminate and that the public interest is best served by restricting the impact of that lesislation as far as possible.' (J. A. G. Griffith, *The Politics of the Judiciary*, Fontana, 1977, p. 201). Parliament has not been over-hasty in re-asserting the principle of non-discrimination.

# AUTHOR INDEX

Bibliographical information will be found on pages printed **bold**.

# SUBJECT INDEX